DISASTER NURSING
Planning, Assessment, and Intervention

Loretta Malm Garcia,
RN, BSN, MSN
University of Utah
Salt Lake City, Utah

AN ASPEN PUBLICATION®
Aspen Systems Corporation
Rockville, Maryland
Royal Tunbridge Wells
1985

Library of Congress Cataloging in Publication Data

Main entry under title:
Disaster nursing.

"An Aspen publication."
Includes bibliographies and index.
1. Disaster nursing — United States. 2. Disaster nursing. I. Garcia, Loretta
Malm. [DNLM: 1. Critical Care — nurses' instruction. 2. Disaster
Planning — nurses' instruction. 3. Disasters — nurses' instruction.
4. Emergencies — nursing. WY 154 D611]
RT108.D57   1985   610.73'49   85-11209
ISBN: 0-87189-227-8

Editorial Services: Martha Sasser

The author and publisher have made every effort to ensure the accuracy of
the information herein, particularly with regard to drug selection and dose.
However, appropriate information sources should be consulted, especially
for new or unfamiliar drugs or procedures. It is the responsibility of every
practitioner to evaluate the appropriateness of a particular opinion in the
context of actual clinical situations and with due consideration to new
developments.

Contributors

Audrey S. Bomberger, R.N., Ph.D.
Director of Nursing Education and Research
McKay-Dee Hospital Center
Intermountain Health Care Corporation
Ogden, UT 84409

Kris L. Brown, R.N., M.S.N., F.N.P.
Instructor, Medical Surgical Nursing
College of Nursing
University of Utah
Salt Lake City, UT 84112

Ralph L. Brown, EMT-P, PA-C
Director, Emergency Medicine and Safety Program
College of Health
University of Utah
Salt Lake City, UT 84112

Loretta Malm Garcia, R.N., B.S.N., M.S.N.
Certification, Nursing Administration, Advanced
Disaster Management Consultant
Associate Instructor, Emergency Medicine and Safety Program
College of Health
University of Utah
Salt Lake City, UT 84112

Susan Smart Gardner, R.N., A.N.P., M.S.
Program Director
WSC/SUSC/Dixie College Cooperative AD Nursing Program
Cedar City, UT 84720

Laraine H. Guyette, R.N., M.S., C.N.M.
Assistant Professor
University of Colorado Health Sciences Center
School of Nursing, Nurse-Midwifery Tract
Denver, CO 80262

Deborah K. Hattan, R.N., B.S.N.
Nursing Coordinator, Nursing Service
Administrative University Hospital

Oregon Health Sciences University
Portland, OR 97201

David B. Lehnhof
Paramedic, Lieutenant
Coordinator, Medical Division
Salt Lake County Fire Department
Associate Instructor, Emergency Medicine and Safety Program, College of Health
University of Utah
Salt Lake City, UT 84112

Roseann P. Lindsay, R.N., B.S.N.
Active Volunteer Instructor
Former Assistant Director of Nursing Health Services, San Diego Chapter
American National Red Cross
3650 Fifth Avenue
San Diego, CA 92103

Richard D. Mickelson, B.S.
Director, Disaster Services
San Diego/Imperial Counties Chapter
American Red Cross
3650 Fifth Avenue
San Diego, CA 92103

Jean R. Miller, R.N., Ph.D.
Associate Dean For Research and Development
·College of Nursing
University of Utah
Salt Lake City, UT 84112

Marilyn M. Pesto, R.N., M.S.N., J.D.
Attorney
Baker and Sterchi
Kansas City, MO 64199-3584

Judith L. Richtsmeier, R.N., B.S.N.
Nursing Development Coordinator
Holy Cross Hospital
Salt Lake City, UT 84103

Michael J. Rogers, M.A.
U.S. Army Patient Administrator
Executive Officer
85th Medical Battalion
Fort George G. Meade, MD 20755

Lloyd A. Schlaeppi, M.H.A.
Consultant, Patient Administration
Office of the Surgeon General
Washington, D.C. 20310

Kathleen H. Switzer, R.N., C., M.S.
Community Health Clinical Nurse Specialist
VA Medical Center
Salt Lake City, UT 84112

Stephen B. Taggart, B.S., M.S., C.H.C.M.
Manager, Safety Services
University of Utah
Salt Lake City, UT 84112

Mary P. Wieland, R.N., M.S.N.
Associate Director of Nursing, Emergency Room & Critical Care
University Hospital
Oregon Health Sciences University
Portland, OR 97201

Table of Contents

Foreword

Natural and man-made disasters present a serious threat to the health and welfare of people in the United States, in the hemisphere, and, indeed, in the world. Disaster-prone countries are increasingly adopting measures for the mitigation and prevention of disasters. Nevertheless, disaster emergencies that threaten to overwhelm the response capacity of health care delivery systems still present a formidable challenge to members of the nursing profession. Unless nurses are involved in preparedness and planning, this challenge may not be met. The results of a lack of preparation are confusion and inadequate improvisation.

The provision of comprehensive health care services to persons and communities involved in disasters is likely to require knowledge and skills not generally taught in nursing or medical schools. This book attempts to fill that educational gap and to provide nurses with practical information about their potential roles in disaster situations. It would be an excellent text for a course in disaster nursing. It would also be a valuable addition to a nurse's personal library or to an emergency room library.

Writing from the perspective of health care and emergency services as they are practiced in the United States, the authors address such practical problems as assessment of patients, triage and tagging, treatment of casualties, and the social, psychological, and mental care of victims. The material presented could be useful to nurses in other countries, provided that they adapt its suggestions to the needs of the systems of health care in their own countries.

Another point stressed by the authors of this book is the disparity between nursing services performed under normal conditions and those performed under the stress of a disaster. The importance of adaptation to the new situation and flexibility under difficult conditions is stressed. Practical, step-by-step procedures are given to assist nurses to prepare themselves to deal with new and sometimes frightening working conditions.

Because every disaster is unique, rigid rules and protocol are impractical. Unless nurses are prepared thoroughly for the unusual demands of disaster management they may find themselves uncomfortable and unable to perform at their best during a disaster. This book offers practical guidelines for nurses hoping to prepare themselves to perform at their best during times of emergency.

If members of the nursing profession are to play decisive roles in the event of disasters, they must be taught disaster preparedness in professional schools, participate actively in community and national disaster planning, and train jointly with members of other helping professions to prepare for effective team effort during a disaster. This book provides insights into the practical aspects of these needs. I heartily recommend it as a valuable resource.

Claude de Ville de Goyet
Director, Emergency Preparedness and Disaster Relief
Pan American Health Organization

Preface

Disaster! The very word creates anxiety in the hearts of many nurses. Some may even say to themselves, "I hope it happens elsewhere." One reason for this dread may be that most nurses, even including emergency room specialists, lack confidence in their ability to function effectively in a disaster. This lack of confidence is attributable to the fact that few nurses have had training or education designed to prepare them to deliver care effectively in disaster or mass casualty situations. Disaster lends a frightening, overwhelming dimension to nursing practice, yet disaster care is not a recognized clinical specialty. Rather, it remains an extension of everyday practice.

Studies of major disasters have shown that improved organization in nursing and medical care could have prevented or reduced the occurrence of many deaths and injuries. This book endeavors to help nurses—especially emergency nurses, public health nurses, and other specialists apt to be involved in disaster planning and care—to increase their understanding, confidence, and skill as they prepare to meet the challenges of disaster settings.

In spite of the technological advances in nursing and medicine today, the many implications of disaster bring a nurse back to the basics. An analysis of the problems frequently associated with disaster or mass casualty incidents can assist nurses to anticipate the commonalities of disaster situations. Nurses must broaden their knowledge in critical areas such as rapid assessment skills, triage decision making in the field and hospital settings, and provision of psychological and supportive care. Leadership and organizational skills specific to disaster settings can be improved with education and practice.

I hope that this book will enable nurses to develop a positive attitude and confidence in assessing and dealing with many situations. Use of all steps of the nursing process related to disaster care should be the ultimate goal of every member of nursing and disaster teams.

Support and belief in the need for improved disaster nursing has come from many persons who have shared their ideas and enthusiasm. For example, a needs assessment helped to define the content for this book. More than 250 nurses were asked what types of information they needed in order to function most effectively in a disaster. Their concerns focused on fifteen major topics. These topics became the subjects of chapters in this book.

Steve, Michaela, and Alaina Garcia have consulted on this material as a graduate program research project since its inception. Carmen Germaine Warner provided the knowledge and the encouragement to enable this idea to become a reality. Lt. Col. Judith L. Richtsmeier, Chief Nurse, and Colonel Howard G. Wilcox, former Commander, of the 328th General Hospital, Fort Douglas, Utah, combined with all unit Army Reserve nurses, were a never-ending source of new ideas and tactics.

I would also like to acknowledge La Delle Blust for her contributions regarding ethical considerations in disaster. John Papasodero and N. Jean Myers contributed greatly in the area of hazardous materials incidents. Dodie Rotherham assisted in the Shelter Management chapter. Ms. Jan Boller provided invaluable content suggestions. Ms. Barbara Halliburton spent countless hours providing editorial comments and direction.

My sincere appreciation is extended to my team of contributing authors. The inevitable frustrations of this project were markedly reduced by their hard work and contributions. The friendship of each means a great deal. I thank them one and all!

Loretta Malm Garcia

Chapter 1

Background and Historical Perspective

Stephen B. Taggart, B.S., M.S., C.H.C.M.

Almost every day, disasters that threaten many lives and much property occur somewhere in the United States. We hear about them in the news: plane crashes, floods, hurricanes, tornados, fires, earthquakes, accidents with hazardous materials, droughts, famines, and wars. From January 1, 1971, to June 3, 1980, various presidents of the United States declared 326 events major disasters.[1] In addition, many localized disasters occur that do not qualify for a presidential declaration. These may result in as many, or more, casualties. As an example, the collapse of the skywalks in a Kansas City hotel on July 17, 1981, did not prompt a presidential disaster declaration; yet it resulted in 113 deaths and 188 injuries. The toll of these disasters in human terms is seldom fully realized by people who have not experienced them personally (Table 1–1).

As public awareness of disasters increases, the demand for better management practices increases correspondingly. The goal of disaster management is to prevent or to minimize death, injury, suffering, and destruction. Many people and many organizations are involved in this effort: local, state, and federal disaster management agencies; private relief organizations; fire and police departments; medical and nursing staffs; political leaders; also administrators, lawyers, engineers, meteorologists, geologists, sociologists, and volunteers. Because disaster management is an interdisciplinary task, all persons involved must understand their respective roles and responsibilities. The purpose of this chapter is to provide some general definitions relating to disasters; to discuss the different types of disasters and disaster agents; to outline phases of disasters and to show how they relate to disaster management; to examine the historical and expanding role of nurses in disasters and emergency preparedness; and to discuss common problems associated with the delivery of health care in disasters.

Table 1–1 Recent Disasters

Location	Date	Type	Deaths	Injuries
San Diego, Calif.	September 25, 1978	Midair collision	144	16
Mt. St. Helens, Wash.	May 18, 1980	Volcanic eruption	85	unknown
Las Vegas, Nev.	November 21, 1980	MGM Grand fire	84	700
Cocoa Beach, Fla.	March 21, 1981	Condominium collapse	11	22
Kansas City, Mo.	July 17, 1981	Hyatt Regency collapse	113	188
Washington, D.C.	January 13, 1982	Plane and subway crash	81	27
Estes Park, Colo.	July 15, 1982	Lawn Lake Dam collapse	4	unknown
Biloxi, Miss.	November 8, 1982	Harrison County jail fire	29	59
Oklahoma City, Okla.	April 6, 1983	Natural gas explosion	0	7
Coalinga, Calif.	May 2, 1983	Earthquake	0	47
Galveston, Tex.	August 18, 1983	Hurricane Alicia	17	3,000+
Buffalo, N.Y.	December 27, 1983	Propane gas explosion	6	70+
Mexico City, Mexico	November 19, 1984	Natural gas explosion	350	2,000
Bhopal, India	December 3, 1984	Chemical leak	2,500	150,000

Source: National Emergency Training Center Library, Emmitsburg, Md.

DEFINITIONS

Disaster

The Red Cross has defined a *disaster* as ''an occurrence such as a hurricane, tornado, storm, flood, high water, wind-driven water, tidal wave, earthquake, drought, blizzard, pestilence, famine, fire, explosion, building collapse, transportation wreck, or other situation that causes human suffering or creates human needs that the victims cannot alleviate without assistance.''[2] In this book, the word *disaster* is used in the sense of any occurrence that inflicts destruction and distress and that creates demands exceeding the capabilities of the community to handle it in a normal or routine way.

An event need not cause any deaths or injuries, however, to be classified as a disaster. A flood, for example, can threaten many lives, can cause widespread destruction of property, and can create economic hardship; yet, not produce any casualties.

Mass Casualty Incident

Alexander M. Butman defines *mass casualty incidents* (MCI) as ''disasters that occur in one location in the absence of similar or related occurrences in neighboring towns or communities."[3] In other words, an MCI occurs if the number of casualties (injured or dead) in a given location exceeds the capabilities of the local emergency medical services.

A disaster can occur without involving an MCI; however, by definition, when there is an MCI, there is a disaster.

Major Disaster

The Disaster Relief Act of 1974, Public Law 93-288, defines a *major disaster* as

> any hurricane, tornado, storm, flood, high water, wind-driven water, tidal wave, tsunami, earthquake, volcanic eruption, landslide, mudslide, snowstorm, drought, fire, explosion, or other catastrophe in any part of the United States which, in the determination of the President, causes damage of sufficient severity and magnitude to warrant major disaster assistance above and beyond emergency services by the Federal Government to supplement the efforts and available resources of States, local governments, and private relief organizations in alleviating the damage, loss, hardship or suffering caused by a disaster.[4]

Emergency

The Federal Emergency Management Agency defines an *emergency* as "Any of the various types of catastrophes included in the definition of a "major disaster" which requires Federal emergency assistance to supplement State and local efforts to save lives and protect property, public health and safety, or to avert or lessen the threat of a disaster."[4]

TYPES OF DISASTERS

Disasters are commonly divided according to their causes into two distinct categories—natural disasters and man-made disasters.

Natural disasters include the following types:

- meteorological disasters: cyclones, typhoons, hurricanes, tornados, hailstorms, snowstorms, and droughts
- topological disasters: landslides, avalanches, mudflows, and floods
- disasters that originate underground: earthquakes, volcanic eruptions, and tsunamis (seismic sea waves)

- biological disasters: communicable disease epidemics and insect swarms (locusts)

Man-made disasters include these:

- warfare: conventional warfare (bombardment, blockade, and siege) and nonconventional warfare (nuclear, chemical, and biological)
- civil disasters: riots and demonstrations
- accidents: transportation (planes, trucks, automobiles, trains, and ships); structural collapse (buildings, dams, bridges, mines, and other structures); explosions; fires; chemical (toxic waste and pollution); and biological (sanitation)

This classification, which is not intended to be fully comprehensive, has its limitations. The distinction between natural and man-made disasters is not always clear (e.g., an earthquake may cause buildings to collapse, and flooding can be caused by dam failure), and this summary does not reflect the chain reaction and the cumulative effects that can occur in a major disaster.

Skeet has provided an example of the cumulative effects of a major disaster that occurred in November 1970, when a cyclone followed by a severe tidal wave struck East Pakistan in the coastal Bay of Bengal.[5] Serious destruction was caused by the impact of the tidal wave and the flooding that followed. Approximately 500,000 people died, most of the livestock drowned, crops were destroyed, the soil was ruined, and the water supplies were polluted.

The demands placed on the Pakistan society as a result of the disaster came at a time when there was widespread discontent in the country because of political, economic, and administrative influences exerted on the territory by West Pakistan. The civil disturbances that followed the declaration of the new state of Bangladesh in March 1971 forced some 10 million people to flee into India—principally around Calcutta—where they were fed and housed in camps run by various voluntary organizations. Overcrowding and poor sanitary conditions led to a cholera outbreak, causing yet another problem.

As the civil strife in Bangladesh grew steadily worse, the administration became powerless, the economy almost collapsed, and communications became difficult. These factors and the poor monsoon rains caused famine to spread through the country.

The relief operations to aid the cyclone victims were temporarily suspended in December 1971 when the Indian Government sent its army into Bangladesh in support of the local freedom fighters. The war was bloody and immensely destructive, producing the usual high number of surgical casualties and the destruction of strategic roads, bridges, and railways. The war also left another serious problem: approximately 750,000 non-Bengalis, who had sided with the previous West Pakistan administration, were now in urgent need of food, shelter, and clothing.

The combined effects of disaster and war from November 1970 to January 1972 had affected the entire population of Bangladesh, some 75 million people. Subsequently, governments, United Nations agencies, the International Red Cross, and other organizations mounted one of the biggest relief organizations since World War II.

DIMENSIONS OF DISASTER AGENTS

Disaster agents have different characteristics. Knowledge of these differences is useful in disaster management because it sensitizes participants to possible variables that have to be taken into account in developing response plans.

Dynes et al. explain:[6]

First, disaster agents vary in terms of their *predictability*. For example, an explosion or an earthquake is considerably less foreseeable than a flood, which is brought about by a series of more precisely measurable factors. In fact, for some weather phenomena it is possible to obtain for specific localities the gross probabilities of a particular disaster agent striking the given area. For example, the chances of hurricane force winds in given Florida cities in any given year have been calculated. Thus, the chances for such winds are 1 in 50 for Jacksonville, 1 in 20 for Tampa–St. Petersburg, and 1 in 7 for Miami.

A disaster agent can also vary in terms of its *frequency*. Although natural disasters may be relatively rare happenings, there are certain locales that can be labeled disaster-prone. To illustrate, some regions in the Ohio Valley are more susceptible to flooding, other areas such as the Midwest are subject to tornados, and the Gulf coast is frequently confronted with the threat or occurrence of hurricanes. Thus, there are geographic, climatic, and other conditions that present the possibility of particular kinds of disaster and represent a sustained threat. Here again, gross figures for frequency can be obtained for some disaster agents. Thus, the National Weather Service has not only calculated tornado incidences by month (May is the highest), by state (Texas has the most), and by square mile (Oklahoma has the highest), but also in terms of threat, which takes high incidence of tornados and dense concentration of population into account (Massachusetts with a rating of 347, Connecticut with a rating of 150, and New Jersey with a rating of 136 are the three highest ranked states).

A third factor to consider is the *controllability* of the disaster agent. Some situations allow for intervention and control which reduce the potential impact of the disaster agent. For example, flooding can often be anticipated and at least partially prevented, while other disasters such as earthquakes and tsunamis (so-called tidal waves), allow no such luxury. For example, in the early months of 1971 the National Weather Service predicted serious snowmelt flooding in the Upper Midwest and certain other areas of the country. But, as a result of effective flood-fighting actions taken by the Corps of Engineers, as well as slow warming with little or no precipitation, spring flooding in the Upper Midwest, the Northwest, and Alaska caused no appreciable damage.

The next three factors all deal with time but should not be confused. Disaster agents differ in their *speed of onset*. For example, impact is sudden in tornados and flash floods, while other floods gradually crest. Also, some types of agents, such as earthquakes, may strike an area repetitively in a matter of hours. *Length of forewarning* is the period between warning and impact. Tsunamis or tidal waves generated by an earthquake illustrate the distinction between the above two time factors. Length of forewarning of tidal waves may be several hours, but their actual speed of onset, once initiated, is very rapid. Disasters also differ in their *duration of impact*. For example, a tornado impacts an area for only a few minutes, but a flood's impact may be sustained for several days. The worst time combination from the viewpoint of damage potential is a disaster agent that is rapid in onset, gives no warning, and lasts a long time. An earthquake with strong aftershocks comes closest to such a threat.

The final differentiating characteristics of disaster agents are their *scope and intensity of impact*. Scope of impact is essentially a geo-graphic and social space dimension. A disaster can be concentrated in a small area, affecting few people, or dispersed over wide areas, affecting large numbers. Intensity of impact reflects a disaster's potential to inflict injuries, deaths, and property damage. These two factors should be clearly distinguished. For example, an explosion, though highly destructive, may affect only a limited geographic area, whereas flood may be of low intensity but affect a broad geographic area and many people. This, of course, has important implications for the degree of disruption of local community affairs. A destructive but focalized disaster, though tragic, may have only minimal consequences for the community at large. Conversely, a diffuse but less destructive disaster may be extremely disruptive to everyday community living.

It should be noted that space or time dimensions underlie all of these features of disaster impact. And these dimensions are often crucial in terms of the actual extent of damage a disaster brings. For example, if there are large concentrations of people in the impact area during a certain time of day (say during the rush hour), this would have important implications for intensity and scope of impact. If there is substantial time between warning and impact, this allows for preventive actions. It should also be noted that by using these characteristics one can distinguish between disaster agents in various ways. Thus an explosion is generally unpredictable, has rapid onset with little warning, is of short duration, and has highly focalized but destructive impact. On the other hand, a flood can sometimes be predicted, has gradual impact with considerable forewarning, and is generally of long duration and diffuse scope.

PHASES OF DISASTERS

Disasters can be divided chronologically into five phases: (1) predisaster preparation, (2) warning, (3) impact, (4) emergency, and (5) recovery (Table 1–2). This chronological organization of disaster activities is helpful because it provides an outline by which to develop disaster plans, to assign tasks and responsibilities and to set priorities for activities in a logical sequence. An amplification of each phase is included to provide examples of the kinds of activities that might take place. The activities listed are intended to be general in nature and not all-inclusive. Also, in many cases, two or more phases may overlap (e.g., predisaster preparation and warning); sometimes one of the phases does not occur (warning).

Predisaster Preparation

The phase before a disaster strikes is of critical importance because it, more than any other phase, determines the impact of the disaster on the community. During this stage, a community undertakes the task of assessing its disaster potential by conducting geological hazard surveys and risk assessment for severe storms, hazardous materials accidents, transportation accidents, fires, and so forth. The community may establish land-use or zoning ordinances and may adopt codes and other laws in an effort to prevent or to mitigate a disaster. An effective disaster plan is developed, distributed, tested in mock disaster exercises, revised and refined, and kept up-to-date. The various disaster response organizations (e.g., fire, police, emergency medical services, social services, and utilities) meet on a regular basis under the direction of local civil defense authorities to coordinate planning and preparation activities. Essential equipment and supplies required to meet the response demands of potential disasters are procured. These include extra emergency medical supplies, communication equipment, rescue equipment, and

Table 1–2 Five Phases of Disaster Activity

Phases	Activities
Predisaster preparation	Governmental, environmental, technical, and economic resources preparation to meet disaster demands
	Prevention and mitigation activities
	Disaster planning and coordination between response groups
	Community education
	Training, "mock disaster" exercises
	Equipment and supply procurement (medical supplies, communication equipment, emergency generators, sandbag supplies, pumps)
Warning	Increased readiness, disaster plan activation, establishment of Emergency Operations Center (EOC)
	Warning population
	Warning hospitals
	Evacuation/in-place protection
	Pre-impact preparation
Impact	Enduring, "holding on"
Emergency	Assessment—advise disaster response organizations
Isolation	Activation of disaster plan/establishment of EOC if not already done
	Mitigation of further injuries or damage
	Summons of additional help, mutual aid
	Preparation for search and rescue activities
	Hospital disaster plans in operation
Rescue	Establishment of command post
	Assessment
	Search and rescue
	Triage, establishment of patient collection points
	Establishment of emergency vehicle routes/patient transportation
Remedy	Arrival of organized assistance
	Relief of disaster workers by groups from unattached areas
	Arrival of additional relief supplies and equipment
	Care of the dead
	Provision for emergency food, shelter, and clothing needs
	Attention to sanitary measures and other public health concerns
Recovery	Restoration of essential community services
	Reestablishment of community order
	Meeting of victims' welfare demands
	Repair of community damage
	Continued damage assessment and procurement of local, state, and federal assistance
	Initiation of preventive measures

Source: Adapted with permission from Dynes RR: *Organized Behavior in Disaster.* Lexington, Mass., Lexington Books, 1970, p 56.

emergency generators. Disaster training is provided to all response agencies to familiarize them with the disaster plan, their roles and responsibilities, and the new tasks or demands generated by a disaster. An important part of the predisaster preparation is to educate the public and to encourage individual preparedness.

Too many organizations and communities fail, however, to take full advantage of this predisaster period. It is usually not until after a disaster that the full resources of the community are devoted to preparation for the next disaster.

Warning

The *warning phase* is the period of time from the first possible danger signal to the moment of impact. Although some disasters (explosions, earthquakes, and transportation accidents) provide little, if any, warning, many disasters occur with some prior indication of danger. With the aid of satellites and networks of weather stations, many meteorological disasters (e.g., hurricanes, tornados, severe winter storms, heat waves, and droughts) can be predicted. In addition, it is possible to predict conditions conducive to avalanches and landslides. In these situations, warning can be the most important aspect in minimizing the loss of lives and in mitigating damage. It is important that a community be well informed about the possibility of a disaster occurring, its intensity, and its duration and scope.

Warning includes detecting and predicting the occurrence of a disaster and disseminating this information and information about ameliorative and protective action to the community. It is during the warning phase that disaster plans are activated, emergency operations centers are established, and the affected area is evacuated or provided with in-place protection. Obviously, an effective communications system is essential. Final preparations are made in anticipation of the impact phase.

Several problems may arise during the warning phase. First, many disasters do not permit dissemination of vital information either because communications systems are inadequate or because there is not enough time. Second, when warning is possible, the community must recognize the threat as legitimate and serious. Third, frequent false alarms are likely to jeopardize future response to warnings.

Impact

Impact is the phase in which the disaster actually strikes and in which little can be done to mitigate damage or to increase the number of survivors. It is essentially a period of enduring the disaster's effects and "holding on." The impact phase can last anywhere from a few seconds or minutes (earthquakes, plane crashes, or explosions) to a few days or weeks (floods and heat waves) to several months (droughts and epidemics). People within the disaster area may not fully comprehend the scope of the disaster. Likewise, neighboring communities that are relied upon to provide assistance may be unaware of the disaster's magnitude. It is essential that a preliminary damage assessment be conducted during the impact phase (if possible), or immediately afterwards to determine emergency response priorities, needs, and limitations.

Emergency

The *emergency phase* begins at the end of the impact and continues until the immediate threat of additional destruction has passed and the community is organized for recovery and rehabilitation. The emergency phase can be divided into three parts: (1) isolation, (2) rescue, and (3) remedy.

The period of isolation is the interval in which immediate mitigative actions are required to prevent additional loss of life. These actions, which take place at the same time the first emergency personnel respond to the disaster, include a preliminary assessment of casualties; fires, broken gas, water, and power lines; blocked roadways; and damage to essential equipment and services. Disaster plans are activated, and the emergency operations center is established— if it has not been done during the warning phase.

The reactions of communities and organizations without previous disaster experience or training are likely to be hurried, uncoordinated, and nonproductive. They concentrate on the speed rather than the appropriateness of their response.

The *rescue* period begins when the first survivors render first aid to the victims, especially their own family members. It continues through the arrival of the first local rescue organization, the establishment of a command post, and the convergence of other local and neighboring rescue organizations.

How many victims are rescued alive and whether they are triaged and treated appropriately depends on the community's prior preparation, organization, and training.

The *remedy* period of the emergency phase begins with the establishment of organized, professional, and voluntary relief operations. The confusion of the rescue period subsides as the remedy period gets underway. Professionally supervised medical aid, clothing, feeding, and shelter needs are provided. There is a directed movement of the injured to hospitals. Morgue facilities are established, and coordinated search and reunion activities are initiated. Definitive mitigative actions aimed at preventing further injuries and damage are undertaken, and attention to sanitary measures and other public health concerns begins.

Recovery

Recovery begins during the emergency phase and ends gradually with the resumption of normal community order and functions. For the persons in the impact area, recovery is a long—perhaps lifelong—readjustment, and assistance may be required to meet their welfare demands. Permanent repair and rebuilding of damaged property, replanting of crops, and the restoration of all public services must take place.

TRADITIONAL ROLES OF NURSES IN DISASTER

An important point to remember in disaster management is that the effectiveness of individuals or groups responding to a disaster depends on not only how well they carry out their own responsibilities but also how well they allow others to carry out theirs. Because nursing is specialized, nurses in different positions bring various skills to a disaster scene. This fact, which is often not recognized outside the nursing profession, should be better understood. Most persons assume that each nurse knows how to do everything in nursing; however, the principle of using persons in functions most closely associated with their daily work holds true for nursing too.[7]

Furthermore, a nurse's role in a disaster may depend on the nurse's location at the time of impact. For example, an emergency nurse obviously performs a vital role in the hospital. If that nurse happens to be near the impact zone, however, a greater contribution may be made by assisting in evacuation, rescue, and first aid efforts until the immediate needs of the situation are met. At that point, the nurse may decide to return to work in the hospital's emergency department. In other words, it is up to the individual nurses to determine, within their particular set of circumstances, where they may best serve the community. For the purpose of disaster planning and preparation, however, it is simpler to categorize nurses as working in either a nonhospital or hospital setting.

Nonhospital nurses

Nonhospital nurses generally include school nurses, private nurses, nursing educators, industrial and occupational health nurses, researchers, nursing consultants, public health nurses, administrators, and members of various volunteer organizations.

An important role for all public health nurses and nursing educators is that of educating the public in principles of personal preparedness and casualty care. The leadership for this program ought to stem from the public health nurse. Public health nurses should know of some of the inactive nurses in the community and so be able to call on them to assist in this effort. (See Chapter 10 for specific information on the role of nonhospital nurses.)

Hospital Nurses

Hospital nurses have two general areas of concern in disaster management: (1) the internal disaster (such as the hospital fire or other disaster) that physically affects the hospital's ability to function and (2) the external or community disaster (such as a bus crash) that places critical demands on the hospital's resources. The hospital nurse should be involved in developing both internal and external disaster plans.

Nurses can help to prevent internal hospital disasters by being well versed in emergency plans and fire and safety codes and by ensuring that hazards within the hospital are corrected immediately. In the case of external disasters, the most important thing a hospital nurse can do is to make sure the hospital has a good disaster plan and then to become familiar with her role in the plan. The goal to provide the best possible patient care can be accomplished only if confusion and delays are minimized. (See Chapter 4 for details on the hospital nurse's role in disaster management.)

COMMON PROBLEMS FOUND AT MCIs

Butman has discussed the common problems that seem to recur in MCIs.[3] His observations are partly based on an in-depth study of MCIs published in December 1977 by the Disaster Research Center of the Department of Sociology, Ohio State University. The study included field work done in 44 communities located in 17 states, Washington, D.C., and the United States Virgin Islands and encompassed 29 disasters. The research included communities of various sizes and with a wide range of emergency medical services (EMS) development—from rudimentary capabilities to complex, well-established systems.

Butman and his colleagues also compiled and studied information on 22 nonenvironmental disasters. After they compared the problems observed in MCIs with the failures and the problems that occurred repeatedly in a wide variety of drills and exercises, they observed that the following problems appeared in the disasters and the disaster drills:

- failure in adequate alerting
- lack of rapid ''primary'' stabilization of all patients
- failure to move, to collect, and to organize patients rapidly at a suitable place
- failure to provide proper (or any) triage
- use of overly time-consuming and inappropriate care methods
- premature commencement of transportation
- improper use of personnel in the field
- lack of proper distribution of patients, which results in improper use of medical facilities
- lack of recognizable EMS command in the field
- lack of proper preplanning and lack of adequate training of all personnel

- failure to compensate for malfunction and remediate problems
- lack of adequate or proper communication

PROSPECTS FOR THE FUTURE

Despite all our efforts to control our environment, the toll from disasters, both natural and man-made, continues to increase. The average number of disasters has remained relatively constant and, if anything, has even declined somewhat. However, the death rates and the economic losses continue to climb significantly because of the increased population and the growth of a technologically advanced society. As we continue to develop land in flood plains, construct taller buildings, and produce larger ships and planes, losses from flood, fire, and transportation accidents seem destined to increase.

Nurses can take action in three areas to help mitigate human and material losses in disaster:

1. Personal preparedness
   - Make sure you are a resource to your community rather than a burden.
   - Maintain your own emergency equipment and supplies (see Chapter 3).
   - Make sure your family knows what to do in an emergency.
   - Use prudence in selecting sites for your home.
2. Community involvement
   - Become familiar with local disaster plans and emergency procedures.
   - Get involved in the political issues in your community that relate to disaster management.
   - Support leaders who opt for long-term, definitive solutions in loss reduction and emergency preparedness programs rather than those who choose the short-term, politically expedient solution.
   - Help to modify land use and development ordinances to reflect the best available knowledge of geologic and hydrologic hazards.
   - Support local voluntary assistance organizations.
   - Help to educate the public in personal preparedness.
3. Professional preparedness
   - Get involved in the development of community or hospital disaster plans.
   - Attend continuing education classes and refresher courses to keep current in disaster management skills.
   - Be supportive of administrative efforts to increase disaster preparedness.

SUMMARY

In an effort to lay groundwork for subsequent chapters, some general definitions and information relating to disaster management have been presented. The practice of nursing actually developed from and matured in response to the demands created by disasters, particularly wars. Nurses, in hospital and nonhospital settings, have played a substantial role in disaster management. They will continue to play that role, and so they are obligated to prepare for that challenge. The demands precipitating from a disaster are unlike those occurring every day; furthermore, experience and training in nondisaster situations do not ordinarily prepare a person to act appropriately in a disaster situation. It is essential that we learn from past mistakes in the delivery of health care to disaster victims. We must place added emphasis in the future on education and training in disaster management.

REFERENCES

1. Logue JN, Melick ME, Hansen H: Research issues and directions in the epidemiology of health effects of disasters. *Epidemiol Rev*, 1981; 3:141

2. *Disaster Relief Program*, ARC 2235. Washington, DC, American Red Cross, revised March 1975.

3. Butman AM: *Responding to the Mass Casualty Incident: A Guide for EMS Personnel*. Westport, Conn, Educational Direction Inc. 1982, pp 14, 33–36.

4. *Disaster Assistance Programs*, DR & R-18, program guide. Federal Emergency Management Agency, March 1983, p 1.

5. Skeet M: *Manual for Disaster Relief Work*. Edinburgh, Scotland, Churchill Livingstone, 1977, pp 2–3.

6. Dynes RR: Quarantelli EL, Kreps GA: *A Perspective on Disaster Planning*, TR-77. Defense Civil Preparedness Agency, December 1972, pp 6–8.

7. Garb S, Eng E: *Disaster Handbook*, ed 2. New York, Springer Publishing Co Inc, 1969, p 112.

SUGGESTED READINGS

Bahme CW: *Fire Officer's Guide to Disaster Control*. Boston, National Fire Protection Assoc, 1978, pp 1–41.

Blanshan SA: *A Time Model: Hospital Organization Response to Disaster*. Beverly Hills, Calif, Sage Publications Ltd, 1978, pp 173–198.

Burton I, Kates RW, White GF: *The Environment as Hazard*. New York, Oxford University Press, 1978.

Butler JE: *Natural Disasters*. London, Heinemann Educational Books Ltd, 1978.

Conway HM: *Disaster Survival: How to Choose Secure Sites and Make Practical Escape Plans*. Atlanta, Conway Publication Inc, 1981, pp 1–101.

Disaster Services Regulations and Procedures: Providing Red Cross Disaster Health Services, ARC 3076-A. Washington, DC, American Red Cross, December 1982, pp 64–80.

Dynes RR: *Organized Behavior in Disaster*. Lexington, Mass, Lexington Books, 1970.

Hays WW (ed): *Facing Geologic and Hydrologic Hazards: Earth Science Considerations*, Geological Survey professional paper 1240-B. Government Printing Office, 1981.

Hurd C: *The Compact History of the American Red Cross*. New York, Hawthorn Books Inc, 1959.

Mahoney RF: *Emergency and Disaster Nursing*. New York, MacMillan Inc, 1965.

The role of nursing in disasters. Pan American Health Organization Newsletter, January 1984, pp 1–2.

Rossi PH, Wright JD, Weber–Burdin E: *Natural Hazards and Public Choice: The State and Local Politics of Hazard Mitigation*. New York, Academic Press Inc, 1982.

Taggart SD: *Emergency Preparedness Manual*. Salt Lake City, University of Utah, 1982.

Thygerson AL: *Disaster Handbook*. Provo, Utah, Brigham Young University Press, 1979.

Turner BA: *Man-Made Disasters*. New York, Crane Russak & Co Inc, 1978, pp 40–48.

Western KA: *The Epidemiology of Natural and Man-Made Disasters*, dissertation. University of London, London, 1972.

Whittow J: *Disasters: The Anatomy of Environmental Hazards*. Athens, Ga, The University of Georgia Press, 1979.

Chapter 2

Skills in Rapid Field Assessment

Susan Smart Gardner, R.N., A.N.P., M.S.

The proverb "first things first" may seem obvious in most nursing situations; but in a disaster, it is not always obvious which patients and which injuries take precedence. What do you do first, for instance, when the unconscious patient with a leg at an odd angle suggestive of fracture is also bleeding profusely from several facial and abdominal wounds? What if you are faced with not just one multiple-injured patient but with dozens? Where do you start when injuries run from the superficial to the fatal and the scene is one of confusion and hysteria? The answer: Establish priorities.

This book is intended to help you assess a disaster situation, to set priorities, and to plan effective interventions. This chapter provides information about the skills necessary for a rapid assessment of the sick and injured. A logical, systematic format for the complete, yet rapid, assessment of the individual patient is presented. Triage decisions are covered in Chapter 3, while care of the multiple-trauma patient is addressed in Chapter 5.

A number of systems have been developed to help the nurse to sort problems of assessment and treatment and to decide the order in which to deal with them. Whatever the system, the essential strategy in managing a disaster victim includes the following:[1]

- rapid initial assessment
- emergency treatment of life-threatening injuries according to the proper sequence of priorities
- more detailed assessment
- safe and quick transfer to the right facility

CHALLENGE OF DISASTER NURSING

Disaster nurses must possess highly developed, knowledge-based skills of assessing and deciding priorities of care. Whether confronting the immediate responsibilities of managing a full-scale disaster or a single severely injured patient, the nurse does not have the luxury of a leisurely assessment; every second counts. The nurse must rapidly assess patients and take immediate action to preserve life and function. The assessment must be thorough enough, however, to identify concealed injuries.

The circumstances and the surroundings are rarely ideal. Patients may be fully clothed, awkwardly positioned, uncooperative, unconscious, or non-English speaking. The environment may present special hazards to victim and rescuer. Rarely are such conditions as lighting, equipment, temperature, or appropriate dress for weather conditions ideal. Furthermore, the nurse must be able to assess the patients as they arrive, despite a lack of knowledge about the patient's medical history or the mechanism of the trauma. To the less injured, waiting patients, they must diplomatically reveal the reasons for delayed treatment while simultaneously initiating necessary life-saving care for the critically ill and injured.[2,3]

Key to the Challenge

Assessment is the key to meeting successfully the challenge of disaster nursing and must precede the initiation of treatment. Priority interventions are carried out on the basis of systematic assessment. In the face of life-threatening conditions, continued assessments may be postponed as lifesaving measures are instituted. As life-threatening conditions are resolved, systematic assessment ensures that all body systems and parts are just as carefully evaluated.[3]

Disaster victims present a unique challenge because they differ from most patients in several ways:[4]

- The injuries often require immediate lifesaving intervention.
- The patients have had no chance to prepare for the situation that now poses a crisis for their families and themselves.
- The patients may sustain multiple-system injuries.
- The injuries may sometimes be so subtle that they escape initial detection.
- The patients have a great potential for developing later complications because of the multiplicity and severity of the injuries.
- The rehabilitation period is extensive, demanding ongoing evaluation and adjustment from the entire health care team.

Assessment of Phases

The seriously injured disaster victim needs the skilled practitioner to do many things at once. In a clinical setting with a wide range of clinicians and therapies immediately available, assessment and treatment by a readily mobilized trauma team can commence simultaneously. In a field situation, where help and resources are too few or inexperienced, the nurse-manager must make the decisions about stabilization and transfer. However, before these decisions can be made, appropriate data must be gathered.

Caring for trauma patients involves three major assessment phases:[4,5]

1. initial survey (Immediate assessment and stabilization of the patient is always the first priority.)
2. secondary survey (After initial resuscitative measures and stabilization, a more thorough examination must be completed in order to identify all existing injuries.)
3. ongoing assessment (A continuing evaluation of the care given and the patient's response has the goal of recognizing impending or actual complications.)

Assessment takes much longer to read about than to perform. In a disaster situation, the nurse works rapidly, assessing several body systems simultaneously from the moment the first victim arrives. Disaster nurses make a complete head-to-toe assessment of all body systems in no more than 3 to 5 minutes—usually while listening to reports and receiving information. Assessments of patients with significant airway, breathing, or circulatory problems take 60 to 90 seconds and concentrate on these priorities.[6]

The guidelines presented provide a systematic approach designed to gain maximum information in a minimum amount of time. Although there are many ways to organize an assessment, the important point is that a routine be developed and followed. A systematic routine is beneficial for a number of reasons:

• The data are collected in a logical, ordered manner.
• All body systems are evaluated.
• Priorities for planning are established.
• The baseline data are secured as reference for future evaluation.
• A foundation is secured for the formulation of nursing diagnoses.

INITIAL SURVEY

The initial survey focuses on the identification of potentially life-threatening injuries. Immediate priorities for care are those functions necessary to sustain life, namely, effective breathing and circulation. If either is absent or inadequate, proper treatment must begin immediately without wasting precious seconds treating less urgent injuries or conditions. A framework for the initial survey can be remembered as readily as the ABCs (airway, breathing, circulation, cervical spine, and consciousness).

Airway and Cervical Spine

The top priority is prompt assessment of the patient's airway. The initial step in oxygen delivery is the movement of air from the atmosphere to the pulmonary alveoli; this action requires a patent airway and adequate ventilation. Inadequate ventilation leads to immediate hypoxemia and hypoxia, and cutoff of oxygen to the brain leads to irreversible damage within five minutes. Quickly consider the patient's position, the nature of the airway obstruction, and how to open the airway. When looking at the airway, keep in mind that if the patient has facial fractures and cuts and is unconscious, there was probably enough force on impact to cause a fracture of the cervical spine. A rule of thumb is to assume that the cervical spine is fractured if there is a serious injury above the clavicle. Manage the patient accordingly until x-ray films prove otherwise.[1,7,8]

The most common cause of airway obstruction is the patient's tongue. When a cervical spine injury is a possibility, however, the usual head-tilt and chin-lift maneuver, which hyperextends the neck, must not be used to clear the obstruction. Such a move could convert a cervical spine fracture without cord injury into one with cord injury. The cervical spine must be kept in a neutral position with in-line traction, which involves getting at the tongue from in front.

The first method that can be used is the chin-lift. Place the fingers of one hand under the chin and lift it forward while simultaneously depressing the lower lip with the thumb, thus opening the mouth slightly. If mouth-to-mouth breathing is necessary, the patient's nostrils can be closed with the thumb and index finger of the other hand. This maneuver is the method of choice for trauma victims because it does not require hyperextension of the head.

A second technique to open the airway is the jaw-lift. Place the thumb around the lower incisors and bring the mandible forward. The disadvantages of this technique are the difficulty in maintaining a grasp in the wet mouth and the danger of being bitten if the patient suddenly regains consciousness.

The third maneuver to open the airway is the jaw-thrust. Grasp the angle of the mandible with both hands, one on each side, and lift the mandible forward. The disadvantage of this technique is that it ties up both hands of the attending person, who is then incapable of rendering further aid.[8]

The cervical spine must be immobilized as soon as possible. Any transfer or movement of the patient should be done only while the attending person keeps the head and trunk in line and log-rolls them as a unit. The patient should be placed on a long, firm board. If a cervical collar is unavailable, sandbags or rolled towels can be placed on either side of the head to prevent the neck from being turned. Two-inch tape is placed across the forehead and the rolled towels and secured to the board. Another strip of tape across the chest ensures stabilization above and below the cervical spine.[9]

Breathing

Second, breathing must be evaluated. Ventilation of the lungs depends not only on a patent main airway but also on pulmonary alveoli, on rigid thorax bones, and on the integrity of nerves and muscles that control the movements of the ribs and the diaphragm.[10] Start the initial examination for breathing by holding your ear over the patient's nose and mouth to assess ventilatory exchange. Palpate the pulse at the wrist or the neck to assess the circulation. Bare the thorax, and observe respiratory motions. If spontaneous breathing efforts are absent or are ineffective, begin and continue assisted ventilation.[8]

Circulation

Circulation is examined next. Measuring blood pressure in the primary survey is, however, not the optimal use of time for this evaluation. Significant information about cardiac output can be obtained from the pulse alone. The pulse can be quickly assessed for quality, rate, and regularity. If the radial pulse is palpable, it can generally be assumed that the systolic blood pressure is greater than 80 mm Hg. If the femoral pulse is palpable, the systolic pressure is greater than 70 mm Hg; it is greater than 60 mm Hg if the carotid pulse is palpable. Capillary filling time can also quickly determine the adequacy of blood volume. A capillary blanch test of the nail bed shows return to normal color within two to three seconds in a normovolemic patient.

If spurting blood indicates arterial bleeding, apply direct pressure to the wound. If this action proves to be unsuccessful, locate the nearest pressure point between the wound and the heart and apply pressure with three fingers, rather than with just a thumb or one finger.

Internal bleeding is more difficult to evaluate, but it can be detected through signs and symptoms of hypovolemic shock. Likely sites of "hidden" blood loss include the thorax, the abdomen, the pelvis, the retroperitoneum, or the thigh. Each hemithorax, for instance, can contain up to two liters of blood.[7,11] For specific signs of "hidden" blood loss, see Appendix 2–A.

Consciousness Level

While these initial assessments and treatments are being carried out, the patient's level of consciousness is evaluated as indicated by the alertness and the orientation of the patient's responses.[12] Orientation to time, place, and person are signs of cerebral functioning. The level of consciousness may mean different things to different people. For the rapid initial survey, the AVPU method is simple, uniform, and easy to remember.[8]

A = alert

V = response to vocal stimuli

P = response to painful stimuli

U = unresponsive

During the ABC survey, try to obtain a description of what happened, focusing on possible mechanisms of injury to help determine which areas or systems were put under particular stress. For example, a survey of the surrounding scene may provide valuable clues to an understanding of the mechanism of the injury and the resulting trauma. Generally, the greater the speed of the vehicle (motor vehicle or the object striking the patient) the greater the injury. In the case of automobile accidents, the position of the steering wheel, the presence of lap belts, the condition of the windshield, and the intactness of inside door latches or window handles should be noted. Burns should alert the care provider to the dangers of smoke inhalation and carbon monoxide poisonings and to burns of the nose, mouth, and pharynx. Gunshot wounds commonly cause internal bleeding, perforations, and fractures. Any such information obtained from the rescue personnel is helpful in a determination of the possibility of specific injuries.[8]

Signs of deteriorating condition include the following:[13]

- cold, clammy skin
- ashen pallor, indicating decreased tissue perfusion and stress reactions from increased activity of the sympathetic nervous system
- diaphoresis, a sympathetic response that occurs in late stages
- cyanosis, signalling sluggish blood flow, proportionally low volume of hemoglobin, and thus decreased oxygen content
- altered level of consciousness, initially seen as anxiety, nervousness, and irritability as the sympathetic nervous system increases the secretion of epinephrine, and later manifest as apathy, lethargy, confusion, and restlessness as the brain receives an inadequate supply of blood and glucose

These initial assessments can be completed in 60 to 90 seconds and ensure that life-threatening conditions can be adequately assessed and treated. Appendix 2–A illustrates the priority sequence of the initial ABC assessment.[2,4,7,10-12,14-17] Potential problems, possible causes for interferences of function, and appropriate emergency treatment are outlined. Further discussion of the care of the multiple-trauma victim is covered in Chapter 5.

SECONDARY SURVEY

A more detailed nursing assessment is completed after the initial survey. As life-threatening injuries are ruled out, a complete secondary survey ensures that no major injuries are overlooked and facilitates the process of setting priorities. The survey takes approximately 3 to 5 minutes and must be tailored to the specific situation. In some disaster situations, there may be time to begin secondary assessments in the field as victims undergo triage, are stabilized, and await transport. Realistically, the field situation may be short of help, and many patients may require treatment for ABC problems. The secondary survey would then be performed at the transfer site as the victims are brought in for more definitive assessment and treatment.

Given the amount of data to be collected and recorded, a careful plan is an absolute necessity. Without a plan, the nurse wastes time backtracking and fumbling. However, a concise, comprehensive plan allows the nurse to move confidently and efficiently through the information that must be routinely covered.

Organization of Assessment

A nurse can conduct a rapid assessment by beginning at the head and moving down to the toes. A consistent order and approach should be used as each body part is examined. Throughout the examination, a comfortable rhythm should be established. General guidelines include the following:[11,18,19]

- *Proceed from head to toe*. Start with the hair and proceed to the bottom of the feet. This sequence keeps track of progress so that no area is overlooked.
- *Progress from the general to the specific*. Look at the patient as a complete organism first; then progressively narrow the focus to areas, organs, and local sites of problems and complaints.
- *Move from external to internal*. Follow the natural order of structures that may be involved when examining an orifice or organ.
- *Proceed from distal to proximal*. This sequence, reflecting the direction of blood flow back to the heart, applies to the examination of the extremities.

Techniques of Assessment

The nurse uses the senses—except taste—in the assessment process. Instruments merely amplify these senses. Four standard techniques are used in the assessment process: (1) inspection, (2) palpation, (3) percussion, and (4) auscultation. Although these techniques require some motor skills and dexterity, they are readily mastered with practice, and their use enhances the nurse's ability to assess effectively and efficiently.

Inspection is the visual examination of the patient to detect significant physical features. Detailed and focused observations are compared with established standards or norms. Although inspection seems to be the least complex skill used in physical assessment, it demands that the assessor have a broad knowledge base and skill in observing. Inspection alone can provide up to 90 percent of all the information a physical examination yields. Rarely does palpation, percussion, or auscultation uncover an abnormality that does not exhibit some sign on careful inspection. Look before you touch.

Palpation uses the sense of touch to determine the characteristics of tissues or organs. Properly performed, superficial light and deep palpation are vital tools for uncovering masses, temperature changes, and tenderness. Watching the facial expressions while palpating gives valuable clues to the degree of pain and tenderness. Knowing the usual shape and texture of underlying structures before palpating an area facilitates identification of fixed or movable masses. Palpation must be done very gently over possibly inflamed structures (such as the potentially injured spleen or liver), phlebotic vessels, or the skin of the elderly; all are friable, easily damaged tissues. Palpation should never be carried out over frozen tissues or possible fractures.

Percussion is a procedure in which the body surface is lightly but sharply tapped or struck to produce sounds that reflect the density, the size, and the position of underlying structures or tissue. The tones elicited by percussion vary according to the underlying density of the tissue. The technique is especially valuable for determining the amount of air or solid material in the underlying lung or abdomen and for determining the boundaries of organs or parts of the body that differ in density. Percussion can also be used to determine whether there is a change in normal density—for example, when percussion reveals dullness over the normally resonant lung. A combination of aural and manual skills is needed to perform percussion accurately.

Auscultation is the process of listening to sounds produced by various organs of the body to detect variations from normal. Except in the assessment of the abdomen, in which auscultation follows inspection, it is traditionally the final step in the four-step process. *Immediate auscultation*, performed without a stethoscope, can be used to evaluate such sounds as wheezing, stridor, bowel sounds, or the inability to speak a complete sentence in a single breath. *Mediate auscultation*, performed with the stethoscope, identifies internal sounds from the heart, the lungs, and the abdomen, as well as friction rubs and bruits.[19,20,21]

Although smell is often the forgotten sense, it may also provide valuable data. From the foul smell of a wound discharge to an overperfumed presence, odors describe a patient. Odors can be recorded as foul, sweet, nauseating, "acetone-like," fecal, mild, strong, or weak.

The Head-to-Toe Approach

It is important for the nurse to keep in mind that the secondary survey is not meant to be a complete physical examination; rather, it serves the purpose of screening all body parts and systems. Because it is easy to be sidetracked by the first positive finding, the nurse must keep asking, What else may be wrong? Appendix 2–B presents a comprehensive overview of the head-to-toe survey and the approximate times for each assessment step.[1,2,5,7–9,11,21–26] The Glasgow Coma Scale (GCS) (Table 2–1) is based on eye-opening, verbal and motor responses and is a quick practical way to monitor changes in consciousness. The graduated numerical scale ranges from 3–15. The lower the rating, the more serious the patient's condition. A response level of below 7 signifies a comatose state where as above 9 indicates a non-comatose state. Key points regarding techniques and findings are provided. The suggested times may seem unrealistic to the beginning practitioner; however, development of an organized, systematic approach followed by diligent practice soon makes the assessment process routine and feasible within the time suggested.

Table 2–1 Glasgow Coma Scale

Organ/Action	Response	Score
Eyes	Open spontaneously	4
	Open to verbal command	3
	Open to pain	2
	No response	1
Best motor response		
To verbal command	Obeys	6
To painful stimulus*	Localizes pain	5
	Flexion—withdrawal	4
	Flexion—abnormal (decorticate rigidity)	3
	Extension (decerebrate rigidity)	2
	No response	1
Best verbal response†	Oriented and converses	5
	Disoriented and converses	4
	Inappropriate words	3
	Incomprehensible sounds	2
	No response	1
Total		3–15

Notes: *Apply knuckles to sternum; observe arms.
†Arouse patient with painful stimulus if necessary.
Source: Adapted with permission from Jennett B, Teasdale G: Aspects of coma after severe head injury. *Lancet* 1977; 1:878.

GATHERING AND RECORDING DATA

Although it may seem impossible, the nurse must be both brief and thorough and must learn to describe findings objectively according to the senses: What was seen? What was heard? What was felt? Vague terms such as ''normal'' or ''no problems'' should be avoided. Keeping in mind what *is* normal, record whatever conforms or does not conform to normal. Remember that norms for such things as skin color, turgor, body proportion, and fat distribution vary according to the person's age and ethnic origin. Rather than label findings, describe them so that an independent reader can arrive at the same conclusion. A comprehensive data-base form that follows the assessment process facilitates the collection and the recording of vital information. A sample form like that presented in Exhibit 2–1 can serve as the initial record of assessment and treatment and as an ongoing flow sheet.

Medical History

Collecting an adequate medical history is as important as performing the physical examination. In a disaster situation, the nurse cannot conduct a leisurely interview that follows the classic format: chief complaint, history of present illness, past medical history, family history, psychosocial history, and review of systems. Essential information must be gathered quickly and concisely.

The patient should be approached in a manner that helps allay fear and anxiety. A calm approach and a few words of quiet reassurance are advisable. During the course of the initial examination, most of the relevant immediate history can be obtained by remembering a convenient mnemonic, AMPLE:[8,21]

A = *allergies* the patient may have—especially allergies to penicillin, other antibiotics, or medications likely to be given in the course of treatment for trauma.

M = *medications* the patient is receiving that might affect the patient's condition. Past or present heart medications, anticoagulants, narcotics, or steroids should be particularly asked about. Find out when the last tetanus immunization was given.

P = *past illness or injury* that could provide important information about the patient's need for or response to treatment.

L = *last meal* or oral intake. Since digestion may be delayed after injury, the possibility of gastric retention, vomiting, and aspiration must be considered.

E = *events* preceding or following the accident. The extent to which the patient recalls them provides some estimate of the level of consciousness and the severity of injury and may provide clues to the site and the mechanisms of injury to the body.

Additional Information

Ideally, the history should be obtained from the patient if the patient is able to provide it. If the patient does not seem to comprehend, consider that the patient

Exhibit 2–1 Multiple Trauma Assessment and Flow Sheet

1. AIRWAY
   Artificial airway____ Size____ Time____
   O_2 therapy: Type____ Liter/min____
   Tracheostomy _____

2. BREATHING
   Ventilatory assistance _____
   Spontaneous respiratory effort _____
   Rate and character _____
   ABGs _____ (see result sheet)

3. CIRCULATION
   External bleeding sites _____
   Pressure dressings _____
   Suturing _____ (to be done later)
   Lab work ordered: SMA–6__ CBC__
   TCM __ Units __ UA __ PT/PTT __
   Cardiovascular status _____
   Pulse rate and character _____
   Arrhythmia ____ JVD __ Edema __
   Peripheral pulses _____
   Capillary filling time _____

4. INTRAVENOUS THERAPY
   Angiocath size: 18 __ 16 __ 14 __
   Sites _____
   Solution: LR __ Other __ Time __
   Rate of flow _____ IV Pump _____
   Dial-a-flow __ Blood: Amt __ Time __

5. VITAL SIGNS
   Repeat every 15 minutes

TIME	BP	P	R	T

6. BRIEF SECONDARY
   EXAMINATION
   Head-neck _____
   Neurologic _____
     Coma score _____
   Chest _____
   Abdomen _____
   Genitalia _____
   Extremities _____
   Skin _____

A. Immobilize
B. Prepare for transport & notify
   receiving facility
C. Prepare for surgery
D. Decadron 50 mg IVP
   Time _____ (given for depressed
   CNS status)

7. EVIDENCE OF MASSIVE BLOOD
   LOSS INTO CHEST OR ABDOMEN
   MAST: time applied _____
   Pressures _____
   Time began removing _____

8. EVIDENCE OF CARDIAC
   TAMPONADE
   Percardiocentesis _____
   MD _____ Time _____
   Notes _____

9. TENSION PNEUMOTHORAX
   Size of chest tube _____
   Applied by _____
   Drainage _____
   Method of drainage: Closed _____
     Two-bottle _____

10. EVIDENCE OF MI OR
    MYOCARDIAL CONTUSION
    ECG _____
    Monitor hemodynamics: Dopamine __
    Solution _____% of Dopamine _____

11. SPLINT ALL FRACTURES
    Locations _____
    Type of splints _____

12. INSERT FOLEY CATHETER
    Time _____ Size _____ Type _____
    Output:

Time	Amount	Color/Consistency

    RBC present __ Order IVP and
    Cystoscopy

Exhibit 2–1 continued

13. INSERT NG TUBE
    Size _____ Suction: Constant _____
    Intermittent _____
    Output: Irrigation type _____
       Time   Amount   Color/Consistency
    _____
    _____

14. ORDER X-RAYS
    Chest ____ C-Spine ____ Extrem ____
    Continue immobilization of head/neck

15. PERITONEAL LAVAGE
    INDICATED
    Yes ____ No ____ Time _____
    Size of angio _____

Performed by _____
Amounts and description _____
_____

16. DRESS WOUNDS
    Areas _____
    Tetanus: Type____ Amt____ Time____
    Antibiotics: Type _____
       Amt____ Route____ Time____
    Other: Type_____ Amt_____
       Route_____ Time____

SIGNATURES _____MD
            _____RN

Source: Adapted with permission from Multiple Trauma or Critical Care Flow Sheet, Valley View Medical Center, Cedar City, Utah.

may be deaf, may speak a foreign language, or may have a neurological impairment. The patient may be in physical or emotional shock and so may be unable to answer questions.

If the patient is unconscious, uncooperative, or non-English speaking, other avenues must be explored to obtain an adequate history. Police or rescue personnel should be queried about the time, the type, and the location of the disaster; the position in which the patient was found; the initial assessment data; any seizure activity noted; and any supportive or therapeutic treatment measures that were undertaken.

The patient may also have been separated from family members or associates and from such identifying materials as a wallet or a purse. However, if family members or close friends are present, they may be able to provide information about allergies, medications, prosthetic devices (including hearing aids or contact lenses), and changes in behavior before admission. In addition, the nurse should look for any Medic-Alert jewelry. These bracelets and necklaces list hidden medical conditions (such as allergies) and give an identification number and 24-hour emergency telephone number. Calling that number and giving the patient's ID number provides access to the patient's medical history from a computerized file. Although it is unlikely that Medic-Alert information can be obtained by persons working in the field, a notation on the patient's record that Medic-Alert jewelry was found will alert personnel at the receiving facility to call for the appropriate information. Regardless of the source of information, document it in the patient's record, along with the source of the information.[11,24,27]

ONGOING ASSESSMENT

At this point, the first two assessment phases are complete. The third phase, ongoing observation and evaluation, quickly identifies changes in condition. Further laboratory and hemodynamic measurements can help to determine the severity of the trauma and the effectiveness of the treatment. Definitive treatment for the problems uncovered in the initial and secondary surveys can be implemented. As long as the patient is entrusted to the nurse for care, the role of assessor, planner, care provider, evaluator, and reporter never ceases. A continuous, systematic assessment enables the nurse to stay alert to changes in the patient's condition that may require quick, decisive intervention or instant notification of the physician.

To summarize briefly, the appropriate sequence for treatment of the disaster victim is as follows:[8,28]

- Make a rapid initial survey of the patient's condition, focusing on the vital functions of respiration, circulation, cerebration, and the possibility of cervical spine injury.
- Evaluate and ensure airway patency.
- Ensure effective respiratory exchange.
- Maintain or restore effective circulation.
- Perform a rapid, complete secondary survey, avoiding excessive movement of the patient—especially if spinal injury is suspected.
- Record important observations such as level of consciousness, pupil size, vital signs, deformities, or abnormalities to serve as baseline data.
- Obtain a history of the injury and of the events before and after the accident. Inquire about allergies, medications, past illness, and last meal.
- Cover open wounds, using pressure to maintain control of bleeding as necessary.
- Splint obvious or suspected fractures, and maintain neck and back immobility in those suspected of spinal trauma.
- Assist with transfer to the appropriate treatment facility.

PITFALLS AND PRECAUTIONS

After the assessment is complete and the findings documented, what should be done? The first part of the assessment process is the adequate collection of data; the equally important second part is the analysis and the interpretation of information for the formulation of nursing diagnoses and the initiation of appropriate treatment. Above all, data analysis must be given the same careful attention as data collection. Avoid drawing hasty (and possibly inaccurate) conclusions. For example, if the patient is restless, belligerent, combative, with bowel or bladder incontinence, poor personal hygiene, and a disheveled appearance, do not automatically assume a drug or alcohol abuse problem or a psychiatric disorder; the patient may have a brain lesion or hypoxia. Similarly, the patient with multifocal premature ventricular contractions does not automatically have severe heart disease but may have a benign, long-standing cardiac arrythmia or may be suffering from digitalis poisoning. Never assume that all the patient's problems can be immediately identified.

The nurse must keep eyes and ears open to sudden changes in condition.[11] A few guidelines may help in avoiding some common pitfalls:[11,29]

- Always validate what you think you are hearing. Patients may be giving answers they think the nurse wants to hear. Use open-ended questions and let patients describe their condition in their own words.
- Remember that what you see is seldom the whole picture. Many injuries lie below the surface, like the tip of the iceberg.
- Conduct a thorough screening assessment that starts with a visual inspection and is followed by palpation, percussion, and auscultation.
- Do not restrict your assessment to only the body part in question or the most obvious signs of the condition. Avoid the tunnel vision that allows you to jump to hasty conclusions.
- Look for causes. There can be one cause or dozens of causes for such conditions as chest pain, dyspnea, or confusion—some benign, some life-threatening.
- Do not rule out a condition just because a typical symptom is absent.
- Carefully tailor your assessment to include all the possible underlying conditions that can produce a particular symptom.
- Search out the facts of the significant past medical history. Patients may underestimate the importance of past illnesses and their effect on their present condition.
- Remember that all psychoneurotic patients eventually die of organic disease. Even repeat patients with multiple, unfounded complaints may come with serious problems.
- When patients say they have an emergency and are in need of help, the burden of proof is not theirs. Do not court disaster by ignoring or discounting a patient's fear. All patients should feel they have been heard and understood and that the seriousness of their condition has been fairly evaluated.

Effective disaster management through the use of rapid yet thorough assessment skill is analogous to a kaleidoscope. The picture changes slightly as each patient is evaluated and treated. Just as the intensity of light increases the colors of the kaleidoscope, the acuity of the condition and the volume of patients intensify the need for nurse assessment and triage skills. The nurse-manager must be aware of the patients waiting for attention and must coordinate the patient flow so that all patients feel cared for and no serious problems go unattended.[29] Skills in rapid assessment increase the effectiveness of disaster management and increase the rate of patient survival.

REFERENCES

1. McSwain N: To manage multiple injury: Establish priorities. *Emerg Med*, November 30, 1982, pp 223–243.

2. Perdue P: Urgent priorities in severe trauma: Life-threatening respiratory injuries. *RN*, April 1981, pp 26–33.

3. Wells-Mackie JJ: Clinical assessment and priority-setting. *Nurs Clin North Am* 1981;16:3–12.

4. Cardona VD: Trauma post-op: The real nursing challenge. *RN*, March 1982, pp 22–29.

5. Sigmon HD: Trauma: This patient needs your expert help. *Nurs 83*, January 1983, pp 33–41.

6. Orr SM, Robinson WA, Campbell PM, et al: The Hyatt disaster: Two physicians' perspectives, two nurses' perspectives. *JEN*, January/February 1982, pp 6–16.

7. Levison M, Trunkey DD: Initial assessment and resuscitation. *Surg Clin North Am* 1982;62:9–16.

8. A primer on trauma care: What primary care physicians should do and how to do it. *Emerg Med*, November 15, 1980, pp 25–140.

9. Warner CG (ed): *Emergency Care: Assessment and Intervention*, ed 3. St Louis, The CV Mosby Co, 1983.

10. Bucknall TE: Assist: A nursing scheme for the management of the severely injured patient. *Nurs Times* 1979;75:1902–1903.

11. Urosevich PR (ed): *Dealing with Emergencies*. Horsham, Pa, Intermed Communications Inc, 1981, pp 8–42.

12. Hoyt KS: Chest trauma: When the patient looks bad, act fast; when he looks good, act fast. *Nurs 83*, May 1983, pp 34–41.

13. Clutter P: Assessment of abdominal trauma. *JEN*, March/April 1981, pp 47–49.

14. Sumner SM, Grau PE: Emergency! First aid for choking. *Nurs 82*, July 1982, pp 40–49.

15. Guidelines for cardiopulmonary resuscitation (CPR) and emergency cardiac care (ECC). *JAMA* 1980;244:453–509.

16. Hall JP, Jackson VD: Adult respiratory medical emergencies. *Nurs Clin North Am* 1981;16:75–84.

17. Perdue P: Stab and crush wounds to the heart. *RN*, May 1981, pp 63–65, 124, 126.

18. Koeckeritz JL: The fine art of giving a physical: Organizing your plan of action. *RN*, November 1981, pp 46–51.

19. King C: Refining your assessment techniques. *RN*, February 1982, pp 43–47.

20. Sana JM, Judge RD (eds): *Physical Assessment Skills for Nursing Practice*, ed 2. Boston, Little Brown & Co, 1982, pp 11–25.

21. Lanros NE: *Assessment and Intervention in Emergency Nursing*, ed 2. Bowie, Md, Robert J Brady, 1983, pp 59–67.

22. Mastrian KG: Of course you can manage head trauma patients. *RN*, August 1981, pp 44–51.

23. Perdue P: Life-threatening head and spinal injuries. *RN*, June 1981, pp 36–41, 102.

24. Miller M: Emergency management of the unconscious patient. *Nurs Clin North Am* 1981;16:59–73.

25. Buchanan LE: Emergency! First aid for spinal cord injury. *Nurs 82*, August 1982, pp 68–75.

26. Bailey M: Emergency! First aid for fractures. *Nurs 82*, November 1982, pp 78–81.

27. Estrada EG: Triage systems. *Nurs Clin North Am* 1981;16:13–24.

28. Committee on Trauma, American College of Surgeons: *Early Care of the Injured Patient*, ed 2. Philadelphia, WB Saunders Co, 1976.

29. Turner SR: Golden rules for accurate triage. *JEN*, July/August 1981, pp 153–155.

Appendix 2–A

The Initial Survey: A 90-Second ABC Assessment

Critical Observation	Indication	Suspect	Priority Action
Airway	Airway obstruction	Maxillofacial trauma Stridor Choking No air movement Skin red to cyanotic Unconsciousness	Collection of blood, mucus, vomitus, or other debris Edematous soft tissue Allergic reaction Tongue obstruction	Find out cause of choking Foreign object: use combination backblows and manual thrusts Finger sweep for visible foreign object (never perform blind sweep) Edema: perform artificial airway or emergency cricothyreotomy Allergy: treatment for anaphylaxis Tongue obstruction: perform head-tilt and chin-lift, or chin-lift, jaw-lift, or jaw-thrust without head-tilt
Breathing	Inadequate ventilation	Absence of spontaneous or even-sided breathing Tracheal shift Subcutaneous air Retractions	Deviated trachea due to tracheal fracture Tension pneumothorax with	No spontaneous breathing after airway opened: begin artificial ventilation Place in semi-Fowlers, if possible, to facilitate breathing Administer supplemental oxygen whenever ventilation is inadequate May require emergency tracheotomy if unable to ventilate

		Paradoxical breathing Inaudible breath sounds and minimal movement of chest wall	mediastinal shift Pneumothorax from fractured ribs and punctured lung	Insert chest tube for drainage of air and bloody fluid from around lung to allow reinflation
Circulation	External bleeding		Arterial injury from fractures or severe lacerations	
		Scalp or temple wound		Compress temporal artery
		Facial wound below the eye		Apply pressure to the facial artery located along lower border of jaw
		Neck wound		Compress wound site; do not compress carotid artery
		Upper-arm or shoulder wound		Compress subclavian artery against clavicle
		Wound on elbow or lower part of upper arm		Compress brachial artery against humerus
		Lower-arm wound		Compress ulnar and radial arteries at antecubital fossa
		Hand wound		Compress ulnar and radial arteries at the wrist
		Thigh wound		Compress femoral artery against femur
		Lower-leg wound		Compress popliteal artery located behind knee
		Foot wound		Apply pressure to all arteries in the ankle
	Internal bleeding	Severe respiratory distress	Bleeding into thorax	Elevate head of bed to ease breathing Administer oxygen

Critical Observation	Indication	Suspect	Priority Action
	Cardiac arrhythmias		Check apical and peripheral pulses Monitor and treat cardiac arrhythmias Prepare for chest tube insertion
	Abdominal distention Rigid, boardlike abdomen Rebound tenderness Vomiting and paralytic ileus Numbness and pain in legs Hematoma over flank	Bleeding into abdomen	Perform gastric ice lavage if related to peptic ulcer Prepare for IV Cimetadine Prepare for paracentesis
	Abdominal or pelvic distention Lower abdominal pain and tenderness Lower back pain Blood in urine Decreased urine output	Bleeding into pelvis	Pelvis fractured: prepare for traction or surgery Immobilize with pelvic sling Insert foley catheter (caution: do not insert if urethral damage is suspected) Observe urine for amount and color
	Erythema on affected leg Painful, boardlike thigh Localized edema and change in size	Bleeding into thigh	Apply ice packs Elevate affected leg Apply plastic air splint

Appendix 2–B

The Secondary Survey: A 3- to 5-Minute Head-to-Toe Assessment

Approximate Time	Assessment Step	Key Points
12–15 seconds	Assess general appearance and level of consciousness: • conscious patient	Check level of orientation: • Test and chart actions the patient is able to perform and any responses elicited by applying standard stimuli. • Check alertness and orientation by asking questions about history. • Note whether patient is restless and combative, whether speech is incoherent or slurred, and whether questions are understood and answers are appropriate.
	• unconscious patient	Check level of consciousness: • Use Glasgow coma scale or other objective scale of value (see Table 2–1). • Look for spontaneous movement of extremities, bilaterally and equally. • Look for evidence of decerebrate posture: adduction, extension, hyperpronation of arms; extension and plantar flexion of lower extremities (usually the result of trauma to the brain stem). • Look for evidence of decorticate posture: flexion of arms, wrists, and fingers; adduction of upper extremities; extension, internal rotation, and plantar flexion of lower extremities (usually the result of severe cerebral trauma). • Test reaction to verbal, tactile, and painful stimuli; classify response as purposeful, inappropriate, or nonpurposeful. If the patient is not fully alert and oriented, suspect— • neurological deficit, • head injury,

- oxygen insufficiency,
- fluid and electrolyte imbalance,
- infections (internal toxins),
- drugs or alcohol (external toxins).

45–60 seconds

Assess face, head, and neck:

- inspect and palpate head and scalp
- inspect face

Check for lacerations, avulsed tissue, deformities, and soft spots (could indicate depressed skull fracture).

Inspect for symmetry, ptosis, pallor, flush, circumoral cyanosis, orbital ecchymosis and conjunctival redness (goggle-like) or grossly bloody conjunctiva (Pircher's sign) indicative of severe abdominal trauma.

If patient is dark-skinned, check conjunctiva, mucous membranes, palms, and soles.

Note any facial lacerations, but do not get sidetracked by superficial bleeding.

- inspect eyes and pupillary reactions

Check pupils for size, movement, and direct and consensual response to light.

Check for intact corneal reflex.

Note evidence of trauma, foreign body, infection, hypovolemia, sympathetic nerve lesion, or the presence of contact lenses.

- inspect ears and nose

Note color, amount, and consistency of any drainage.

Check for evidence of leaking cerebrospinal fluid (fluid does not clot; ring sign, and positive glucose). In the case of a positive ring sign, blood dropped onto a sponge or filter does not form the usual single spot; instead, blood components form one or two rings in the periphery while the center remains clear.

- inspect mouth

Check buccal mucosa and under tongue; note inflammation, cyanosis, bleeding, or missing teeth.

Approximate Time	Assessment Step	Key Points
		Smell breath odor (fruity, acetone, alcohol).
		Check for presence of adequate gag reflex.
	• inspect and palpate neck	Ask whether the patient has neck pain; palpate for muscle spasms while maintaining immobilization; palpate spinous processes; note local pain, limitation of motion, crepitus, or deformity of spinous processes.
		Inspect and palpate jugular veins for distention, pulsation, or collapse.
		Palpate trachea: if deviated, check lung sounds and suspect atelectasis, tension pneumothorax, or pleural effusion.
		Palpate for crepitus, subcutaneous emphysema; if present, suspect fractured trachea and pneumothorax.
		Neck injury in the unconscious patient is suspected by the presence of flaccid areflexia, especially with flaccid rectal sphincter; diaphragmatic breathing; ability to flex, but not to extend, the forearms; pain response above, but not below, the clavicles; priapism.
50–60 seconds	Assess chest	Inspect symmetry of chest expansion, position of comfort, retractions or use of accessory muscles, ecchymosis, lacerations, puncture wounds, drainage, or deformities.
		Check stability of chest and rib cage with a sternal press and barrel push against sides of ribs toward center; feel for subcutaneous emphysema.
		Percuss and auscultate bilaterally.
		Note normal and abnormal breath sounds.
		Count respiratory rate and note rhythm.
		Note distant or muffled heart sounds.
		Count apical pulse rate.

Time	Assessment	Description
30 seconds	Assess abdomen	Inspect for distention, obvious masses, scars, skin conditions, lacerations, puncture wounds, contusions, ecchymosis, or drainage. Auscultate, beginning in the right upper quadrant lateral to the umbilicus and moving clockwise through all quadrants; note bowel sounds (intermittent gurgling sounds from 5 to 30 times per minute), bruits (murmur-like sounds), or friction rubs (like two pieces of leather rubbing together). Percuss to note size and location of organs and masses; note tympany (hollow or air-filled structures), or dullness (dense tissue). Palpate last to avoid disruption of bowel sounds; perform light palpation to relax musculature and to evaluate generally, deep palpation to detect masses and enlargements. Note localized pain, spasm, rigidity, or rebound tenderness. Palpate iliac crests; apply pressure to anterior superior iliac spines and symphysis pubis (tenderness suggests pelvic bone fractures or joint separations).
10 seconds	Assess genitals and perineum	Inspect for lacerations, swelling, discharge, incontinence, blood at meatus (do not catheterize if suspect urethral damage).
60 seconds	Assess extremities	Inspect for obvious deformities, wounds, fractures, ecchymotic areas, and burns, splint suspected fracture. Assess limb movements: if patient is unconscious, note decerebrate or decorticate postures; if conscious, equality and adequacy of strength. Assess the 5 Ps bilaterally: • *Pain.* Ask patient to locate and to describe the pain; ask if it is increasing or decreasing; palpate limbs, starting

Approximate Time	Assessment Step	Key Points
		farthest from the pain and feeling for deformities of crepitus.

- *Pulse.* Check all peripheral pulses, carefully noting those distal to any injuries.
- *Pallor.* Note color of palms and soles; note capillary filling time (normal, 3–5 seconds); note skin temperature.
- *Paresthesias.* Ask patient to describe feeling (no feeling, numbness, or "pins and needles"); test sensation with point of paper clip or pen cap.
- *Paralysis.* Assess grip strength; ask patient to flex, extend, adduct, and abduct limbs within limits of pain (if patient is unable to move arms and legs, do not increase anxiety by continuing to ask).

Suspect spinal cord injury if the patient has back pain or tenderness, the level of consciousness is impaired, head or neck injury is present, sensory or motor loss is evident, or if the mechanism of injury suggests it.

Any patient who can forcibly flex both arms at the elbow, who can open and close both hands with ease, and who can vigorously wiggle the toes and lift each leg off the stretcher may be presumed to have no spinal injury. Patterns of weakness may vary; however, arm and hand weakness generally means cervical injury, but leg weakness with normal arms suggests thoracic or lumbar spine injury.

Take blood pressure bilaterally.

Note edema, pedal or sacral.

If time and condition permit, turn patient over for a head-to-toe assessment of the back. Never turn the patient with suspected cervical spine injury or fractured pelvis.

30–45 seconds	
Assess head, scalp, and neck	Continue inspection; palpate for lacerations, deformities, and tenderness. Note any discolorations, abrasions, or deformities.
Assess posterior thorax	Assess pain, tenderness, and deformity along entire spine. Check for ecchymosis, open wounds, penetration or exit wounds, flail segments, or blood. Palpate/percuss for costovertebral angle tenderness. Percuss and auscultate lung sounds for equality and adventitious sounds.
Assess flanks and buttocks	Note retroperitoneal bleeding and discoloration over flanks.
Assess perineum	Perform a rectal examination to determine the presence or absence of sphincter tone and the presence or absence of gross blood.
Assess extremities	Inspect and palpate extremities for discolorations, tenderness, deformities, and wounds.

Chapter 3

Management and Triage at the Disaster Site

Ralph L. Brown, E.M.T.-P., P.A.-C.

A disaster scene is one of the most challenging environments in which nurses have to practice. Most disaster scenes are noisy, dangerous, and confusing. There, nurses are expected to work closely with unfamiliar personnel, to use equipment with which they may not have had experience, and to follow procedures that are different from normal clinical procedures. Without question, emotional and physical stress factors are extreme.

This chapter examines closely the challenges nurses face at a disaster scene, the steps they must take to overcome these challenges, and the way they can apply their skills to have a positive influence on patient care. The organization of a disaster scene and the process of triage at the scene are emphasized. The chapter concludes with suggestions that nurses can use to prepare for a disaster.

CHALLENGE OF A DISASTER SCENE

The nurse's patient care skills are desperately needed in a disaster situation; however, before nurses can be effective in caring for patients at a disaster scene, they must understand the many challenges that can distract from their efforts. These challenges can be broken down into three main types: (1) hazardous environments, (2) overwhelmed systems, and (3) inappropriate patient care.

Hazards at the Disaster Scene

The disaster scene may be full of hazards to life and limb. The very act of walking through rubble or climbing on steep slopes can cause injury to the nurse or further injury to the disaster victim. Some major hazards that may exist include the following:

- fire
- explosive material
- smoke or other toxic gases
- downed power lines
- falling debris
- collapsing buildings
- floods
- landslides or avalanches
- crowd violence

The nurse must be aware of the threat of disaster hazards and must assess the area for these problems before entering the scene. Obviously, these hazards can make it difficult to reach the patient and to carry out treatment; they can also make it more difficult to move medical supplies into the disaster area and to move patients out. If the nurse is injured or killed in a disaster, a greater burden is placed on the already taxed rescue system: an incapacitated nurse means that patients lose the benefit of the nurse's skills. In addition, an injured nurse becomes one more patient for the disaster personnel to care for. It is absolutely vital, then, that nurses be cognizant of disaster hazards and avoid them at all times.

Overwhelmed Systems

Emergency medical services (EMS) have progressed rapidly since the 1960s. Highly trained and well-equipped emergency medical technicians (EMTs) or paramedics exist in almost all communities. These EMTs and paramedics are backed up by fire departments, police departments, rescue teams, and other organizations that can be called out in a disaster. In many communities, nurses serve on the EMS team as prehospital personnel. Hospitals and their staffs have likewise progressed in their ability to care for mass casualties. Regardless of this progress in disaster preparedness, however, any event classified as a disaster causes the community's emergency medical systems to be overloaded, and so they fail to function as they would normally do. For example, the nurse who is accustomed to working in a controlled environment can be caught off-guard when faced with the confusion of a disaster. To counter the breakdown of an over-whelmed emergency system and to remain an effective practitioner in a disaster, the nurse must understand the failures that can occur. Perhaps Murphy's Law, which states that "anything that can go wrong will go wrong and at the worst possible time," is a good rule to go by when anticipating emergency system failures in a disaster.

Communication

One of the universal disaster problems is miscommunication. Nurses should not count on being able to receive or send out reliable information—especially early in a disaster.[1] Because EMTs, paramedics, fire fighters, police, hospitals, and government officials may initially have little understanding of the extent of the disaster, radio frequencies may be full of erroneous information. Many times emergency agencies or hospitals are not notified of a disaster, and valuable personnel do not respond until late in the event. Communication equipment may fail as telephone lines are knocked out, electricity goes off, or radio batteries are drained. Further assistance or medical supplies may be impossible to summon. Because nurses caught in this situation can find it difficult to know how to help, they should anticipate these communication problems and take steps to work around them so that they can continue to function.

Equipment

Another problem that can be expected is the lack of medical or rescue equipment. The limited number of ambulances and rescue vehicles in a community can prove to be inadequate for a disaster. Because stretchers, bandages, intravenous fluids, splints, and other medical supplies will be used up immediately, many patients will face the possibility of going without these supplies. Furthermore, disaster caches in most communities are inadequate or outdated. Extra equipment may not be dispatched to the disaster scene because of poor communications, or it may be sent to the wrong location. Most community disaster plans have provisions for mutual assistance agreements by which neighboring communities agree to help each other in the event of an overwhelming situation, but it takes time for this backup equipment to arrive. Nurses facing a disaster must understand the equipment restraints they may be forced to work within.

Command

Amid the confusion and dangers of a disaster, a third problem usually occurs: poor command.[2(p271)] The first responding units to arrive at a disaster scene are usually unsure about who the leader is. As more and more personnel arrive, too many leaders can emerge. Orders are contradicted, and important commands are overlooked. This problem lessens later in the disaster as local command of the scene evolves.

The nurse who arrives early at a disaster has to anticipate the possibility of conflicting leadership. Nurses must understand, then, their role in a disaster and, if necessary, must be able to function with minimal supervision.

Personnel

One of the most disturbing situations that develops in a disaster is the improper use of personnel. When medical or rescue personnel are used inappropriately, an already bad situation becomes even more desperate. Medical personnel who are needed to deliver their valuable skills to patients are often directed to perform rescue operations or are placed in administrative positions. Nurses should be aware of this problem and, whenever possible, avoid tasks that detract from direct patient care.

MEETING THE CHALLENGE

A review of disaster challenges can paint a gloomy picture of what may occur. Nurses who participate at a disaster scene should not be discouraged, however, because these challenges can be met if they establish the following three goals as they attempt to handle a disaster scene:

1. to assure the safety of personnel and patients
2. to organize an effective disaster system
3. to deliver appropriate patient care

Any nurse participating in a disaster scene must realize that the ability to care for patients will be severely compromised unless all three goals are somehow met. Nevertheless, it may be necessary at first to address the goals of safety and organization before concentrating on patient care (Exhibit 3–1).

Assuring Safety

All disaster personnel, including nurses, should have as their foremost consideration the protection of (1) themselves, (2) their fellow workers, and (3) their patients—in that order.[3] Nothing is more important that assuring that no more injuries occur. An incapacitated rescuer places a great strain on the entire disaster scene. In lieu of formal safety training, the nurse must rely on common sense in order to employ the necessary safety precautions. Some guidelines to remember include the following:

- Always quickly assess the scene for dangers before rushing in.
- Stay at least 100 yards away from fires.
- Never enter a burning structure.
- Stay at least 300 yards from explosives.
- Never enter an area that may contain toxic gases.
- Always remain upwind from toxic gases.
- Protect yourself from oncoming traffic by placing flashing lights or flares several hundred feet toward traffic.

The nurse must remember that some disaster environments are so dangerous that those entering them may be injured or killed. If this is the case, the nurse

Exhibit 3–1 Evaluating the Disaster Scene

The nurse who enters a disaster scene should begin an evaluation of the three steps used to control a disaster. If one of the goals is not being met, the nurse may need to address that problem before going on to provide patient care.

Goal 1: Safety of the area

Ask yourself,

- Can I safely enter the scene?
- What hazards should I be avoiding?
- Are there hidden dangers that need marking?

Goal 2: Organization of the disaster system

Ask yourself,

- Where is the disaster zone?
- Where is the treatment zone?
- Where is the transportation zone?
- Is the leadership functioning in each zone?

Goal 3: Provision of the most appropriate patient care

Ask yourself,

- Do I need to perform triage?
- How many priority levels should I set up?
- What personnel should be assigned to each level?
- What types of patients are assigned first priority level?
- Have someone direct traffic away from you.
- Place vehicles in a position to protect you when working on a highway (Figure 3–1).
- Completely avoid downed power lines.
- Never try to remove a patient who may be in contact with a power source.
- Mark hazards that are not obvious so that others do not walk into them.

should never enter that environment and should discourage others from entering it. This action may mean that the nurse can not render care to certain victims.

Organizing the System: Personnel at the Scene

The key to handling a disaster properly and caring for patients rapidly is the organization of an effective disaster system that is based on the proper utilization

Figure 3–1 Vehicle Placement for Safety at Disaster Scene

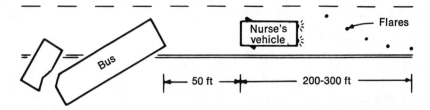

Note: Protect the scene of an accident on a road by placing your vehicle 50 ft. towards traffic with emergency lights blinking and wheels turned away from the scene. Place a flare pattern towards traffic for 200 to 300 ft. in order to give rapidly moving vehicles time to slow down.

of personnel at the most appropriate sites. The system that local, state, and federal disaster preparedness agencies have developed to handle large emergencies is usually unfamiliar to nurses. Because the roles of different personnel and the legal line of authority at a disaster site must be known before the nurse can fit into the disaster organization, a brief explanation of the different types of personnel that participate in a disaster and their roles can help the nurse to understand better how the disaster is handled.

Police Department

Because law enforcement officers are generally the first personnel to be notified of a disaster they are usually the first to arrive at the scene. Often, it is the police officer who recognizes that a disaster has taken place and notifies other agencies that their help is needed.

A number of law enforcement agencies may respond to a disaster scene (e.g., highway patrol, state police, county sheriffs, and local police officers). These officers can become involved in rescue work or patient care, but their most important job is to secure the disaster area. Law enforcement officers are invaluable for keeping traffic moving, keeping crowds out of the way, and directing rescue equipment into the area. The overall safety of disaster personnel is also a concern of police officials.

Fire Department

Fire fighters, too, play an extremely active role in most disasters. Besides caring for patients, fire fighters are responsible for controlling fires and other hazardous environments. They also usually have the expertise and the equipment to extricate patients from collapsed buildings or crushed vehicles. The nurse should be aware that the legal responsibility for the command of a disaster scene usually rests with the fire chief and his officers, although in some communities, the county sheriff or the chief of police has the responsibility.[2(p269)]

EMS Personnel

EMS personnel are responsible for providing prehospital patient care in most communities. Because the nurse probably works most closely with these persons in a disaster, the nurse's skills are combined with the skills of the EMT or the paramedic to deliver maximum patient care. EMS personnel at a disaster consist of either EMTs, who can provide basic life support and basic trauma management, or advanced EMTs and paramedics, who can provide advanced life support and advanced trauma management. Although EMTs and paramedics do not have the medical background of a nurse, they are well trained to deliver patient care in prehospital environments.

EMS personnel work under the authority of a local or regional medical system that provides them with direct radio link to a physician or nurse or provides them with standing protocols in order to carry out patient care. In many communities, the EMS system provides for a nurse at the scene to supervise the personnel. Regardless of whether the EMTs and the paramedics continue to work under their normal medical system or rely on the nurse at a disaster for authority, the nurse and the EMS personnel must work well together, for they both have valuable skills that can benefit patients.

EMS personnel may be provided by a number of agencies. Fire departments, police departments, and ambulance organizations all may provide EMTs or paramedics. In rural areas or small cities, the majority probably come from the local volunteer ambulance associations.

The nurse should note that many community disaster systems call for the senior EMT or paramedic to act as triage officer. These people receive extra training to perform this function and may have experience as triage officers from participating in mock disasters or performing this role in real life disasters.

Medical Staff

Some disaster plans call for teams of physicians and nurses to respond to a disaster scene. Their role may be to provide patient care, triage, or both. In many instances, nurses find themselves at a disaster by chance. In either of these situations, the nurse is in an ideal position to fill one of the greatest needs at a disaster: advanced life support.[4(p135)] Although the assessment of patients and the administration of more sophisticated treatment is the most important role nurses can play, the nurse may find it necessary to address other roles. Whenever possible, however, the role of providing patient care should be the highest priority.

Government Leaders

Few local, state, or federal government leaders attempt to direct a disaster scene; the fire department or police department officials are best suited for this job. Government officials perform their important role through the emergency operations center (EOC).[2(p269)] Most counties and all states have a sheltered structure of some sort that can house various officials and can provide them with maps of the disaster area, lists of hospitals, emergency agency capabilities, and a sophisticated radio communications system. The EOC coordinates assessment of the needs at a disaster site and the sending of support units to be used by the leaders at the scene. EOCs can also direct the flow of patients from the disaster to the hospitals most capable of handling the patients.

Organizing the Site

Once the nurse is familiar with the various personnel who work at a disaster, the nurse must gain an understanding of where these personnel should be concentrating their skills. To provide for the best organization of personnel, a disaster scene should be broken up into three zones: (1) disaster, (2) treatment, and (3) transportation (Figure 3–2). Different types of personnel are assigned to each zone.

The Disaster Zone

The disaster zone is the actual location of the incident (e.g., the wreckage of a plane or the rubble of a collapsed building). Patients may be scattered throughout this hazardous environment. Because this site is, by its very nature, the most confusing and dangerous area of a disaster, it is a difficult location in which to deliver adequate patient care. If disaster personnel try to treat patients there, they can be defeated by the difficulty of moving supplies to the patients and by the

Figure 3–2 Zone Organization at Disaster Site

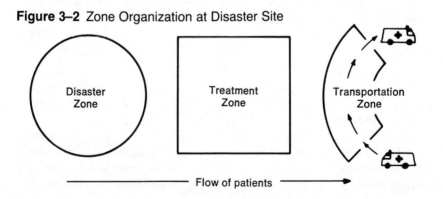

spreading out of their personnel. Therefore, disaster zone activities should include the following:

- providing site safety
- achieving access to patients
- stabilizing life-threatening conditions for patients
- moving patients to a better zone for treatment

The majority of disaster personnel are sent to this zone initially in order to stabilize and to move patients. As more and more patients are removed from this zone, a shift in personnel takes place. EMTs, paramedics, and nurses should then be reassigned to stay with patients at the site of treatment; fire fighters and other rescue personnel should continue the work of extricating patients and moving them away from the disaster zone.

Patients must be removed from the disaster zone as soon as possible, even before they have received a thorough assessment. To protect patients from hidden injuries, move them on wooden backboards, not stretchers. Good rescue plans call for large caches of backboards, which can be made inexpensively from plywood and can be stored until needed.

The first triage decisions are made at the disaster zone. The first EMTs or nurses to arrive should identify the patients to be moved to the treatment zone first, either because they appear to have more serious injuries or because they are in the way of rescue teams moving in and out of the area.

The Treatment Zone

A second zone should be established to which patients can be moved to receive treatment. This site is usually situated within 50 feet of the disaster zone, unless a dangerous environment forces it to be located farther away. The treatment zone is a better area in which to carry out patient care because equipment and personnel can be concentrated at this site, which is somewhat removed from the confusion of the disaster zone. Nurses should spend most of their time in this zone during a disaster. Activities carried on in this zone include the following:

- triage of patients into treatment categories
- thorough assessment of each patient
- treatment of injuries
- preparation for transport

Patients should be laid out in rows according to the severity of their condition. Highest priority patients are put in the row that will be transported first, second priority patients are put in the next row, and so on. The end of each row should border the transportation zone so that rescuers can move patients to the ambulances without having to step over other patients (Figure 3–3).

Transportation Zone

Disaster leaders must establish the transportation zone as soon as the disaster and treatment zones have been designated. The transportation zone should be situated directly next to the treatment zone and should have clear passage for emergency vehicles to enter and exit. Emergency vehicles are directed by the EOC to enter the transportation zone and for unloading supplies or personnel. Ambulances and other suitable vehicles then load up patients and leave for hospitals. The personnel who work in this site are primarily police officers or fire fighters. (See Chapter 5 for the role of the nurse during transportation.)

Leadership

The division of labor and the establishment of different zones will not provide, however, an effectively functioning disaster system. Strong leaders must assume control of the disaster area. Most disaster plans call for three important leadership positions: (1) the disaster officer, (2) the triage officer, and (3) the transportation officer.

Disaster Officer. The overall management of a disaster area falls to the fire chief in most communities. As disaster officer, the chief (or one of his subordinates) is responsible for establishing the three zones and assigning personnel to those sites. Because the majority of the disaster officer's efforts must go towards directing work at the disaster zone, the command post should adjoin this zone.

Triage Officer. The triage officer may be an EMT, a paramedic, a nurse, or a physician at the treatment zone. This officer has two functions: (1) to assess the

---

Figure 3–3 Patient Arrangement in Treatment Zone

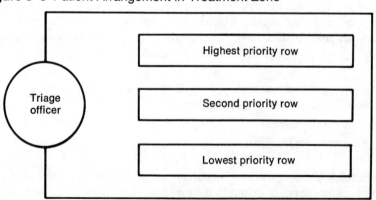

patients' conditions quickly and to assign them to a priority category in the treatment zone, and (2) to assure that medical personnel have been assigned to care for these patients in the zone.

Many experts feel that nurses should leave triage to someone with less clinical background inasmuch as this position involves only basic assessment and no patient treatment.[4(p69)] The nurses' skills can be better used in thoroughly assessing patients and carrying out treatment.[5(p156)] Regardless of who acts as triage officer, nurses must understand the principles of making triage decisions. Nurses continue to assess the patients and may need to advise the triage officer about a change in a patient's condition that necessitates a change in the patient's priority category.

The triage officer should be located at the entrance to the treatment zone so that all patients entering this site pass by this officer for assignment to a category.[6(p346)] The triage officer must perform this task in less than 30 seconds to assure a rapid flow of patients through the zone. If the flow of patients into the treatment zone is too great for one triage officer, assistants may be assigned to help assess patients as they enter this zone.

This triage assessment can be performed competently with practice and is similar to the initial survey discussed in Chapter 2. The nurse who is called on to perform this examination as the patient enters the treatment zone can base an assessment on four things:

1. the patient's pulse and respirations
2. the patient's level of consciousness
3. a description of the patient's condition by rescuers moving the patient
4. a quick examination of major body areas for obvious problems.

The category assigned after the triage officer's examination is only tentative. EMS personnel or a nurse immediately begin a more thorough assessment and may advise the triage officer of the need to reassign the patient to another row. This type of teamwork between personnel at the treatment zone allows for the best care of a large number of patients in a short time.

Transportation Officer. The person responsible for directing emergency vehicles into the disaster area and out again is the transportation officer. Probably a police officer, this person is stationed in the transportation zone but near the treatment zone. The transportation officer must work with medical personnel to assure that patients in the higher priority rows are transported to hospitals first.

Delivering Appropriate Patient Care

Patient Triage

The nurse who supervises or treats patients in a disaster finds several types of patients. Essential to the success of the disaster system, then, is the correct treatment of each type of patient and the knowledge that the appropriate care for a patient in nondisaster situations may be inappropriate in disaster conditions. For example, critically ill patients in nondisaster situations may have a good prognosis because of the excellent care they receive through the EMS and hospital systems. Whole teams of medical personnel can concentrate on saving a single patient who has suffered a horrible automobile accident or who has a severe surgical emergency. The patient with these types of problems in a mass casualty situation, however, probably cannot be saved because the manpower and the equipment necessary to care for a single critical patient are being used on a large number of patients. Normal priorities change in a disaster. The critical patient who would normally receive heroic, lifesaving efforts may have to be placed in a low priority category in order to save the patients who have better prognoses in a disaster situation. To understand how best to make these triage decisions, the nurse should review the following types of patients found in a disaster and their position in priority categories.

Probable Fatal. There may be patients in a disaster who have sustained an injury or illness that will probably be fatal, regardless of the care they receive. Patients with massive head injuries, patients in cardiac arrest, and persons with extensive chest trauma are examples of extremely critical patients who have poor prognoses even in normal conditions. This type of patient is almost always placed in one of the lowest priority categories during a disaster.

Critical. Many patients in a disaster will be critically injured. These patients may have life-threatening conditions, such as tension pneumothorax or intraabdominal hemorrhage, but if they receive hospital care within 30 to 60 minutes, they have good prognoses. If these patients can be transported and treated at a hospital quickly, they fit into a high priority category; if they can not get to a hospital quickly, their prognosis may be so poor that the nurse must put them in a low priority category.

Serious. The patient with the best prognosis in a disaster is the patient in serious condition. These types have injuries such as multiple fractures or pneumothorax. Death is not imminent and the treatment of these patients does not tie up the whole medical team. Because the seriously injured patient is most likely to be salvaged in an overwhelmed system, this type of patient is placed in the highest priority for treatment and transportation.

Stable. Patients who do not have life-threatening conditions but who do need medical attention in a hospital are numerous in most disasters. A patient who has sustained a closed leg fracture or who has a second-degree burn over a small area of the body is an example of this type. Such a patient can wait several hours for treatment in a hospital and still have an excellent outcome. These stable patients may be placed in a middle or lower category.

Minor. Patients with abrasions and contusions who can receive medical care at the disaster scene and go home or who can take themselves to their own physicians are examples of minor injuries that can be placed in a low priority category.

Fatal. Deaths are commonly associated with disasters. A patient who has died at the scene should be placed in the lowest priority category.[7] CPR is seldom performed in a disaster. It is nearly impossible to resuscitate a patient who has a cardiac arrest in disaster circumstances. Treatment would use personnel and equipment that could provide better results if used on more viable patients.[6(p341)] The deceased's body should be treated with respect and moved to a remote area of the treatment zone. In a simple triage system the deceased patient may be placed in the same row with the obviously fatally injured patient.

Triage Systems

Many types of triage systems exist. Most communities have already designed a system into their disaster plans. Some systems call for the placement of the different types of patients into one of three priority categories. Other systems may have five or six levels of priority. A look at two typical triage systems can help nurses work with any system.

Three-Tier System

The simplest triage has only three levels of priority in which to place patients (Exhibit 3–2).[8(p34)] This type of system works well with smaller numbers of patients or when confusion at the scene is extreme. The three-tier system is also a good system to establish when the nurse must start a triage plan without help from other personnel. This system can always be expanded to a four-tier or five-tier system when the need arises.

In the three-tier system, patients who are viable if they receive treatment in the first 30 to 60 minutes are placed in the highest priority row in the treatment zone. Stable patients are placed in the second priority row. Patients who are likely to die or who have already died are placed in the third priority row, along with patients who have minor injuries that can wait several hours for care. The patients with minor injuries should be separated from the fatalities.

Five-Tier System

A more complicated system with five levels of priority may be used by the nurse (Exhibit 3–3). This triage system is used in many communities and is patterned after the military systems.[5(p158)] The primary difference between this system and the three-tier system is the addition of separate categories for minor and deceased patients.

Exhibit 3–2 Three-Tier System of Triage

First priority

- airway problems of any type
- most types of chest wounds
- deteriorating vital signs
- suspected internal hemorrhage
- severe uncontrolled external bleeding
- head injuries with decreasing level of consciousness
- partial- and full-thickness burns of 20%–60% of body surface
- some types of medical emergencies, such as status epilepticus or insulin shock

Second priority

- open fractures
- multiple fractures
- spine injuries
- large lacerations
- partial- and full-thickness burns of 10%–20% of body surface
- medical emergencies, such as angina pectoris or diabetic coma

Third priority

- minor burns
- closed fractures
- sprains and strains
- minor lacerations
- abrasions and contusions
- probable fatal injuries, such as severely crushed heads or full-thickness burns of 80%–100% of body surface
- cardiac arrest
- obviously dead

Special Cases

The vast majority of patients fit into one of the priority levels discussed so far; however, a few unusual circumstances must be kept in mind. Injured disaster personnel are usually put in the highest priority row for treatment and transportation even though they are not seriously injured. This basic rescue rule helps to keep the morale of fellow disaster workers high. Likewise, if family of rescue personnel

Exhibit 3–3 Five-Tier System of Triage

First priority

- airway problems of any type
- most types of chest wounds
- deteriorating vital signs
- suspected internal hemorrhage
- severe uncontrolled external bleeding
- head injuries with decreasing level of consciousness
- partial- and full-thickness burns of 20%–60% of body surface
- some types of medical emergencies, such as status epilepticus or insulin shock

Second priority

- open fractures
- multiple fractures
- spine injuries
- large lacerations
- partial- and full-thickness burns of 10%–20% of body surface
- medical emergencies, such as asthma or angina pectoris

Third priority

- minor burns
- closed fractures
- sprains and strains
- minor lacerations
- abrasions and contusions

Fourth priority

- severe blood loss with long-standing profound shock
- acute whole-body exposure of 500 rads radiation
- crushed-head injuries
- partial- and full-thickness burns of 80%–100% of body surface

Fifth priority

- cardiac arrest
- obviously dead

are found to be disaster victims, they are put with the highest priority category for the same reason. Special consideration should also be given to extremely agitated or violent patients. Because these patients can distract personnel from their jobs and can decrease morale, the nurse may decide to put these patients in the highest priority row to remove them from the scene as soon as possible.

Tagging Patients

Most communities have a method for marking patients with a tag to help disaster personnel know the status of each victim. These tags may also contain important charting information, such as the patient's vital signs and the medications administered.[6(p341)]

Tagging systems are convenient, but they have limitations when communities use different methods for marking the tags. Some methods use a red tag to indicate the highest priority patient; others use red tags to indicate the lowest priority patient. Many communities use drawings on the tag—a rabbit or a stop light—to indicate the patient's priority.

In some instances, disaster tags may not arrive until after many patients have already been transported from the treatment zone. When the nurse is without tags, a small piece of note paper can be taped to the patient's arm or chest, and charting information can be written on the note.

Nurses who must face the dilemma of a confusing or absent tag system can often clarify the problem by placing a piece of tape on the forehead of the patient and writing on it, "first priority," "second priority," and so forth. These written words can not be misunderstood; some symbols may be misunderstood. These words can also be superimposed over existing tags to assure that everyone understands the patient's triage category. If a reassessment of the patient waiting for transportation shows that the patient's condition has changed, the tag can be changed or written over to reflect that change.

PUTTING IT ALL TOGETHER

To illustrate the effective handling of a disaster, imagine the events involving two fictitious participants in a disaster (Exhibit 3–4). The scene is a ball park, and the emergency is the collapse of a section of bleachers. One participant is a young man who has been injured when the bleachers collapsed; the other, a nurse who arrives shortly after the disaster happened.

PREPARING FOR A DISASTER

Nurses can greatly enhance their ability to handle disasters by making preparations in advance. Dedicating a few hours per month over a year or two toward

Exhibit 3–4 Case Example

The bleachers collapsed at about 10:30 on a summer night, injuring 70 victims and causing a power outage that plunged the whole scene into darkness.

The emergency dispatcher of the 911 emergency number, which had been called by neighbors, sent a police officer to investigate. Assessing the situation, the officer summoned an ambulance and a fire truck. When the EMTs arrived, they and the officer climbed over the rubble of the bleachers, discovering many injured and trapped people. Realizing that the scope of the disaster was greater than the normal EMS system handles, they summoned the dispatcher, who activated the community's disaster plan. Immediately more police, EMTs, and fire fighters arrived with emergency apparatus and supplies. The fire chief, the county EOC, and other authorities were notified. The EOC notified local and regional hospitals, which in turn took steps to coordinate disaster support.

Driving by the ball park, a nurse saw fire trucks arriving and stopped to help. She observed a scene of chaos—rushing figures, screams for help, and jumbled metal. Unsure at first of how to help, the nurse saw police officers keeping people away from the downed power lines and EMTs and fire fighters trying to move victims from the wreckage. She realized that by performing these actions they were securing the scene, thus meeting the first goal in disaster management.

At this point, the nurse realized that she could help best by helping to organize the disaster area—the second goal in disaster management. An area of grass on the playing field and next to the road provided an ideal location for a treatment zone, and several EMTs helped her to move the first three patients to this area. The condition of these patients was assessed and treatment begun before the EMTs returned to the disaster zone.

In the meantime, officials started to staff the EOC, to receive reports of the disaster situation, to call neighboring communities for help, and to summon extra personnel and equipment. All local hospitals had activated their disaster plans and had notified the EOC as to numbers and types of patients they could handle.

One of the victims, a young man whose early warning of impending disaster had been a rumbling of the bleachers and a flickering of lights, found himself pinned beneath wooden planks and metal beams. Unable to move to help anyone else, he could only wait until a rescuer shined a flashlight on him and told him to hold on.

The nurse, meanwhile, finding that the EMTs felt uncomfortable performing triage, began the process herself for the patients who now began to arrive in increasing numbers. She moved to the entrance of the treatment zone and quickly examined each patient brought to her. She worked rapidly, determining each patient's level of consciousness and pulse rate. She also glanced at each victim's body to determine whether there was serious injury and received reports from rescue personnel as to what they had found when they rescued the patients and brought them to the treatment zone.

The nurse now began to classify victims according to their needs, using the simple three-tier triage system. Patients needing immediate treatment and transportation were placed by the EMTs in the first row, and the nurse instructed the medical personnel with her to concentrate their efforts on these patients. The nurse also placed on the forehead of each patient a piece of tape on which was written the level of priority.

As the numbers of patients increased, the number of rows for patients of the second priority increased to two and then to three. Hard decisions had to be made: a patient with massive deep wounds leading to fatal hemorrhage had to be placed at the end of the third row so that other, more viable patients could receive care.

Exhibit 3–4 continued

> The young man under the rubble was finally reached, freed, and brought to the treatment zone on a backboard by personnel who did an initial survey to determine whether he had any life-threatening injury. When he arrived at the treatment zone, the nurse checked his pulse, examined his head, palpated his chest and abdomen, and glanced at his extremities to determine whether he had hidden bleeding. The rescuer reported to the nurse that the young man had a suspected fracture. It proved to be the only obvious injury, and so the patient was placed in the second-priority row. Now his blood pressure was taken for the first time, as it would be several more times before he reached the hospital. Fifteen minutes after his rescue, the nurse and the EMT had his leg splinted, his abrasions bandaged, and a blanket covering him.
>
> Upon the arrival of support units from neighboring communities (30 minutes after the disaster started), the nurse asked the newly arrived paramedics to continue with the triage so that she could start working on patients who had not received treatment. A team of nurses, paramedics, and EMTs worked closely to administer IVs, suction, antishock trousers, nasotracheal intubation, and other treatment procedures. Having been assessed and treated, the patients were ready for transport, according to their assigned priorities.[9] Fatalities were transported to the city morgue by local morticians.
>
> One and a half hours after the bleachers collapsed, the nurse returned to the hospital at which she worked. She returned to work in the same ambulance that transported the young man with the broken leg, assisting the EMT in caring for the patients as they rode to the hospital.

disaster preparedness may mean the difference between ineffectively stumbling through a disaster or competently applying nursing skills to save patients' lives.

Predisaster Personal Preparation

Many nurses prepare themselves personally to handle disasters by upgrading their emergency medical skills. A nurse may practice starting IVs or may spend extra time in an emergency department reviewing special treatment procedures for orthopedic problems, burns, and other wounds. A busy emergency department is also an excellent place to practice triage. The nurse would benefit from taking a first aid class or even completing an EMT course. A nurse can also gain experience in working on patients outside a hospital by riding with EMTs or paramedics on the local ambulance. Many communities offer inservice meetings or conferences on disaster handling. Periodically reviewing this book can help the nurse to be prepared for a disaster.

The nurse who faces the likely prospect of working outside the hospital in a disaster should take the time to become familiar with the local disaster plan. Local fire departments and the EOC are usually happy to explain their roles in a disaster and to describe what they would expect from nursing staff in the event of a disaster.

One of the most effective ways to prepare for a disaster is to take part in local mock disasters. These simulated mass casualty incidents are invaluable for the practice of the skills discussed in this book. The nurse can obtain considerable feedback by taking part in these mock disasters. Such an experience can quickly improve their ability to perform in a real disaster.

Disaster Supplies

Many communities call upon the nursing staff to prepare disaster supplies that can be stored in a secure place and pulled out to be used during a disaster. It is usually best to keep these caches of supplies in several locations. One cache may be kept in the central service of the hospital, and other caches may be stored at the fire department or at the location of a possible disaster, such as an airport. Bulk trauma dressings and IV fluids are the most important medical supplies to put into most caches. Other needed supplies include backboards, splints, and blankets (see Appendix 3-A). Items with expiration dates should be rotated annually into active hospital stock.

Personal Supplies

Nurses should also give thought to their own needs in preparing for a disaster. Personal and family supplies are essential for the safety and comfort of anyone associated with a disaster. The nurse may start preparing personal disaster supplies by building a medical "jump kit"—an expanded first aid kit that the nurse can carry in the trunk of a car (see Appendix 3-B). The kit provides some medical supplies for the nurse to use at a disaster site if emergency vehicles have not yet arrived with their supplies. The jump kit can also be used by the nurse to treat family members or other patients in nondisaster emergencies.

A small quantity of survival supplies should also be gathered by the nurse preparing for a disaster (see Appendix 3-C). These supplies should provide the nurse and the nurse's family with extra clothing, shelter, food, and water. Survival items should be kept at home and in the car trunk. Small preparations such as these can go a long way in helping the nurse survive a disaster and remain efficient in caring for patients.

SUMMARY

A disaster is one of the most severe challenges to a nurse's ability to care for patients. The disaster scene is a foreign environment characterized by confusion, urgency, and perhaps even danger. A nurse functioning in a disaster may have to address the problems of scene safety and organization while she delivers nursing skills to numerous patients. To do this successfully, the nurse must know who will be working at a disaster. She must also know how personnel will be organized. Basic to the concept of good patient care during a disaster is the change from normal medical procedures to disaster medical procedures. The nurse's understanding of triage concepts helps to provide the best care for patients in an overloaded medical system. Preparation for disasters enables the nurse to fulfill a valuable role during a disaster.

REFERENCES

1. Sellers T: Mass casualty picture is EMS at its worst. *Emergency Department News,* April 1982, 1–11.

2. Bever DL: *SAFETY: A Personal Focus.* St. Louis, Times Mirror/Mosby, 1984, pp 269, 271.

3. Caroline NL: *Emergency Care in the Streets,* ed 1. Boston, Little Brown & Co, Inc, 1979, p 441.

4. Butman AM: *Responding to the Mass Casualty Incident: A Guide for EMS Personnel.* Westport, Connecticut, Emergency Training, 1982, pp 69, 135.

5. *Emergency War Surgery.* United States/NATO, Comville, Ariz.: Desert Publications, 1982, pp 156, 158.

6. Grant HD, Murray RH Jr, Bergeron DJ: *Emergency Care,* ed 3. Bowie, Md, Robert J. Brady Company, 1982, pp 341, 346.

7. Gazzaniga AB, Iseri LT, Baren M: *EMERGENCY CARE: Principles & Practices for the EMT-Paramedic,* ed 2. Reston, Va.: Reston Publishing Co, Inc, 1982, p 383.

8. American Academy of Orthopaedic Surgeons: *Emergency Care and Transportation of the Sick and Injured,* ed 2. Chicago, George Banta, 1977, p 34.

9. Hafen BQ, Karren KJ: *Prehospital Care & Crisis Intervention,* ed 2. Englewood, Colorado, Morton Publishing Co, 1983, p 543.

Appendix 3-A

Disaster Supplies

Trauma Trunks

Ten trunks full of basic trauma supplies are kept in each cache. Each trunk contains the following:

Airway equipment

10 assorted oropharyngeal airways
2 50-mL irrigation syringe with suction catheter
2 bite sticks

Instruments

2 flashlights with extra batteries
2 bandage scissors
4 disposable scalpels
4 disposable hemostats

Trauma material

200 sterile 4 × 4s
50 ABD pads
100 nonsterile 3-inch kling rollers
50 triangular bandages
10 petroleum jelly gauze pads
10 rolls of 1-inch tape
5 pint bottles Betadine

IV Trunks

Three IV trunks to be used by nurses or paramedics should be available in each cache. Each trunk contains the following:

    20 1000-mL lactated Ringer's solution
    20 adult IV tubing
     5 pediatric IV tubing
    40 assorted Angiocath needles
    10 assorted scalp vein needles
     5 1-inch Penrose drain tourniquets
    50 alcohol wipes
     5 rolls 1-inch tape

Supplementary Equipment

The following equipment is cached to accompany the trunks as the situation dictates:

    50 backboards
    50 stretchers
   100 blankets
    50 cardboard leg splints
    50 cardboard arm splints
    10 half-ring traction splints
    25 cervical collars

Appendix 3-B

Jump Kit

Kit should be put in a sturdy tackle box or tool box container and kept in the car trunk.

Airway section

    5 assorted oropharyngeal airways
    1 50-mL irrigation syringe and suction catheter
    1 bite stick
    1 pocket mask or bag-valve-mask
    1 cricothyrotomy set

Instrument section

    1 stethoscope
    1 sphygmomanometer
    1 pair of bandage scissors
    1 pair of hemostats
    1 pair of pick-ups
    2 disposable scalpels
    1 thermometer

Trauma section

  20 sterile 4 × 4 gauze pads
  10 sterile 5 × 9 gauze pads
    2 sterile 10 × 30 dressings
  10 nonsterile 3-inch kling roller bandages
    4 nonsterile 2-inch kling roller bandages

2 nonsterile 1-inch kling roller bandages
2 kerlex roller bandages
4 triangular bandages
1 roll 1-inch tape
1 roll 2-inch tape
2 vaseline pads
2 wire splints
50 1-inch bandaids
2 chemical cold packs
2 chemical hot packs
1 pair sterile gloves
1 thin, foam cervical collar (medium size)

IV section

2 1,000-mL bags lactated Ringer's solution
2 extension tubing sets
2 IV tubing set-ups
4 scalp vein needles
6 Angiocath needles
1 Penrose drain tourniquet
20 alcohol preps

Medical section

syrup of ipecac
glucose
aspirin
acetaminophen (Tylenol)
aluminumhydroxide, magnesium hydroxide, and simethicone (Mylanta)
pseudoephedrine hydrochloride (Sudafed)
tripolichine hydrochloride and pseudoephedrine hydrochloride (Actifed)
antibiotic ointment
snakebite kit
umbilical clamps
prescriptions and injectible medications (depending on the individual nurse)

Miscellaneous section

tongue blades
cotton-tipped applicators

safety pins
notebook and pen
dimes and quarters
matches
flashlight and extra batteries

Appendix 3-C

Personal Disaster Equipment

This list suggests appropriate equipment for personal survival situations as well as for disasters. Most of the equipment can be kept in one or two sturdy containers and should be stored in a closet or the trunk of the car for easy access when an emergency occurs.

Work clothes: leather gloves, sturdy boots, overalls, safety goggles, hard hat, and filter masks

Warm clothes: extra socks, long underwear, sweater, coat, wool cap, and gloves

Shelter & warmth: blankets or sleeping bag, foam pad, poncho or tarp

Light: flashlight, hand lantern, or head lamp, extra batteries and bulb, candles and matches

Nutrition: canteens or plastic water bottles, snacks and canned foods, utensils, pocket stove and fuel tabs, can opener

Tools: pocket knife; shovel; saw; axe; rope; jumper cables; road flares; fire extinguisher; small toolbox with hammer, hacksaw, pliers, wrench, and screwdrivers

Communications: portable AM-FM radio with extra batteries, pad and pencils, survival and medical reference books, road maps and compass, CB radio

Medical: jump kit, c-collar, newspaper and cardboard splints, personal prescriptions

Sanitation: toilet paper, soap, toothbrush and toothpaste, small plastic garbage bags

Chapter 4

Disaster Decision Making in the Acute Care Facility

Mary P. Wieland, R.N., M.S.N., and
Deborah K. Hattan, R.N., B.S.N.

Disaster! The very word activates a stress response in any nurse working in an acute care facility.

Disasters can and do occur in acute care facilities such as hospitals and major civilian and military medical centers. Also, acute care facilities have often been the recipients of casualties from disasters that occur in the surrounding communities. These internal and external disasters are unanticipated catastrophies that tax the care facilities. The usual pattern of patient care activities is disrupted as the facility is forced to supply personnel and resources to meet the demand. The decisions that nurses working there need to make when the disaster strikes can be overwhelming, particularly if adequate preparation has not been given.

Each acute care facility should be prepared, then, for a disaster by having a simple, organized, well-defined disaster plan. A disaster committee with representation from nursing services must be formed. In addition, frequent, planned drills are essential to the implementation of a disaster plan. (See Chapter 14 for specifics of designing and evaluating a disaster plan.)

Note: The authors would like to express sincere appreciation to the following facilities who submitted copies of disaster plans for incorporation in this chapter: Ballard Hospital, Seattle, Wash; Charity Hospital, New Orleans, La; Desert Samaritan Hospital, Mesa, Ariz; Harborview Medical Center, Seattle, Wash; Illinois Masonic Medical Center, Chicago, Ill; Kuakini Medical Center, Honolulu, Hawaii; Letterman Army Medical Center, San Francisco, Calif; Long Island Jewish Medical Center, Long Island, NY; Madigan Army Medical Center, Tacoma, Wash; Memorial Hospital, Colorado Springs, Colo; Mercy Hospital and Medical Center, Chicago, Ill; Merle West Medical Center, Klamath Falls, Ore; Portland Bureau of Fire, Portland, Oreg; Southwest Washington Hospitals, Vancouver, Wash; St. Francis Hospital, Honolulu, Hawaii; St. Vincent's Medical Center, Portland, Oreg; University Hospital, Oregon Health Sciences University, Portland, Oreg; University Hospital, University of Illinois, Chicago, Ill; Valley View Medical Center, Cedar City, Utah; Veteran's Administration Medical Center, Salt Lake City, Utah; Yale–New Haven Medical Center, New Haven, Conn. Special thanks to the following people for sharing their expertise: Carolyn Garrison, R.N., Oregon Trail Chapter, American Red Cross, Portland, Oreg; Phillip Picard, Newberg Fire Department, Newberg, Oreg.

The objectives of this chapter are—

- to present the concept of decision analysis and the corresponding use of the nursing process in an emergency situation;
- to discuss briefly the stress factor and its effect on nurses during a disaster situation;
- to emphasize the factors of communication, personnel, and resources when the nurse is making decisions during an internal or external disaster situation.

DECISION ANALYSIS AND THE NURSING PROCESS

Decision analysis is a systematic approach to decision making in areas of uncertainty. This topic has been presented thoroughly in the publications of business and administrative circles. Five steps are involved in decision analysis:

1. Identify the decision problem.
2. Structure the decision problem over time, and generate alternative solutions.
3. Characterize and assign priorities to the information gathered.
4. Choose a preferred course of action.
5. Evaluate the action taken.

Nursing has used similar steps for decision analysis in the nursing process: assess and analyze, plan, implement, and evaluate. The nursing process can be used during an emergency or during a disaster. The goals of care tend to be broad, and the steps are carried out much faster than they are in a normal decision-making situation (Figure 4-1).

The basic components included in decision making are the decision, the decision-making process, and the decision maker. These decision-making components are complicated during a disaster because of the following factors:

- The decisions very often involve life-threatening or immediate problems.
- The decision-making process includes making decisions based on rapidly obtained data that have high levels of uncertainty.
- The decision maker, the nurse, is faced with making decisions in a stressful and an uncertain climate.

A decision-making checklist should be used at each stage of the nursing process. Such a list would ask two general questions:

1. What exactly are we trying to decide?
2. Which stage of problem solving are we in?

Figure 4-1 The Nursing Process Applied to Emergencies

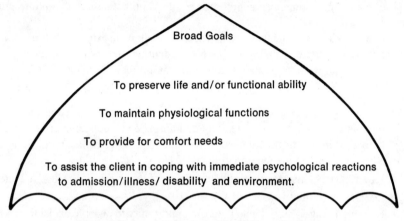

Broad Goals

To preserve life and/or functional ability

To maintain physiological functions

To provide for comfort needs

To assist the client in coping with immediate psychological reactions
to admission/illness/ disability and environment.

Acute emergency care — sequence of events and action:
   Initial encounter with client

   Instant data collection (assessment) added to pertinent information
      acquired prior to encounter

   Instant analysis

   Decision for action to provide for broad goals (listed above)

   Execution of action

Source: Reprinted from Nicholls ME and Wessells WG (eds): *Nursing Standard and Nursing Process,* Rockville, Md, Aspen Systems Corporation, 1977, p 98.

For each stage, it would ask additional questions:

- Who needs to be involved?
- How? (directly? consulted? informed?)
- When?
- Is someone in charge of making certain that things get done?

That decision making during an emergency has its peculiar facets is underlined by I. Janis and L. Mann: "Emergency decisions made during a disaster differ from executive or professional decisions and the usual decisions of everyday life in two aspects. One, there is more at stake during a disaster (patient survival) and two, the amount of time available to make a decision before crucial options are lost."[1]

These two aspects further suggest that decision making in a disaster setting must be accurate and rapid. Nursing research has identified the following factors as being influential when nurses are faced with making rapid decisions:[2]

- Knowledge—Nurses are continually expanding their knowledge base by reading current literature, attending continuing education courses, and participating in practical simulated drills such as disaster drills and basic and advanced cardiac life support courses.
- Experience—This area helps the practitioners to set priorities, to anticipate needs, and to modify plans of action.
- Role modeling—Nurses who have the opportunity to observe decision making by more experienced nurses in practice disaster drills and in actual disasters may be able to use this experience as part of their own decision making.
- Values (intuitive nature)—Nurses need to realize that the decisions made in a disaster may conflict with those made during normal operations. For instance, because of the complexity of the situation and the number of disaster patients, the decisions made must be focused on saving the greatest numbers of patients and resources, as opposed to assisting with the care of just a few.
- Flexibility—Some flexibility is appropriate in the ordering of rapid decisions, as long as they are made within the time limit applicable to the patient situation.
- Stress—Decision making has been identified as a stressor to nurses. In the initial stages of a disaster, stress may be accountable for the prompt, accurate decisions and interventions nurses make, but this quality of thinking may deteriorate as the environmental stressors increase.

INTERNAL DISASTER

An *internal disaster* is an emergency situation that occurs within an institution. Casualties may overload the system, and services to patients may be disrupted. A threat of physical harm to patients, staff, and visitors may exist. The establishment of a triage and patient receiving station near the disaster site may become necessary.

Action taken by the nursing staff should seek to achieve these goals:

- safeguard patients, visitors, and staff
- provide emergency care at the site
- confine the disaster area and evacuate those in danger of injury
- reassure those not immediately involved in the disaster situation
- limit the disruption of services as much as possible

Assessment

A primary step in the achievement of these goals is a careful assessment of the situation. Crucial areas that must be assessed are communication channels, personnel, evacuation, and equipment.

Notification of an internal disaster may come from a number of sources. Unless notification comes from members of the hospital administration, they should be requested to verify the information. If a disaster occurs on a nursing unit, a protocol must be established for use in notifying the administration and the rest of the hospital. For example, the protocol for communicating information about a fire in most hospitals requires that the person discovering a fire call the operator at a designated number, as well as sounding the fire alarm.

Each nursing unit should have preestablished guidelines for internal disasters that include unique considerations for the unit and the type of patients on the unit. When an internal disaster has been declared, several key questions must be answered:

- What is the exact location of the disaster site in the hospital?
- Can the disaster be confined to one area?
- Is there a threat of harm to staff, patients, or visitors?
- Is evacuation of an area required?
- Is hospital evacuation required?
- Are the usual disaster triage sites functional?
- Are there sufficient casualties at the disaster site to necessitate the establishment of a triage station?

In the event of a disaster notification, all personnel return immediately to assigned areas, avoiding, of course, use of the elevators. The charge nurse must assemble the personnel to do the following:

- count the number of personnel present on the unit
- compile a list of patients currently on the unit
- determine the mobility of patients (ambulatory, wheelchair, stretcher)

- assess the need to evacuate patients and the appropriate number of personnel
- determine location of the nearest unobstructed exit for evacuation

An internal disaster may also necessitate the need for evacuation. The hospital administration is responsible for making such a decision; however, unit preplanning is necessary to ensure that the evacuation occurs in an orderly fashion. An early assessment of patient priority for their removal, their mode of transport, and the precise route to follow are all essential and should begin when the disaster notification is received.

During an internal disaster, it is important that nurses know the location of wheelchairs and stretchers that can be used if evacuation becomes necessary. Alternative transport devices must also be considered, such as blankets to drag patients across the floor. It is helpful if the personnel have been trained to use various types of lifts and carries. They must also be familiar with all evacuation routes.

Intervention

These assessment data can be used in the implementation of the internal disaster plan. The decision to evacuate an area is usually made by the hospital administration or the fire department personnel. If there is immediate danger to patients, staff, or visitors, the decision may be made by the first person involved in the incident. The person discovering a disaster should do the following:

- sound the nearest fire alarm
- inform other staff members of the incident
- designate a staff member to notify the switchboard operator of the exact location and nature of the incident
- evacuate those in immediate danger
- close all doors and windows

Evacuation may occur when any situation renders the hospital unsafe for occupancy or prevents the delivery of necessary patient care. It is important that personnel have predetermined evacuation guidelines. Such guidelines should be prepared by a joint nursing and medical committee. The guidelines should include establishment of priorities to determine which patients are to be evacuated first.

An evacuation is either partial (patients are transferred within the hospital) or total (patients are transferred from the hospital to an outside area).

If a disaster is contained in one area, it may be necessary to evacuate only the immediate vicinity. All doors and windows must be closed to guard against the spreading of a fire. Unit evacuations should occur horizontally first—that is, evacuees move beyond the fire doors. Then, if necessary, people can be evacuated vertically—that is, down the stairs. Vertical evacuation is much more difficult, because stairways must be negotiated and nonambulatory patients must be carried.

If a disaster has occurred on one unit, and there is a possibility that it could spread to the rest of the hospital, then preparations must be made to evacuate the entire hospital. If time allows, the building should be evacuated from the top down because the evacuation of the lower levels can be accelerated more easily if the need arises or if the danger increases rapidly. Evacuate horizontally first, closing all doors after exiting. Evacuate vertically if necessary, using the stairs. Do not use the elevators. The evacuation team should be available to help the unit nursing staff to remove patients according to preestablished criteria (Exhibit 4-1).

The nurse in charge of the unit is responsible for assigning a staff member to monitor the traffic flow at the main entrance of the nursing unit and at any designated exits; for providing a roster of all patients and a list of the staff members present so that staff activity can be monitored and everyone's safety can be assured; and for assigning teams (including a charge person) to evacuate patients. The person in charge must designate an exit, must determine the location of patients to be evacuated, must assure that the patients have been assigned priorities for the evacuation, and must remind the staff to remain in the relocation area until they are relieved.

It is important to verify who is on the unit at the beginning of a disaster alert and to double-check this list when everyone has been evacuated to safe areas. The staff should be given as much information as possible about the disaster and their roles in coping with it.

In the case of an internal disaster, very few equipment or supplies are removed; however, it is important to remove patient records so that care can return to normal as soon as possible. Consideration should be given to having patients carry their own medical records away from the disaster site. Any personal item important to the functioning of the patient should also be removed with the patient when time allows (glasses, dentures, prostheses).

An attempt should be made to disconnect patients from all equipment possible, even those patients in the intensive care unit. The following guidelines are suggested for such activities:

- For patients with tracheostomies, take an obturator and spare tube, as well as a bulb syringe.
- Allow nasogastric or gastrostomy tubes to drain by gravity.
- Clamp chest tubes and disconnect the collection system if it is too cumbersome to move.
- Disconnect the patient from any monitors, but do not take time to remove the chest leads.

Exhibit 4–1 Duties of the Evacuation Team

The evacuation teams are to assist the unit staff in the removal of patients according to these suggested criteria:

Patients closest to danger

- Move them by any means possible to a safe area.
- If there is danger of fire, shut the doors and windows to help prevent the spread of smoke and flames.

Ambulatory patients

- Incorporate these patients as volunteers, as needed, to help move other patients in stretchers or wheelchairs.
- Designate one staff member to lead the group.
- Have all patients and staff hold hands when exiting.
- Have the staff member monitoring the exit check off the staff and patients as they leave.
- Have all visitors leave with the patients and record their names as they go.
- On mother-baby units, evacuate the baby in the mother's arms, if possible.

Wheelchair patients

- Assign a team of nursing staff members to evacuate these patients, incorporating ambulatory patient volunteers as well.
- Use volunteer visitors to move these patients, if possible.
- Check the patients and the staff on the list as each one leaves the unit.

Stretcher patients

- Assign a team of staff members to move these patients.
- Use any means necessary to move these patients; there may not be enough stretchers to go around.
- Check the patients on the list as they leave the unit.
- Last, move those patients requiring the constant care of a nurse.

The evacuation team must also remove patient records if at all possible (perhaps, send them with the patient), and to prevent the spread of fire, they must turn off the lights and main oxygen valves and shut the door as the last person leaves the unit.

- Clamp peritoneal dialysis tubing and cap the tubing ends after removing them from the bottle or bags.
- Heparin-lock intravenous lines whenever possible.
- Use portable oxygen tanks and Y-connectors with oxygen tubing for neonates being evacuated in the same crib.

Patient and staff safety are of concern in any internal disaster. Providing safety measures includes a knowledge of how to prevent problems, how to use patterns of communication, and how to cope with fire and related problems.

Hospital staff members are required by the Joint Commission on Accreditation of Hospitals (JCAH) to have regular in-service programs about fire and electrical safety. They need to know the location of all fire extinguishers and how to determine which extinguisher is the correct one to use for the fire. All staff members must know the locations of the fire alarms and which procedures to follow when a fire is discovered. This program should include information on how to alert the hospital operator (usually on a priority line) and the fire department.

Anytime a fire occurs in a hospital, the fire department must be alerted immediately—no matter how small the fire appears to be. They will ensure that the fire is contained and that it is completely extinguished.

The presence of a fire means that there is also a potential for smoke or noxious fumes, intense heat, and other problems (Table 4–1). The key points to remember in a fire are as follows:

- Stay calm.
- Stay near the floor if smoke or heat are present.
- DO NOT open a door that is warm or hot to the touch.
- Know the exits and their alternatives.

Evaluation

Once the patients have been safely evacuated and the disaster is over, it is necessary to assess the damage and to determine when the unit will be safe for reoccupancy. Electrical equipment must be checked by the instrument safety department to assure proper function. Supplies must be evaluated for contamination and replacement needs. The paperwork necessary to operate a unit may need to be replaced. An assessment of the staff available for work may need to be made, and structural damage may need to be repaired in order to make the unit operable. When the equipment, the unit, and the staff are all functioning appropriately or substitutes have been found, the unit is ready for reoccupancy. Efforts should be made not to reoccupy a unit until the safe delivery of care can be assured.

EXTERNAL DISASTER

An *external disaster* is any situation within a community that results in an abnormal patient load, requiring emergency care and resources beyond that which is usually available. The situation may be a natural event such as a tornado or an earthquake, or it may be a man-made disaster such as an explosion.

Table 4–1 Potential Problems Associated with Fire

Problem	Action
Sound the fire alarm!	
Darkness due to disruption of the electrical system	Keep flashlights and batteries on each unit. Have ambulatory patients join hands for evacuation.
Smoke and noxious fumes	Close all doors and windows.* Stay near the floor. Put wet rags at base of door from which smoke is issuing.
Heat	Close all doors and windows. Stay near the floor.
Flames	Close all doors and windows. Evacuate people. Do not open warm or hot doors.
Water (from sprinklers)†	Beware of slick floors. Remove babies from open bassinets. Unplug electrical equipment. Turn off electricity at main switch at direction of fire department.
Blocked exit	Know alternative exits. Communicate to the outside to let the fire fighters know you are trapped.

Notes: *Regulation fire doors keep a fire contained for 2 hours; wooden doors last 20 minutes.
†Overhead sprinklers deliver 25 gal/min and cover a 100-sq-ft area.

Action taken by the nursing staff should seek to achieve these goals:

- preserve life or functional ability
- maintain physiological functions
- provide for comfort needs
- assist the patient in coping with the immediate psychological reaction to the disaster

Assessment

When a call is made to the emergency department or to the appropriate hospital communication center, the emergency department personnel or receiver of the call obtains and records the following information:

- name and title of the caller
- time of the call
- nature of the disaster (location and scope)

- estimated number and type of casualties
- estimated arrival time of first casualties
- mode of arrival (i.e., helicopter or ambulance)

The administrative disaster office is then given this information. A disaster notification form used by some facilities to remind the staff of the questions they are to ask appears in Exhibit 4–2.

Role of the Emergency Department

When the emergency department is notified that the external disaster plan is in effect, it sets in motion a series of activities. The information obtained from the call is given to the charge nurse; the nursing and medical personnel in the department are notified of the impending arrival of casualties; and the emergency

---

Exhibit 4–2 Disaster Notification Form

Date: _____ Time: _____ Person taking report: _____
Who is calling? _____
What has happened? _____
_____

Location of disaster: _____
_____

Estimated number of casualties: _____
Estimated severity of injuries: _____
_____

Anyone at the scene providing care? _____
Who is currently in charge? _____
Estimated time of arrival of first victims: _____
Other information: _____
_____
_____
_____
_____

Notified: Time:

Medical Director   _____
Nursing Supervisor   _____
Charge Nurse   _____

Disaster plan activated? Yes_____ No_____ Time activated: _____
If no, explain: _____
_____

Source: Courtesy of Harborview Medical Center, Seattle, Washington.

department's plan for calling additional staff is activated (see Chapter 14 for phone tree).

One to five minutes after the disaster notification, an initial assessment is conducted. The nurse and the physician in charge of the emergency department evaluate the current status of the patients in the department and make the appropriate decisions concerning their care and disposition. Among the decisions are those related to the admission and the discharge or transfer of patients and decisions about patient priority in the giving of care. Those in charge must also designate a waiting room area for family members that is located away from the emergency department so that congestion of people does not occur when casualties arrive. In addition, they determine how many patients the department can receive on the basis of its current patient load. The nurse and the physician in charge then assign staff to those areas in the department to be used during the disaster (Figure 4–2).

Equipment and Supplies

An emergency department nurse is assigned to the appropriate treatment areas to evaluate the equipment and the supplies in preparation for the arrival of the

Figure 4–2 Casualty Flow Chart

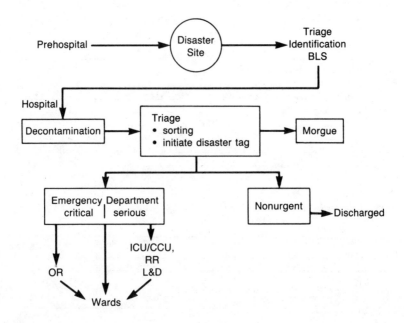

casualties. Basic guidelines to consider when assessing and stocking disaster supplies include the following:

- All disaster supplies should be kept in one location.
- A stocking and supply rotation schedule should be established. (This schedule will depend on the amount of supplies already available in the department and the system designed for restocking during a disaster.)
- A mobile triage cart must contain enough supplies to treat the maximum number of patients the facility can handle. An example of the contents of such a triage cart is shown in Exhibit 4–3.
- The ambulance pack should contain the basic supplies needed to restock the field treatment areas—depending on the guidelines in the community disaster plan—and should include dressings, intravenous supplies, and fluids.
- A major treatment area's disaster cart should contain enough supplies to last 1 to 2 hours (Exhibit 4–4). The materials management department would be mobilized to check and to restock the cart at least hourly.

Exhibit 4–3 Triage Disaster Supply Cart Checklist

Safety pins _____
Log book _____
Clipboard _____
Triage team II (armbands) _____
Plastic bags _____
Ambubag _____
Bandages

- 2 × 2s _____
- 4 × 4s _____
- Kling Abd. pads _____
- Kerlix _____

Bandage scissors _____

IV poles _____
Splints (cardboard) _____
Emesis basins _____
Tourniquets _____
Disaster tags _____
Pens _____
Penlights/flashlights _____
Adhesive tape _____
Oral airways (adult & pediatric sizes) _____
All-purpose scissors _____
Blankets _____
Stethoscopes _____
Kleenex _____
Alcohol sponges _____

To be obtained with the disaster cart:

- wheelchairs _____
- stretchers _____
- ambulance field packs _____
- backboards _____

Exhibit 4–4 Major Treatment Area Disaster Cart Checklist

Denture cup _____	Clipboards _____	Nonsterile gloves _____
Plastic bags _____	Safety pins _____	Blood pump _____
Pens _____	Envelopes for patient	Kleenex _____
Tongue blades _____	valuables _____	Rubber bands _____
Flashlights _____	Thermometers _____	Blankets _____
Penlights _____	Sphygmomanometers _____	Stethoscopes _____
Bandages (4 × 4s) _____	Kerlix _____	Splints _____
Ace bandages _____	Fluffs _____	Kling _____
Adhesive tape _____	Paper tape _____	Eye pads _____
Needles (all sizes) _____	Syringes (various	Hypoallergenic tape _____
Lidocaine 1% _____	sizes) _____	Blood tubes (red & purple) _____
Betadine _____	Suture (silk & nylon) _____	Sterile water (3000 mL) _____
Muslin slings _____	Sterile saline	Surgical prep trays _____
Suction bottles _____	(3000 mL) _____	Chest drainage tube _____
Sterile gloves _____	Chest tubes (variety) _____	Suction tips (variety) _____
X-ray requisitions _____	Suction extension tubing _____	Laboratory requisition forms _____
Emesis basin _____		

IV supplies:

- Lactated Ringer's (1000 mL) _____
- Normal saline (1000 mL) _____
- D$_5$W (500 mL) _____
- IV set _____
- IV extension tubing _____

IV tray:

- Tourniquets _____
- Alcohol sponges _____
- Sponges (2 × 2) _____
- Syringes (35-mL, 20-mL, 2-mL) _____
- Heparin locks _____
- IV catheters (16–20 gauge) _____

- The minimal treatment area requires first aid supplies (Exhibit 4–5). Stocking is accomplished by having a prepared requisition filled and delivered at the time the disaster is declared. Additional items to obtain for this area include blankets, pain medication (morphine, meperidine HCL (Demerol), hydroxyzine HCL (Vistaril), and tetanus toxoid.

The emergency department nurses are assigned to work in the following treatment areas:

- triage (sorting area)
- major (resuscitation room)
- minimal (first aid)
- morgue
- delayed
- decontamination

Exhibit 4–5 Minimal Treatment Area Supply Requisition Checklist

Bandages:	Applicators _____
	Stethoscopes _____
• 2 × 2s _____	Emesis basins _____
• 4 × 4s _____	Kleenex _____
• Kling _____	Alcohol sponges _____
• Kerlix _____	Tourniquets _____
• Abd. Pad _____	3-mL Syringe with Needle _____
	10-mL Syringe _____
	18-gauge and 25-gauge needles _____
Muslin slings _____	Lidocaine 1% _____
Bandaids _____	Suture set (disposable) _____
Steri-Strips _____	Prep set (disposable) _____
Ace bandages _____	Betadine _____
Tongue depressors _____	Suture (nylon & silk) _____

The emergency department charge nurse assigns personnel to appropriate treatment areas. If there are not enough emergency department nurses to assign to all areas, priority should be given to assigning them to the triage and major treatment areas. Cards are handed out to remind staff members of their particular duties (Exhibit 4–6).

The emergency department charge nurse then communicates information about personnel placement and space availability to the disaster control center.

Triage Area

Personnel working in the triage area determine the severity of the casualties and designate the treatment area to which each victim is sent. They also provide for the smooth flow of information. The triage team communicates to the emergency department or the control center the number of casualties arriving and the need for additional resources. This process may be handled by the use of runners or by the use of portable radios.

The triage team consists of any number of the following personnel:

- emergency department physicians
- an experienced emergency department nurse who is familiar with the disaster plan
- an emergency department admitting clerk
- security personnel to direct the flow of traffic
- runners who are familiar with the layout of the facility

Exhibit 4–6 Disaster Action Card

	RN in charge
RN in charge	1. Notify ED physician and share all available information 2. Call Nursing Supervisor at extension ____ or page a. advise of extent and type of disaster b. request immediate response to ED to help evaluate staff needs 3. Survey department for available treatment areas; help determine which patients can be discharged, admitted, or transferred 4. Assign triage nurse and technician; hand out cards 5. Assign one critical care team; hand out cards 6. Assign staff to ED and delayed treatment areas; hand out cards 7. You will be responsible for nursing disaster coordination until relieved by ED nursing supervisor or assistant 8. Notify waiting room patients of situation 9. Assign arriving staff to patient care responsibilities
A. (front of card)	**B.** (Back of card)

Source: Reprinted with permission from Simoneau JK: Disaster aspects in emergency nursing. In Budassi SA, Barber JM (eds): *Emergency Nursing*. St. Louis, The CV Mosby Co, 1981, p 666.

The cart containing the listed supplies and wheelchairs should be located here (see Exhibit 4–3).

The medical and nursing staff assess the severity of the casualties by obtaining prehospital information from the patient or the paramedics. A rapid assessment of injuries and complaints offered is obtained, and the triage nurse obtains an allergy and tetanus immunization history from the patient or the paramedics.

Role of Triage Team

The responsibilities of the triage team include the following:

- Assign disaster patients to appropriate treatment areas according to the assessment of their immediate needs and the availability of the department.

- Implement basic life support measures, such as CPR and the control of hemorrhage.
- Place a hospital disaster identification tag on each patient.
- Triage nurse and the admitting clerk: obtain registration information (name, sex, age, address) for the disaster tag (Exhibit 4–7). If unable to obtain this information, describe the physical characteristics of the patient (hair color, eyes, body build) on the tag.
- Keep clothing and valuables with the patient; insert these articles in plastic bags and pin to the patient's gurney.
- Assist the runners in transporting victims onto stretchers or to wheelchairs; make certain that safety measures are considered.

Evaluation

The outcome of the implemented plan in the triage area is the rating of the urgency of the patient's problems (Table 4–2) and the appropriate transfer of the patient for further care. After the casualties have undergone triage, the emergency department personnel receive assignments and provide patient care in the department.

In general, the most serious cases (critical) should be placed as near as possible to the emergency department's resuscitation room; the least serious ones (nonurgent) should be sent to an area farthest from the resuscitation room. (This area would be a room designated for first aid and holding patients.) Segregation of the sexes is not necessary.

Category II cases (serious) may be treated in an area of the emergency department or perhaps in another area (recovery room, labor and delivery) in which lifesaving equipment is available. Emotionally shocked patients should be sent to a room located outside the emergency department—a room designated for the care of these patients.

Documentation of the patient's hospital course starts in the triage area. Proper tagging with a hospital disaster tag is essential for proper identification; supplying information for relatives and the news media; and as a basis for later medical-legal reports (see Exhibit 4–7). This information is entered into a department log and is also placed in a triage logbook.

Patients who come to the emergency department for treatment but who are not associated with the disaster should be encouraged to seek treatment elsewhere. If the patients cannot be transferred, they should be assigned to a treatment area and reassessed.

Triage personnel need to be informed about the status of the treatment areas and other facilities that may be able to handle specialty problems (such as burns). They also need to know about the establishment and location of overflow areas.

Exhibit 4–7 Disaster Tag

Front of Tag — Back of Tag

Triage Tag

Indicate Injuries

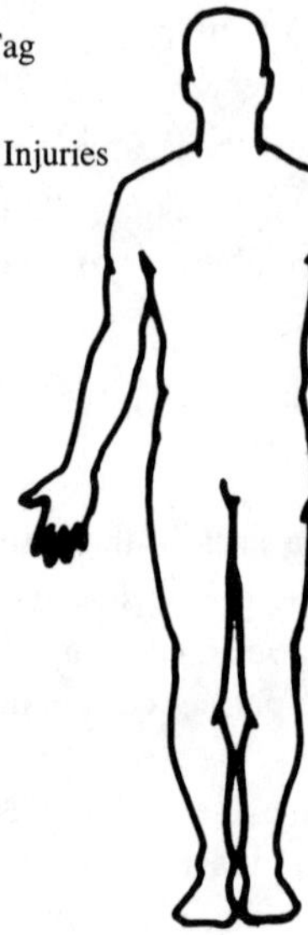

Front ☐
Back ☐

Additional Information

Pt. Destination

Description of injury

Pt. Name   Age

Pulse   B/P   Resp.   Triage Team

Loc.   Allergies   #1   #2

Treatment Given

Table 4–2 Sample Disaster Triage Model or Rating Scale

First Priority Category I: Critical	Second Priority Category II: Serious	Third Priority Category III: Nonurgent
Multiple trauma	Moderate lacerations (without severe hemorrhage)	Simple lacerations
Penetrating chest and abdominal wounds		Minor wounds
Incomplete amputations		Minor eye injuries
Shock		
Open fractures	Closed fractures of major bones	Sprains, strains, contusions
Burns, 40%+ BSA*	2nd° burns, 20%–40%+ BSA*	2nd° burns, <20% BSA*
Smoke inhalation		
Critical CNS injuries	Noncritical CNS injuries	
Facial injuries with airway impairment	Chest pain	Facial injuries without airway impairment
	OB patients	
Unconsciousness		Stress reactions (hysteria, hyperventilation)

Note: *May have separate areas of treatment for these victims.

Source: Reprinted with permission from Wieland MP: General principles of emergency care. In Dickson EJ, Armstrong ME, Howe J, et al (eds): *McGraw-Hill Handbook of Clinical Nursing.* New York, McGraw-Hill Book Co, 1979, p 1289.

To prevent confusion and congestion in the immediate area, visitors, family members, and the news media should be directed to designated areas by the triage members.

Emergency Department

Ongoing communication needs to take place between the triage and emergency department management personnel (medical director and nurse manager), the emergency department managers and the control center, and the emergency department managers and the personnel working in the treatment areas. If the telephone lines or the electricity lines are overloaded or are not functioning, the emergency department personnel can use ambulance radios, a CB, or walkie-talkies as a means of communication.

The critical patients are placed in the resuscitation-trauma area of the department; the serious patients are placed in other emergency department treatment areas. Every attempt should be made to move these patients out of the emergency department as soon as possible.

Each emergency department nurse in the treatment areas should be responsible for periodically checking the supplies and informing the emergency department nurse manager of any deficiencies.

The emergency department nurse-manager should be clearly identified by the use of an armband, colored vest, or name tag (large enough to be easily visible) to designate the role. The nurse-manager is responsible for the following:

- assigning to specific rooms nursing personnel who arrive from the nursing pool
- instructing volunteers and ancillary personnel about where to go, what to do, and where to find materials (Functions that ancillary services can provide during a disaster should have been planned ahead of time—e.g., getting water for patients, reinforcing dressings, watching IVs.)
- providing breaks or periods of rest for the triage nurse and nursing personnel working in the resuscitation and minor treatment areas
- communicating the need for additional personnel to the control center (The exact type of person needed should be specified—i.e., a strong person able to lift heavy patients or an RN capable of monitoring stable patients.)
- assuring that all personnel who work in the department are wearing the appropriate disaster identification (arm band or colored vest)
- posting a wall map in the area to help assist in giving directions to others

The emergency department nursing staff or other personnel designated by the disaster plan work closely with the department's medical and surgical teams. Their responsibilities include assigning specific tasks to nurses, orderlies, and technicians working in the area; assisting assigned staff with the locating of charts and supplies and with the documentation of procedures and the care given; and communicating to the department's charge nurse the need for supplies and additional personnel to assist with specific tasks.

Specific Emergency Treatment Areas

Like the triage areas, specific emergency treatment areas have their goals and must be concerned with nursing assessment and intervention.

Major Treatment Area

To provide expedient care to a large number of patients while observing the need for quality treatment is the goal of the major treatment area.

As each patient arrives in the appropriate treatment area, the emergency department nurse reassesses the patient thoroughly, giving special attention to the patient's airway, breathing, and circulation (see Chapter 2 for patient assessment). These nursing assessments or interventions may take place simultaneously with life-threatening emergency treatment. If possible, perform a complete assessment. It includes the following:

- eliciting the patient's chief complaint
- performing a head-to-toe objective survey
- taking vital signs and monitoring pain
- obtaining a past medical (and surgical) history related to heart disease, respiratory problems, diabetes mellitus, allergies, present medications, and tetanus prophylaxis

After the initial survey, formulate patient priorities and institute appropriate nursing interventions. These include:

- administering oxygen
- starting IV lines
- drawing requested blood specimens. (Be sure that disaster labels are attached to requested laboratory and x-ray requests.)
- reinforcing bandages
- administering prescribed medications

Use all available staff in carrying out these nursing interventions:

- obtain respiratory therapists for airway management and delivery of supplemental oxygen
- obtain IV therapists and laboratory technicians
- summon additional personnel for pressure dressings
- have nursing pool members ready to administer medications

Notify the emergency department charge nurse of available space, the need for additional supplies and personnel, and the number of patients needing surgery or admission to the ICU/CCU. Document all nursing assessments and interventions on the patient's disaster tag, the emergency department record, and/or the flow sheet.

When carrying out the nursing assessment or intervention, eight priority points should be kept in mind:

1. Maintain a patent airway.
2. Assist with or maintain ventilation.
3. Stop or control hemorrhage.
4. Order laboratory (typing and matching blood takes precedence over urine analysis and wound cultures) and x-ray tests (in general, chest films would be done first, limbs last) only if their results can make an immediate difference in the treatment of the patient.
5. Use available equipment and supplies wisely; they may be at a premium.

   - Use cardiac monitors only when truly indicated.
   - Use available equipment to immobilize the spine.
   - Heparin lock IVs that are just to be kept open.
   - While the nurse is waiting for blood to arrive, infuse the patient with IV fluids and volume expanders.

6. Use personnel wisely.

   - Ancillary personnel trained in CPR can deliver chest compressions in code while the emergency department nurse starts IVs, administers medications, and sets up for procedures.
   - Nursing personnel not used to working in the area can document care on the appropriate forms and monitor vital signs (see Chapter 14 for disaster forms).
   - Additional helpers should be used in their areas of expertise. (Anyone can be shown how to apply pressure to a wound.)

7. Make certain that the disaster tag is always on the patient and on the patient's valuables.
8. Communicate with your patients, team members, and people in charge. Don't forget the families, if they are present.

Minimal (Nonurgent) Treatment Areas

To provide first aid or basic nursing interventions is the goal of the minimal treatment area.

The nurses assigned to this area must reassess the patients according to their chief complaint. Appropriate nursing interventions are then instituted in order to immobilize fractures, sprains, or strains; to administer medications; and to provide care for basic wounds. In addition, the interventions should provide reassurance and support and prepare the patient for discharge (e.g., information sheets, need for later x-ray films, or follow-up care). Nursing assessments and interventions and the appropriate mode and time of discharge are documented on the disaster tag. Patients are assisted in the discharge process (e.g., buses are made available and families are called to help).

Decontamination Area

The goals of a decontamination area are more extensive. The staff must determine the type and the extent of injuries, must ascertain the level of radioactive contamination or exposure to hazardous materials, and must provide for safety measures for the patients and the staff. Meanwhile they must keep in contact with the radiation officer or hazardous materials officer and the control center. Ongoing consultation with the radiation officer and control center about the status of the patient and the need for additional supplies and assistance is mandatory.

Nursing assessment or intervention in this area includes the assessment of patients for any obvious life-threatening problems; categorization of the status of the radiation by the radiation officer; and the assessment of the availability and the number of supplies on the decontamination cart.

Plan/Implementation

Follow the protocol designed by the hospital for the care of radiation accident victims and according to the radiation officer's directions. (See Chapter 7 for specific nursing care involved.)

Delayed Area

When decisions are made at the triage area to send victims to a delayed area, several factors must be taken into consideration: the magnitude of the disaster (numbers and types of injuries); the hospital's available resources (personnel, supplies, surgery facilities); and the status of the patient. The staff working in this area need to reassess the patient's status, and to provide comfort measures (such as intravenous analgesics).

Morgue Area

Ideally, the morgue should be located away from the emergency department. There, the deceased can be treated with dignity, and families can be allowed to visit and grieve over the deceased victim. Appropriate hospital personnel (psychiatric nurse, chaplain, social worker, administrator) are assigned to assist the bereaved.

Supplies located in this area may include linens, towels, Kleenex, and refreshments for the family.

Assigned personnel should do the following:

- Evaluate the area for adequate space to accommodate the number of fatalities and the arriving family members.
- Assess the need for any crisis intervention or sedation for distraught family members.
- Provide for optimal temperatures in the morgue area—cold enough to provide for slow body decomposition (consider use of a refrigerated truck).
- Receive patients as they arrive and cover bodies with a sheet.
- Keep the bodies covered and located on the floor, because the stretchers may be needed at the triage and treatment areas.
- Make sure that the disaster tag is in place on the victim's body and valuables; keep a record of the patients in a log book; and send information about the casualty status to the control center.
- Ask the appropriate personnel to photograph unidentified casualties.
- Assist the relatives with the identification of the body when necessary.
- Provide emotional support to bereaved family members.
- Record the final disposition of the body in the log (e.g., coroner, funeral home).
- Evaluate the need for additional information about the identification of the body.
- Evaluate the need for additional crisis intervention and support for the family members.

Evaluation

After the initial triage and treatment of the casualties, there may be a large number of patients in the minimal treatment area who need treatment. The nurses working in the morgue may be reassigned to this area. The final disposition log should be completed and sent to the control center. Arrangements should be made for the transportation of discharged patients. Reassessment of equipment and supply needs should be performed in all emergency department areas. All borrowed equipment should be returned to the ambulance crews and to the nursing floors. Urgent cleaning, tidying, and restocking of the areas must be done so that normal operations may resume.

The members of the emergency department staff must also take care of their own needs. They have just been through a disaster—an organized stress test—and may need counseling to help them to deal with their feelings. Consideration should be given to *mandatory* counseling for staff—depending upon the extent of the disaster.

Moreover, the emergency department management team should be in contact with the community agencies about the aftermath and the potential health care problems. Additional staff may need to be scheduled for handling immunizations or answering telephone calls requesting information about the disaster. Involvement in the disaster critiques is essential for making needed adjustments to the disaster plan.

The emergency department nurses should be made aware of the potential of patients arriving at the department with a disaster-related stress action. Security guards should be readily available to assist with crowd control and to search for possible weapons. Postdisaster nursing interventions require additional skills and information: knowledge of disaster reaction phases, community resources, referrals, and general crisis intervention skills. Chapter 8 contains additional information on psychiatric interventions that may be needed.

Nursing Units

A defined mechanism to alert nursing units to an external disaster must be in place. It may take the form of calling key units and having them send runners to other units, or the emergency department may send runners to the nursing units directly. A cascade phone-tree may be in place; however, a phone-tree should have a manual backup in case the telephone system has been damaged. It is advisable for most institutions of any size to have a specific telephone number for the staff to call to verify that a disaster has been declared. Each unit must have a method of notifying the staff of the emerging need for additional help. This plan is usually in the form of a phone-tree initiated by the nurse in charge at the time the disaster alert is first given (see Chapter 14). In addition, it is recommended that the person calling have a predetermined statement for notification (Exhibit 4–8).

A regular communication channel must also be established between the bed control area and the units. The personnel pool should respond to any request for additional personnel or supplies from any area of the hospital.

Exhibit 4–8 Staff Notification of Disaster

Statement to be used for notification by telephone:
  "Hello _____.
  The disaster plan at Community Hospital has been activated because of (fire, air crash, etc.).
  Can you report to work immediately?
  How long will it take you to get here?"

If the telephones are not working, a message should be broadcast by the radio and television media:
  "All staff of Community Hospital are requested to report for duty at once. Please use _____ entrance and report to (unit or personnel pool, including room location).

The staff on the units have the responsibility of informing the patients and the visitors of the disaster situation. Patients should be asked to make only urgent requests of the staff. All personnel should restrict outside telephone calls to a minimum to avoid tying up the lines. The staff should be encouraged to use pay telephones if they must make a call home to check on their own families.

Space Allocation

The allocation within the hospital of bed space for disaster victims must be controlled through one department. The consolidated report would then go to the emergency department nurse-manager. This information would include the unit, the time, the number of beds available, and the names of the patients being discharged.

The evaluation of patients for discharge or transfer should be started immediately upon notification of a disaster. Ideally, this evaluation is done by a team of one registered nurse and one physician per nursing unit. There should be general guidelines to direct the team in deciding who should be discharged or transferred.

The evaluation should be made with the use of a patient classification system, if one is in place. Patients should be classified according to the level of care required and their resources at home. One such system is as follows:

- Level I—discharge; no special care required
- Level II—discharge; some support required (dressing change, meals, medication)
- Level III—transfer; institutional care of a limited nature required
- Level IV—transfer; critical care and staff to accompany on transfer required

Patients to be discharged include mothers and babies without complications, ambulatory patients near discharge, and ambulatory patients with minimal care needs. Patients to be transferred include those in levels III and IV as well as patients with inadequate home environment for discharge (e.g., their home may have been destroyed).

Patients being sent home should leave through one location established to process discharges. This area would be staffed by a clerk, social services, and a nurse functioning as discharge coordinator; they would be responsible for keeping records of all discharges, arranging transportation, notifying families, assuring adequate home resources, and, if necessary, notifying home health care services for follow-up. Patients transferred to other facilities should be processed through a separate site; however, they should have a name tag securely attached before they leave the nursing unit. Patients' valuables, dentures, prostheses, glasses, charts, nursing care plans, and other documents should be sent with the patient.

Transportation may be a problem for patients, whether they are discharged to go home or transferred to another facility. Public transportation may be adequate for some ambulatory patients, or family or friends may be able to help. Because most ambulances would be in use transporting disaster victims, other means would have to be found to transport stretcher patients. Delivery vans may be useful; they have a lot of room and their drivers usually know the area well. Also, buses could be used to transfer large numbers of patients at one time.

All personnel should be assembled to be informed of the nature of the disaster and of their individual assignments for the disaster situation. At the time a disaster is declared, all nonessential functions cease. All personnel should report to their departments for briefing and assignment if they are on duty during a disaster announcement. If it is determined by the charge nurse on the nursing unit that more help is required (the point at which units will call in staff should be indicated in the disaster plan), some guidelines should be followed to ensure that help is available for more than just the immediate crisis:

- If the time is close to the change of shift, retain the off-going shift, allowing them to call home to make certain their own families are safe.
- Call in only those employees not scheduled to work during the next 24 hours.
- Switch to 12- to 16-hour shifts if possible.

During a prolonged disaster, consideration must be given to the need for relief help, meals, and sleeping quarters. After the initial rush, it may be advisable to send some of the staff to rest so that they can be ready to provide relief a few hours later. It is important to provide breaks for the staff in an area that is away from families and patients.

The use of supplies and equipment needs to be rationed. Extra wheelchairs, stretchers, and IV poles should be collected and placed in a central area close to the elevators or stairwell for pickup and delivery to the emergency department.

Nursing care should include only that which is essential. Regular nursing care such as baths, bed changing, and dressing changes should be delayed or curtailed completely if at all possible (Exhibit 4–9).

Evaluation

After the disaster is over, steps must be taken to put the nursing unit back in functional order. Supplies must be restocked; future staffing needs and the avail-ability of personnel must be assessed. In addition, a critique of the disaster plan responses should be done as soon as possible. It should include such questions as the following:

Exhibit 4–9 Nursing Unit Disaster Checklist

All information, personnel, or supply requests are coordinated through the charge nurse. All nursing personnel should take the following action:

- Remain calm.
- Inform patients and family of disaster situation and request cooperation.
- Notify on-duty staff and call in off-duty staff as needed, sending extra personnel to the personnel pool.
- Obtain an initial count of available beds.
- Evaluate patients to determine who can be discharged or transferred, should the need arise.
- Determine minimum care required and revise bed availability as patients are discharged.
- Reallocate resources to the treatment areas (e.g., wheelchairs, stretchers, IV poles).
- Conserve supplies and resources left on the units.
- Avoid use of the telephones and elevators except for disaster activities.
- Assign someone to inventory supplies, IV poles, wheelchairs, and stretchers; to submit requisitions; and to keep a running count of supplies.
- Have patients, staff, and visitors entering or leaving the unit sign in or out so that an accurate head count can be maintained.
- If the need to evacuate patients arises, run through preparation for evacuation (i.e., chart preparation, transportation, dress of patients, essential items to send with patients) and make staff assignments for assisting with the evacuation.

- Was there adequate notification that a disaster was in progress?
- Were there adequate staffing and supplies to meet the patient care needs of the unit?
- What areas went smoothly? What areas were the problems?
- What are the recommendations for improvement?

CONCLUSION

Disasters—internal or external—that affect the acute care facility can be managed in an orderly and systematic fashion by the nurses involved by use of the normal nursing process. In a disaster situation, however, the primary areas of communication, personnel, and resources must be emphasized in the decision making.

A concise, clear disaster plan provides personnel with guidelines on how their units will be affected and what their roles will be during a disaster. Regular drills give personnel an understanding of what to expect before the situation occurs. Staff roles on each unit should be well defined. They should be written in their

Table 4–3 Staff Role and Nursing Action Flow Sheet

Time	Emergency Department	Nursing Units
Initial notification (1st 5 min)	Obtain an initial report; verify information; and alert the hospital administration.	Receive the disaster alert; notify unit personnel; and obtain an initial bed count.
5 min–2 h	Assess the impact on the hospital; call additional staff; set up triage area and treatment areas; and assess the need for additional equipment or supplies.	Assign priorities to patients for possible discharge or transfer; call in additional staff if needed; and send extra personnel to central personnel pool; conserve supplies and inventory their current levels; brief patients and staff on status; and maintain a disaster update board.
2–12 h	Assess the disaster for its possible duration; reevaluate personnel and supply needs; and provide rest and meal breaks for the staff.	Determine the need to implement discharges or transfers; provide for staff relief; and update bed count hourly.
12h+	Determine when the acute phase of the disaster will end; evaluate the need to provide sleep area and relief for staff; provide staff meals; and assess personnel and supply needs.	Reevaluate the need to continue patient discharge or transfer; evaluate the need to provide a sleep area and relief for staff; provide staff meals; and assess ongoing personnel and equipment needs.
Evaluation	Address any need for community health (see Chapter 12). Identify and provide for follow-up care for patients' needs. Assess staffing, and revert to normal ED routine; restock ED and disaster carts. Assist the staff to deal with the physical and psychological effects of the disaster by holding a debriefing session; recognize the effects of the disaster on patient and staff behavior. Assess the strengths and weaknesses of the disaster response, and begin action to correct any deficiency in the response.	Assess staff availability to resume normal routine; restock supplies; resume regular nursing care, and prepare to readmit those patients transferred out. Hold a debriefing session; recognize effects of disaster on patient and staff behavior. Assess the strengths and weaknesses of the disaster response, and begin action to correct any deficiency in the response.

order of priority and in simple format. Table 4–3 provides a summary of these roles and of the nursing actions to be taken during the course of a disaster.

REFERENCES

1. Janis I, Mann L: Emergency decision making: A theoretical analysis of responses to disaster warning. *J Human Stress* 1977;3:35–48.
2. Baumann A, Bourbannais F: Decision making in a crisis situation. *Can Nurse* 1983;79:23–25.
3. Kennedy J: Evacuation of a neonatal unit. *Can Nurse* 1979;79:26–29.

SUGGESTED READINGS

Bailey JJ, Hendricks D: Decisions, decisions. *Nurs Life,* July/August 1982, pp 45–47.

Baumann A, Bourbannais F: Nursing decision-making in critical care areas. *J Adv Nurs* 1982;7:435–446.

Best R: Mississauga, Ontario, Canada evacuation. Unpublished report from the National Fire Protection Association, 1980.

Budassi S, Barber JM (eds): *Emergency Nursing: Principles and Practice*. St Louis: The CV Mosby Co, 1981.

Campbell M, Pribyl C: The Hyatt diaster: Two nurse's perspectives. *JEN* 1982;8:12–16.

Cross RE: The team approach to disaster care. *JEN* 1977;3:17–19.

Demi AS, Miles MS: Understanding psychological reactions to disaster. *JEN* 1983;9:11–16.

Feldman S, Monicken D, Crowley MB: A systems approach to prioritizing. *Nurs Admin Q* 1983;7:57–62.

Henderson V: The nursing process—is the title right? *J Adv Nurs* 1982;7:103–109.

Jones R: It can happen to you! *JEN* 1978;4:24–27.

Lancaster W, Lancaster J: The leader as decision maker. *Nurs Leadership* 1981;4:7–12.

Marriner A: *The Nursing Process,* ed 2. St Louis, The CV Mosby Co, 1979.

Prato SA: Ethical decisions in daily practice. *Supervisor Nurse* 1981;12:18–20.

Readings in Disaster Planning for Hospitals. Chicago, American Hospital Association, 1966.

Rund DA, Rausch JS: *Triage*. St Louis, The CV Mosby Co, 1981.

Weinstein MC, Fineberg HV: *Clinical Decision Analysis*. Philadelphia, WB Saunders Co, 1980.

Zimmerman JM: Mass casualty management, in Ballinger WF, Rutherford RB, Zuidema JD (eds): *The Management of Trauma*. Philadelphia, WB Saunders Co, 1968, pp 769–793.

Chapter 5

The Trauma Patient in the Disaster Setting

Kris L. Brown, R.N., M.S.N. *and*
Ralph L. Brown, E.M.T.-P, P.A.-C.

The nurse who responds to the site of a disaster will find confusion, disorganization, and danger. There may be only a few patients or an overwhelming number. Their injuries may be minor or catastrophic. A few years ago most personnel who responded to a disaster site were poorly trained and knew little about the management of the seriously injured patient; thus treatment consisted only of loading the patient in an ambulance and providing transportation to the hospital. This practice resulted in a high mortality rate during disasters. In most disaster situations, nurses were rarely used; if they did respond to the emergency call, their expertise was often used in the capacity of triage and organization of the scene rather than in patient care. The evolution of the emergency nurse has put a new focus on the role of the nurse at the scene of a disaster. Advanced training in trauma assessment and treatment has prepared the nurse for a unique position in the care of trauma patients during a disaster.

The ultimate treatment of disaster victims with multiple injuries rests with critical care and surgical facilities; however, the initial management may be the responsibility of the nurse who first sees the patient. Field triage and stabilization of patients have been credited with reducing mortality.[1] Nurses too, as the initial advanced life support providers at the scene of a disaster, can have great impact on the trauma patient's outcome.

This chapter discusses the role of the nurse in treating trauma patients at a disaster scene with special emphasis placed on assessment, stabilization, and transportation of the seriously traumatized patient.

ROLE OF THE NURSE

Nurses may be presented with a number of conflicting roles during a disaster. They may be asked to perform triage, serve as stretcher bearers, bandage minor wounds, or provide advanced life support to seriously injured patients. Nurses can easily perform all of these roles, but many of these activities may be an inappropriate use of their valuable skills. Nurses should be cautious about which roles they accept. In most disaster settings, there is an excess of nonclinical personnel to carry out rescue tasks such as extrication, patient transportation, and management of various zones (see Chapter 3). The greatest need in disasters is for personnel who can provide sophisticated medical treatment to patients in an established treatment zone. The clinical skills that nurses possess make them extremely valuable to patients who require medical attention. It would be a misuse of talent to assign the nurse to perform rescue or management tasks while nonclinical personnel are assigned to patient care tasks. The most important role the nurse can assume is the care of patients in the treatment zone.

The exact role of the nurse in patient care may vary, depending on the nurse's skills and the needs of the patients. Severely traumatized patients in the more urgent triage categories (see Chapter 3) require highly specialized skills that all nurses may not possess. In order for the nurse to treat these patients successfully, they need training in emergency nursing or intensive care nursing. Lack of essential trauma management skill, such as the ability to insert chest tubes, perform endotracheal intubation, start IV lines, and accomplish thorough assessment of severe injuries may prevent the nurse from treating these patients successfully. Nurses may choose, therefore, to develop a philosophy of ''do no harm'' when they evaluate their ability to treat these patients. Nurses without strong backgrounds in treatment of severely injured patients should avoid being assigned to the more urgent category patients, whenever possible. There are many other patient care roles the nontrauma oriented nurse can perform. Caring for less urgent category patients is one such role; another major role may be to meet the psychosocial care of the victim or the family in a disaster. All of these roles are essential to good patient care, and each is important during a disaster.

The nurse who has established a role in a disaster setting must then consider three keys to the successful management of patients. These keys can help the nurse adapt to the unusual circumstances that may exist during a disaster. The three keys are orientation, improvisation, and aggressiveness.

Orientation

Many times the nurse has been oriented to the hospital setting; there personnel and equipment are readily available. It must be emphasized, however, that the normal treatment protocols for a trauma patient may not be appropriate in a mass casualty situation because large numbers of patients must be treated simultaneously.

The nurse can easily become caught up in the treatment of an extremely critical patient and lose several more viable patients in the process. Most nonviable patients are removed from the high priority category by triage, but, occasionally, a viable patient deteriorates to an obviously fatal status. Do not waste valuable equipment and time on patients that have no hope of recovery, given the medical limitations during a disaster. For example, there may be only one or two antishock trousers available and a dozen victims that could benefit from this device; apply the antishock trousers to the most viable patients, not necessarily to the most seriously injured patients. Also, because surgical intervention may not be readily accessible to patients in a disaster setting, focus on those victims who can and will survive without immediate surgical care. Decisions may have to be made to direct time and energy toward victims who have a good chance for recovery based on the materials and the resources available.

Improvisation

The scene of a trauma site may be in a dirt field or on a crowded highway. Patients may be laid out on the ground without stretchers or blankets under them. Setting up a sterile field may be difficult. The availability of sterile equipment may be at a minimum. The nurse who refuses to put an intravenous line in a hypo-volemic patient because there is no alcohol wipe will not be able to function effectively at the scene of a disaster. Be willing to improvise and to remain flexible. Clean bandages may have to do instead of sterile ones. Moreover, be conservative in the use of equipment because supplies can be depleted rapidly and new supplies slow in arriving. Some medical equipment may have to be improvised from items at hand, such as splints made from newspapers or stretchers made from an airplane seat. Conserving medical supplies and making appropriate decisions about their use permits better care for disaster patients.

Aggressiveness

Patients who have been traumatized can easily die from their wounds within minutes to hours. Many patients who are potentially salvageable can bleed to death or asphyxiate quickly unless medical personnel are aggressive in treating their problems. Trauma patients need immediate action on the part of the nurse if they are to be saved.

When responding to a disaster realize that many patients with life-threatening injuries may have subtle or no signs to indicate how seriously injured they are. By the time the extent of the injuries becomes apparent, the patient is too far gone to be saved. It is imperative to have a high index of suspicion when dealing with injured patients. If you do not think about the possibility of a particular injury, you are not going to find it.[2] The aggressive nurse must suspect the worst and treat trauma patients before their injuries cause deterioration. For example, the key to success in saving seriously injured patients is to stay ahead of the development of shock or the malfunction of essential body functions. Before the patient with a ruptured spleen develops shock, the aggressive nurse will have started two large bore intravenous lines and infused one to two liters of lactated Ringer's solution into the patient. The nurse will have already put the patient on oxygen and started to search for a pair of antishock trousers before the patient's blood pressure drops. This is the type of aggressiveness the nurse must exhibit in order to save the trauma patient. At disaster sites, be prepared, then, to move quickly from patient to patient, making such rapid, aggressive decisions about treatment.

SYSTEMS APPROACH TO PATIENT CARE

The treatment of multiple patients with various and difficult problems is a challenge. Add the confusion of a disaster site, and the result is a combination of factors that may blunt the intervention of even the most skilled nurse. To overcome this problem, employ a logical step-by-step approach in the treatment of each trauma patient. A tool that is simple to learn and that provides a quick and thorough system for handling even the most challenging patients is known as the systems approach to patient care (Table 5–1).

Table 5–1 Systems Approach to Patient Care

Sequence	Problem/Goals	Action
Step 1: Priorities—1 to 3 min	airway breath circulation bleeding spinal fracture shock	Use a primary survey to find the problems and correct them with basic life support skills. This step can be applied to several patients in a disaster before the next steps are taken.
Step 2: Assessment—2 to 4 min	history vital signs physical examination	Use this time to gain an understanding of the patient's problem and to formulate a care plan. This is essential before proper treatment can be rendered.
Step 3: Treatment—3 to 5 min	most serious injury next most serious injury least serious injury	Address the most serious problems first. Periodically repeat step 2 to reassess patient's condition.

The systems approach has the nurse follow three steps to care properly for the trauma patient: (1) priorities, (2) assessment, and (3) treatment. Each step is completed before going on to the next step. Memorize all three steps and practice them before they are ever needed in a disaster. (See Chapter 2 for an in-depth discussion of rapid assessment techniques.)

Step 1: Priorities

Treatment of the multiple-trauma patient must first be directed to survival.[3] The majority of trauma patients present six major problems that can lead to death within minutes: airway, breathing, circulation, bleeding, spinal fractures, and shock. (The mnemonic device *A, B, C, B, S, S* can be used to remind the nurse of the six life-threatening problems.) Step 1 calls for a search for these problems and the provision of relief. Employ a brief primary survey to find the priorities in a patient. Quickly address each of the priorities in the order of sequence. Do not carry out time-consuming or complicated treatment at this step. Step 1 can normally be accomplished in one to three minutes on each patient. You are simply looking for the immediate threats to life and correcting them with basic life support skills and, occasionally, with the use of some advanced life support techniques. If you have the luxury of concentrating on only one patient in a disaster, you can then go on to perform Step 2 and Step 3 on that patient. More often, you have several patients requiring immediate care, and so you will have to handle this challenge by moving from patient to patient, carrying out Step 1 on each patient. When the patients have been stabilized, go back and carry out Step 2 and Step 3 on each patient.

Airway

The first priority in the case of a trauma patient is to assess the status of the airway (Exhibit 5–1). Careful observation of the patient is essential when making this evaluation. Always treat unconscious patients as if they have an airway obstruction. Be alert for signs of injury or trauma to the face that may lead to obstruction of the airway. Any noisy breathing is an indication of partial airway obstruction. If lacerations or bruises are noted about the face or neck, be suspicious of a cervical spine injury and immobilize the neck while caring for the airway. (See Chapter 2 for a detailed presentation of airway problems.)

The three main causes of airway obstruction are anatomical structures, foreign objects, and fluid. The most common cause of airway obstruction is the victim's own tongue.[4] If no cervical spine injury has occurred, the airway can easily be opened by hyperextending the head; however, if a cervical spine injury is suspected, hyperextending the head may sever the spinal cord. When in doubt, do not hyperextend. Keep the head in a neutral position with manual traction, and remove

Exhibit 5–1 Airway Management

Airway problem indicators:

- noisy breathing
- face trauma
- neck trauma
- fluids in the airway
- loss of consciousness

Airway problem treatments:

- head tilt/chin lift
- jaw thrust
- patient rolled on side
- airway suction
- oropharyngeal airway
- esophageal obturator airway (EOA)
- endotracheal tube (ET)
- nasotracheal tube (NT)
- cricothyrotomy

---

the tongue from the back of the throat by using the jaw-thrust maneuver or the jaw-lift maneuver.

Foreign objects should be suspected in the airway if hyperextension or the jaw thrust do not open the airway. A partial obstruction may cause a crowing noise. Sweep the mouth of foreign objects such as teeth or bone. The Heimlich maneuver can be used on a patient who has a foreign object obstruction. If blood or vomitus are found in the airway, logroll the patient to the side and allow the fluid to drain out. Use suction equipment if available.

If the patient needs assistance in keeping the airway open, consider the use of mechanical aids (oropharyngeal airway, esophageal obturator airway, endotracheal tube, or cricothyrotomy).

Breathing

After the airway has been evaluated or treated, rapidly assess the patient's breathing. This can be done by observing the chest and the abdomen for motion and by listening for respirations. If there is no respiratory effort, ventilate the patient by using a bag mask resuscitator or mouth-to-mouth breathing. If breathing returns, go on to further assessment. Then make a decision about the priority of a patient who remains apneic. In most disaster situations, an apneic patient is placed in a low-priority triage category. If excess personnel are available and hospital facilities are not burdened by the disaster, the nurse may choose to attempt to resuscitate the patient.

Assess any patient who is breathing for respiratory distress. The cardinal signs of inadequate ventilation are dyspnea and cyanosis.[5] Also look for nasal flaring, retraction of the intercostal muscles, and the use of the diaphragm and neck muscles—all are signs of respiratory distress. The rate and rhythm of respirations as well as the symmetry of chest movement may also determine respiratory effectiveness.

Begin stabilization of the patient with respiratory distress with the administration of oxygen. Deliver 25 to 40 percent oxygen to a patient by applying a nasal cannula and setting the oxygen regulator at 6 liters per minute. Place a face mask on patients who need higher concentrations of oxygen and set the regulator at 12 liters. This setting will deliver 40 to 60 percent oxygen.

Patients need further ventilatory assistance when they exhibit any of the following signs:

- no improvement with the application of oxygen
- respirations more than 35 per minute
- respirations less than 8 per minute
- chest wall trauma (includes sucking chest wounds or flail chests)

A bag-mask resuscitator is an efficient way of assisting a patient with respiratory difficulty. When an open airway is established, the mask is formed in an airtight seal over the patient's face. The bag is fully or partially squeezed to enhance the patient's respirations or to interspace breaths between bradyapneic respirations. The nurse manipulating the bag must be efficient at maintaining a seal around the patient's face, or the procedure will be completely ineffective. A bag mask using room air delivers 21 percent oxygen; connected to a high-flow oxygen source, the mask delivers up to 40 to 50 percent oxygen to the patient. A reservoir connected to the bag can increase the oxygen level to as high as 90 percent.

Endotracheal or nasotracheal intubation may be necessary, however, for patients who do not respond to the above treatment (see Exhibit 5–1).

Circulation

The absence of circulation (i.e., cardiac arrest) can be prevented in most patients by attending to the other priorities. A patent airway, adequate ventilation, control of hemorrhage, immobilization of spinal fractures, and treatment of shock can assure good circulation in nearly all patients.

Cardiac arrest is diagnosed by the absence of a carotid or femoral pulse. When the nurse finds a patient in cardiac arrest, the nurse must realize that attempts to resuscitate this patient in a disaster are almost always futile and can tie up valuable resources that could better be used to treat more viable patients. If excess personnel and medical facilities are available to handle an arrest, cardiopulmonary resuscitation and advanced cardiac life support can be initiated. If a trauma patient has arrested, the resuscitation will be unsuccessful unless the patient's lost blood volume has been replaced by crystalloids and blood. Most disaster situations call for cardiac arrest patients to be placed in the lowest triage category.

Bleeding

A patient can bleed to death in only a few minutes. Many times a patient's hidden wounds cause exsanguination while medical personnel are treating other areas of the patient's body. The nurse working on a trauma patient must quickly search for serious bleeding and effectively stop it in order to keep the patient alive. Take care not to focus on minor wounds and waste valuable time bandaging them. A small scalp wound can present a ghastly picture, covering the face and shirt of the victim with blood; but, in reality, this blood loss is insignificant. Such minor wounds and bleeding can be ignored initially or covered by a 4 × 4 gauze pad as the nurse continues to perform the primary assessment, looking for the priorities.

External Bleeding. Blood loss can be categorized as external or internal. External blood loss is the easiest to find, though at times it may be hidden underneath thick clothing or masked by darkness at night. Do not hesitate to cut or tear away clothing that may get in the way of the search for bleeding.

External bleeding is most effectively stopped by applying direct pressure to compress the open vessels.[6] When brisk, heavy, or pumping bleeding is discovered, stop it immediately by pressing the cleanest object available firmly against the wound. Even pressing a bare hand against a seriously bleeding wound is preferable to wasting time in search of a sterile dressing. Furthermore, adjust the location and application of pressure, if necessary, to compress all the bleeding vessels in a wound. Even severe bleeding from a horribly mangled or amputated extremity can be stopped by direct pressure effectively applied.

After the bleeding has been stopped by direct pressure, a pressure bandage may be applied over the wound in order to free the nurse's hands so that the assessment and stabilization of the patient may continue. Place a sterile dressing, or the cleanest material available, over the wound and tightly wrap it with a bandage. (Gauze rollers make the best bandage material, but torn sheets or folded triangular bandages also work well.) Apply the pressure bandage so that it is wide enough and tight enough to stop the bleeding but does not stop blood flow to the extremity. If blood soaks through the pressure bandage, it may not be tight enough or wide enough. To remedy the problem, apply a new dressing and bandage over the top of the old one.

In rare circumstances, the application of a tourniquet to a bleeding extremity may be necessary. Tourniquets can effectively stop bleeding, but their use has a number of serious side effects—including extremity necrosis and death from releasing the tourniquet. The release of a tourniquet in a prehospital environment may trigger ventricular tachycardia secondary to released acids from the metabolic acidosis in the affected limb. Use a tourniquet only when bleeding cannot be stopped with direct pressure against a wound or when there are a large number of bleeding patients and not enough personnel to apply direct pressure. If a tourniquet is necessary, use the following guidelines in its application:

- Apply the tourniquet close to the wound but proximal to the heart.
- Make the tourniquet material three to four inches wide.
- Wrap the material tightly around the extremity, and tie a knot in it.
- Insert a small stick under the knot, and twist the tourniquet tight until the bleeding stops.
- Secure the stick so that it will not unwind.
- Plainly mark the patient's forehead with the letters *Tk* and the time of application.
- Do not release the tourniquet until the patient is in a hospital.
- Transport a tourniquet patient as soon as possible.

Internal Bleeding. Internal bleeding is often much more difficult to diagnose than external bleeding. Suspect blood loss with all forms of chest trauma. The abdomen and the pelvic cavities are also prime areas for internal bleeding. Bilateral femur fractures can cause enough blood loss into the thighs to create critical problems in many patients.[7] If the patient has a distended abdomen or evidence of chest trauma, rapid pulse, and decreasing blood pressure without large amounts of external hemorrhage, strongly suspect internal bleeding.

The patient who is suffering hemorrhage inside the body is a challenge to the nurse at a disaster site because it is difficult to stop the bleeding. Surgical intervention is required for many patients with internal hemorrhage. In the meantime, thigh, pelvis, or abdomen bleeds can be stopped or slowed by the application of antishock trousers to these patients.

Spinal Fractures

Most nurses realize the danger of moving a patient who may have a spinal fracture. Irreversible respiratory arrest, neurogenic shock, and permanent paralysis can easily result from even the slightest manipulation of a fractured spine. The difficulty in dealing with a spinal fracture comes in not recognizing the indicators of this injury. Search for these spinal fracture indicators as the priorities are investigated:

- pain in the neck or back region
- wounds to the head, the neck, or above the clavicles
- unconsciousness
- multiple injuries
- neurological symptoms such as tingling, numbness, or paralysis.

When any of these signs or symptoms are discovered, immediately treat the patient as one who has a serious spinal fracture, even if the patient is up and walking about. The treatment for spinal fracture, like that for any fracture, is complete immobilization. Because immobilization can be done in a number of ways, ingenuity is required to figure out the best way to prevent movement of the back.

Possible spinal fracture patients who are in respiratory distress should have their airways opened by the jaw-thrust rather than the head-tilt method. Patients with suspected spinal fractures who are conscious should be told to hold perfectly still and not to move, and a device should be applied to the patient's neck to prevent motion. When cervical collars are not available, they can be improvised from blankets or articles of clothing.

The preferred method of immobilizing a possible spinal fracture is through the use of a rigid backboard. Stretchers, army cots, and improvised carrying rigs are usually too flexible to provide the protection the spine needs. There are numerous types of commercial backboards available. If there is no access to a rigid backboard, improvise; use a door taken off its hinges or the tailgate of a pickup truck. A community that is well prepared for disasters has many simple wooden spine boards in its disaster supplies. Many communities plan to transport patients from the disaster zone to the treatment zone on a backboard.

The nurse must ensure that all patients with suspected spinal fractures are placed on a backboard as soon as possible. Because many patients receive permanent injuries when they are incorrectly put on a backboard, be careful not to move the spine of a patient when transferring the patient from the ground or another stretcher onto the board. Three to five practiced persons are needed to logroll or to loglift a patient onto a backboard correctly. If a Robertson Orthopedic Stretcher is available, two persons can safely scoop a spinal injury patient onto the board. The nurse at a disaster site will probably rely on emergency medical technicians or paramedics to move spinal injury patients, inasmuch as this is an area in which they have expertise.

The patient who has been placed on a backboard should be securely strapped in place to avoid a shifting of the body when the board is transported. The patient's head should be stabilized by sandbags and straps even when the patient is wearing a cervical collar because, in reality, collars offer only moderate cervical spine protection.

Shock

Shock is the most common cause of death among trauma patients. It occurs when body tissues are not being perfused because of decreased cardiac output from the loss of circulating blood volume, massive vasodilatation, or heart failure. In a disaster setting, the usual cause of shock is internal or external hemorrhage. Remember, however, that the obvious signs and symptoms of shock may not appear in a patient until considerable blood loss has occurred. A trauma patient can lose 1200 mL of blood and exhibit no indications of shock.

Shock can be divided into two categories: early and late. *Early shock* occurs with the loss of 750 to 1500 mL of blood. The usual signs and symptoms accompanying this condition include mild to moderate anxiety, slight increase in cardiac rate, and a delay in the refilling of capillary beds. A capillary perfusion test should be done on all patients with suspected blood loss. This test consists of compressing, then releasing, the nail of a finger and observing for the return of blood into the nail's capillary beds. If it takes longer than two seconds (about the time it takes to say "capillary perfusion") for the color to return to the nail bed, the patient is suffering decreased perfusion from shock. Other signs in early shock are normal, including blood pressure and respiratory rate.

Late shock occurs when the patient loses 1500 to 3000 mL of blood. These patients exhibit tachycardia with rates over 120 beats per minute, tachypnea with rates over 25, and a decreasing blood pressure with systolic values of 80 mm Hg or below. Do not wait for a low blood pressure to be documented before suspecting shock in a patient; hypotension is a late sign. Because the hallmark of late shock is the decreasing level of consciousness, the nurse must realize that the patient is rapidly progressing toward death by the time lethargy or coma is seen. Immediate intervention is required.

Treatment for shock must be aggressive and must be initiated early; all areas of bleeding must be brought under control. Place the patient in the Trendelenburg position or elevate the feet 12 to 16 inches. Keep the airway open, and administer oxygen. Maintain the patient at a comfortable temperature. The most important treatment for early shock is the establishment of one or two large bore IV lines and the rapid infusion of 1 to 3 liters of lactated Ringer's solution or other crystalloid solutions.

If the patient shows any of the signs of late shock, apply and inflate antishock trousers until the patient's systolic blood pressure returns to 100 to 110 mm Hg. The inflation of the antishock trousers often causes dilation of the extremity and neck veins, making it easier to establish peripheral IV lines. Establish no fewer than two IV lines in late shock victims. A third line may also be established, using the subclavian vein or other central routes. Late shock patients should have 3 to 6 liters of lactated Ringer's solution infused; many patients require more. Although whole blood transfusions are desirable for patients in late shock, they are usually not available until the patient reaches a medical facility.

Step 2: The Assessment

The nurse, once the priorities have been addressed, must examine the patient in more detail before treatment can be initiated. Step 2 in the systems approach to patient care is essential for proper treatment and should never be skipped. Assess each patient by taking a history when possible, recording vital signs, and performing a head-to-toe physical examination. Remove or cut away clothing to provide access to the areas being examined. This assessment should be quick but thorough enough to discover any hidden injuries. It usually requires two to four minutes to complete. Step 2 allows the nurse to find all the patient's injuries, to organize an approach to the patient's condition, and to set priorities for further treatment.

History

The nurse is able to care for the trauma patient better if an adequate history is obtained. The history should be brief but should cover several important points. Whenever possible, try to elicit a chief complaint, mechanism of injury, present illness, current medical problems, allergies, and current medications.

The chief complaint is usually obvious; nevertheless, ask the patient what the main problem is. Knowing the mechanism of injury is important because gaining an understanding of the forces applied to the body can help in understanding the resultant injuries. For example, the nurse who discovers a history of blunt trauma to the abdomen is likely to be more sensitive to early abdominal symptomatology.

Obtaining a description of the present illness helps the nurse to understand the patient's chief complaint and is best developed in a limited time by use of the mnemonic device *COLDERR*. Each capital letter stands for an aspect of the chief complaint that must be developed:

- Character
- Onset
- Location
- Duration
- Exacerbation
- Relief
- Radiation

Information about any pertinent medical problems such as diabetes, pregnancy, or heart disease is important because such problems can affect the outcome of the patient if they are not acted upon. Information about allergies and current medication should also be collected.

If the patient is unconscious or unable to communicate, rely on the patient's friends or family to supply the history. However, this source may not be available in a disaster and necessitates the use of ingenuity on the nurse's part. Look then for Medic-Alert tags or ask the attending EMTs where the patient was found and what forces may have been applied to the patient. When it is impossible to obtain a history, be particularly thorough in performing the physical examination.

Vital Signs

The EMTs and paramedics have little time to assess a trauma patient's vital signs in the confusion of the disaster zone. Instead, their main goal must be to prevent death and to move the patient as soon as possible to the treatment zone where more detailed assessment and treatment can be carried out. There the nurse takes the vital signs as part of Step 2 in the systems approach to patient care.

The most valuable vital sign in the majority of trauma patients is the pulse. A rapid pulse is one of the earliest indicators that the patient is suffering shock or deteriorating. In the case of a critically injured or unconscious patient, palpate the pulse over the carotid or femoral artery rather than a peripheral vessel because of the possibility of vascular shutdown in distal extremities. Pulse rates below 60 beats per minute or above 100 are usually indications of patient deterioration.

Respirations can be counted by observing or palpating the rise or fall of the chest and the abdomen. Blood pressure is obtained through the use of a stethoscope and a sphygmomanometer. Different size sphygmomanometers are usually not available in a disaster, so the standard adult-size cuff must be used on children and obese patients.

The nurse seldom takes a patient's temperature in a disaster unless there is a suspicion that the patient is suffering heat stroke or hypothermia.

The vital signs and the time they are obtained should be recorded on each patient's triage tag or on a piece of tape attached to the patient. The nurse should repeat and record the vital signs every 10, 15, or 20 minutes, depending on the seriousness of the patient's condition.

Physical Examination

The physical examination of the trauma patient gives the nurse the greatest amount of data on the patient's physical condition. This examination must be thorough as outlined in Chapter 2 in order for the nurse to discover all of the patient's injuries. Many trauma patients may have subtle or hidden injuries, which are easily overshadowed by obvious wounds. Following the systems approach for doing a methodical physical examination helps the nurse to avoid the mistake of missing injuries. A physical examination also helps the nurse in formulating an approach to treatment.

The nurse should employ the physical assessment skills of observation, palpation, percussion, and auscultation on every trauma patient. Examine in a rapid, organized and sequential manner each of the following areas:

- head and neck
- shoulders and upper extremities
- chest
- abdomen and pelvis
- lower extremities
- back

After performing the head-to-toe physical examination, make a neurological assessment, using the Glasgow coma score (see under Head Injury).

Step 3: Treatment

Treatment is started once the life-threatening problems have been dealt with and the patient has been thoroughly assessed. More definitive treatment of the priorities may be necessary; then treat other major injuries, such as chest and abdominal trauma. Minor problems, including wounds and minor fractures, can be addressed last.

Chest Trauma

The danger of chest trauma is the disruption of the integrity of the chest cavity. Most injuries to the chest decrease the ability of the heart to pump blood, or they prevent the lungs from oxygenating the blood. The resultant hypoxia quickly leads to death. Effective management depends upon prompt diagnosis and treatment.

Do not judge the severity of the patient's condition by appearance.[8] Chest trauma patients with severe injuries may be initially relatively symptom free. A careful history, including mechanism of injury, may prove valuable in evaluating the chest trauma patient. For example, a patient who describes a blow to the chest may often have rib fractures or a flail chest. Observe, palpate, percuss, and auscultate the thoracic cavity; look for clues that give a better understanding of the type and the extent of the injury. A patient who has decreased breath sounds or asymmetrical respirations has damaged the integrity of the thoracic cavity. Any patient who has a suspected chest injury should be reevaluated frequently to assure that the condition is not deteriorating.

Chest trauma is considered one of the most serious insults to the body and can rapidly lead to death. If the chest trauma is identified and treated early, however, the patient has an excellent prognosis. The nurse's primary goal in the management of the chest trauma patient should be immediate treatment and early transport. There are many types of injury to the chest, but, in this chapter, only life-threatening injuries are reviewed. These include simple pneumothorax, open pneumothorax, tension pneumothorax, flail chest, and cardiac tamponade.

Simple Pneumothorax. A simple pneumothorax is usually caused by blunt trauma to the chest. Injury to the chest wall or pleura from the trauma causes leakage of air into the pleural space. The air prevents the lung from expanding and leads to partial lung collapse. The collapse of the lung decreases oxygen exchange in the lung. The signs and symptoms of a pneumothorax are as follows:

- dyspnea
- pain
- cyanosis (late)
- diminished or absent breath sounds on the affected side
- hyperresonance to percussion

Treat the patient with a pneumothorax with oxygen therapy and position on the affected side. Consider the placement of a chest tube for anyone in respiratory distress unrelieved by oxygen therapy.

Hemothorax. Hemothorax is usually caused by a tear in the lung or chest. The accumulation of blood in the pleural cavity can cause partial or complete collapse of the lung. Symptoms of a hemothorax are often the same as those of a simple pneumothorax, compounded by the development of hypovolemia from loss of blood. Treatment of a hemothorax is the same as for a pneumothorax. In addition, the patient may need volume replacement and treatment of shock. A larger chest tube is needed for these patients to allow the blood to drain.

Open Pneumothorax (Sucking Chest Wound). An open pneumothorax is caused by an object that penetrates into the chest wall, creating an opening to the outside. The pressure inside the pleural cavity equalizes with the atmospheric pressure, resulting in a loss of the vacuum in the lung. This loss in negative pressure prevents the lung from expanding and leads to collapse of that lung. Signs and symptoms of an open pneumothorax are as follows:

- pain with breathing
- visible wound with possible passage of air
- subcutaneous emphysema

- absent or decreased breath sounds on the affected side
- cyanosis

Treat an open pneumothorax by immediately covering the wound with a sterile occlusive petroleum gauze dressing. If there are no sterile dressings available, plastic wrap or a rubber glove can be used. The bandage should cover the wound and should be taped on all sides; however, taping all sides may cause a buildup of air in the pleural cavity, creating a tension pneumothorax. This condition can be relieved by raising the edge of the dressing for a few seconds to allow the air to escape. Patients with this condition need to be observed closely and transported as quickly as possible; they may need high-flow oxygen therapy and placement of a chest tube.

Tension Pneumothorax. A tension pneumothorax may be caused by blunt or penetrating trauma. The lesion allows air to enter the pleural cavity during inspiration, but the air cannot escape during expiration. The accumulated air in the pleural space causes a collapse of the lung. The air continues to accumulate in the pleural space, displacing the heart and the opposite lung. Unless this pressure is relieved, this patient may die from cardiac or respiratory failure. Signs and symptoms of tension pneumothorax are as follows:

- pain with breathing
- dyspnea
- jugular venous distension
- tracheal deviation
- absent or decreased breath sounds on the affected side
- muffled heart tones
- cyanosis
- tympany and percussion
- deteriorating vital signs
- decreasing level of consciousness

The treatment of a tension pneumothorax must be carried out immediately. The preferred method is the insertion of a chest tube. In the field, however, this procedure may not be possible because of lack of proper equipment or training. Nevertheless, the nurse can relieve the pressure by doing a needle thoracentesis.

To do a needle thoracentesis, locate the second intercostal space of the mid-clavicular line on the affected side. Scrub the site with antiseptic and locally anesthetize it if the patient is conscious. Use a number 12- or 14-gauge over-the-needle catheter attached to a 50-mL syringe. The needle should go over the top of the ribs as it is inserted into the intercostal space. Puncture the parietal pleura, and aspirate the air. Then firmly anchor the needle to the chest wall and close it with a three-way stopcock. Watch the patient carefully for a recurrence of the tension, which necessitates a brief opening of the stopcock. Transport the tension pneumothorax patient as quickly as possible.

Flail Chest. A flail chest is caused by blunt chest trauma resulting in multiple rib fractures. The segment of fractured ribs moves paradoxically inward with inspiration and outward with expiration. The flail segment does not participate in respiratory effort, impairing normal chest excursion. This loss of proper lung movement quickly leads to severe hypoxia and the death of the patient. The fractured ribs may also puncture the lung and lead to a pneumothorax. Signs and symptoms of a flail chest are as follows:

- pain with breathing
- dyspnea
- tenderness to palpation
- paradoxical chest movements
- cyanosis
- subcutaneous emphysema
- crepitus over the fractured site
- decreased or absent breath sounds on the affected side
- decreased level of consciousness

The treatment of choice is internal immobilization with endotracheal intubation and positive pressure ventilation. In the field, this procedure may not be possible because of lack of training and equipment. High-flow oxygen, splinting the chest with pillows or sandbags, and turning the patient onto the affected side can all help relieve the flail chest. Most complications are attributed to the lack of chest movement. There is now strong evidence that respiratory compromise is a consequence of the underlying pulmonary contusion.[9] This contusion can be increased by overhydration with crystalloids. Care should be taken that the patient is not given too much solution unless there are signs of hypovolemia.

Cardiac Tamponade. A blunt or penetrating injury to the chest can cause blood or fluid to accumulate in the pericardial sac. The accumulation of blood in the sac impairs ventricular filling and pumping and leads to decreased cardiac output. These patients deteriorate rapidly from shock. The following signs and symptoms of cardiac tamponade are present:

- jugular venous distention
- cyanosis

- muffled heart tones
- pulsus paradoxus
- hypertension followed by hypotension

Cardiac tamponade is an emergency that must be treated immediately. The preferred treatment is pericardiocentesis, which requires sophisiticated monitoring equipment that is not usually available in the field. In lieu of this equipment, the nurse may choose to treat the patient with high-flow oxygen, high Fowler's position, and intravenous volume replacement. Without rapid transportation, this patient may become a low-priority patient. Do not confuse this syndrome with a tension pneumothorax, which resembles cardiac tamponade. When in doubt as to which injury the patient may have, choose to do a needle thoracentesis into the apparently injured lung.

Great Vessel Injury. A sudden narrowing of the chest's anterior-posterior diameter followed by a rapid expansion may exert enough force to tear the aorta or other great vessels. Foreign objects may also puncture vessels. Signs and symptoms of a great vessel injury are chest pain, hypovolemia, and a decreasing level of consciousness. There is no specific therapy that can be used in the field. Ten percent to 20 percent of victims survive to reach the hospital.[10] Treatment for shock and immediate transport to the hospital are needed. If transport is slow, these patients may have to be placed in the low-priority category.

Abdominal Trauma

The abdomen is a complicated area of the body containing numerous delicate organs and tissue. Forces applied to the abdominal region can easily cause ruptures, contusions, or lacerations. The resultant hemorrhage or spilling of intestinal contents can be catastrophic. Because the signs of abdominal trauma can be confusing or hidden, the nurse must maintain a high index of suspicion with any patient involved with this type of injury. The two types of abdominal injury include blunt trauma and open wounds.

Blunt Trauma. The signs and symptoms of abdominal injury in blunt trauma are often dependent on the organs affected. Ruptured solid organs bleed heavily. This condition can lead to early hypovolemia and late peritonitis. Rupture of hollow organs may lead to early peritonitis and late hypovolemia.

It is usually impossible to differentiate between these two injuries in a disaster setting. Both are life-threatening. The following signs and symptoms may be apparent in the early development of blunt trauma:

- fractured lower ribs
- abdominal contusions

- abdominal pain
- abdominal tenderness
- rebound tenderness
- referred pain to the shoulder (Fehr's sign)
- absent bowel sounds

Other signs and symptoms may develop later:

- distended abdomen
- rigid abdomen
- nausea and vomiting
- evidence of hypovolemia

An aggressive approach to the treatment of the abdominal trauma patient is paramount to his survival. The primary factor in the successful outcome of this patient is not the accurate diagnosis of a specific type of injury, but rather the determination that an acute abdominal emergency is present, requiring rapid transport to a surgical facility. Stabilize these patients by the application of antishock trousers if hypotension is present. Antishock trousers can slow down or stop abdominal bleeding as a result of the indirect pressure they exert on the internal bleeding lesion; they also transfuse blood from the lower extremities to the vital organs in the chest and the head. Start large bore intravenous lines on all abdominal trauma patients, and be prepared to infuse large quantities of lactated Ringer's solution. A nasogastric tube can be inserted to decompress the stomach and to empty the abdominal contents. Other supportive measures include the administration of oxygen and the placement of the patient into a Trendelenburg position.

Open Abdominal Wounds. Open abdominal wounds include penetration of objects into the abdominal cavity, impaled foreign objects, and evisceration of abdominal contents. All of these injuries can lead to hemorrhage or peritonitis. Evisceration of the intestines can also cause necrosis of the bowel. These conditions are medical emergencies that require surgical repair. The signs and symptoms of these injuries are similar to those for blunt trauma. In addition, the nurse may find wounds about the abdomen, impaled objects, or protruding bowel.

Treat open wounds by covering them with sterile bulk dressing. Impaled objects should be removed only in the emergency room, inasmuch as their removal may lead to increased hemorrhage. Minimize the motion of an impaled object by surrounding it with supportive bulky dressings. Never place eviscerated organs back into the abdomen; cover them with moist sterile dressing. Further treatment is the same as for blunt trauma.

Head Trauma

A nurse in the disaster setting frequently sees head injuries. Cerebral contusions and lacerations are the most common results of this type of trauma and may result in increasing intracranial pressure and massive tissue damage. Intracranial hematomas, which may also occur, lead to the shifting of brain tissue and increasing intracranial pressure. Skull fractures are of less significance, unless they are associated with underlying soft tissue damage, which may be the case with depressed skull fractures. Open fractures are also serious, because they usually allow communication with cerebral spinal fluid or brain tissue. Patients with serious head injury are often placed in the low-priority categories of triage. A patient with simple contusions that receive good care has an excellent prognosis. Epidural and subdural hematoma patients who can receive early surgical intervention also have a good chance of survival.

It may be difficult for the nurse to decide exactly what injury has occurred inside the patient's head. More importantly, the nurse must recognize that an intracranial lesion is occurring in the patient. Assessment of head injuries in a disaster setting can be based on the following:

- Glasgow coma scale
- vital signs
- breathing patterns
- pupil size and reaction to light

Tachycardia and hypotension almost never occur with head trauma unless the patient is suffering shock from another injury. Cushing reflex, in which the patient exhibits rapid development of hypertension and bradycardia, is a grave indication of prognosis. Depressed and irregular respirations often accompany cerebral dysfunction as a head injury progresses. Pupilar dilation in the eye of an unconscious head injury patient may indicate development of a lesion in the contralateral hemisphere or a compression of the oculomotor nerve by herniation of the ipsilateral hemisphere. Patients with both pupils fixed and dilated have an extremely poor prognosis. Because of the high incidence of associated spinal injury, the nurse should not check for doll's eyes in a patient before x-ray films have ruled out spinal fractures. Rotation of the head from side to side as the eyes are observed worsens a spinal cord lesion.

The most valuable indication of the development and progression of head injury is the serial recording of the patient's level of consciousness. The Glasgow coma scale is rapidly becoming the most accepted method of measuring and communicating a patient's mental status after trauma (see Table 2–1 in Chapter 2). Though the coma score is only a rough guide, it is quick and easy to use. To assess a patient's level of consciousness simply measure the response of three body areas to a verbal or painful stimulus. A patient's ability to open the eyes is worth 1 to 4 points; a patient's verbal response can have a value of 1 to 5; the ability to move extremities is worth 1 to 6 points. Each body area is tested and the total points are recorded. Scores range from 3 points in a dead or nearly dead patient to 15 points in a conscious patient. A head trauma patient should be evaluated frequently by use of this test. The score recorded measures improvement or deterioration.

It is not necessary for the nurse to diagnose the exact nature of the head injury in order to initiate treatment. Initial steps in head injury management are always addressed to stabilizing the priorities. Unconscious patients can develop numerous airway problems, and the nurse must frequently check for airway patency. Intubation of unconscious patients assists greatly in relieving airway problems. Respiratory efforts often need assistance, though a shortage of personnel in a disaster may not allow for this. Head injury patients usually need immobilization or a backboard to protect possible spinal fractures. The head trauma patient should always have a large bore IV line established to provide a slow infusion of lactated Ringer's solution. If the patient develops signs of shock, the head injury becomes a second priority and the shock should be aggressively treated with the infusion of crystalloids and the application of antishock trousers. Attempt to keep blood volume replacement at 75 percent of estimated needs in the shock patient with head trauma. This practice prevents increased intracranial pressure. Hypovolemic shock in the head injury patient often reduces cerebral hypoxia.

Most head-injured patients develop cerebral hypoxia immediately after an injury. This hypoxia can easily lead to permanent brain damage and should be relieved by the administration of high concentrations of oxygen. Take steps to decrease intracranial pressure by elevating the patient's head 30 to 45 degrees and by hyperventilating the patient, using a rate of 20 to 25 breaths per minute. Because the administration of drugs to relieve increasing intracranial pressure has several undesirable side effects, it should be reserved for patients who show deterioration and who do not respond to other methods. Mannitol, an osmotic agent, may be given in a 0.25-g/kg IV push every 1 to 4 hours as necessary in the adult patient. Administer furosemide (Lasix) to patients who do not respond to mannitol. The adult dose is a 40- to 80-mg IV push. The use of cortico-steroids to reduce cerebral edema, though unproven at this time, is widely recommended. Dexamethasone administered in a 4- to 10-mg IV push every six hours is a standard recommendation, though some institutions recommend much higher dosages.[9]

Do not remove objects impaled into the head; rather, pad and tape them to immobilize them. Pad depressed skull fractures and protect them from the application of force that may further damage the soft tissue under the fracture site. Do not occlude orifices and wounds that leak cerebral spinal fluid, because this practice may contribute to an increase in the intracranial pressure. Place several layers of sterile gauze dressing over a cerebral spinal fluid leak to help prevent contamination of the meninges from outside bacteria.

Patients who have a high Glasgow coma score or patients just recently exhibiting decrease in the loss of consciousness should be transported as soon as possible in order to have their exact injuries diagnosed and to have surgical or other intervention initiated.

Burns

Burns may be one of the worst forms of trauma the patient can receive in a disaster. They can quickly prove fatal if they are not recognized and treated rapidly. Burns can occur when body tissue is exposed to flame, heated objects, and steam. Explosions, electrical currents, and caustic chemicals also cause burns.

Two major indicators of the seriousness of a burn patient's condition are the thickness category and the percent of body surface burned. Burn depth is usually categorized as superficial, partial-thickness, and full-thickness.[11] *Superficial burns* are red and painful but cause few systemic complications; they heal well without sophisticated treatment. *Partial-thickness burns* are characterized by blisters or a wet mottled appearance. They are also painful. These burns can lead to fluid loss and other complications but respond well to treatment. Healing usually takes place in two to three weeks. *Full-thickness burns* are leathery and dry with a dark, tan, or white coloration. The surface of this burn is usually painless. Patients with full-thickness burns have the greatest incidence of severe complications, and long-term therapy is needed to help them recover.

Nurses may use the "Rule of Nines" to approximate the percentage of body surface burned[12] (Figure 5–1). Patients with partial- and full-thickness burns of less than 20 percent of the body surface usually have an excellent prognosis for recovery. The same burns over 60 percent of a patient's body might well prove fatal in a disaster.

Probable fatal or minor burns are assigned by triage to low-priority categories of care. The burn patients who should receive the most attention in a disaster are those who have partial or full-thickness burns of 20 to 60 percent of the body surface or burns about the face, neck, and chest. These patients suffer massive fluid loss from damaged tissue and quickly develop hypovolemic shock. Patients with burns about the chest, neck, or face often have pulmonary involvement that leads to hypoxia, pulmonary edema, and respiratory arrest.

All serious burn patients should receive two large bore intravenous lines of lactated Ringer's solution or normal saline. The fluid should be run at the flow rate of 3 mL/kg/percent of surface area burned.[13] Fifty percent of the total volume should be administered in the first 8 hours. The patient who is already in shock

Figure 5–1 Rule of Nines for Burn Patients

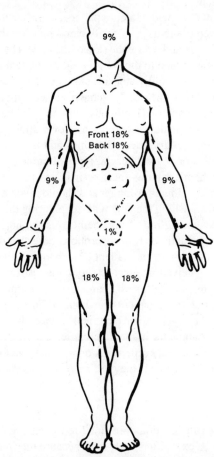

Note: The rule of nines is used to measure the percent of body burned. Adding together the percent burned will give the nurse an estimate of the extent of body surface burned.

Source: Reprinted with permission from Cardine NL: *Emergency Care in the Streets.* Boston, Little, Brown & Co, 1983, p 359.

---

should be placed in the Trendelenburg position, receive oxygen, and have the antishock trousers applied and inflated if systolic blood pressure is below 80 mm hg. Administration of pain medication to the burn patient is a controversial topic. If analgesics are used, they should be administered intravenously in small increments.

Patients who show any signs of respiratory distress such as dyspnea, tachypnea, or hoarseness indicate a need for endotrachael or nasotracheal intubation. Those patients with neck, facial, or chest burns who do not have respiratory distress should receive oxygen.

The most important treatment of a burn patient is directed to correcting hypoxia and shock. The burned tissue itself is easily cared for after these life-threatening complications are addressed. Expose the skin of the patient by gently removing the clothing. Cloth that has melted to the skin should not be removed; it may damage viable tissue. Do not apply cold water or cold packs to patients who are burned over 20 percent of the body surface. The compromised temperature regulation of these patients causes them to develop hypothermia if they are cooled. This development worsens the patient's condition. Never apply topical preparations. Cover the burned skin with dry, clean dressings and loosely bandage the area.

Nurses may be called on to treat special types of burns from chemical spills or electrical currents. Chemical burns must be irrigated before they are bandaged. Irrigation should last 20 minutes or longer and should involve copious amounts of running water. Gently washing the area with soap during the irrigation process is usually advisable. Neutralization of the chemical is not normally attempted. Be alert for systemic toxic reactions from absorption of the chemical. Such a reaction calls for further stabilization of the patient or a change in the triage category.

Patients who have received an electric shock may suffer a variety of injuries including fractures, respiratory arrest, cardiac dysrhythmias, and neurological changes. Always search these patients for both an entrance wound and an exit wound. The primary problem with electrical injuries is the underlying tissue destruction that is not apparent immediately after the incident. The burned area observed on the surface usually represents only a small part of the actual injury. Always treat electrical burns as if they are more serious than they appear.

Orthopedic Trauma

Most fractures and dislocations are not life-threatening. Spine, pelvic, and femur fractures may be exceptions, however, because they may cause neurogenic shock due to blood loss. Complications from poorly treated fractures may leave a patient with permanent disabilities. It is, therefore, essential for the nurse to know how to recognize and to treat orthopedic problems at the disaster site. The signs and symptoms of a fracture or dislocation may include the following:

- pain
- crepitus
- deformity
- ecchymosis
- loss of use
- asymmetrical extremities

- open wounds
- swelling

The primary goal of treatment is the effective immobilization of the bone fragments, usually accomplished through the use of a splint. Characteristics of an adequate splint include the following:

- extension past proximal and distal joints of the fracture
- strength and rigidity
- padding at bony prominences
- snugness without vascular compromise

The precise diagnosis of a fracture or dislocation during a disaster is impossible. If the nurse suspects an orthopedic problem, the area should be immobilized immediately. Elevation of the extremity and application of cold packs can also benefit the injury. Certain orthopedic injuries present special problems.

Deformities. Whenever possible, a deformed extremity should be returned to anatomical position. This procedure is best performed by applying gentle traction along the long axis of the extremity and returning it to anatomical position. The extremity is then placed in a split.

Joint Fractures or Dislocations. When a fracture exists in a joint or a possible dislocation has occurred, the injury is best treated in the field by forming a splint around the joint in the position found. No straightening of the extremity should take place.

Neurological and Vascular Involvement. The patient who has numbness, tingling, cyanosis, or loss of pulse distal to the fracture site may have compression of nerves or vessels. If a patient is more than two hours away from a hospital facility, attempt to relieve this pressure through gentle traction and manipulation of the dislocation or fracture until the neurological or vascular function returns.

Open Fractures. Open fractures leave the patient with a high likelihood of osteomyelitis secondary to wound contamination. Any fracture associated with a wound should be treated by irrigation with povidone-iodine and the application of a sterile dressing before a splint is applied.

Fractures of the Femur. Fractures of the femur trigger spasms of the powerful muscles in the thigh which lead to overriding of the fractured femur and increased soft tissue damage. Suspected femur fractures should, therefore, be placed in a traction device such as a Hare traction splint. This traction splint helps to relax the muscle spasms and immobilizes the injured bone. When a traction splint is not available, some form of traction may be improvised or the leg can simply be placed in a rigid splint. Femur fractures can cause a large amount of blood loss inside the thigh. A patient with a femur fracture should have a large bore IV line of lactated Ringer's. Be alert also for signs and symptoms of hemorrhage, such as swelling around the fracture site. An increase in diameter of 1 centimeter represents a loss into the thigh of 2 liters of blood.[14]

Fractures of the Pelvis. Pelvic fractures often sever large vessels, thus leading to massive blood loss inside the pelvic cavity. The bladder or urethra may also be lacerated, causing their contents to leak into the pelvis. Either of these problems may develop into a life-threatening condition. Suspect a pelvic fracture if the patient complains of low back, hip, or pubis pain. Other signs of a pelvic fracture include the flexion of lower extremities or pain on heavy palpation of the iliac crest. This fracture is best treated with a scooping device such as a Robertson orthopedic stretcher or a backboard. Antishock trousers may also provide immobilization of the pelvic fracture, but should only be inflated upon signs of shock. Patients with suspected pelvic fractures should have volume replacement with lactated Ringer's solution and should be monitored closely for signs of shock or peritonitis.

Additional Treatment

The nurse may consider additional treatment for any trauma patient if equipment is available and time permits. All suspected trauma patients should have two large bore IV lines of lactated Ringer's solution inserted and oxygen applied. These patients should be placed on rigid backboards to prevent spinal cord injury from hidden fractures. If there are antishock trousers available, they should be placed on suspected trauma patients but inflated only if the systolic blood pressure drops below 80 mm hg.

Scarce supplies, such as advanced invasive equipment, should be reserved for high priority but viable patients. Those adult patients with any suspected severe injuries should have number 18 nasogastric tubes and number 16 French Foley catheters inserted.

Medication availability at a disaster scene may be limited. Analgesics should be used sparingly and only on patients who are not likely to suffer respiratory or cardiovascular depression from their administration. Serious trauma patients or patients suffering large open wounds can benefit from the administration of an antibiotic such as cefazolin sodium (Ancef), 1 to 2 grams administered intravenously, as soon after their injury as possible.

Record on the patient tag or note attached to the patient any treatment performed—especially invasive techniques and the administration of medications. Monitor closely all patients with invasive lines or tubes until they are in the care of the hospital staff.

TRANSPORT

Treatment of patients at the scene of a disaster is always limited by a number of facts—which include lack of sophisticated personnel and equipment. This limitation makes transportation of the trauma victim to an advanced care facility an essential element of the care in a disaster. The nurse who is involved with patient care at the scene may need to assist in the transportation of patients to advanced care facilities in order to assure the survivability of the more seriously injured patients. Nurses are either preparing patients to leave the treatment zone or accompanying the patient on the way to the hospital. Therefore, they must be prepared to make decisions about patient transport.

One of the first transportation questions the nurse needs to address is when to transport patients away from the disaster. Several problems can occur when transportation timing is inappropriate. Most hospitals cannot activate their disaster plans and gear up for an onslaught of patients in less than an hour. The nurse who assists in transporting 25 seriously injured patients to the local hospital emergency department that has a staff of six has not benefitted the patients. The nurse should not allow the transportation of a patient with a large pneumothorax to a distant hospital unless the patient has had a chest tube or needle inserted to prevent death from a tension pneumothorax.

Several guidelines should be used by the nurse to decide when to transport patients:

- Time patients' transportation so they arrive at hospitals that are prepared for them.
- Transport patients first who are exhibiting a deteriorating condition but who will be salvageable when they arrive at the hospital.
- Whenever possible, transport seriously injured patients after IVs and tubes have been placed to help keep patients stable while they travel.
- Begin the transport of patients only when adequate vehicles have arrived.
- Transport patients only when there is adequate staff to accompany them.

Other important decisions, such as where the patients go and who accompanies them, may have to be made concerning transportation. In most communities, the destination of a patient during a disaster transport is decided by the emergency operations center. The decision is based on communications with the receiving hospitals. The nurse may assist the EOC by advising them of special circumstances—such as burn patients who should be referred to a hospital with a burn unit or head injury patients who would be best treated by a facility that has a neurosurgeon. If the EOC is not able to advise the disaster team on transportation, the nurse may need to decide where patients should be transported. The following directions may be used when determining where to transport patients:

- Distribute patients among as many hospitals as possible.
- Send patients who do not need immediate care to the most distant hospitals.
- Send patients who need specialist care to the most appropriate facilities.
- Consider sending patients with minor injuries to local clinics rather than to hospitals if the hospitals are overburdened.
- Attempt to communicate with the hospital before deciding where to send the patients.
- Always notify the hospital in advance of how many and what type of patients you have sent them.

When there are adequate personnel to treat patients at the treatment area, nurses may accompany the more seriously injured patients and may continue treatment during transportation.

Nurses must make sure that patients have been adequately prepared before they are loaded into a vehicle and rushed away. The longer the travel time, the more important adequate preparation becomes. Follow the general rule for the preparation of a patient for transport: if you suspect that a serious condition might develop during transport, treat the condition in advance of the transport.

Starting an IV or inserting a chest tube in a hypovolemic patient in the back of a small, crowded, moving ambulance may be impossible. Make sure then that the patient has been prepared in advance. Before a patient leaves for the hospital, ensure that this checklist has been accomplished:

- Assure the proper placement of all IV lines and other invasive tubes.
- Make sure all chest tubes are sealed.
- Make sure IV lines are working.
- Consider nasogastric tube placement in serious patients to prevent aspiration.
- Securely tape down all tubes to prevent accidental removal during handling.
- Make sure all splints and bandages are secure.
- Strap all patients to backboards or stretchers to prevent shifting during travel.
- Attach a record of vital signs, physical assessment findings, and treatment to each patient, either in the form of a disaster tag or a small note.
- Inform transportation personnel of any special care the patient needs during the ride.

Patients may be transported in several types of vehicles during a disaster. However, because most patients will leave by ambulance, the nurse should have some orientation to the capabilities of an ambulance. Most ambulances are designed to carry four patients in the back. One patient is placed on the ambulance's wheeled stretcher, and another patient is placed on the long bench along the the vehicle's right side. The nurse must make sure that both of these stretchers are securely locked into the ambulance floor or strapped to the bench. Two more patients can be suspended in stretchers from the ceiling. It is possible to place a fifth patient who has minor injuries sitting upright in the front passenger seat of an ambulance. This arrangement of patients leaves almost no room to work on patients during transport. Whenever possible, then, limit the capacity of ambulances carrying serious patients so that there is room for the staff to administer care during transport.

Ambulances are equipped with at least two sources of oxygen. One source is usually a portable oxygen set up; the other is a large cylinder usually located in a closet-like container of the vehicle wall. This large container has to be turned on by reaching into the closet and twisting outlets near the front of the patient compartment. Intravenous fluids can be hung from small hooks located in the ambulance's ceiling. Suction apparatus and other airway maintenance equipment is usually located on the shelves of the patient compartment. Extra stretchers and backboards are located in compartments outside the ambulance or just inside the back door. A nurse who is riding in the back of an ambulance should wear a seat belt or be well braced because a vehicle that is being driven by even the most cautious driver often provides a bumpy ride for its occupants.

Ambulances take patients to hositals and return to pick up more patients as fast as they safely can; however, when there are larger numbers of patients and not enough ambulances, other vehicles may be pressed into service. Vans, buses, and trucks can substitute for ambulances. Private cars can carry patients with minor injuries. Whenever nonambulance vehicles carry patients, the following rules should be applied:

- Medical personnel should always accompany the patients in the vehicle.
- The driver should not be regarded as the person caring for the patient.
- All patients should be strapped down or should wear seat belts.
- Oxygen or other equipment should accompany the patient if needed.
- Drivers should be given clear directions as to which hospitals they are going to and where they are located.
- The vehicle should always be driven in a safe manner and the speed limit should not be exceeded, even in emergencies.

Some communities may have access to helicopter transport during a disaster. Hospital-based medical helicopters, state or county police helicopters, or a variety of military helicopters may be called on to respond to the disaster. A helicopter can be a valuable asset, but it has many limitations. If the helicopter is a nonmedical aircraft, it should be prepared according to the same guidelines as those for nonambulance vehicles outlined in the previous paragraph. Never base the transportation of disaster patients solely on helicopters, because they frequently are grounded by weather, darkness, terrain, and mechanical problems. Large military helicopters have the capacity to transport many patients, but most hospital and other helicopters can transport only one or two patients simultaneously.

The nurse who is planning to use a helicopter for patient transportation has to initiate preparations for this vehicle in advance. Fire department or police department personnel can assist the nurse in these preparations. An area adequate in size and free of overhead obstructions should be located close to the treatment zone for the helicopter to land. Helicopter pilots prefer the following characteristics for a landing zone:

- The location should be free of power lines, tall trees, or other overhead obstructions for several hundred feet.
- Landing zone size should be at least 50 feet by 50 feet for small helicopters and 100 feet by 100 feet for larger helicopters.
- The landing zone should be relatively flat and level without objects that stick up.
- No objects should be near the landing zone that could be blown up into the helicopter rotors.
- The landing zone should be marked with road flares or traffic cones when possible.
- At night, any lights available should be directed down onto the landing zone—never up at the helicopter as it approaches.
- All personnel should be kept as far back from the landing zone as possible.
- To help the pilot assess wind direction, a smoke grenade should be set off or a thin strip of cloth should be held up as the pilot makes the final approach.
- If other wind direction markers are not available, one person should stand at the upwind side of the landing zone with back to the wind, holding both arms in front, pointing to the landing zone.

Preparing the landing zone is, however, only one aspect of helicopter transportation. Working around helicopters can be extremely dangerous. To prevent other accidents from occurring at a disaster site, then, the following helicopter safety rules should be enforced:

- Tie down all blankets and other loose articles near the landing zone.
- Protect your eyes from the dust kicked up by the rotor wash as the helicopter lands or takes off.

- Never approach a helicopter until signalled to do so by the crew.
- Always approach in view of the pilot—from the front or side.
- Stay entirely away from the back of a helicopter.
- Do not run toward a helicopter—walk.
- If the helicopter rotors are moving, stoop down when you approach.
- Do not hold IV bottles or other equipment upright when approaching the helicopter.
- Let the helicopter crew open and close doors and supervise the loading of patients.
- Remember, the safest place to be when a helicopter is landing or taking off is as far away as possible.

Transportation is a continuum of treatment in which the nurse plays a vital role. Nurses must direct their talents towards helping the patient to move safely and rapidly toward the most appropriate care facility.

SUMMARY

Treating trauma patients at a disaster scene can be a challenging role for the nurse. Most success will be achieved if treatment is aggressive and rapid. The care of trauma patients should always be organized and systematic. Use of the systems approach to patient care assures that the priorities of airway, breathing, circulation, bleeding, spinal fractures, and shock are located and treated. Early assessment and treatment of the patient at the scene are also a part of the systems approach and allow the nurse to offer the best possible care to a trauma patient in the disaster setting. Following transportation guidelines and safety rules will ensure that the patient arrives at the hospital with an optimal prognosis.

REFERENCES

1. Hicks TC, Danzl DF, Thomas DM, et al: Resuscitation and transfer of trauma patients: A prospective study. *Ann Emerg Med* 1982;11:296–299.

2. A philosophy for blunt trauma: Your assumption must always be that he is injured more seriously than you think. *Emerg Med*, January 15, 1983, pp 96–107.

3. Shaftan GW: The initial evaluation of the multiple trauma patient. *World J Surg* 1983;7:19–25.

4. McSwain N: To manage multiple injury: Consider mechanisms, establish priorities. *Emerg Med*, February 29, 1984, pp 56–72.

5. Eckert C: *Emergency Room Care*, ed 4. Boston, Little Brown & Co, 1981, p 34.

6. American National Red Cross: *Advanced First Aid and Emergency Care*. New York, Doubleday & Co Inc, 1973, p 30.

7. Trunkey, DD: The first hour. *Emerg Med*, March 15, 1984, pp 93–107.

8. Hoyt KS: Chest trauma: When the patient looks bad, act fast; when he looks good, act fast. *Nurs 83*, May 1983, pp 34–41.

9. Meislin HW: *Priorities in Multiple Trauma*. Rockville, Md, Aspen Systems Corp, 1980, pp 59, 84.

10. Wilson RF, Murray C, Antonenko DR: Nonpenetrating thoracic injuries. *Surg Clin North Am* 1977; 57:17–36.

11. Gillespie RW: Life-threatening injuries: The burn at first. *Emerg Med*, May 15, 1979, pp 186–191.

12. Caroline NL: *Emergency Care in the Streets*. Boston, Little Brown & Co, 1979, p 303.

13. Committee on Trauma, American College of Surgeons: *Advanced Trauma Life Support Course*. Omaha, The Lincoln Medical Education Foundation, Creighton University/University of Nebraska School of Medicine, 1981, pp 19, 131.

14. Collins JA: Until the specialists arrive: Keep the patient alive in the meantime. *Emerg Med*, February 28, 1983, pp 178–190.

Chapter 6

The Traumatized Pregnant Woman

Laraine H. Guyette, R.N., M.S., C.N.M.

And woe unto them that are with child, and to them that give suck in these days![1]

In 1981, the estimated birthrate was 16 per 1000 population. On the basis of this ratio, one can anticipate that for every 1000 disaster victims 18 to 20 are in some stage of pregnancy.

"Accidental injury during pregnancy is both common and unique," Baker says,[2]

> not only because two lives are involved but also because of alterations in the nature of and response to injury. Today's women are more exposed to the rigors and dangers of our society. Because of economic necessity, and by choice, more women are working outside of the home; their jobs are more hazardous and require more traveling in faster but smaller cars, as well as motorcycles. Contemporary women have increased exposure to injury because of greater participation in sports, both conditioning and competitive. Moreover, today's woman does not seclude herself when pregnant.

She will be part of any disaster.

The physiologic changes of pregnancy influence the type and the severity of the injuries sustained, the assessment and diagnosis of the problems, and the management and response to the treatment. When the traumatized pregnant woman appears for treatment, it is the responsibility of the health care provider to determine the status of the mother and the fetus and to implement an appropriate plan of care. In most situations, the mother and the baby are treated as a unit, and so one may assume that what is good for the mother is good for the baby. The health care provider is faced with the responsibility of managing two patients as one.

Understanding the physiologic changes of pregnancy and the altered response to trauma can facilitate the development of an appropriate plan of care. For example, manifestations of these changes would frequently be considered pathologic in the nonpregnant state, but in a trauma situation, these manifestations may confuse the clinical picture. Cruikshank cites four complicating factors the health care provider must keep in mind when treating a pregnant trauma victim:[3]

1. The fact that the patient is pregnant may alter the pattern of severity of the injury.
2. The pregnancy may alter the signs and symptoms of the injury, and the results of laboratory tests used in diagnosis.
3. The management of the trauma victim needs to be modified to accommodate and preserve the physiologic changes induced by pregnancy.
4. The injury may have initiated or have been complicated by pathologic conditions peculiar to pregnancy (e.g., abruptio placentae, amniotic fluid embolism, ruptured uterus), or a pregnancy-related disease may occur coincidental to trauma and thus complicate the diagnosis and therapy (e.g., eclampsia complicating possible head trauma).

Baker further warns that

the pregnant patient with significant trauma should be closely observed and records carefully documented. Patients with minor injuries usually require only brief attention whereas more significant injuries such as vaginal bleeding, uterine irritability, abdominal tenderness or pain, evidence of hypovolemia, a change in or absence of fetal heart tones, or leakage of amniotic fluid require longer periods of observation. Management should primarily be directed toward guaranteeing the health of the mother, which better insures the health of the fetus.[2]

Because emergency department personnel lack familiarity with the anatomic and physiologic changes of pregnancy and fear the impending delivery they often view major trauma to the pregnant woman as a complex tragedy.[2] That a woman is pregnant should not alter the plan of immediate management; shock, lacerations, and fractures should be treated as they would be in a nonpregnant patient. The signs, symptoms, and laboratory indexes of injury in the pregnant patient may be changed, however, and the pattern of injury may be altered. "Injury may be complicated by conditions peculiar to pregnancy, and often therapy must be modified to accommodate the anatomic and physiologic changes of gestation."[3] For example, because the pregnant woman is prone to abdominal trauma that may be complicated by hidden blood loss, the fetus may experience anoxia before the mother is symptomatic. Hesitancy to institute appropriate stabilization measures could result in the loss of the fetus and the loss of the mother.

The changes of pregnancy as they affect resuscitation, assessment, and management of the individual traumatized pregnant woman are discussed at the beginning of this chapter. This information will serve as a basis for the triage and management of pregnant women in a mass casualty situation. Because there are also pregnant women who escape trauma but then begin their labor or experience a complication of their pregnancy, a nurse may be the most prepared person available to assume responsibility for them and their babies. The nursing management of the traumatized pregnant woman (including support during labor and emergency delivery) is discussed in the remainder of this chapter.

IN THE EMERGENCY DEPARTMENT

Assessment of the Woman

When the pregnant woman comes to the emergency department, the immediate assessment of respiratory, circulatory, and neurological stability should not be changed because of her pregnancy. The initial focus is the stabilization of the mother; then consideration is given to the fetus. The major cause of fetal demise related to trauma is the death of the mother.

Resuscitation

Maintenance of an airway and subsequent ventilation are the same for the pregnant or the nonpregnant adult. Likewise, techniques of chest compression are not altered by pregnancy. Proper placement of the hands on the sternum gives maximum efficiency and does not traumatize the enlarged uterus.

The Heimlich maneuver, however, must be modified for use with the pregnant woman. The enlarged uterus inhibits the inward and upward direction and the force of the abdominal thrust; furthermore, a strong blow to the uterus might cause the separation of the placenta. To clear an airway obstruction for a woman in advanced pregnancy, then, requires chest thrusts. The American Heart Association recommends that the rescuer stand behind the victim, encircle the chest with arms under the woman's armpits, grasp one fist with the other hand and place the thumb-side on the lower and middle parts of the sternum, then, press directly back with four quick thrusts.[4]

Head-to-Toe Assessment

A rapid head-to-toe assessment of life-threatening situations in the case of a pregnant woman varies slightly from that of a nonpregnant woman. Table 6–1 illustrates findings that may be altered because of pregnancy or that may be indicative of problems in the pregnant patient.

Women in early to midpregnancy may respond to shock with peripheral vasodilatation; therefore, they may not demonstrate the usual cold, clammy skin.[5] The other change of note is the loss of the usual abdominal guarding and rigidity in the presence of a concealed abdominal hemorrhage.

Vital Signs

The normal alterations in the vital signs that result from the physiologic changes of pregnancy could be considered pathologic in the nonpregnant woman (Table 6–2).[6–9]

It has been observed that the mother can maintain homeostasis at the expense of the fetus. She can also maintain stable vital signs and an adequate circulation and perfusion with a 30–35 percent gradual blood loss or a 10–20 percent acute blood loss.[2] Therefore, blood pressure and pulse need to be assessed frequently in order to recognize early change; shock can develop rapidly once these values begin to change.

History

During stabilization of the patient, the nurse should obtain information about the possibility or the duration of pregnancy. As soon as the woman is stabilized, a basic prenatal history should be obtained (see Exhibit 6–1).

Diagnostic Tests

During pregnancy, the accepted range of normal in diagnostic tests is variable. Significant examples are discussed below.

Urinalysis. A small amount of glucosuria can be a normal finding in pregnancy because of the increase in glomerular filtration and the impaired tubular reabsorption of glucose. Proteinuria is an abnormal finding and may be indicative of pregnancy induced hypertension (PIH). Occasional white blood cells (WBC) are within normal limits (5–10 per high power field), but gross or microscopic hematuria indicates renal disease or urinary tract injury.[3]

Hematology. During the second trimester of pregnancy, there is an average increase in blood volume level of about 45 percent and an increase in erythrocyte and hemoglobin mass level of about 30 percent. Because of a greater increase of plasma volume over red blood cell (RBC) mass, the hematocrit level falls—the physiologic anemia of pregnancy.[10] Hematocrit and hemoglobin levels are of little value in assessing hypovolemia. Serial studies are required to demonstrate

Table 6–1 Head-to-Toe Assessment—Modifications for Pregnancy

Area	Altered Findings	Potential Problems
Head and neck	Seizures without obvious head injury	Eclampsia
	Moderately enlarged thyroid	Normal in pregnancy
	Hyperemia of mucous membranes	Increased bleeding from nose and gum injuries
Thorax and chest	Widened subcostal angle	Normal findings in pregnancy
	Lateral expansion of thorax	
	Elevation of diaphragm	
	PMI—4th ICS lateral to MCL	
Abdomen	Uterus-abdominal organ	Normal finding
	Contractions	Pre-term labor
	Tenderness, irritability, increased size, decreased fetal movement	Placental separation
	Diastasis recti	Normal finding
	Displaced abdominal organs	Liver and spleen more susceptible to injury
	Guarding and rigidity	May be absent with hemorrhage
Back	Lordosis	Normal finding
Pelvis	Relaxation of pelvic joints	Separated symphysis
	Presenting part fixed in pelvis	Fractured pelvis, usually bilateral
	Increased vascularity	Retroperitoneal hemorrhage
Genital-rectal	Labial edema	Normal finding
	Bleeding	Menstruation vs abortion in early pregnancy
		Separated placenta, or placenta previa in late pregnancy
		Labor
	Fluid from vagina	Ruptured bag of waters
Extremities	Warm dry skin	Shock
	Relaxation of ligaments	Dislocation of joints
	Edema	Legs, normal finding; hands & face, PIH
	Hyper-reflexia, hypertension	Pregnancy-induced hypertension

Table 6–2 Vital Signs in Pregnancy

Temperature	37.0 °C (98.6 °F)
Pulse rate	Up 10–20 beats/min (80–95 beats/min)
Respirations	16/min
Blood pressure	Both pressures down
	15 mm Hg/in (2nd trimester)
	Returns to baseline near term
Central venous pressure	10 cm H_2O
Fetal heart tones	120–160 beats/min

ongoing bleeding or hidden blood loss. Table 6–3 provides a detailed list of changes in these hematology values.

Additional hematologic and biochemical laboratory studies include these:

- sedimentation rate (It has little or no value in the diagnosis of injury or disease during pregnancy.)[3]
- leukocyte count (Because the level can reach $1.8 \times 10^3/\mu L$ in the last trimester of pregnancy, the finding of leukocytosis is only of limited value, although it may be a clue to peritoneal irritation.)
- biochemical panel (Because there is no change in serum glutamic-oxaloacetic transaminase (SGOT), serum glutamic-pyruvic transaminase (SGPT), lactic dehydrogenase (LDH) and serum amylase in pregnancy, the study is not useful.)

Exhibit 6–1 Basic Prenatal History

LMP: EDC: Wks Gestation:

Gravida: Para:

Problems this Pregnancy: Blood Type: Rh:

Past OB History:
    Problems with pregnancy, labor, or delivery
    Length of Labor
    Type of delivery
    Pregnancy outcome
    Weight of child

Name of physician or nurse-midwife:

Table 6–3 Hematology Changes During Pregnancy

	Normal Nonpregnant	*Pregnant (3rd Trimester)*
WBC (total)	4500–10,000/μL	5000–14,000/μL
Platelets	175,000–250,000/mm.^{3}	200,000–350,000/mm.^{3}
Plasma volume	2400 mL	3700 mL
Red blood mass	1600 mL	1900 mL
Blood volume	4000 mL	5250 mL
Hemoglobin	12–16 gm./dl.	10–13 gm./dl.
Hematocrit	37%–47%	32%–42%
RBC indexes	Normal	Normal
Polymorphonuclear leukocytes	54%–62%	60%–85%
Lymphocytes	38%–45%	15%–38%
ESR	Less than 20 mm./hr	30–90 mm./hr
Amylase	60–180 Somogyi units/dL	60–180 Somogyi units/dL
Alkaline phosphatase	4–13 King-Armstrong units/dL	17–19 King Armstrong units/dL
Total protein	7 g/dL	5.5–6.0 g/dL
Serum albumin	3.5–5.0 g/dL	3–5 g/dL
α globulin	0.8 g/dL	0.9–1.4 g/dL
β globulin	0.71–1.20 g/dL	0.9–1.5 g/dL
γ globulin	0.8–1.4 g/dL	0.5–1.2 g/dL
Fibrinogen (plasma)	300 mg/dL	450 mg/dL
Glucose	90–110 mg/dL	90–110 mg/dL
Uric acid	2.0–6.4 mg/dL	2.0–5.5 mg/dL
Creatinine	0.6–1.2 mg/dL	0.4–0.9 mg/dL
Sulfobromophthalein retention at 45 min	5%	10%
Cephalin flocculation	Negative	Positive in 10%–15% of patients
Thymol turbidity	Negative	Positive in 10%–15% of patients
Bilirubin, total	0.1–1.2 mg/dL	0.1–0.9 mg/dL
SGOT	10–40 U./mL	10–40 U/mL
SGPT	15–35 U./mL	15–35 U./mL
LDH	60–100 U./mL	60–100 U./mL
Lipase serum	> 1.5 U./mL	> 1.5 U./mL
Serum iron	75–150 μg/dL	65–120 μg/dL
Total iron-combining capacity	250–450 μg/dL	300–500 μg/dL
BUN	10–18 mg/dL	4–12 mg/dL
Plasma lipids		
Total cholesterol	175 mg/dL	245 mg/dL
Free cholesterol	216 mg/dL	231 mg/dL
Cholesterol esters	74%	77%
Serum lipids (total)	700 mg/dL	1000 mg/dL
Phospholipids	250 mg/dL	350 mg/dL
Free fatty acids	700 mEq/L	1200 mEq/L
Electrolytes		
pH (arterial)	7.30–7.44 mol/L	7.41–7.46 mol/L
Chloride	98–109 mEq/L	90–105 mEq/L
Bicarbonate	24–30 mmol/L	19–25 mmol/L

Table 6–3 continued

	Normal Nonpregnant	Pregnant (3rd Trimester)
Phosphorus (inorganic)	2.0–5.2 mg/dL	2.0–4.5 mg/dL
Magnesium	1.5–2.5 mEq/L	1.2 mEq/L
Sodium	135–145 mEq/L	132–140 mEq/L
Potassium	4.0–4.8 mEq/L	3.5–4.5 mEq/L
Calcium		
Total	4.5–5.4 mEq/L	4.5 mEq/L
Ionized	2.0–2.6 mEq/L	2.0–2.6 mEq/L
Plasma base		
excess	0.7 mEq/L	3.5 mEq/L
Arterial carbon dioxide		
partial pressure	38.5 mm Hg	31.3 mm Hg
Carbon dioxide	24–30 mmol/L	19–25 mmol/L
Plasma osmolality	284–295 mosm/kg	275–285 mosm/kg

Source: Adapted with permission from Barber HRK, Graber EA: *Surgical Disease in Pregnancy.* Philadelphia, WB Saunders Co, 1974, pp 110–111.

Blood coagulation tests include the following:

- platelet function (unchanged)[11]
- fibrinogen levels (increase up to 600 mg/dL)[12]
- activated partial thromboplastin time (aPTT) and prothrombin time (PT) (unchanged)[11]
- concentration of factors VII, VIII, IV and X (increase)[6]
- levels of factors V, XI, and XII (unchanged)[6]
- clotting time and bleeding time (unchanged)[11]

Electrocardiogram. The electrocardiogram does not show characteristic changes attributable to pregnancy. Premature beats, atrial or ventricular, are relatively common.[13]

Radiologic Examinations. Abdominal and chest films, skeletal films of the pelvis and back, cystograms, and limited intravenous pyelograms are often essential to diagnose perforated viscus, severe fractures, and ruptured bladder.[2] Findings of note include the following:

- Marked dilation of the renal pelves and ureters occurs as early as ten weeks gestation, and persists until six weeks postpartum. The right side is usually more dilated than the left, with dilation below the pelvic brim.[3]

- The altered position of the heart and the increased size of the heart shadow are evident on chest films.
- Abdominal and pelvic x-ray films show the fetal skeleton.

Although irradiation risks are known to exist for the fetus, the mother's life should not be jeopardized. Needed radiologic examinations should be ordered; however, unnecessary studies and duplicate films should be avoided, and the uterus should be shielded as much as possible to avoid total-body irradiation of the fetus.

Assessment of the Fetus

Although resuscitation and stabilization of the mother is usually in the best interest of the fetus, the status of the fetus must be determined as soon as possible. The quickest and simplest assessment of fetal well-being is to count the fetal heart rate (FHR) with a fetoscope or stethoscope. Heart tones ranging from 120 to 160 beats per minute can be heard when the mother is more than 18 to 20 weeks pregnant. To prevent confusion, the maternal pulse should be palpated as the FHRs are auscultated. Heart tones can be heard with an ultrasonic pulse monitor (doppler) as early as the 12th to 14th week of gestation. If a beat is present, the fetus of any age should be continuously monitored sonographically until there is presumptive evidence that the fetus has tolerated the traumatic episode.

If there is a question of fetal status and if the equipment, the time and the expertise are available, the following tests should be considered:

- nonstress test (NST)
- contraction stress test (CST)[2]
- realtime ultrasound[2]
- amniocentesis[2]
- Kleihauer-betke Staining (modified Singer's test)[14]

When assessing fetal status, the nurse must remember that conditions affecting the mother are also affecting the baby. Likewise, the baby requires the same reevaluation or monitoring as the mother. Stuart suggests that if the fetus does not demonstrate evidence of distress over a period of 24 hours it probably was not significantly compromised by the accident.[14]

Management of the Woman

Management of the pregnant woman who has experienced a traumatic episode differs only slightly from that of the nonpregnant patient. The usual stabilization procedures should be followed—but with consideration for the modifications identified in Table 6–4.

Drugs

"With rare exception, any drug that exerts a systemic effect in the mother will cross the placenta to reach the embryo and fetus."[7] This warning by Pritchard and MacDonald is a reminder to anyone who must consider administering drug therapy to a traumatized pregnant woman that it is necessary to weigh the needs of the mother against the long-term effects on the fetus. The gestational age of the fetus and the drug dosage must also be taken into account. Table 6–5 provides a list of some drugs that might be considered in an emergency situation and gives their known or potential side effects.

Shock

The physiologic hypervolemia of pregnancy is a mechanism of the body that meets the increased demand for perfusion of the uterus and kidneys. At term, blood flow through the uterine artery is approximately 500 to 700 mL/min. "Thus, at term, the total circulating blood volume flows through the uterus every 8–11 minutes. Women in shock may not have the typical cold and clammy skin which characterizes the shock syndrome, and hypovolemia may therefore go unrecognized."[15]

When traumatized, the pregnant woman's body releases catecholamines. These cause peripheral vasoconstriction and marked reduction in blood flow to the uterus, the kidneys, and the intestines, which has a protective effect for the mother by shunting the increased blood volume to the brain and the heart. The reduced perfusion to the placenta results in reduced fetal PO_2 and fetal bradycardia.[16] The mother may lose 10–20 percent of her blood volume in acute hemorrhage or as much as 35 percent in a slower blood loss before hypotension and tachycardia become evident.[3,5] Therefore, fetal bradycardia may be the first sign of hypovolemic shock.

The pregnant woman demonstrates the same progression in her physiologic response to shock as the nonpregnant patient does: decreased cardiac output, decreased capillary perfusion, vasoconstriction to nonvital organs, hypoxia, metabolic acidosis, and death. A tachycardia more rapid than 140 beats per minute or a systolic blood pressure less than 80 mm Hg indicates that she may be near irreversible shock. A systolic blood pressure less than 80 mm Hg results in inadequate perfusion to the fetus.

Baker observed that "the mother can survive hypovolemic shock for a considerably longer period of time than the fetus."[2] Crosby suggested that "otherwise unexplained post-traumatic fetal death may be due to transient and unrecognized maternal shock."[16] Baker has further advised that a vasoconstrictor should not be

Table 6–4 Modified Management of Traumatized Pregnant Women

Action	Rationale
1. Establish and maintain adequate airway. Do not delay tracheostomy or endotracheal intubation.	Hypoxia is a major cause of fetal loss.
2. Control bleeding. Avoid supine position.	Maternal hemorrhage results in fetal hypoxia. Enlarged uterus obstructs circulation in lower extremities, which results in upper body hypotension and increased bleeding from leg injuries.
Avoid MAST trousers after 20 weeks.	Supine hypotension is increased.
3. Maintain fluid volume.	The mother has a 50% increase in blood volume accompanied by increased pelvic vascularity. Her body maintains homeostasis by vasoconstriction to the pelvic organs. She can lose 30%–35% of her circulating blood volume without changes in blood pressure or pulse. The pelvic cavity can hold a 500–ml concealed hemorrhage.
Intravenous infusions with 14-gauge lumen in both upper extremities	This gauge is large enough for large volume fluid replacement; Lower extremities are obstructed by the enlarged uterus.
Aggressive fluid replacement with lactated Ringer's solution	Procedure prevents hypotension and reduces third spacing of fluids
Central line (CVP or Swan-Ganz)	Procedure is best clinical guide to fluid replacement.
Type and cross-match whole blood equaling blood loss	Procedure replaces RBC mass to oxygenate fetus.
Autotransfusion preferred to uncrossed O-negative blood	Atypical antibodies can lead to erythroblastosis.
Plasma expanders—last choice	Procedure restores mother's BP but does not oxygenate fetus.
4. Laboratory studies	Hematologic and biochemical changes in pregnancy (Table 6–3).
Venous Blood Type and cross-match, indirect Coomb's CBC Electrolytes, glucose, Amylase BUN, creatinine	Serial changes are of most value.
PT and PTT Fibrinogen Hourly clotting times	Placenta and uterine injuries may release thromboplastin and plasminogen activators, which increases susceptibility to DIC.

Table 6–4 continued

Action	Rationale
Arterial blood gases	
Pregnancy Test	Serum Beta HCG is most accurate; urine HCG is most rapid
5. Vital signs	
FHR by continuous ultrasound	Changes in FHR usually precede maternal changes in BP and pulse before severe shock.
Pulse	Pulse greater than 140 bpm and systolic
Blood Pressure	blood pressure less than 80 mm Hg indicate impending irreversible shock.
6. Monitor renal function.	
Indwelling urinary catheter	Use accurate measurement of output.
Urinalysis and micro for blood	Bladder becomes abdominal organ with increased vascularity in pregnancy, and so it is more susceptible to trauma.
I & O	Procedure indicates amount of fluid loss and fluid replacement.
Lie on left side.	Move weight of uterus off renal veins for better perfusion of kidneys.
7. Monitor intraabdominal bleeding.	
NG tube	Pregnancy causes prolonged gastric emptying, reduced intestinal motility, increased gastric relaxation and regurgitation.
Peritoneal lavage	Procedure can be safe and valuable in pregnancy; use "open" technique and a lateral tap.
Laparoscopy	Procedure is safe and useful up to 14 weeks.
Culdocentesis	Procedure may be used instead of peritoneal lavage.
Paracentesis	Procedure is not helpful in pregnancy.
Ultrasound for uterine rupture	Procedure can demonstrate fetal parts outside the uterus.

used in an attempt to maintain maternal blood pressure; rather, blood volume loss should be rapidly corrected with volume expanders and blood replacement unit-for-unit.[2] Vasoconstrictors worsen fetal hypoxia and increase the chance of fetal death.

Supine hypotension (mentioned earlier) results from obstruction of the inferior vena cava by the growing fetus as early as the 24th week of pregnancy. The decreased returning blood flow to the right side of the heart and the reduced cardiac output result in maternal hypotension, which can trigger the vasoconstrictive response—another reason to keep the pregnant woman off her back. This change in position may be all that is needed to prevent fetal hypoxia.

Table 6–5 Drugs with Potential Adverse Effects on the Fetus

Drug	Action
Analgesics	Depression in fetus
indomethacin	Arteriosis
salicylates	Premature closure ductus arteriosis, diminished factor XII activity, and platelet dysfunction
Anticoagulants: coumarins	Teratogenesis
Antiinfectives	
chloramphenicol	Gray baby syndrome
streptomycin	Nerve deafness
tetracycline	Stains teeth
chloroquine	Death, deafness
Diuretics: thiazides	Fetal acidosis
Sex hormones	
diethylstilbestrol	Cancer when fetus reaches teens
androgens, progestins	Masculinization of fetus
Hypotensives	Fetal hypoxia
Psychotropics	Withdrawal, hyperactivity
lithium	Teratogenesis
Sedatives	Depression in fetus
barbiturates	Withdrawal, apnea
thalidomide	Teratogenesis
Anticonvulsants: dyphenylhydantoin	Birth defects
Vasoconstrictors	Fetal hypoxia

Another significant risk of prolonged hypotension to the pregnant mother is pituitary necrosis, which results in Sheehan's syndrome. The prevention or the rapid treatment of shock could preserve all or part of the function of the anterior pituitary.[3]

Hemorrhage

The pregnant woman is especially vulnerable to hemorrhage. Because the increased venous pressure in her legs, which is secondary to the enlarging uterus, is an impingement on the circulation from the lower extremities, it can result in increased blood loss from leg wounds.[3] Turning the woman to one side reduces the peripheral venous pressure.

As the uterus enlarges, the abdomen becomes an obvious target for trauma. With increased pelvic vascularity, the pregnant woman is subject to retroperitoneal, retroplacental, and intraperitoneal hemorrhage. It has been suggested that there is an increased frequency of ruptured spleens among pregnant women. Increased bleeding in and around the pregnant uterus has also been reported in cases of pelvic fracture. With 500 to 700 mL of blood flowing through the uterine artery every minute, pelvic or uterine trauma can result in a large volume of blood loss very quickly.[16]

The most serious source of hemorrhage in the traumatized pregnant woman is a retroplacental bleed, which is also known as placental abruption or premature separation of the placenta. This condition should be suspected whenever a woman has received a blow to the abdomen (no matter how minor) or any significant bodily trauma. It has also been suggested that a serious hypotensive episode, which involves decreased perfusion to the uterus, may be associated with placental abruption.[16] The woman experiencing placental abruption usually complains of continuous abdominal pain. She may have vaginal bleeding; a tender, tense, boardlike uterus; contractions; a fundus that is rising in the abdomen; and hypotension out of proportion to visible blood loss. Frequently, the fetus exhibits bradycardia before the mother shows any change in vital signs. If the area of separation is large enough to influence fetal oxygenation, labor or fetal death occurs within 48 hours.[16] The height of the fundus should be marked on admission and observed for signs of increased height. Maternal vital signs should be monitored frequently, and the fetal heart tones should be continuously monitored electronically until the danger of abruption or intraabdominal hemorrhage is past.

Baker believes that the hypervolemia of pregnancy improves maternal tolerance for hemorrhage. The increase in fibrinogen and the concentrations of factors VII, VIII, and IX—coupled with a decrease in circulating plasminogen activators—are a potential maternal benefit. A problem arises when there is injury to the placenta (causing it to release thromboplastin) or injury to the uterus (causing it to release plasminogen activators into the circulation).[2] The release of these substances after trauma can occur in cases of placenta abruptio or amniotic fluid embolus and can lead to a consumptive coagulopathy or disseminated intravascular coagulation (DIC).[2]

Bleeding time, clotting time, and prothrombin time are unchanged in pregnancy, and serum fibrinogen is increased; therefore, these tests can identify a developing coagulation problem. If bleeding is present or suspected, blood should be drawn hourly to observe for clot formation; if poor, the blood should be assayed for serum fibrinogen.[16] D. Cruikshank proposed a management plan of supportive therapy with fresh whole blood, fresh frozen plasma, or cryoprecipitate and delivery as soon as possible.[3] The problem may resolve with delivery. The use of heparin is contraindicated in this type of DIC.

Crosby stated that the "immediate priorities for the hemorrhaging pregnant woman are the same as those for the nonpregnant victim."[16] Bleeding must be stopped by ligature or compression. Setting and immobilizing fractured extremities, vertebrae, and pelvis also reduce blood loss in the surrounding tissue. Blood replacement is mandatory if the patient is in hypovolemic shock, and because blood volume is normally increased during pregnancy, replacement should be generous.

Burns

Baker presented the following general conclusions about thermal injuries to pregnant women. They are based on studies performed at the Burn Center, Brooke Army Medical Center.

1. Pregnancy does not alter the maternal outcome after thermal injuries;
2. Maternal survival is usually accompanied by fetal survival;
3. When the mother does have a lethal injury but is adequately supported, the fetus is usually delivered liveborn prior to maternal death;
4. Obstetric intervention is not necessary and might further compromise both mother and infant;
5. Obstetric intervention is indicated only (1) in the gravely ill woman in whom complications (hypotension, hypoxia, sepsis) might jeopardize the life of a salvageable infant and (2) to anatomically remove the uterine mass in order to operate in the retroperitoneal area;
6. Survival of the infant is related to its maturity.[2]

He has recommended the following management of the victim:

Outpatient
    Stabilize cardiac system (electrical)
    Insure open and effective airway, O_2 therapy
    Early fluid and electrolyte replacement
    Clean and irrigate wound (chemical)
    Control pain
    Transfer to burn treatment center

Inpatient
    Continue electrolyte and fluid stabilization
    Administer tetanus prophylaxis
    Open versus closed wound management, escharotomy
    Administer topical and systemic antibiotics
    Prevent hyponatremia, hypoxia, anemia, and sepsis for fetal well-being[2]

Postmortem Cesarean Section

When a pregnant woman dies, a postmortem cesarean section is considered. H.J. Buchsbaum recommends cesarean section in the case of all pregnancies beyond 28 weeks gestation (1000 grams of estimated fetal weight) and in which fetal heart tones are present (regardless of rate).[17] At 28 weeks, the fundus of the uterus is usually 28 cm above the symphysis or halfway between the umbilicus and the sternal xiphoid. C.E. Weber concluded that the chance of fetal survival remains good if no more than ten minutes elapse from the time of maternal death to fetal delivery.[18] Fetal salvage is more likely when appropriate respiratory and cardiovascular resuscitation of the mother is continued until delivery.

Psychological Support

The traumatized pregnant woman and her family have three concerns:

1. Am I going to be all right?
2. Is the baby all right?
3. Is my family all right?

Usually a direct answer cannot be given. The following information may be helpful as you attempt to reassure a woman and her family:

- Maternal morbidity and mortality are related primarily to the severity of maternal injury.[2]
- There does not seem to be an increase in fetal loss from noncatastrophic trauma in pregnancy.[19]
- During the first trimester, the fetus is protected by the bony pelvis; in the second trimester, it is cushioned by the amniotic fluid, uterine muscles, and gas filled bowel; late in the third trimester, the protection is diminished, and fetal injury is more likely.
- Direct fetal injuries are rare; however, skull fractures may occur after the head has descended into the pelvis, close to term.[16]
- Fetal injury and morbidity are related primarily to injuries of the uterus, the placenta, and the umbilical cord; they are related secondarily to maternal death, maternal shock, and sepsis.[2]

The nurse attempting to reassure the parents should use the term *baby* rather than the term *fetus*—this fetus is their baby, not an object. Using the premise that it is easier to cope with the known than the unknown, the nurse should keep the mother informed of the baby's status (e.g., "the heart beat is slow, but I can hear it" or "I am not hearing the baby's heart beat.") and should encourage the mother to report signs of fetal activity. Otherwise, the mother may perceive that if nothing is said, then something is wrong. Caring concern for the mother and her family can help them cope with this crisis.

Follow-up Care

Follow-up for the pregnant woman who has experienced a trauma should include continuous external fetal monitoring until all signs of labor or fetal distress have been eliminated. In cases of serious trauma this time could be as much as 24 to 48 hours. The woman should be instructed to keep a record of fetal movement. Killien and his associates reported that "an exact standard for the number of fetal movements indicative of fetal well-being has not been established, but it is generally accepted that a decided reduction in fetal activity may be an indication of deterioration of fetal status."[10] They advocated that all women be taught to monitor fetal activity as a simple means of monitoring fetal well-being. If decreased fetal movement is noted, the woman should return for additional fetal assessment. The fundal height should be measured on a weekly basis to ensure that the fetus is growing appropriately. Any indication of inadequate fetal growth should be evaluated by serial ultrasounds performed a month apart and by weekly nonstress tests. These measures can give the mother some reassurance of her baby's well-being, but, as with all mothers, she will not be satisfied until she sees and holds her baby and has counted the fingers and toes.

The Rh-negative mother who has experienced abdominal trauma should have an atypical antibody screen performed and, if negative, should be given Rh_o,D immune globulin prophylactically within 72 hours to prevent Rh sensitization and erythroblastosis in the newborn.

The woman who has undergone pelvic surgery can be assured that it is safe to undergo vaginal delivery even a few hours after surgery. Women who have pelvic fractures must be evaluated, however, on an individual basis. Delivery by cesarean section may be necessary in 5–10 percent of women who have suffered pelvic fracture secondary to pelvic deformity. The risks are that the healed fracture may have reduced the diameter of the pelvis, making it impossible for the fetus to pass through, and the soft tissue of the pelvis (including the urethra and the bladder) may be traumatized when it is compressed between sharp bones and the fetal skull.

DURING A MASS CASUALTY SITUATION

In any disaster (natural or man-made) there are pregnant women—in labor, aborting, experiencing a complication of their pregnancy, traumatized, and seeking reassurance. Those women who experience trauma undergo triage on the basis of their injuries. All others are assigned to the third priority category in which they may be cared for by insufficient numbers of nursing and auxiliary help. Green suggested that a separate maternity area should be established.[20] Those persons who were not actively laboring or in need of immediate attention would be assigned duties to help those in need. "The professional nurse will be called upon to organize, deputize, and supervise the women under her care, and she may have to permit some of these to deliver others. Self-help and neighbor-help are going to be all important to the pregnant women in the event of a disaster."[20] White suggested that during a disaster, normal labor and birth are low priority, and so the woman may get more attention at home with family support and with less risk of exposure to infection.[21]

Labor Support

The needs of the laboring woman are essentially supportive.[22] Birth is a normal physiologic process and nursing measures to facilitate this process can prevent most problems. If the mother has maintained her fluid and caloric intake, has voided periodically, has rested, and has stable vital signs, the nurse may be reassured of the mother's status. If the baby moves periodically, and the heart rate is within the range of 120 to 160 beats per minute, the nurse can be reassured of the baby's status. Labor can then be allowed to continue until delivery without undo concern. For some women the time can be 24 hours or more.

Most labors can be successfully managed without vaginal assessment of labor progress. The physical and behavioral signs of transition from active labor to imminent delivery described in Exhibit 6–2 indicate that labor is progressing.

Exhibit 6–2 Signs of Transition and Imminent Delivery

Transition
  Increased agitation, irritability, restlessness
  Increased apprehension
  Resistance to touch
  Hiccoughs or vomiting
  Narrowing focus centered on contractions
  Alternating feelings of hot and cold
  Leg tremors
  Profuse perspiration with beading on upper lip or between eyes
  Overwhelming discouragement with progress—"I can't take it anymore."
  Difficulty relaxing with contractions
  Increased bloody show

Delivery
  Involuntary catching of breath or grunting with contractions
  Desire to defecate
  Spontaneous bearing down
  "Blossoming" of the anal orifice
  Bulging of the perineum
  Crowning of the baby's head
  Mother says, "The baby is coming."

An increase in maternal temperature greater than 37.0 °C (100 °F); a blood pressure elevation of more than 30 mm Hg, systolic, or 15 mm Hg, diastolic; bright red vaginal bleeding; or signs of shock indicate a mother in distress. Meconium-stained (green) amniotic fluid, loss of fetal heart beat, or loss of fetal movement for 24 hours indicate a baby in distress. In any of these situations, attempts should be made to transfer the mother to a facility that can handle these complications. If transfer is not possible, supportive care can be given as the outcome of labor is awaited.

Emergency Delivery

By the time the signs of imminent delivery are present (see Exhibit 6–2), the person to assist at the delivery should have been identified, the equipment accumulated (Exhibit 6–3), and a clean private place prepared for the birth. The nurse can be reassured that most babies deliver with little or no assistance. If nurses are not trained birth attendants, they should not place that expectation upon themselves. If there is any doubt about what to do or if the nurse does not understand what is happening, White's advice is to stand by and to do nothing until the needed action becomes evident.[21] Remember: First do no harm. The following five principles of emergency delivery offer the nurse further guidance:

1. Provide reassurance
2. Provide a safe environment
3. Control the delivery
4. Resuscitate the baby
5. Control bleeding
6. Recover the mother and baby

Exhibit 6–3 Equipment for an Emergency Delivery

Clean, dry, absorbent material for cleaning the mother and drying the baby
Blankets for mother and baby (warmed if possible)
Soap and water
Sterile scissors, knife or razor (can be boiled or heated over a flame)
Sanitary napkins or absorbent material
Diapers and baby clothes
Blanket-lined drawer or box for a bassinet
Identification for the baby (adhesive tape with mother's name)
2 pieces fibrous material to tie baby's cord (shoe string, torn strips of cotton cloth)

Provide Reassurance

If the nurse has been providing the labor support, the provision of reassurance is a continuation of the relationship already established. If the nurse is a stranger to the mother or has newly arrived on the scene, it is important to provide reassurance that the nurse is capable and can provide help: "My name is Laraine, and I'm going to help you. What is your name?" The tone of voice should be soothing, almost hypnotic, and the manner calm. This manner provides reassurance to the mother, to the other people involved, and also to the nurse. Keep talking; tell the mother what is happening step by step. This process also helps the nurse to clarify what needs to be done.

If the situation is out of control, the nurse must take control. Assess the situation and briefly assign tasks to specific people (e.g., to get equipment or to support the mother's head). By word and action, the nurse should promote a calm, controlled atmosphere. Focus the mother's attention on the directions she is receiving. Maintaining eye contact gives support to the mother and increases her cooperation in the delivery. Give the mother clear, specific, simple directions; use her first name to retain her attention.

Provide a Safe Environment

Escort the mother to a clean, private area for the birth. If you must use the floor, place clean linen or the mother's own clothing under her. Remove her underwear and any restrictive clothing. Place the mother in a semi-recumbent position with her head and shoulders propped so that you can maintain eye-to-eye contact while having easy access to her perineum. Remember to keep talking to her. Direct a specific person to assemble any remaining materials that you may need. Wash your hands. If any attempt at cleanliness is possible, this one has the highest priority. Birth is not a sterile process, but attempts should be made to avoid introducing bacteria into the birth canal. Wash the mother's perineum with soap and water if time permits.

Control the Delivery

Once the baby's head appears at the vaginal opening, if the mother is not already pushing with her contractions, encourage her to do so. If she is in control, reinforce her pushing pattern; if she is out of control, attempt to establish a pushing pattern in response to your command. "Push, 2, 3, 4, 5. Now breathe and push." Once the perineum is thinning and distended and the head is crowning, birth is about to occur. Encourage the mother to blow or pant through this last contraction, and allow the force of the uterine contraction to deliver the head. You may also have her push after the contraction if needed to complete delivery of the head. As the head becomes progressively more visible with pushing, place the palm of your hand and your fingers on it. With each push offer gentle resistance to the progress of the baby's head as it delivers. Do not hold the baby in; rather, allow the baby's head to slowly push your hand away as it comes out. This procedure reduces the potential for lacerations as the head crowns and then delivers.

As the baby's head turns to face one of the mother's thighs, feel at the base of the neck for the umbilical cord. If the cord is present, gently pull to gain some slack. The cord can then be lifted over the baby's head or be allowed to slip over the baby's shoulders as they deliver. If the cord is very tight, it may be necessary to clamp or to tie it off in two places, cut between the clamps, and then unwrap it before the rest of the baby can be delivered.

It is now time to deliver the shoulders. Wipe any fluid from the baby's face with your hand or a clean cloth. Place one of your hands on each side of the baby's head, over the ears. Exert gentle downward traction to the head until you see the anterior shoulder and axilla appear at the vaginal opening. Then exert upward traction to lift the posterior shoulder over the perineum.

Deliver the body by sliding your hands down over the back and chest while holding the baby's arms close into the body. The unrestrained arms can "pop out" and lacerate an otherwise intact perineum. You may have to tug on the trunk to complete the birth because the baby may not come sliding out over an intact perineum. As the body is delivered, slide one hand down to cradle the buttocks while the other supports the head. Keep the head down. Remember the baby is wet and slippery. Place the baby on the mother's abdomen on its side with the head down to facilitate drainage of mucous from its mouth and nose. Encourage the mother to hold onto the baby.[23]

Resuscitate the Baby

Before the baby's body is delivered, attempt to wipe the fluid away from the mouth and nose. As the baby is delivered, keep the head down to facilitate drainage of the oral and nasal passages. The baby can drain its own respiratory passages. A bulb syringe may be used if available. Dry the baby off and place it "skin-to-skin" on the mother's abdomen; then cover both mother and baby with warm, dry blankets. Cold stress will be avoided if the baby is kept dry and covered. The uncovered head accounts for a lot of heat loss. With a normal, unmedicated labor and delivery, the stress of the birth gives sufficient stimulation to produce crying. Gentle stimulation such as drying the baby, massaging its back and chest, or flicking its feet may be used. Avoid such methods as vigorously rubbing the spine, hanging the baby by its feet and spanking, or immersing the baby in alternately hot and cold water. These methods are potentially harmful and may put the baby into shock.

If more vigorous methods are required, mouth-to-mouth breathing for a new-born requires that your mouth cover the baby's mouth and nose while giving gentle puffs. (A puff is the amount of air one can hold in the cheeks.) Closed chest cardiac massage is easily accomplished by placing one hand under the chest and then compressing the chest with the first and middle fingers of the other hand placed on the sternum. The desired respiratory rate is 30 respirations per minute and heart rate is 120 beats per minute—a 4:1 cardiac to respiratory ratio.[24]

Control Bleeding

Once the baby is stable, encourage the mother to put the baby to her breast. The baby's exploring behavior at the nipple is sufficient to stimulate the release of oxytocin, which then causes uterine contractions and aids placental separation. Signs of placental separation are a gush of blood from the vagina, lengthening of the cord, and the fundus rising in the abdomen. Do not rush the placenta; it can take from 5 to 30 minutes to separate. An attached placenta does not bleed. Place one hand above the symphysis to support the uterus and encourage the mother to push. Grasp the cord close to the vaginal opening, apply gentle downward traction until the placenta appears, then lift the placenta up and out of the vagina by the cord. Grasp the trailing membranes gently to ease them out. If there is any resistance, encourage the mother to cough or to bear down as you tease them out.

Once the placenta is delivered, gently massage the fundus of the uterus until it is firm. Avoid massaging a firm fundus, which can lead to muscle fatigue and relaxation. The uterus controls bleeding from the placental site by clamping the open blood vessels between contracting muscle fibers. If the uterus does not contract, massage the fundus, then grasp it between the two hands (one at the fundus and one just above the symphysis) to provide bimanual compression. Bleeding from vaginal or perineal lacerations can be controlled with a pressure dressing of several sanitary napkins. Have the mother keep her legs closed for constant pressure.

Recover Mother and Child

The baby's umbilical cord does not have to be cut immediately. The umbilical vessels constrict at birth and the stagnant blood soon clots. The cord can be clamped or tied with any strong, clean, fibrous material such as boiled shoe strings, or torn strips of cotton cloth. It must be clamped or tied in two places and then cut between the two clamps to prevent blood loss from the baby. Sterile scissors, razor, or knife is essential to prevent neonatal tetanus, a highly fatal disease. The cutting instrument can be boiled or heated over an open flame. The placenta can be wrapped with the baby until sterile equipment can be secured. A plastic bag for the placenta reduces the mess.

Watch the mother for signs of bleeding. She can be taught to check her uterus and massage it, if it is relaxed. It is not unusual to soak one to two super sanitary pads per hour at first. The mother will be hungry, thirsty, and tired. She should have time with her baby and her family, be encouraged to void, and allowed to rest.

In addition to being kept warm and dry, the baby needs an opportunity to eat within the first 30 minutes of life. It will then sleep for as much as two hours; during this time it does not readily respond to stimuli. Because the baby's systems are adapting to extrauterine life, additional stresses should be minimized (e.g., the baby does not need a bath). A piece of tape with the mother's name or a piece torn from the mother's clothing (preferably a distinctive print) can be tied to the baby's wrist or ankle for identification if the baby and mother are separated.

Postpartum Support

The postpartum woman goes through a rapid correction of the anatomic and physiologic changes of pregnancy (the birth of a child is a normal bodily process). Care should be taken to encourage sleep and to prevent caloric and fluid deprivations. A woman who has experienced a normal birth should be able, however, to care for herself and her baby with minimal supervision. She may need assistance to walk immediately after birth, but she will soon do that without difficulty.

The nurse can reassure the mother that frequent voiding in large amounts is normal. Her vaginal flow will be heavy for the first 24 hours (one to two super sanitary napkins every two hours) but will gradually subside to a small amount in two to three days. Her milk will come in by the second or the third day, but the baby needs only the colostrum that is already present. She should have a normal bowel movement by the third day.

The mother should be observed for signs of infection (fever) and hemorrhage (blood loss, tachycardia, hypotension). The potential for infection is reduced by good handwashing before nursing and frequent perineal care with pad change. The potential for hemorrhage is reduced by breast feeding, frequent voiding, and avoidance of massaging a firm uterine fundus.

Bonding is the process by which the mother and her family identify with and claim the new baby. During the entire childbirth process, the family should be allowed to participate actively to the extent the mother wishes. During a mass casualty situation, separation of the family is very stressful. Bonding can be facilitated by keeping the baby with the mother, by allowing the mother and her family undisturbed time with the baby, and by pointing out normal behaviors or familial features of the baby. Compliment the mother on a job well done.

Newborn Nursing Care

The newborn needs support in adaptation to extrauterine life. Breast feeding should be established as soon as the baby acts hungry and should continue on demand (usually every two to four hours). Breast feeding ensures a readily available, sterile supply of adequate nutrition. If breast feeding is not the planned method of feeding, the baby can be weaned to a bottle as soon as the crisis is over.

Prevention of hypothermia is also essential. The baby should be kept warm, dry, and free of drafts. Because the mother is an excellent source of constant heat, the baby can initially be kept with her until she becomes more active. Then a bassinet can be made from a blanket-lined box or drawer.

The baby's intake and output should be monitored. The baby's intake is probably adequate if it sleeps at least two hours between feedings and voids six times a day. A breast-fed baby frequently has a loose stool after each feeding.

The Nonlaboring Pregnant woman

The nonlaboring pregnant woman frequently arrives at a shelter or health care facility seeking reassurance about her pregnancy or offering assistance. The woman should be reassured about the baby's status and then sent home to her family with suggestions to avoid large crowds, ill children, and environmental hazards, such as toxic chemicals and radiation. The woman may also be put to work at tasks within her physical capabilities. She should avoid heavy lifting; exhaustion; and exposure to infection, toxic chemicals, or radiation.

PREGNANCY WITH COMPLICATION

In a mass casualty situation, the nurse in a third-priority setting may be responsible for providing care to women who are experiencing a complication of their pregnancy. These women should be referred for specialized care as soon as possible. Nurses may find themselves, nevertheless, in a shelter situation with minimal supplies and help but with seriously ill pregnant patients for whom to care. Then they need to be aware of some common obstetrical complications.

First Trimester Bleeding

Bleeding in early pregnancy can be due to several causes. Many women experience implantation bleeding, which is usually minimal and does not produce adverse symptoms in the mother. This type of bleeding is also self-limiting and disappears within a day or two. The most common cause of bright red profuse vaginal bleeding in early pregnancy is an impending or actual abortion of the fetus. Nothing can prevent this process once it has started. The nurse's role is to provide whatever emotional and physical support the particular situation allows.

Differential diagnosis of this bleeding is difficult, if not impossible, in an emergency shelter situation. Any pregnant woman experiencing profuse vaginal bleeding becomes a first-priority patient and should be transferred as soon as possible. If this is not possible or if there may be a delay, know these practical measures to treat shock:

1. Place the woman in the most physiologically desirable position

   - Elevate her head on a pillow.
   - Keep her trunk horizontal.
   - Elevate her legs about 20 to 30 degrees, keeping the knees straight. (For second- and third-trimester pregnancies, position the woman on her side.)
   - Avoid the Trendelenburg head-low position. (After the initial increase of blood-flow to the brain, a reflex compensatory mechanism causes vaso-constriction that then decreases blood-flow to the brain. Also abdominal organs in the head-low position tend to fall against the diaphragm, which causes dyspnea and inadequate ventilation.)

2. Keep the patient warm.
3. Provide reassurance and display confidence in order to allay the woman's fear.

Vaginal Bleeding During Late Pregnancy

The dividing line between abortion and premature labor is the 20th week of pregnancy. Vaginal bleeding during the latter half of pregnancy (after the 20th week) occurs in approximately three percent of all pregnancies. This symptom is abnormal, and it is associated with increased maternal and fetal risk. Vaginal bleeding can be either maternal or fetal in origin, but most often it results from a placental abnormality or a lesion in the reproductive tract. Table 6–6 compares the findings of the two most common placental problems: (1) placenta previa and (2) placenta abruptio (premature separation of the placenta).

Generally, any patient with painless, bright red vaginal bleeding during the latter half of pregnancy should be suspected of having a placenta previa until

Table 6–6 Comparison of Placenta Previa and Placenta Abruptio

Previa	Abruptio
Painless	Constant pain
Bright red bleeding	Dark red bleeding
Visible bleeding	Concealed bleeding
Uterus normal tone	Uterus tense
Shock appropriate to blood loss	Shock inconsistent with visible blood loss

proven otherwise.[25] Do not do a vaginal examination on a pregnant woman who is bleeding vaginally. There is always a danger of putting the examining fingers through a placenta previa and causing intractable hemorrhage. It must be assumed that, despite the cause, this bleeding is ominous and requires immediate medical attention. Transfer these women to a first-priority area as soon as possible while supporting them and instituting measures for shock. Again, the differential diagnosis in a shelter situation is difficult, but do not overlook the possibility that intermittent abdominal pain associated with vaginal bleeding and mucous suggests the bloody show of labor.

Preterm Labor

Premature labor can be defined as regular uterine contractions with progressive cervical dilation after the 20th week of gestation and before the 37th week. In an emergency shelter situation, methods to stop labor would be purely practical because the appropriate medications would not be available. Five practical measures can be instituted in an attempt to stop or to slow a preterm labor:

1. An ample intake (2 to 6 oz.) of whiskey or any type of "hard" alcohol may slow or stop uterine contractions. Also, force clear fluids, such as water or juices.
2. It is essential that the woman stop all activity, get off her feet, and rest.
3. The environment should be made as quiet, calming, and restful for the mother as possible.
4. Local application of heat may slow uterine contractions (a warm bath, hot water bottle, or heating pad).
5. Sometimes, postural tilting of the pelvis (elevating the hips) can slow uterine contractions by taking the weight of the baby off the cervix. This procedure may not be successful, but in an emergency, all options should be explored.

Delivering a preterm infant outside a hospital setting is hazardous. The main consideration is protection of the very fragile head. The best one can do in an emergency is to attempt a slow, controlled delivery of the head in order to decrease the risk of trauma.

If the infant is viable, the main consideration for its care is maintenance of body temperature. Preterm infants are prone to hypothermia because of insufficient body fat reserves. Dry the baby, place it skin-to-skin with the mother, and cover them both. The placenta can be wrapped up with them for added warmth. Make sure the infant's head is covered at all times. (Heat is lost most rapidly from the head because this is the largest surface area on a preterm infant.)

Make a bassinet for the baby. Two cardboard boxes (one inside the other) can be used. Line the inner box with blankets and place hot water bottles between the outer box and inner box to provide warmth. A drawer or other similar container can also be used to contain the baby, the smaller the better to conserve warmth. Handle the preterm baby as little as possible.

Preterm infants have difficulty maintaining blood glucose levels. A feeding of sugar water (1 tsp sugar to 8 oz water) can be given with an eyedropper. Molasses or honey can be substituted if sugar is not available. The infant who is able should be encouraged to breastfeed. This feeding can be supplemented then with sugar water feedings.

Pregnancy-Induced Hypertension (Preeclampsia)

Hypertension is defined as a BP of 140/90 or a rise of 30 in the systolic and 15 in the diastolic pressures over the woman's baseline BP. Proteinuria and third-spacing of body fluids are also associated with pregnancy-induced hypertension (PIH). Appropriate care can be provided in an emergency because the majority of measures are practical, essentially nonmedical, and designed to prevent seizures. The first measure should be environmental control. Excess stimulation of the mother should be avoided. Her activity should be curtailed; ideally, she should have long periods of rest—preferably on her left side. Fluid intake should be encouraged to ensure optimal functioning of the kidneys.

Maintenance of adequate nutrition may not be easy in an emergency, but every effort should be made to see that the hypertensive pregnant woman has an adequate caloric intake, especially protein. Plasma proteins affect the movement of intra-vascular and extravascular fluids, and so they help the body to eliminate excess fluid. Normal salt intake should also be maintained; it is an essential nutrient that is important in water and electrolyte balance. Excessive salt intake, however, contributes to increased water retention, which may worsen a hypertensive condition.

Pregnant women with hypertension (and obvious facial edema) should be monitored closely for signs of severe preeclampsia. Danger signs that can be easily identified in a shelter situation include the following:[25]

- hyperreflexia—especially with clonus
- headaches (frontal or occipital—usually resistant to customary effective treatment)
- visual disturbances—e.g., blurring of vision, scotoma, flashing lights, or spots before the eyes
- epigastric pain
- oliguria—less than 500 mL in 24 hours.

Again, reducing environmental stimulus is the best procedure for treating PIH until the woman can be referred to a second-priority area. If the woman begins to experience convulsions, preparation should be made to assist with a rapid, spontaneous or precipitous delivery.

PIH has been associated with an increased risk of placental abruption. Because hypertension results in decreased blood flow to the uterus, which can result in fetal oxygen and nutrient deprivation, assessment of fetal well-being is essential. In an emergency, the clinical assessment may be difficult if one is unable to auscultate or to monitor the fetus electronically. One method of assessing fetal well-being is noting the frequency of fetal movement. Have the mother keep track of how many times her baby moves during the day. A healthy, well-adapted fetus should move at least 12 times per day.

Abnormal Labor and Delivery

Dysfunctional labor is any labor that fails to meet certain time criteria for any of its phases. For the nurse whose specialty is not obstetrics, criteria that may be used to assess the well-being of mother and fetus during the labor process include the following:

- The mother is not exhibiting signs of exhaustion.
- Fetal heart tones are steady at 120 to 160 beats per minute without severe drop in rate during or after a contraction.
- Fetal movement is apparent.

Labor can take more than 24 hours. If the indications of maternal and fetal well-being are present, the plan of care should be rest, fluids, calories, and wait-and-watch. Dysfunctional labors are associated with an increased incidence of maternal and fetal morbidity and mortality. If progress has not occurred and either the mother or the fetus are showing signs of stress, she should be referred to a second-priority area.

Breech presentation is associated with a threefold to fourfold greater risk for the baby than vertex presentation. Delivery trauma and anoxia due to cord compression or cord prolapse are two factors that account for the increased perinatal morbidity and mortality. When dealing with a breech delivery in an emergency situation, the nurse should not attempt to handle, pull, or manipulate the baby. Allow the entire body to be expelled by the natural forces of labor without any traction or manipulation. Basically, keep hands off the baby until it is completely delivered. Manipulation by someone who is unskilled in the techniques of this type of delivery may do more harm than good.

Emergency delivery of a multiple gestation entails much of the same actions and philosophy as that of an emergency breech delivery. Twins deliver by the same process as a single baby—just one at a time, and so the same delivery procedure should be followed.[21] Twins are frequently premature, however, and one of the twins frequently comes breech. The woman should be referred to a second-priority area, if possible.

The possibility of intrauterine fetal demise is great during natural disasters and emergencies when maternal injury is likely. Once it has been reasonably determined that the fetus is dead (e.g., loss of fetal heart tones and cessation of fetal movement), the nurse has the responsibility of supporting the mother's physical and emotional condition. Be honest with the mother; always inform her of your suspicions about the baby's status. Allow the mother to grieve and encourage her to release her emotions. Be as supportive as possible and provide her with positive guidance while she is dealing with the tragedy. If the nurse is unable to remain with her, a supportive person should be assigned to do so.

In cases in which the baby is stillborn, the family should be allowed and encouraged to grieve for this baby in ways that are helpful to them. Seeing the baby, holding, kissing, taking pictures, saying good-bye have all been described as necessary by grieving parents.

The parents may wish to baptize the baby. Baptism can be performed by anyone as long as the procedure is done properly. The baptism is accomplished by pouring water on the bare skin of the baby (on the head, if possible), while saying, ''I baptize you in the name of the Father, and of the Son, and of the Holy Spirit.'' This exact form should be used because it is acceptable to almost all Christian groups that believe in baptism.[21] A record should be kept of the baptism; include the date, the names of witnesses, and the person performing the rite.

The obvious signs of fetal death are the cessation of movement for more than 24 hours and the absence of fetal heart tones. Without radiologic or ultrasonographic evidence, it is difficult to diagnose fetal death with certainty; however, it is reasonable to rely on a lack of movement and heartbeat when no other means of determination are available. Often labor commences normally, and the dead fetus is born without adverse effects to the mother. Labor may not begin spontaneously, however, for days or weeks after fetal death. Retention of a dead fetus carries certain risks, one of them being the development of DIC. The risk of DIC increases when the mother has carried the dead fetus for two to six weeks. Maternal sepsis and the development of blood disorders also becomes a concern as the time between fetal death and the onset of labor increases.

THE NURSE'S ROLE

Knowing what to do in an emergency, wherever it may occur, is by heritage a nurse's role. Although delivery experience is not included in basic nursing education today, the unwritten rule is that in an emergency, the nurse knows what to do.[26] Nurses in an emergency or disaster situation are expected to assume a role beyond that expected in their daily professional activities and usually beyond that for which they were prepared in their basic program. The nurse is expected to assume responsibility for the management of a variety of patients in the absence of physician direction. The expectation includes assuming command of the situation and directing the activities of less prepared or untrained assistants.

The nurse who may one day have to deal with a disaster (probably all of us) would be wise to prepare for that possibility—to review personal resources for coping with a disaster. To prepare for an emergency delivery, the nurse should periodically review the mechanisms of labor, the stages of labor, and the behavioral signs of imminent delivery. Helen Varney's *Nurse-Midwifery* textbook gives step-by-step hand maneuvers for delivery and would be available from a library with a health care collection or through inter-library loan.[24] Nurses should also be familiar with community resources and the community's disaster plan.

The nurse is always accountable, of course, for actions expected of a reasonable and prudent person with such a background. Every effort should be made to seek medical consultation and assistance as soon as possible. A record of observations and actions should be kept. Minimum information for a birth should include date, time, sex, name of parents, complications, and birth attendant.

Faced with an emergency childbirth, the nurse should remember that the baby usually comes without assistance. When in doubt as to what to do, do nothing. The maxim "first do no harm" is always a good guide. Comfort measures and bodily care help the mother cope with her labor, but reassurance and moral support are frequently the major contributions of the birth attendant.

REFERENCES

1. Matthew 24:19 (KJV).

2. Baker DP: Trauma in the pregnant patient. *Surg Clin North Am* 1982;62:275–289.

3. Cruikshank DP: Anatomic and physiologic alterations of pregnancy that modify the response to trauma, in Buchsbaum HJ (ed): *Trauma in Pregnancy*. Philadelphia, WB Saunders Co, 1979, pp 21–39.

4. *Red Cross CPR Module: Respiratory and Circulatory Emergencies*. Washington, DC, American Red Cross, 1980.

5. Hochbaum SR: Diseases of pregnancy, in Rosen P, Baker FJ II, Braen GR, et al (eds): *Emergency Medicine: Concepts and Clinical Practice*. St Louis, The CV Mosby Co, 1983, vol 2, pp 1198–1202.

6. Hytten FE, Leitch I: *The Physiology of Human Pregnancy*, ed 2. Oxford, Blackwell Scientific Publications Inc, 1971.

7. Pritchard JA, MacDonald PC: *Williams Obstetrics*, ed 16. New York, Appleton-Century-Crofts, 1980.

8. Jensen MD, Benson RC, Babcock IM: *Maternity Care: The Nurse and the Family*. St Louis, The CV Mosby Co, 1977, p 132.

9. Cugell DW, Frank NR, Gaensler EA, et al: Pulmonary function in pregnancy: I. Serial observations in normal women. *Am Rev Tuberculosis* 1953;67:568–592.

10. Killien MG, Poole CJ, Jennings B: Essentials of pre-natal care, in Sonstegard L, Kowalski K, Jennings B (eds): *Women's Health*. New York, Grune & Stratton Inc, 1983, vol 2, pp 45–79.

11. Meyer JE: Clinical chemistry, in Abrams RS, Waxler P (eds): *Medical Care of the Pregnant Patient*. Boston, Little Brown & Co, 1983, pp 99–104.

12. Bonnar J: Hemostatic function and coagulopathy during pregnancy. *Obstet Gynecol Annu* 1978;7:195–217.

13. Wolf PS: Cardiovascular disorders, in Abrams RS, Wexler P (eds): *Medical Care of the Pregnant Patient*. Boston, Little Brown & Co, 1983, pp 183–199.

14. Stuart GCE, Harding PGR, Davies EM: Blunt abdominal trauma in pregnancy. *Can Med Assoc J* 1980;122:901–905.

15. Rosen P, Baker FJ II, Braen GR, et al (eds): *Emergency Medicine: Concepts and Clinical Practice*. St Louis, The CV Mosby Co, 1983.

16. Crosby WM: Trauma during pregnancy: Maternal and fetal injury. *Obstet Gynecol Surv* 1974;29:683–699.

17. Buchsbaum HJ: *Trauma in Pregnancy*. Philadelphia, WB Saunders Co, 1979.

18. Weber CE: Post mortem cesarean section: Review of the literature and case reports. *Am J Obstet Gynecol*. 1977, 129:479.

19. Fort AT: Management of the injured gravida. *Contemp OB/GYN* 1978;3:41–46.

20. Green JM: Emergency care of the obstetric patient. *Nurs Outlook* 1958;6:694–696.

21. White GJ: *Emergency Childbirth: A Manual*. Franklin Park, Ill, Police Training Foundation, 1958.

22. Lesser MS, Keane VR: *Nurse-Patient Relationships in a Hospital Maternity Service*. St Louis, The CV Mosby Co, 1956, p 100.

23. Jennings B: Emergency delivery: How to attend to one safely. *MCN*, May/June 1979, pp 148–153.

24. Varney H: *Nurse-Midwifery*. Boston, Blackwell Scientific Publications Inc, 1980, pp 587–599.

25. Taber BZ: *Manual of Gynecologic and Obstetric Emergencies*, 2nd Ed. Philadelphia, WB Saunders Co, 1984, p 219.

26. Butnarescu GF, Tillotson DM: *Maternity Nursing: Theory to Practice*. New York, John Wiley & Sons Inc, 1983.

SUGGESTED READINGS

Anderson CL: Emergency delivery, in Sonstegard L, Kowalski K, Jennings B (eds): *Women's Health*. New York, Grune & Stratton Inc, 1983. vol 2, pp 185–191.

Barber HRK, Graber EA: *Surgical Disease in Pregnancy*. Philadelphia, WB Saunders Co, 1974.

Buchsbaum HJ: Accidental injury complicating pregnancy. *Am J Obstet Gynecol* 1968;102:752–769.

Buchsbaum HJ: Traumatic injury in pregnancy, in Barber HRK, Graber EA: *Surgical Disease in Pregnancy*. Philadelphia, WB Saunders Co, 1974, pp 184–203.

Crosby WM: Automotive trauma and the pregnant patient. *Contemp OB/GYN* 1976;8:115–119.

Dolezal A, Figar S: The phenomenon of reactive vasodilation in pregnancy. *Am J Obstet Gynecol* 1965;93:1137–1143.

Hogan A: Bomb born babies. *Public Health Nurs* 1951;43:383–385.

Stafford PL: Protection of the pregnant woman in the emergency department. *JEN* 1981;7:97–102.

Chapter 7

Management of the Irradiated Patient

Audrey S. Bomberger, R.N., Ph.D.

Radiation disaster! The words themselves conjure up images of unreal devastation. We seldom think of radiation disasters as including less than massive numbers of casualties. But what about the victims of an accidental radiological spill—the types of accidents that result in a trauma victim whose injuries are complicated by the presence of low-level radiation? What care do they require? What preparation is needed to provide proper management of this level of radiological emergency?

Few hospitals have had to provide care and treatment for the radiological accident victim in the absence of nuclear war. Furthermore, it is unlikely that most hospitals will receive victims who have been involved in life-threatening radiation accidents. A more likely event is the possibility of their receiving a routine trauma victim whose condition is complicated by the presence of low-level radioactive contamination or exposure—the result of a transportation, industrial, mining, or reactor accident. The numerous transportation modes (rail, truck, air, and sea) used to deliver radioisotopes and industrial waste products make the transportation category the most likely to provide a radiological accident victim.

The Joint Commission on Accreditation of Hospitals (JCAH) is requiring hospitals to develop radiation disaster plans and treatment capabilities for the subsequent victims.[1] JCAH recommends that hospital emergency departments seek out persons who are knowledgeable in radiation terminology, isotope handling procedures, and radiation detection and evaluation to assist in the preparation of a medical radiation emergency plan (MREP). Persons with such qualifications can be found in hospitals in which sources of radiation are routinely used (e.g., in radiology, nuclear medicine, clinical pathology, or radiation therapy departments).

This chapter provides a conceptual framework for developing a MREP to treat several or numerous irradiated victims. Presented are the following:

- types and sources of radiation
- management of the radiological emergency

- a system of classification using a standard medical system and irradiation information to classify irradiated victims
- decontamination procedures
- components of a MREP
- the clinical course of acute radiation sickness

RADIOLOGICAL OVERVIEW

An elementary school child, who lived near Three Mile Island in 1979, defined radiation as ''something in the air that could kill me.''[2] Her definition may be correct; however, it is a child's definition that needs to be expanded for adults and providers of health care.

Nuclear Radiation

The term *radiation* can be used in various ways. *Nuclear radiation* is the emission and the movement of energy through space or across a distance. It occurs when unstable atoms split or undergo fission and produce smaller and more unstable particles. These unstable particles are called *fission fragments*. The process is known as radioactive decay, and the product of the change is known as nuclear radiation.

Four types of radiation are emitted from the unstable atom undergoing radioactive decay: alpha particles, beta particles, gamma rays and the neutron (Table 7–1).

The *alpha particle* is the largest of the four radiations, though it, too, is quite minute. These particles, which travel several centimeters in the air, are stopped by a sheet of paper or by skin tissue. They cannot damage body tissue except when a substance emitting alpha particles remains in direct contact with the unprotected

---

Table 7–1 Comparison of Alpha and Beta Particles and Gamma Rays

Radiation	Range in Air	Speed
Alpha particles	5–7 cm	2,000–20,000 miles/second
Beta particles	200–800 cm	25%–99% the speed of light
Gamma rays	100s of feet	Speed of light (186,000 miles/second)

Source: NATO Handbook on the Medical Aspects of Nuclear, Biological and Chemical Defensive Operations, AMedP–6. Brussels, Military Agency for Standardization (MAS), August 1973, p 2–16.

tissue for a long period of time; then the radiation could cause considerable damage or could result in functional disease.

Lighter and much smaller than alpha particles, *beta particles* travel a few hundred centimeters in the air and are stopped by an inch of wood or a thin sheet of metal. They can penetrate up to one-third of a centimeter of body tissue. Like alpha particles, they can cause a functional disease if too many get inside the body and remain there.

Gamma rays, similar to x-rays, are invisible waves of energy-like light and radio waves and are very penetrating. These rays travel hundreds of feet in the air and are stopped by thick lead or concrete. Exposure to gamma rays can cause severe damage.

Neutrons are particles about the size of a proton. Produced primarily in nuclear reactors used for research or power production, they travel hundreds of feet in the air. They are stopped by several feet of water or special concrete. Exposure to neutron radiation can result in whole-body irradiation, similar to that caused by gamma rays, but with the exception that they deposit the energy in a nonuniformed manner.[3]

Sources of Radiation

The human race has always lived with radiation exposure produced by natural sources. Natural background radiation comes from the sun, the stars, and other natural radioactive materials distributed in the soil and the rocks. Each of these major elements—natural hydrogen, potassium, and carbon—has a small radioactive part. The level of natural radiation varies according to the geographical location. For example, the cosmic radiation dose approximately doubles when one moves from sea level to higher elevations, such as the Rocky Mountains in the west or the White Mountains in the east.

With the increased development of technology, humans have found many uses for radiation, which add to our everyday exposure. Alpha-emitting particles are used in some smoke detectors and on the dials of watches, clocks, and other luminous instruments. Beta particles are used in industrial gauges to measure the thickness of materials produced for quality control measures, for medical treatment for certain tumors or skin lesions and in many scientific studies. Gamma rays are also used by industry for quality control, in airports for safety inspections, and by the medical profession in diagnostic studies and in the treatment of various selected disease processes.[4]

Effects of Radiation Injury

The effects of radiation injury are not solely dependent on the dose or the amount of the radiation received. They are also dependent upon both genetic and nongenetic variables (Table 7–2).

Table 7–2 Variables Affecting the Degree of Radiation Injury

Nongenetic	Genetic
Amount and rate of radiation exposure	Age of the person
Type of radiation	Parts of the body irradiated
Tissue exposed	Extent of the body irradiated
Type of radioactivity involved	Biological variations
	Internal vs external radiation

One nongenetic factor affecting radiation injury is the penetration power of the radioactive material. Gamma rays and neutrons, for example, cause more injury because they are more penetrating than alpha or beta particles. The amount of tissue exposed to the radiation source is also a consideration and whether it is exposed internally or externally. If internal exposure is involved, the radio-chemical nature and the biological path must also be considered.

The biologic factors affecting sensitivity to radiation injury include the age of the exposed person. Sensitivity is highest when organs are developing, and so the differentiating cells and cells undergoing rapid division are more easily damaged by radiation. Therefore, an adult is more resistant to the effects of radiation than a small child or infant.

When the upper abdomen is irradiated, the radiation effects tend to be more severe than when a body area of similar size elsewhere is exposed to the same dose for the same amount of time. This difference is due to the presence of vital organs in the upper abdominal area. Irradiation of a small part of the body surface has much less general effect than if an equal dose were delivered to the whole body. The non-irradiated portion of the body can aid in the recovery of the affected portion. Although it is possible to determine an average dose of radiation to produce certain effects, it is not possible to predict individual responses from that average.[4]

The relative sensitivity of an organ to direct radiation injury depends upon the individual tissues that make up that particular organ. Table 7–3 lists various organs in the decreasing order of their radiosensitivity and on the basis of a relatively direct radiation exposure.

MEASUREMENT OF RADIATION

To conform to the same terminology as that used in other fields of science, definitions of radiation units are undergoing change. These changes are being introduced gradually in the United States and in other countries. Table 7–4 defines radiation measurement terms.

Table 7–3 Relative Radiosensitivity of Various Organs

Relative Radiosensitivity	Organs
High	lymphoid organs, bone marrow, testes and ovaries, small intestine
Moderately high	skin; cornea and lens of eye; gastrointestinal organs: cavity, esophagus, stomach, rectum
Medium	growing cartilage, fine vasculature, growing bones
Moderately low	mature cartilage or bone, lungs, kidneys, liver, pancreas, adrenal gland, pituitary gland
Low	muscle, brain, spinal cord

Note: Based on relatively direct exposure to radiation.

Source: NATO Handbook on the Medical Aspects of Nuclear, Biological and Chemical Defensive Operations, AMedP–6. Brussels, Military Agency for Standardization (MAS), August 1973, p 5–8.

Maximum Permissible Dose

The National Council on Radiation Protection and Measurements (NCRP) is one of the agencies that establishes the maximum permissible dose (MPD) of irradiation. As additional knowledge is gained about the effects of irradiation the recommended MPD has changed over the years.

The average yearly radiation dose for persons living in the United States has been estimated by geneticists to be 200 millirems per year.[4] This average in no way implies a hazardous dose level. The NCRP makes specific recommendations for the hazardous occupational worker, the rescue worker, and the nonhazardous occupational worker.[5] Efforts should be made, however, to keep the exposure level as low as is reasonably achievable (ALARA).

Exposure Versus Contamination

It is important to understand the difference between the terms *exposure* and *contamination* in their application to a radiological accident victim. Exposure occurs at the accident site and is not capable of being transferred. There is no potential hazard to those providing care. However, contaminated victims are those who are carrying the radiation source on their persons in the form of dust particles or liquid spillage. Radioactive contamination can be transferred to other persons, objects, or to the environment. When in doubt as to whether the victim has been

Table 7–4 Measurements of Radiation

Unit	Definition
millirem (mrem)	A basic measure of radiation for dose equivalent. One rem equals 1000 mrem.
rad—SI unit = Gray (Gy)	Radiation absorbed dose. A measure of the energy imparted to matter by ionizing particles per unit mass of irradiated material at the place of interest.
rem—SI unit = Sievert (Sv)	Roentgen equivalents man. The unit or dose of any ionizing radiation that produces the same biological effect as a unit of absorbed dose of ordinary x-ray.
roentgen (R)—not used as an SI unit	unit of exposure to gamma rays or to x-rays

Source: Bomberger AS, Dannenfelser BA: *Radiation and Health: Principles and Practice in Therapy and Disaster Preparedness.* Rockville, Md, Aspen Systems Corp, 1984; Saenger EL (course director): *Radiation Accident Preparedness.* Washington, DC, Edison Electric Institute, 1981.

exposed to, or contaminated by, radiation, always treat the victim as contaminated.

Types of Exposure

Four types of radiation accident victims may be seen:

1. those with external radiation exposure of the body (whole or partial)
2. those with external contamination of the body or the clothing by radioactive liquid or dirt
3. those with external contamination of the body, complicated by a wound
4. those with internal contamination of the body by inhalation or ingestion of radioactive substances

Victims with external whole- or partial-body radiation exposure may have received exposure to large doses of radiation, but they are no hazard to attendants, other patients, or to the environment. This type of victim is no more hazardous than the patient who has had radiation therapy or a diagnostic roentgenogram.

Victims suffering from external contamination of body surface or clothing by liquid or dirt present problems similar to those caused by vermin infestations.

Surgical isolation technique and cleansing should take place before the victim enters the radiation emergency triage area. The potential hazard must be confined and removed as soon as possible.

Victims with external contamination complicated by a wound present an environmental hazard. Care must be taken not to cross-contaminate personnel, other patients, or the environment. The wound and the surrounding surfaces must be cleansed separately and sealed off after they are cleansed. When crushed dirty tissue is involved, preliminary wet debridement after wound irrigation may be indicated.

Those victims who have internal contamination resulting from the inhalation or the ingestion of a radioactive substance also pose no hazard. After cleansing the minor amount of contaminated material deposited on the body surface during airborne exposure, the victims are treated like victims of chemical poisoning. Body waste should be collected and saved for the measurement of the amount of nuclides to help determine the appropriate therapy.[4]

Acute Radiation Sickness Syndrome

Acute radiation sickness syndrome follows a large sudden whole-body dose of radiation. This syndrome follows total-body irradiation by neutrons or gamma rays, or both. The physiological response in humans is especially dose dependent. The acute radiation syndrome is subdivided into the hematopoietic syndrome, the gastrointestinal syndrome, and the central nervous system (CNS) syndrome. Table 7–5 shows the acute clinical effects of single high-dose rate exposures of whole-body irradiation to healthy adults.[3]

The clinical course of radiation sickness after large exposure of the whole body to penetrating radiation is characterized by four successive phases:

1. transitory prodromal
2. latent
3. main
4. recovery

The first phase, the transitory prodromal phase, develops within a few hours after exposure and lasts for up to 48 hours. During this phase the following symptoms may be noted: anorexia, fatigue, fever, nausea, perspiration, respiratory distress, and vomiting.

This first phase is followed by the latent phase, which is relatively asymptomatic. It may last as long as two weeks.

The third phase, the main phase of the illness, is also a symptomatic phase. During this phase, the following symptoms may be seen: agitation, anorexia, aspermia (non-emission of semen), ataxia, convulsions, coma, diarrhea, disorien-

Table 7–5 Acute Clinical Effects of a Single, High Dose of Whole-Body Irradiation in Healthy Adults

Phase of response	0–100 rads (subclinical range)	~100–800 rads (low lethal range)		600–800 rads	Over 800 rads (supralethal range)	
		100–200 rads	200–600 rads		800–3000 rads	Over 3000 rads
Initial response						
Incidence of nausea and vomiting	0%–5%	5%–50%	50%–100%	75%–100%	100%	100%
Time of onset		~3–6 hr	~2–4 hr	~1–2 hr	<1 hr	<1 hr
Duration		<24 hr	<24 hr	<48 hr	<48 hr	~48 hr
Combat effectiveness	100%	>80%	can perform routine tasks; sustained combat or comparable activities hampered for 6–20 hr	can perform only simple routine tasks; significant incapacitation in upper part of range; lasts more than 24 hr	progressive incapacitation following an early capability for intermittent heroic response	progressive incapacitation following an early capability for intermittent heroic response
Latent phase						
Duration		more than 2 weeks	approximately 7–15 days	none to approximately 7 days	none to approximately 2 days	none
Secondary response						
Signs and symptoms	none	moderate leukopenia	severe leukopenia; purpura, hemorrhage; infection; epilation after about 300 rads and above		diarrhea; fever; disturbance of electrolyte balance	convulsions; tremor; ataxia; lethargy

Time of onset postexposure	2 weeks or more	several days to 2 weeks		2–3 days	1–48 hr
Critical period postexposure	none	4–6 weeks		5–14 days	
Organ system responsible	none	hematopoietic system		gastrointestinal tract	CNS
Hospitalization					
Percentage	<10%	up to 90%		100%	100%
Duration	45–60 days	60–90 days	90–120 days	2 weeks	2 days
Incidence of death	none	0%–80%	80%–100%	90%–100%	90%–100%
Average time of death	—	3 weeks to 2 months		1–2 weeks	2 days
Therapy	hematologic surveillance	blood transfusion, antibiotics, rest		maintenance of electrolyte balance	supportive treatment

Source: Reprinted from *NATO Handbook on the Medical Aspects of Nuclear, Biological and Chemical Defensive Operations*, AMedP–6. Brussels, Military Agency for Standardization (MAS), August 1973, p. 6–8.

tation, epilation (loss of body hair), erythema, fever, hemorrhage, ileus, infection, lassitude, tanning, shock, weakness, and weight loss. This phase may last from two to six weeks.

The final phase—the recovery phase—full recovery without residual damage from radiation sickness is determined by the severity of the body's response to the exposure and the dose received.

There is no known medication or specific treatment to cure radiation sickness; therefore, irradiated victims who have received whole-body exposure to neutrons or gamma rays are given palliative treatment to ensure maximum comfort. Radiation sickness is not contagious and requires no isolation precautions unless the victim has open wounds; then reverse isolation may be desirable to protect the patient.

HANDLING THE RADIOLOGICAL EMERGENCY

Any emergency is successfully managed when all persons involved cooperatively share the responsibility. No single agency or health care facility can function as an entity; activities must be integrated. In the case of a radiation accident, procedures initiated at the scene of the accident must be carried through to those sites to which the victims and properties are relocated. This integration requires the establishment of standardized techniques and a quality communication network. The network includes all activities concerned with scene management, medical triage, the transportation of victims, and their hospitalization (Exhibit 7–1).

Exhibit 7–1 Management of the Radiation Accident Scene

First responder (usually paramedics or ambulance crew)

- assesses the situation
- notifies authorities
- restricts area

Authorities (the receiving hospital)

- notify radiological surveillance team
- notify appropriate agencies
- coordinate the emergency medical system

Field Management

The sequence of actions at the scene is entirely dependent on the situation found there. First steps usually include measures to assess the situation rapidly and to summon help. Assessment includes the recognition that a hazardous situation exists through visual identification of the container labels.

In the presence of radiation, minimize actions until the radiological surveillance team arrives, and seal off the accident site immediately. Furthermore, detain all persons and properties at the scene for radiological monitoring and any needed treatment. In a life-threatening situation, transport the victims immediately while instituting precautions for safe handling of the contaminated victims. Make a record of persons and properties at the scene.

Medical triage should be instituted (see Chapters 3 and 4). Like victims of trauma, irradiated victims should be classified medically; however, triage systems should make provisions to include the victim's radiological status (see Table 7–6).

A variety of triage systems are currently used by rescue units and health care facilities. Medical care for those victims with critical and serious injuries is given priority. Conversely, radiological care may be given priority for victims without injuries or for those with nonserious injuries. Whatever the system, all provide for the following:

- care of the victim
- protection of the health care provider
- protection of the vehicle
- notification of the receiving facility
- accurate documentation

Furthermore, during all phases of triage and transport, segregate victims into contaminated and noncontaminated groups. Likewise, use personnel, transport vehicles, equipment, and supplies with either the contaminated or the noncontaminated victims.

Hospital Management

Upon arrival at the hospital, the irradiated victims are met at a specific emergency department entrance and are monitored there for radiation. Remember, if there is doubt about whether a victim has been exposed or contaminated by radiation, always treat the victim as contaminated.

The hospital should be prepared to receive and to treat irradiated victims by establishing clean and contaminated areas. Each victim must be medically stable, however, before the decontamination procedure is begun.

Table 7–6 Classification of Irradiated Victims

Classification	Severity of Injuries	Irradiation Care Needs
Critical	Major injuries, compromise of body functions	Radiation status is unknown; transport is immediate; treatment is not delayed
	Life-saving care at the scene	Precautions are required in handling if not disruptive to life-saving medical care.
	Immediate transport	Radiation status is determined, and the victim is decontaminated when medically stable.
Serious	Major to minor injuries, minimal compromise of body functions	Care is same as that for critical if radiation status is known.
	Minor care at scene	Precautions are taken as applicable if status is unknown.
	Transport usually immediate	Decontamination is done at scene per medical physician's orders.
Non-serious	Minor injuries, little or no compromise of body functions	Radiation monitoring and decontamination is usually carried out at scene.
	Minor care at scene	
	Transport may or may not be required	
Follow-up	No physical injuries	Radiation monitoring and decontamination at the scene.
	Care usually not required at scene	All irradiated victims should return for follow-up care.

Source: Reprinted from Bomberger AS, Dannenfelser BA: *Radiation and Health: Principles and Practice in Therapy and Disaster Preparedness.* Rockville, Md, Aspen Systems Corp, 1984, p 225.

The objectives of decontamination are—

- to prevent injury caused by the presence of radioactive substances on the body;
- to prevent the spread of contamination;
- to protect the attending personnel from becoming contaminated themselves or, in some cases, from being exposed to a source of radiation.

Ninety to 95 percent of the decontamination procedure is accomplished by removing the patient's clothing. The contaminated clothing is placed in bags, tagged, and removed to a remote section of the contaminated area to be disposed of later by qualified personnel. The remaining decontamination is accomplished by washing the patient. See Exhibit 7–2 for a summary of actions required.

When performing a radiological monitoring survey, first remove the victim's clothing and systematically conduct the survey with a geiger counter. If an open wound is involved, swab the area and remonitor the swab to determine whether radiation is present in the wound. When monitoring a patient without injuries, have the person to be monitored stand, with legs spread and arms extended. Begin by moving the geiger counter probe over the head and subsequently the upper trunk, the arms, the lower trunk, and the legs. Ask the person to turn around, and repeat the procedure. Care must be taken, however, not to allow the detector probe to touch any potentially contaminated surfaces. Special monitoring techniques must be used for hairy body areas and body orifices. After all victims have been treated, the same procedure is followed for all personnel assigned to the contaminated area.

RADIATION DISASTER PLANNING AND EDUCATION

A radiation disaster or accident can involve many victims or as few as one. If the influx of victims taxes an emergency area, the situation rapidly becomes a disaster—even when only one victim is involved. This classification depends, however, upon the placement and the usability of a MREP. The components of a MREP are outlined in Exhibit 7–3.

Once the MREP has been developed, it must be used to educate the personnel and must be tested through drills that include the use of mock-contaminated victims. Education of the emergency department, support personnel, and the disaster response team is imperative for successful implementation of the MREP.

Comprehensive, quality care of irradiated victims, the management of the emergency department, and the safety awareness of the care givers require effectively coordinated techniques and procedures by all persons involved. When developing protocols for the care of the irradiated victim, items to be considered include the following:

- medical and nursing care
- radiological care of the victim
- protection for personnel and the environment
- area clean-up
- documentation of the event

Exhibit 7–2 Radiation Emergency Actions for Hospital Emergency
Department Personnel

1. Upon notification of the imminent arrival of a radiation accident victim, notify the responsible staff physician, nurse, allied health personnel (health physicist and trained technicians from radiology and nuclear medicine), and the hospital administrator.
2. Obtain the required samples for supplies for handling radiation accident patients.
3. Prepare for decontamination:

   • Designate and label treatment areas as "dirty" and "clean."
   • Cover the floor of the designated dirty area with absorbent material large enough for a stretcher, personnel, containers, and medical equipment.
   • Put on isolation apparel and use isolation technique, as appropriate, to contain the contamination within the designated areas.
   • Assign specific staff members only to each designated space.

4. Upon arrival of the ambulances, give life-saving assistance. Fear of contamination must never interfere with the delivery of necessary medical and nursing care to save life and limb.
5. Survey the victims to determine the extent of contamination:

   • Segregate the contaminated patients from the non-contaminated.
   • Survey the transport equipment and ambulance personnel for contamination.
   • Take measures to protect the patient from self-cross-contamination: i.e., remove all articles of clothing, cover uncontaminated areas and/or small contaminated areas with plastic drapes.
   • Extensive wounds and other forms of internal contamination may require immediate attention.

6. Identify and save all personal effects and body wastes for analysis.
7. Decontaminate the victims as soon as they are medically stable:

   • Decontaminate the body areas with the highest levels of radiation first.
   • Pay special attention to hair, body orifices, and body folds.
   • Avoid cross-contamination.
   • Use soap and water; avoid organic solvents and abrasives. The patient may take a shower if medically able.
   • Decontaminate any wounds by irrigating them with sterile water or an isotonic solution.

8. Schedule all contaminated patients for long-term medical follow-up care.
9. Maintain patients in the clean area until they are found to be free of all contamination.
10. Examine all personnel for contamination before allowing them to leave the area.
11. Decontaminate personnel if necessary.
12. Dispose of equipment and supplies according to recommended procedures and decontaminate the entire treatment areas after disaster.

Source: Bomberger AS, Dannenfelser BA: *Radiation and Health: Principles and Practice in Therapy and Disaster Preparedness.* Rockville, Md, Aspen Systems Corp, 1984, pp 219–230.

Exhibit 7–3 Outline of a Medical Radiological Emergency Plan

I. General information
   A. Definition of terms used
   B. Expectations
II. Types of radiation accident victims
   A. External whole- or partial-body exposure
   B. Internal contamination by inhalation or ingestion
   C. External contamination of body surface or clothing by radioactive liquid or dirt
   D. External contamination complicated by a wound
III. Sample of forms to be used
   A. Radiation accident response form
   B. Radiation accident victim body tags
   C. Radiation accident victim flow chart
   D. Others, as predetermined
IV. Hospital procedures
   A. Chain of command and responsibilities
   B. Triage and admission procedure: classification of irradiated victims
   C. Traffic flow
   D. Decontamination procedure
   E. Precautions for handling the irradiated patient
   F. Collection and handling of specimens for radioactive analysis
   G. Care of the expired patient
V. Disposition of contaminated supplies and equipment
VI. Copy of local standard operating procedure of local radiation emergency plan

Establishing an area within or adjacent to the emergency department need not be an overwhelming or expensive task. Areas that could be appropriately designated as a radiation triage area are the hydrotherapy department, the morgue, or any combination of rooms or hallways. Direct access to the outside is essential to protect the hospital environment. The walls do not need to be lead-lined. It is desirable, however, to select an area that has painted walls and linoleum or tile floor covering for ease in decontaminating the area later. An isolated air conditioning system is also desirable; however, ordinary air conditioning or furnace filters can be placed over the exhaust outlets of the selected triage area.[6]

Three types of supplies are required in the designated radiation triage area:

1. standard crash cart and specific equipment for treating the traumatic injuries
2. supplies to handle a contaminated patient
3. radiation sampling material supplies

These supplies can be preestablished on two types of carts: (1) a standard crash cart and (2) a radiation treatment supply cart, which is relatively inexpensive to

Table 7–7 Supplies for a Radiation Treatment Cart

Usage	Supplies*
Patient care	Linens (disposable if possible): towels, sheets, washcloths, gowns, robes, slippers, blankets, etc. Cleansing supplies: soap or recommended cleansing agent, mechanism for connection to a water supply (preferably a shower), basins, isotonic solutions, irrigating syringes, soft scrub brushes Wound dressing and debriding supplies: suture sets, scissors, forceps, gauze pads, sponges, plastic drapes Miscellaneous items for medical care
Radiation sampling analysis	Specimen supplies: labels, containers, requisitions Container for highly radioactive foreign bodies (This should be made of lead, and walls should be about 1 inch thick, 6 inches high, and 4 inches in diameter.) Large plastic garbage cans with plastic liners (can be used for contaminated materials) Copy of sampling procedures Skin wipes (a piece of ordinary filter paper about 1 inch in diameter) Variety of small and large plastic, paper, or glass containers to collect hair, nails, tissue, small foreign bodies (dirt, etc.), wound exudates, vomitus, urine, fecal samples, etc. Cotton-tipped applicators (used to collect swab specimens of wounds, nasal cavities, and mouth)
Environmental protection	Plastic or paper floor covering Sealing tape Signs: radiation, precaution, clean area, dirty (contaminated) area Barricades to segregate areas Paper and plastic bags of various sizes
Radiation detection	Survey instruments Film badges or dosimeters
Personnel protection	Head coverings Surgical masks Gowns Shoe coverings Scrub suits Plastic aprons Plastic or rubber gloves

Table 7–7 continued

Miscellaneous	Writing utensils and paper Radiation specific forms Flashlight (for neurologic checks) Clipboards Copy of decontamination procedure Labels and signs

Note: Items designated for patient care should be separated and removed from the cart to the clean area before patients arrive.

stock (Table 7–7). The radiation treatment cart should be placed in the radiation triage area designated as dirty (contaminated). Establishing well-defined areas within the designated radiation triage area is of paramount importance in order to regulate traffic flow (see Figure 7–1).

The triage area must have direct access to the outside to receive irradiated patients in order to eliminate the possibility of contaminating the general hospital environment. Irradiated victims are admitted directly to the dirty treatment area; there immediate medical care is provided to those victims who are determined to

Figure 7–1 Radiation Triage Area at Hospital

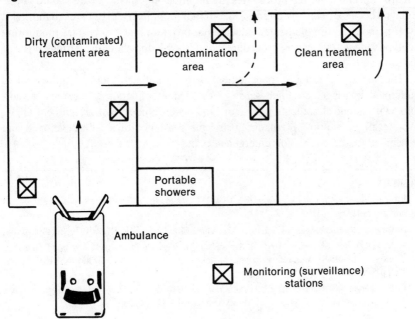

be in a life-threatening situation. Once they are determined to be medically stable, they are surveyed and enter the decontamination area for cleansing. This area is a "buffer zone" equipped with the necessary water supply and portable showers, if they are available. A light-weight portable bathtub that can be attached to an ordinary stretcher is a convenient method for cleansing the nonambulatory victim while collecting the water containing radioactive material. At least one hospital stretcher should be modified for such use in the decontamination procedure.[7]

If medical treatment is required, the victim enters the clean treatment area after monitoring and decontamination. If no care is required, the victim is released to the general hospital area after another radiological monitoring is completed. All personnel requiring decontamination must go through the decontamination procedure before entering the hospital area or returning to the community.

SUMMARY

We live in an environment filled with radiation from natural and man-made sources. These sources produce alpha and beta particles and gamma rays. Neutrons are seen only in a commercial or research reactor or in the event of nuclear war.

The irradiated victim the nurse is most likely to see is the transport accident victim. Special handling procedures are required, but medical care should not be delayed because of an unwarranted fear of radiation. Fear can be reduced through a well-planned and implemented educational program that emphasizes monitoring methods, decontamination procedures, and knowledge about the various types of radiation.

The successful nursing management of the irradiated victim requires sound judgment in triage, common sense in the decontamination procedures, a radiological patient classification system, and specific personnel assignment areas. Above all, it requires preplanning and the existence of a well-developed and rehearsed medical radiation emergency plan.

REFERENCES

1. *Accreditation Manual for Hospitals,* ed 1983. Chicago, Joint Commission on Accreditation of Hospitals, 1982, pp 1–11.

2. Lesher DC, Bomberger AS: Experience at Three Mile Island. *Am J Nurs* 1979; 79:1402–1408.

3. *NATO Handbook on the Medical Aspects of Nuclear, Biological and Chemical Defensive Operations,* AMedP–6. Brussels, Belgium, Military Agency for Standardization (MAS), August 1973, pp 5-17–5-19.

4. Bomberger AS, Dannenfelser BA: *Radiation and Health: Principles and Practice in Therapy and Disaster Preparedness.* Rockville, Md, Aspen Systems Corp, 1984.

5. *Management of Persons Accidentally Contaminated with Radionuclides*, NRCP report No. 65. Bethesda, Md, National Council on Radiation Protection and Measurements, April 1980, pp 14–17.

6. Galvin MJ Jr: Hospital makes itself center for treatment of radiation victims. *Hospitals*, May 1, 1979, pp 37–40.

7. Saenger EL (course director): *Radiation Accident Preparedness*. Washington, DC, Edison Electric Institute, 1981, pp 40–42.

SELECTED READINGS

Breo DL: Nuclear scare tests hospital's disaster plans. *Hospitals*, May 1, 1979, pp 33–36.

Cunningham AM: Is there a seismograph for stress? *Psychology Today*, October 1982, pp 47–52.

Garman AAW, Lesher DC, Bomberger AS: Radiation accidents, in Lewis SM, Collier IC (eds): *Medical-Surgical Nursing: Assessment and Management of Clinical Problems*. New York, McGraw-Hill Book Co, 1983, pp 1667–1677.

Jankowski CB: Radiation emergency. *Am J Nurs* 1982;82:90–97.

Miller, KL, DeMuth WE Jr: Handling radiation emergencies: No need to fear. *JEN*, May/June 1983, pp 141–144.

Operational Radiation Safety Program, NCRP report no. 59, Bethesda, Md, National Council on Radiation Protection and Measurement, December 1978.

Richter LL, Berk HW, Teates CD, et al: A systems approach to the management of radiation accidents. *Ann Emerg Med* 1980;9:303–309.

Upton AC: *Radiation Injury: Effects, Principles and Perspectives*. Chicago, University of Chicago Press, 1969.

Vinsel DB: Hospitals must plan for nuclear accidents. *Hospitals*, August 16, 1980, pp 113–121.

Chapter 8

Psychological Aspects of Disaster Situations

Judith L. Richtsmeier, R.N., B.S., B.S.N., and
Jean R. Miller, R.N., Ph.D.

Disasters produce physical, social, and psychological consequences that are exhibited to various degrees in different persons, families, communities, and cultures. Fortunately, because most afflicted persons pass through predictable stages during a disaster, health professionals and families can prepare for the effects of a disaster.

This chapter is intended to assist with that preparation by providing the following information:

- factors that affect the victim's psychological responses to disaster
- phases of disaster and related psychological responses
- general therapeutic approaches
- issues for children, the elderly, and those with chronic illness
- care of the caregivers

Disasters can be natural or man-made through human error, civil disorder, war, or nuclear attack. Examples of natural disasters are hurricanes, floods, drought, fire, transportation accidents, or other situations that cause human suffering to the degree that affected persons cannot effectively handle the situation without external aid. *Disaster* can be defined as a "situation that causes human suffering or creates human needs that the victims cannot alleviate without assistance."[1]

For the purposes of this chapter, a disaster is described as any occurrence that creates a demand exceeding the capabilities of the system to handle it in a normal or routine way. A crisis occurs when basic needs can no longer be met because of an overload of this system. The system can be as small as an individual self-system or as all-encompassing as a community, national, or international system. The focus of this chapter is on the situation of massive collective stress that occurs when individual stress reactions are combined with changes in the social milieu.

185

FACTORS THAT AFFECT INDIVIDUAL RESPONSE

Major disasters have an effect on both physical and psychological response. Logue et al[2] summarized the results of 32 studies of various major disasters reported in the literature between the years 1943 and 1980. Disasters ranged from the Cocoanut Grove fire in Boston, Massachusetts, 1942, to Tropical Storm Agnes and resulting flooding, in Wyoming Valley, Pennsylvania, 1972. In all studies reviewed, various health effects were reported:

- gastrointestinal complaints—gastritis, nausea and vomiting, diarrhea, constipation
- increased mortality, especially among the aged and those with chronic illness
- increased morbidity, with emphasis on cardiopulmonary diseases, hypertension, and arthritic diseases
- decline of general health during a 1- to 2-year period following the disaster
- increased number of spontaneous abortions and miscarriages
- physical and nervous exhaustion among those in leadership positions who experienced role conflict
- neuropsychiatric problems such as depression, anxiety, difficulty concentrating, sleep disturbances, emotional distress among family members, increased incidence of substance abuse, neuroses, and psychoses

Although there are predictable patterns of behavior surrounding a disaster, there is variation among individuals. The differences in psychological response can be explained by the nature of the disaster and the mediating personal and the social and treatment system variables (see Figure 8–1).

The Event Itself

The disaster can be described by the type or nature of the event: fire, flood, earthquake, train wreck, tornado, explosion, blizzard, nuclear accident, chemical spill, riot, and so forth. The duration of the event is also an important factor to be considered. An explosion is over very quickly, in a matter of minutes; a flood may be prolonged over a period of days; and a nuclear accident may occur over a period of hours or days with far-reaching, prolonged effects due to radiation contamination.

The amount of warning is another relevant factor that affects psychological response to the disaster. This factor is usually associated directly with the type or nature of the event itself. For instance, because hurricanes are often predicted by general weather conditions, direct visual sightings, tracking of storms by weather radar, and so forth, individual persons and communities can receive advance

Figure 8–1 Major Factors That Affect Psychological Responses to
Disaster

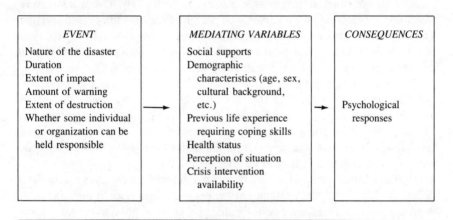

EVENT	*MEDIATING VARIABLES*	*CONSEQUENCES*
Nature of the disaster Duration Extent of impact Amount of warning Extent of destruction Whether some individual or organization can be held responsible	Social supports Demographic characteristics (age, sex, cultural background, etc.) Previous life experience requiring coping skills Health status Perception of situation Crisis intervention availability	Psychological responses

warning of the storm by hours or days. By contrast, earthquakes strike suddenly and usually without warning; even the after-shocks, although expected, are generally unpredictable.

Both the extent of impact and the extent of the destruction can be correlated with the amount of stress experienced and the psychological response to the event. One additional relevant factor that concerns the event itself is whether the disaster is considered to be an act of God (a natural disaster), or the result of human error or negligence (a man-made disaster). In other words, can some individual or organization be held accountable for the disaster?

Mediating Variables

Personal and social factors have a strong influence on a person's reaction to any stressful situation. Some factors that should be considered include the following:

- demographic characteristics (e.g., age, sex, cultural background, socioeconomic status)
- social supports (e.g., family, church, neighborhood, social groups, community groups)
- general health status (preexisting disease or ill health)
- coping skills (usually developed from previous life experience)

The victims' "reality" or perception of the situation is probably the most important factor in mediating the type of psychological response to disaster.

Disasters are significant for individual persons only insofar as they experience them as meaningful in affecting their lives. For example, a person who does not perceive the situation as severe as it actually is will likely have a less severe psychological reaction than a person who perceives the situation as catastrophic. The perception, however, often changes over time as the person allows reality to be truly sensed. The human mind is capable of allowing perceptions to be only as disastrous as the mind can cope with at a given time.

Community, state, and federal emergency systems may also have an impact on individual response to disaster. The extent to which services are available or not available probably determines whether this impact is a positive or a negative one. To maximize positive response, such services should include the availability of crisis intervention and counseling from the earliest possible point through the recovery stage, up to a year or more after the event.

Demi and Miles[3] categorized the factors that influence a person's reactions to disaster as situational and personal. *Situational* variables refer to the amount of warning, the nature and severity of the disaster, physical proximity, and support systems. A person's reactions to a disaster would be greater under the following circumstances: there is little or no warning; the disaster is man-made, not an act of God; the extent of death, injury, and destruction is great; the victim is in close proximity to the disaster; and available support systems are limited. Survivors of Hiroshima can be cited as examples fitting these criteria.

Personal variables include psychologic proximity, coping skills, concurrent losses, role conflict and role overload, and the victim's previous experience with disaster. A survivor's risk of developing severe psychological consequences is greater if the person is psychologically close to affected individuals, has limited coping skills, experiences concurrent losses, is involved in role conflict and overload, and has had little or no previous experience with disaster. An example of survivors fitting these criteria is the survivors of a devastating earthquake in Nicaragua, 1972.

PHASES OF A DISASTER

The phases of disaster referred to throughout the book are clearly defined in Chapter 1: predisaster preparation, warning, impact, emergency, and recovery. In Table 1–2, each phase is described according to the activities that occur during that phase. Refer to this table as the psychological aspects of each are described in the following portion of this chapter.

Remember, phases often overlap or a phase such as the warning phase may be absent entirely. In the following discussion of psychological reactions and possible intervention strategies, some phases again overlap according to the application of general psychiatric nursing principles. The guidelines are meant to be general rather than all inclusive inasmuch as the focus is on assessment and intervention techniques appropriate for all nurses (regardless of area of specialty) who find themselves in a disaster situation.

Predisaster Preparation and Warning

Sadly, these two phases are too often both absent. In these instances, the most severe psychological reactions are possible. During such disaster situations, the lack of resources, planning, prevention, education, supplies, and general and psychological preparation lead to devastating feelings of hopelessness and helplessness. Add to this a lack of warning, and the impact on the individual can be catastrophic.

Predisaster preparation is an activity in which all health care providers should be actively involved—on both a professional and a personal level. It is one of the most effective means we have available to attenuate the effects of disaster on ourselves, our families, and those we may be called upon to care for.

Education and training through mock disaster exercises provide excellent preparation for a disaster when they are conducted in an organized, well-planned, and regularly scheduled basis. Such exercises are an excellent means of "desensitizing" individuals and groups to disaster, thus averting a large measure of the panic that would otherwise occur. When a situation is well rehearsed, it is naturally met with an elevated sense of competence and confidence. Locally, such programs can be designed with realistic threats to the community in mind. For example, a community surrounding a major air terminal might plan exercises simulating a major aircraft crash into an area of the community. A community near a major waterway might plan mock disaster exercises involving a flood, and so forth. (See Chapters 12 and 14 for the planning and conducting of such activities.) The major purposes of these exercises, from a psychological point of view, include the following:

- to increase awareness
- to facilitate a psychological desensitization
- to increase confidence in ability to function and to cope
- to decrease the incidence and the magnitude of negative psychological reactions, such as denial, panic, and shock

The predisaster and warning phases are usually a time when persons with lack of preparation experience anxiety of some magnitude. In mild form, this anxiety is most often managed with a variety of subconscious defense mechanisms. Commonly, people either deny that a potential disaster exists ("It'll *never* happen to me!"), develop a fatalistic attitude ("It's inevitable and there's *nothing* we can do about it"), or employ rationalizations to convince themselves that the disaster will not occur ("There hasn't been an earthquake here in over 50 years, so the chances of it happening again decrease every day").

While actions and reactions during the predisaster phase typically vary from inactivity and apathy to mild anxiety (with the *ideal* of planning and preparation falling somewhere between), overactivity and anxiety increasing to panic levels are more characteristic of the warning phase. Remember that many disasters such as earthquakes, tornados, and transportation accidents, usually do not have a warning phase.

When a warning is issued, unprepared individuals and groups often panic and frantically seek information on how to survive the oncoming disaster. Acute fear during this time is often associated with loss of control and irrational flight behavior. Ironically, flight may be the best survival technique in certain situations. It is important, however, that persons flee in the proper direction and use good judgment in deciding whether to take flight or to seek shelter. In making such a judgment, consider the amount of time involved and the nature of the disaster.

Moreover, during the warning phase, responsibility is often displaced onto leaders and authorities who are viewed as "parent figures." Address this behavior simply by giving very authoritative direction and explicit communication about such matters as evacuation, movement to shelters, and so forth.[4]

Intervention strategies during the predisaster preparation and warning phases should be geared toward education and reality-oriented work. The goal is to decrease denial so that citizens can mobilize and protect themselves. Provide information on the type, the source, and the degree of danger, as well as the plans for evacuation, if indicated. Competent leaders must understand the relevant aspects of the impending danger and must transmit the appropriate defensive or evasive measures that should be followed. Significant factors that affect intervention at this time are the degree of previous planning and preparation and the effectiveness of the communication network.

Impact and Emergency

Survival instincts are primary during the impact and emergency phases of a disaster; saving one's life and the lives of loved ones becomes paramount. Research conducted by Canadian physician J.S. Tyhurst[5] indicates that 12 to 25 percent of the victims are tense, excited, yet capable of functioning effectively and often find themselves too busy to worry. Seventy-five percent are dazed, stunned, and bewildered. This reaction is referred to as the "disaster syndrome"[6]: absence of emotion, inhibition of activity, docility, indecisiveness, lack of responsiveness, automatic behavior, and physiological manifestations of fear. The remaining few percent (0%–12%) exhibit grossly inappropriate behavior, anxiety, hysterical reactions, and pyschosis. It must be emphasized that these latter reactions are rare, in spite of popular belief and media portrayal to the contrary.

The figures show that most of the immediate reactions to a disaster are accompanied by some sign of emotional disturbance. The vast majority of these responses are transient and the victims recover spontaneously with supportive management alone. Flexibility is the best rule of thumb during this period when reactions are transient and changing.

Immediately after the impact phase and during most of the emergency phase, medical skill and expertise are appropriately directed toward saving lives. Psychological needs are usually given a low priority or are deferred until a later time. Research suggests that simple supportive management at the earliest possible time after impact often prevents or attenuates psychiatric disturbances that may occur during the recovery phase.[2,4–6]

At the disaster site, in shelters, or at the earliest triage point, both professional and lay workers should be made aware that simple human compassion and common sense support are the best preventive measures for psychological casualties. Some measures can be taken without special training:

- Facilitate keeping families together, especially keeping children with parents.
- Do not leave frightened or injured people alone; assign another survivor-victim to stay with them or place people in groups.
- Assign meaningful tasks or purposeful activity to keep victims busy and to enhance shattered self-esteem.
- Provide warmth, food, shelter, and rest.
- Maintain a good communications network to prevent rumor, which leads to irrational and impulsive behavior.
- Provide leadership—someone to give direction and to make decisions.
- Encourage victims to talk about what they are experiencing by placing them in groups to share feelings and to support one another.
- Isolate any persons who display panic or hysterical behavior—behavior that can be contagious; someone should stay with them until professional help can assess and intervene.

When such simple supportive measures fail to help or when a person is the victim of physical and psychological injury that places them into the treatment system, intervene quickly with an evaluation of the situation that is as accurate as possible. Take a quick history to identify the person, to ascertain the family's whereabouts, and to learn what happened. Exhibit 8–1 provides a simple format for documentation and assessment.

Exhibit 8–1 Abbreviated Mental Health Assessment Form

Date _____ Time _____

Location (shelter, facility, etc.) _____

Name _____
        Last   First   Middle

                                                    Permanent _____
Address _____Temporary _____
         Street   City   Zip   County

Sex _____ Age _____ Date of birth _____ Cultural background _____

Marital status _____ Vocation _____ Next of kin _____
                                                      Address _____

Presenting problem/situation: (Include client's own words describing his or her perception of
                               the situation.)

Description of losses (property, family, etc.):

Concurrent losses (occurring within the past year):

General health before the disaster (list any specific conditions or illness):

Current medications (OTC or prescription):

Use of alcohol? _____ Tobacco? _____ Drugs _____
                 (Amount and frequency of each)

Coping skills ("How have you handled crises in the past?"):

Exhibit 8–1 continued

Assessment: Brief summary of findings/description of client.

Disposition:

_____
Name and Title

When assessing psychological responses to disaster, keep in mind the uniqueness of each person. Factors discussed earlier in the chapter, such as demographic data, previous life experiences, and cultural background, are all important in determining the individual's response to the situation. There is no right or wrong way to react to a disaster. The type of response can be classified according to general categories such as those found in Table 8–1; however, over-generalization must be avoided and the individual aspects of the response must be considered during assessment and intervention planning.

Evaluate the casualties as quickly and as accurately as possible. Locate significant others, if possible, because they can assist in providing emotional support. Identify the victim's strengths and channel them into constructive behavior that helps others and decreases the anxiety. Reassurance should be straightforward and pity and sympathy should be avoided. Make those with physical problems or injuries as comfortable as possible by having them lie down, by keeping them warm, and by feeding them (if not contraindicated). Encourage victims to talk and to ventilate their feelings.

Significant factors that help to alleviate distress during this phase are similar to those in the previous phases. Good communication and leadership are important in guiding large groups of people (see also Figure 8–1). Past experience with crises and successful prior coping help to alleviate the stresses of this period. Cultural and religious beliefs along with basic support from family members provide strength. For most, the reactions of this period are generally transient and recovery is spontaneous.

Recovery Phase

In the prior phases (impact and emergency), it was demonstrated that much of the indicated intervention can be accomplished by supportive family members, lay volunteers, or health care professionals regardless of area of specialty. Mental

Table 8–1 General Types of Disaster Reactions: Assessment and Intervention

Type	Assessment	Intervention
"Normal" or most common reaction	Mild anxiety (tearfulness, etc.) GI symptoms (nausea & vomiting, diarrhea) Diaphoresis Urinary frequency Muscular tremors or tension Palpitations or tachycardia Hyperpnea	Provide the following support measures: • group activity & group identification • open communication with an empathic listener • information • leadership • warm food & rest Engage in purposeful activities.
Depressive reaction	Immobile Nonverbal Flattened affect Verbalizing a "numb" feeling toward the events	Establish rapport. Encourage ventilation. Provide empathic listening. Legitimize feelings. Engage in simple, routine tasks. Provide warm food, drink, or a smoke. Avoid excessive pity; administration of sedation; and telling victim to "snap out of it."
Psychosomatic reaction (physical symptoms caused by psychological reaction)	Conversion reaction (partial paralysis without physical cause, inability to use some part of their body) Extreme nausea & vomiting	Make victim comfortable. Be aware of your own personal feelings. Show interest in the victim as a person. Try to find some simple task to divert victim's attention from the symptoms and the situation. Avoid ridicule or blame; telling victims that there is nothing wrong with them; and calling attention to their symptoms.
Anxiety reaction	Rapid, continual talking Very short attention span Inappropriate use of humor Argumentativeness	Encourage ventilation. Assign tasks requiring physical activity. Supervise closely.

Table 8–1 continued

	Physical hyperactivity	Provide warm food, drink, or a smoke.
		Avoid sedating, arguing with victims or telling them not to feel the way they do.
Hysterical reaction (an *uncommon* reaction!)	Attempts at blind flight Uncontrolled crying or screaming Severely impaired judgment Unreasoning attempts to flee the area Uncontrolled, wild, running about	Isolate; these can be contagious in a group Try firm kindness and empathy. Get assistance if required. Offer food or warm drink. Avoid the use of brutal restraint or physical force if at all possible. Do not attempt to shock the patient out of it (throwing water, slapping, etc.). Avoid the use of sedatives, except as a last resort.

health care workers (psychiatrists, psychiatric nurse specialists, psychologists, social workers) are involved largely in a consultative, supervisory role and become directly involved mainly with victims who exhibit the most severe reactions and require specialized care.

During the recovery phase, the mental health care system plays a key role. This phase continues for months after the disaster, and, for many, for the rest of their lives. Social and individual stresses surface as the reality of what the disaster has meant in terms of loss is fully experienced. As McLeod states, "Without psychological help the emotional ripples can continue indefinitely."[7]

At this time, the ego defense mechanisms of denial and repression—so prevalent in the previous phases—are replaced by grief, depression, anger, guilt, posttraumatic neuroses, psychosomatic illness, and increased physical illness. The reactions at this point are similar to those defined in psychiatry as anxiety and depressive states.

It is common in disasters to experience the phenomenon of the "rise and fall of the postdisaster utopia." The initial tendency after a disaster is generous giving and acceptance without restraint, but this is soon followed by feelings of hostility, greed, independence, suspicion, envy, and competition.[6]

Although survivors are relieved to be alive, anger often develops and may be expressed individually and collectively. The anger may be directed toward individuals or groups—e.g., minority ethnic groups, the financially successful, civic leaders, care providers, or the government. This type of scapegoating helps release pent-up feelings, but it may also lead to feelings of guilt.

Guilt is a prevalent feeling during the recovery phase. Victims may experience "survivor guilt"—guilt experienced when individuals realize that they survived while others died or that their damage was less than that of others. Some wonder whether they could have done more to rescue those who perished, and so they feel guilty that they did not do more. Others feel as though they were being punished or even that they were responsible for the disaster. Guilt sometimes motivates persons to heroism in an effort to eliminate the guilty feelings within themselves.

Grief for lost objects and loved ones is a long-term process. On a massive scale, it may begin with incineration and mass burial. This type of mass burial can be traumatic for the survivors who cannot mourn until they "know" by identification that their loved one is truly among those who died. It is not uncommon for relatives to spend days searching the rubble for corpses from the disaster.

During this period of reconstruction and recovery, new equilibrium in family and social relations must occur (Exhibit 8–2). Alterations in attitudes, values, and morale change the way people relate to one another. Life-style must change for many whose economic base is less than it was before the disaster.

Exhibit 8–2 Case Example

In January 1982, a freak storm inundated the California coast at night with 20 inches of rain. Mud and water rushed down the mountains into the homes and the businesses of Santa Cruz County. Residents awoke to hear that 22 people had been killed, over 100 families were homeless, and 3,000 other homes were severely damaged. After the initial shock, denial, then euphoria at being spared, many survivors discovered that regaining emotional equilibrium was as difficult as shoveling the mud and the water out of their shattered homes.

Within a few days of the flood, a model program was set up to provide mental health care for disaster victims. Project COPE (Counseling Ordinary People in Emergencies) was set up to provide immediate counseling for victims of the flood.[7]

COPE coordinated the volunteer services of more than 100 private mental health professionals with federal and local government resources. Hundreds of residents were recipients of COPE's services. For more than a year after the disaster, individual and group counseling were provided free of charge to anyone who sought help. The final report of the organization described classic reactions to all types of disaster: grief, guilt, anger, depression, anxiety, vulnerability, and relationship problems.

The organizers of COPE were sensitive to the fact that the majority of the victims had never sought mental health care. Because victims were unlikely to seek help, the counselors continued to make themselves available at schools, shelters, churches, day care centers, and government relief offices. Therapists downplayed their role as mental health professionals and involved themselves in all aspects of the relief effort. For example, by conducting seminars on disaster preparedness they provided not only a valuable educational service but a natural forum to discuss psychological reactions to disaster in a nonthreatening manner. The community response was exceptionally positive and the program has been cited as a model program for other communities to follow.

REACTIONS OF SPECIAL GROUPS

Children

The major factors contributing to children's reactions to disaster are children's developmental level at the time of the disaster, their perceptions of the reactions of their families, and the amount of their direct exposure to the disaster.[8] Normal reactions include the following:

- general anxiety and fear
- separation anxiety from parents
- restlessness
- irritability
- disturbances of bodily functions such as enuresis
- difficulty in concentration
- refusal to go to school
- guilt that they could have done something to prevent the disaster and its effects

Reactions can be more severe than those in this list. Children under 12 years of age in the Buffalo Creek flood experienced chronic and traumatic anxiety reactions, hyperactivity, immaturity, developmental deviations in cognition, inability to take a bath without screaming, bed-wetting, terrifying nightmares, trembling hands, tension, inner tremulousness, difficulty sleeping, sleepwalking, and visual hallucinations. Adolescents in the Buffalo Creek flood had special vulnerabilities to the loss of community and the psychological effects of the disaster. They often chose between rebellious predelinquent behavior or compliant social withdrawal. Some, however, expressed creative solutions for reconstructing the environment. Older children often followed the lawsuit and psychiatric interviews with great interest. In their themes in school, they wrote about safety regulations and dam construction. They talked of being nurses and lawyers in later life.

Children and adolescents who have experienced disaster in their families and communities are affected by their perceptions of their parents' or other adults' reactions. Their perceptions are also influenced by the social and legal processes associated with the disaster. According to Newman, the "common heritage of most children of disaster is a modified sense of reality, increased vulnerability to future stresses, an altered sense of powers within the self, and a precocious awareness of fragmentation and depth."[8] Many have a sense of hope and creativity along with developmental limitations and some psychological pathology. These children and adolescents often need special help to respond constructively to the traumas they have undergone.

The Elderly

Disasters have serious consequences for the elderly, but the results of research suggest that the aged cope better than do their younger counterparts.[8,9] The difficult aspects of disaster for the elderly are their lack of resources, declining physical capacity, and limited time to replace losses. Because many elderly persons have chronic illnesses, this too can present serious problems. For example, access to medications such as insulin and pain relievers is particularly important. Those with heart disease may be under undue stress and should be watched closely. The symptoms of those with psychiatric histories may be exacerbated during disasters. Some psychotic patients become more rational, while paranoid patients may blame themselves for the disaster. Severely agitated patients may become more excited. Patients with severe neurosis may behave rationally and severely depressed patients may show no change.[10] Such reactions, however, are no different for the elderly than for the young.

The responses of the elderly toward losses from disaster do not show excessive feelings of personal disorganization. In studies done after a tornado[9] in Nebraska in 1975 and the breaking of the Teton Dam[11] in 1976, the results suggested fewer adverse emotional effects and feelings of deprivation among the elderly than among younger victims. After the tornado, younger victims experienced more change in interpersonal spheres of family, friends, and neighbors. Younger victims also experienced higher anxiety and physical stress levels than the aged, regardless of the damage sustained. Results from both of these studies suggested that the coping potential of the aged surpassed that of their younger counterparts.

That the elderly cope better than younger persons on an emotional level does not mean the elderly are without needs. Huerta and Horton[11] listed what professionals can do for the elderly after a disaster:

- Provide assistance with the physical problems of cleanup and repair.
- Advise in the elderly person's language style what financial, legal, and tax actions need to be taken.
- Provide income and social assistance through socially accepted agencies such as religious organizations rather than specialized agencies, which carry a stigma for many elderly persons.
- Provide opportunities for the elderly to be information and opinion disseminators rather than passive recipients.

If psychotherapy is needed, it should be brief, goal-directed therapy. The general guiding principle to be used with the elderly is that minimal interference with established life patterns should be followed. The therapist should take care of the problem and then get out. The basic steps in any problem-solving task are (1) to define the problem, (2) to collect the facts, (3) to gather alternative solutions, (4) to pick the best solutions, and (5) to act. The elderly person needs to be actively involved in the process and to focus on the here and now.

CARE OF THE CAREGIVERS

Historically, health care professionals, like the rest of the population, have become victims of disasters. Hiroshima shows how realistic survival concerns can be for health care professionals. Of a total population of 245,000, there were 75,000 people killed and 100,000 injured. Of 150 physicians in the city, only 30 were left alive. Of 1,780 nurses, only 126 were left alive.[12]

Those caregivers and relief workers who survive are able to remain objective observers for only a short time unless they maintain an adaptive psychological, and often physical, distance from their patients. This objectivity is rapidly lost when they become an actual part of the social sequence. Research on disaster responses is difficult because of this very factor; researchers assigned to gather data have often abandoned their work to provide assistance as relief workers.[13]

Psychological reactions can easily overwhelm relief teams of caregivers unless careful attention is given to meeting basic biological needs—especially the need for rest and sleep. In disaster situations, caregivers may easily work harder than they have ever worked before. Therefore, the workload must be paced, and caregivers must accept the human limitations that prevent them from working night and day over a prolonged period. If their basic biological needs are not met, the health care providers cease to function as professionals and have only enough energy to look after themselves and their families.[13]

Edwards studied the sources of stress experienced by nurses during short-term civilian disasters in Great Britain.[10] His findings revealed the following stressors:

- concern over personal safety
- concern over safety of their own families
- concern over deficiencies in the relief organization and supply systems
- increased responsibility
- excessive demands
- need to avoid role-conflict with co-workers
- identification of nurse-mothers with pediatric victims
- need to do something significant
- feelings of possessiveness toward victims

Triage is also a stressor to health care providers. Life and death decisions must be made quickly. There is little opportunity or place for nurse-patient, or physician-patient relationships. Scarce resources, including manpower, must be allocated in the most effective, judicious manner. This climate is foreign to most modern areas of practice.

According to Burkle, "the essence of the traumatic situation is an experience of helplessness on the part of the ego."[13] Health care professionals should avoid expecting others to behave or to feel as they do. What is perceived as threatening to a person depends on the degree of psychic pain that person can tolerate. Acceptance of others' rights to their feelings and personal limitations can ease the burden of caregiving.

Health care professionals should be encouraged to use three of humans' most adaptive defense mechanisms: suppression, acceptance, and humor. *Suppression* is the intentional exclusion of material from conscious thoughts. In this instance it is the surrounding atmosphere of emotional and physical threat to the individual that is suppressed. *Acceptance* is the recognition that things happen far beyond one's control. It helps to avoid dwelling on "could-have-beens." A *sense of humor* is the ability to laugh at oneself and one's own vulnerabilities.

The pressure of decision making in a disaster situation differs considerably from the everyday decision making that caregivers face. There is generally more at stake and less time before critical options are lost. Disaster can be described as a prolonged, organized stress test for the caregiver.

Stress and anxiety for workers at all levels can be attenuated by such things as the following:

- a concise, clear disaster plan
- regular, well-planned disaster exercises or drills
- clearly defined staff roles
- regular relief periods such as breaks, meals, and sleep time

After the disaster, or at least the impact and emergency periods, is over, caregivers need some of the same types of support as the disaster victims. This support includes time to work through their feelings about the event and their roles. This process can be done most effectively in groups with their peers and perhaps with a mental health worker as group facilitator to lead or to guide the discussion and ventilation process. An opportunity to critique the disaster relief process is also an important staff need after the disaster; it is also a vital part in the evaluation and revision of disaster plans to effectively prepare for subsequent events. Group and individual therapy should be made available to the caregivers to assist them in working through any psychosocial distress after the disaster. It must be recognized that caregivers have the same types of psychological reactions as the survivor-victims, in addition to intense frustrations associated with their very roles. Such feelings and reactions must be legitimized and addressed openly.

One last, but extremely important postdisaster staff need, is the need to receive expressions of appreciation and recognition from supervisors and leaders. In the atmosphere of frustration, loss, and continual stress that is created by a disaster, ego strength and self-esteem are easily shattered. There is great therapeutic value in recognition by superiors that in spite of the terrible situation, you as an individual did your best and are appreciated for it.

SUMMARY

Psychological responses to disaster vary according to the nature of the disaster, individual strengths, and environmental factors. Assessment of individual and family responses must be done quickly and accurately. Sensitivity, flexibility, and empathy toward a wide spectrum of emotions and reactions are requirements during the intervention process. Leadership must be calm and confident with straightforward directions being given. Victims should be encouraged to engage in purposeful activity when possible. During these times of high stress, it is imperative that the caregiver obtain the necessary rest and sleep as well as emotional support. Good communication networks help to alleviate the pressures and to enhance the decision-making abilities of all persons involved.

Education and preparation in advance are essential at all levels in order for each of us to maximize our chances for physical and psychological survival in a disaster. Personally and professionally, nurses must accept this challenge.

REFERENCES

1. *Disaster Relief Program,* ARC 2235. Washington, DC, American National Red Cross, revised March 1975, p 2.

2. Logue JN, Melick ME, Hansen H: Research issues and directions in the epidemiology of health effects of disasters. *Epidemiolog Rev* 1981;3:140–162.

3. Demi AS, Miles MS: Understanding psychologic reactions to disaster. *JEN* 1983;9:11–16.

4. Allen J: Psychological aspects associated with major disaster. Presented before Disaster Planning Conference, University of Utah College of Nursing and the 328th General Hospital (US Army Reserve), Salt Lake City, 1982.

5. Tyhurst JS: Individual reactions to community disaster. *Am J Psychiatry* 1951;107:764–769.

6. Kinston W, Rosser R: Disaster: Effect on mental and physical state. *Psychosom Res* 1974; 18:437–455.

7. McLeod B: In the wake of disaster. *Psychol Today,* October 1984, pp 54–57.

8. Newman CJ: Children of disaster: Clinical observations at Buffalo Creek. *Am J Psychiatry* 1976; 133:306–312.

9. Bell BD: Disaster impact and response: Overcoming the thousand natural shocks. *Gerontologist* 1978;18:531–540.

10. Edwards JG: Psychiatric aspects of civilian disasters. *Br Med J* 1976;1:944–947.

11. Huerta F, Horton R: Coping behavior of elderly flood victims. *Gerontologist* 1978;18:541–546.

12. Lown B, Chivian E, Muller J, et al: Sounding board: The nuclear-arms race and the physician. *N Engl J Med* 1981;304:726–729.

13. Burkle F: Coping with stress under conditions of disaster and refugee care. *Milit Med* 1983; 148:800–803.

SUGGESTED READINGS

Glass AJ: Psychological aspects of disaster. *JAMA* 1959;171:222–225.

Hoff LA: *People in Crisis: Understanding and Helping*. Menlo Park, Calif, Addison-Wesley Publishing Co, 1978.

Koegler RR, Hicks SM: The destruction of a medical center by earthquake: Initial effects on patients and staff. *Calif Med,* Feb 1972;116:63–67.

Chapter 9

Establishing and Managing a Shelter*

Richard D. Mickelson, B.S.

A major disaster can displace large segments of the population from their normal residences and places of work. Such a situation places a requirement on local governments to provide temporary lodging, food, health care, and other essential services for an indefinite period of time. The combined resources of government and the private sector are essential in order to accomplish this task successfully.

Ideally, trained managers would be assigned to all shelters upon activation. Although government authorities or the American Red Cross Chapter in a given community may have assigned a trained manager, there is no guarantee that the manager can reach that facility in an emergency. Experience has demonstrated that nurses by necessity have had to assume leadership in many cases. The purpose of this chapter, therefore, is to assist the nurse in the following:

- to understand the organization for mass care shelters and some common definitions
- to understand how the need for shelters is determined
- to understand how shelters are located and selected
- to identify the functions or activities within a shelter
- to identify the responsibilities of a shelter manager
- to understand and to deal with problems and potential conflicts in shelter living
- to understand the role of the nurse within a shelter

Source: Adapted with permission from *Disaster Services Regulations and Procedures: Disaster Health Services,* ARC 3050. Washington, DC, American National Red Cross, revised February 1976, p 33.

It should be noted at the onset that the contents of this chapter are based essentially upon two sources. The first is the American Red Cross's *Disaster Services Regulations and Procedures Series*[1] and the second is the Federal Emergency Management Agency's *How to Manage Congregate Lodging Facilities and Fallout Shelters*.[2] The associated training and operational experience these documents afforded this chapter were essential for its preparation.

BACKGROUND

Most counties and cities have adopted and published emergency operations plans. These plans generally define the emergency services organization of a given jurisdiction and assign emergency responsibilities to the various departments and agencies. In addition, many jurisdictions have prepared specific plans designed to expedite local response to a particular type of disaster—an earthquake response, for example. An emergency plan normally consists of a basic plan and a number of annexes or sections that deal with specific functions.

The provision for sheltering disaster victims is normally found in the mass care annex of most emergency plans. *Mass care* can be defined as "meeting the needs of disaster victims and emergency workers through the provision of supplies and services."[3(p10)] A *mass-care shelter* is "a facility adequate to provide temporary shelter for groups of disaster victims unable to continue their living arrangements in separate family units."[4] One also hears or reads such terms as *evacuation center, mass-care center,* or *congregate-care facility,* which are all synonymous with mass shelter.

In many situations, shelters either are established and managed by or operated in conjunction with the American Red Cross. The American Red Cross, chartered by the United States Congress in 1950 to provide disaster relief to the American people, has over the years become the nation's primary volunteer agency when a natural disaster occurs. The role of the Red Cross disaster program under federal law has been restated in federal disaster legislation through the years. Further clarification is achieved by means of state and local laws and ordinances, executive proclamations, and formal and informal understandings negotiated between the state and local governments and the appropriate Red Cross operations headquarters and chapters.

Agreements concerning the use of facilities as mass-care shelters are frequently made between school districts and the local Red Cross chapter. Similar arrangements are made with churches for the use of their facilities and with cities for the use of such buildings as community centers and park and recreational facilities. The popularity of these agreements is understandable inasmuch as the Red Cross essentially assumes financial and liability responsibilities whenever such facilities are used as mass-care shelters under the control of the Red Cross. Agreement about Red Cross support to shelters and feeding centers operated by other volunteer agencies is in accordance with prearranged plans or ad hoc agreements. A church, for example, that has the facility, the equipment, and the trained personnel to establish a shelter may lack only financial resources. In such a case, the Red Cross could agree to accept financial obligations and establish the shelter in conjunction with the church. It is basic Red Cross policy, however, "that administrative responsibility and financial control are inseparable."[3(p4)] In assuming responsibility for relief, therefore, the Red Cross requires that all funds used by it in extending relief be expended in accordance with its established policies and regulations. For this reason, the Red Cross system for records and reports is in common usage within the mass-care environment. Moreover, Red Cross training courses like "Shelter Management" and "Providing Red Cross Disaster Health Services" are popular.

Although the American Red Cross has a clear mandate in natural disaster and other emergencies, the relationship changes in time of war. "In war-caused situations, the Red Cross will use its facilities and personnel to support and assist mass care and emergency operations activities of the Federal Emergency Management Agency to the extent Red Cross considers possible, while carrying out its other essential responsibilities and assignments."[5] In this situation, however, both administrative and financial control rests with the federal government.

DETERMINING THE NEED FOR A MASS SHELTER

The need for shelters varies according to the nature and the extent of the disaster. Normally, emergency plans call for their designation and activation by local government in collaboration with the local Red Cross chapter. A hurricane warning along the Gulf Coast, for example, would result in several predesignated mass-care shelters being established for precautionary measures. Precautionary mass-care shelters may be opened in advance because of the threat of fire, flood, snow, and so forth. A shelter may be open for only a matter of hours if the threat diminishes or for a prolonged period if there has been extensive damage in the area. Whenever the local government recommends or enforces the evacuation of a given area, mass shelters are established. Given the opportunity, the majority of people will take responsibility for themselves by arranging to stay with friends or relatives or in commercial facilities. If only two or three families arrive at a designated shelter, they may be provided individual shelter in a motel or hotel, which would enable the mass-care shelter to close. Remember that mass shelters are only an emergency and temporary means of caring for people; they are also expensive to operate. As soon as a shelter is opened, plans are made to close it as quickly as possible. A shelter will be kept open, however, until every family in it can be returned to their own homes or until some alternative plan is made for them.

LOCATING AND SELECTING A SHELTER

Although mass shelters are only a temporary means of caring for people and certainly not the most desirable of living accommodations, they are often the only means of caring for large numbers of people quickly and effectively. Accordingly, some preplanning is desirable. The American Red Cross recommends that a committee be formed at the local chapter level to be responsible for predisaster planning and for operating shelters during a disaster or a threat thereof. A written plan of action is prepared in advance, which allows, in part, for the selection of satisfactory shelters. Predisaster planning is an important process for most communities and vital for those with a history of major disasters.

In many communities, the predesignation of mass shelters is a collaborative effort between local government and Red Cross. Shelters are preselected for each area of the community, with both primary and secondary designations. This allows for expanding the number of shelters if a situation so dictates.

When selecting a good shelter location, first determine the potential hazards for the community. If your community is flood prone, it would make little sense to select shelters located within flood boundaries. By the same token, it is desirable to locate shelters in close proximity to the affected area. The size of the building is also a consideration. Disaster planners consider a small shelter to be one capable of handling 50 to 200 people. In most communities the majority of shelters fall into this category. A shelter that can hold 200 to 500 people is classified as medium; 500 and over, large. Some additional considerations are as follows:

- Sleeping accommodations (40–60 square feet per person).
- Food services (cooking facilities for the number of people sheltered, and providing each person 2,500 calories per day).
- Water (5 gallons per person per day for all uses).
- Sanitation (1 toilet for every 40 persons).
- Storage areas that can be secured.
- Separate rooms for such groups as the ill, the elderly, and families with small children and for office spaces.
- Recreation area.
- Parking.

A building should not be rejected simply because one or more of these requirements is missing. Many Red Cross chapters maintain organized lists of characteristics (including floor plans) of buildings selected as shelters. It is normal procedure, once suitable structures have been located, to enter into agreements for their use and to establish entry procedures for setting them up when a shelter is needed.

FUNCTIONS OR ACTIVITIES WITHIN A SHELTER

Functions or activities vary according to the length of time the shelter is in operation and the functions that the "normal" community can no longer handle because of damage caused by the disaster. Certain major functions are common to all shelters.

Common Major Functions

Food Service

Food represents security and the feeling of being taken care of. Eating eases tension and calms anxiety. If food is available or if its delivery can be arranged, a simple meal or snack is usually provided to incoming victims. When a shelter initially opens, food service may not be in operation. Also, should a shelter be opened as a precautionary measure, the activation of a cafeteria for one meal may not be feasible. In such cases, fast food outlets are normally used. Shortly after the opening of a shelter, food is usually prepared on the premise or delivered from fixed feeding stations. Cafeteria hours are planned and food is prepared by trained personnel and inspected by local health authorities. The goal is to provide a feeding capability inside the shelter or to locate one outside the facility that occupants can use. Additionally, insofar as possible, the special food needs of such groups as infants, the elderly, and the sick must be met.

Sleeping Accommodations

Shelters are characterized by a lack of privacy, and so community living is usually required because of the number of people involved. Because sleeping requires more time and space than other activities, shelter sleeping arrangements influence the physical organization of space within the building and the scheduling of other activities. Frequently the sleeping accommodation consists of a high school gymnasium or other similar rooms in buildings such as community centers. If only a single sleeping space is available, sleep positions are assigned to single men and women at opposite ends of the space, with family groups in between. A head-to-toes arrangement is recommended as the best position for sleep. The idea is to increase distance and to decrease risk of airborne infection. If a number of rooms are available, it is possible to separate groups for sleeping. Special consideration can be given to children, the elderly, and the infirm; they require more sleep than the average adult. In all probability, at least initially, there will not be enough cots or beds for all occupants. If a limited number of beds or cots are available, they are normally assigned to the emergency aid station and to the elderly. Comfort can be increased for the majority of the occupants by using gym mats, blankets, carpets, or fiberboard box material. Many victims, especially those who have previously experienced an evacuation, will bring their own bedding or sleeping bags.

Health Services

The role of health services is to see that the injured and the ill receive essential care, to plan for health protection and maintenance and to provide emotional support. Medical supervision and plans for 24-hour continuous nursing coverage are essential to maintain standards and to assure quality care. Health services should be given a high priority in the allocation of resources. Again, requirements vary according to the nature and the scope of the disaster.

Shelter occupants may normally use their own physicians and other medical personnel and hospitals or other treatment facilities within the community. Shelter nurses may make referrals to other agencies and to hospitals. If local health authorities request that the shelter be used to house the severely ill or injured victims, temporary infirmaries must be established. There have been occasions when entire nursing home populations have become shelter occupants. In these cases the nursing home staff is given a separate area adjacent to health services in which they can care for their patients.

Family Services

Often individuals or families come to a shelter because they are in need of assistance beyond a temporary place to eat or sleep. The American Red Cross has the responsibility for meeting the emergency disaster-caused needs of each family or person on an individual basis after a disaster. Emergency assistance is given for a variety of verified needs—all designed to enable family members to resume living as a family unit. Normally, emergency assistance workers are not present at the time a shelter opens; however, as soon as a need is determined, workers are assigned and casework begins. All emergency assistance is provided on a grant, not loan, basis. Information about training as an emergency assistance worker can be obtained by calling a local chapter of the American Red Cross.

Psychological Counseling

Counseling services can normally be made available to shelter occupants, depending on their need. Professionals such as psychiatrists, psychologists, nurses, social workers, mental health workers, vocational counselors, and the clergy are often available as volunteers. Victims with possible psychiatric disorders may be referred for evaluations or hospitalization if they cannot adapt to shelter living. The goal of this service is to reduce the mental anguish of persons suffering from reactions to the circumstances and to prevent psychological problems of disturbed individuals from affecting other residents' successful adjustment to shelter living.

Recreation and Religious Activities

One of the most difficult tasks in shelter management is to keep people occupied. Planned activities within and without the shelter are extremely important and should begin as soon as possible. Special services activities (e.g., caring for young children, helping with the elderly), physical fitness activities, training education classes, arts and crafts, rented movies, and social activities help to make time pass more quickly. Such activities raise morale and reduce anxiety. Concurrently, they control undesirable and unproductive behavior such as gambling, quarreling, and aimless wandering about. Religious activities can normally be established within a few days. In the absence of denominational services, non-denominational services of inspirational talks, singing, and periods of silent meditation may be offered. Remember, however, that although shelter occupants should be encouraged to participate in these activities, they should not be forced. Participation must be voluntary. Some persons prefer to be by themselves and should be left alone.

Administration

Systematic administrative procedures (records and reports) are vital to the successful operation of any shelter; they help to control and to account for shelter occupants and the supporting functions and activities. They should be instituted at the onset of the operation and continue until the operation is terminated.

Supportive Considerations

In addition to the major functions common to all shelters, several supportive functions should also be mentioned. They range from the provision of water to decontamination.

Water

Although normally not a problem, water, next to good air, is the most essential requirement of the shelter's occupants. It is important, therefore, to determine quickly how much water is available to the shelter. A minimal amount of water is needed to prevent dehydration, and, if possible, to provide water for fire fighting, washing, sanitation, and cooking. Assurance of safe water is the responsibility of local health authorities.

Sanitation

Shelters in which living conditions are crowded require the highest possible sanitation standards to prevent the spread of disease and to maintain morale. When developing duties and responsibilities, remember that the general population often has a very poor understanding of sanitation. Again, assurance of sanitation is the responsibility of local health authorities.

Ventilation

Although ventilation is not a serious problem in most shelters, an adequate supply of good air is critical. Be aware of the kinds of air problems you may face when doors or windows are kept closed during bad weather or when limited power is available for air circulation and air conditioning or heating.

Power and Lighting

Control the use of electric power; available power may be limited or subject to intermittent overloads or outages. Even when no problem exists, efforts should be made to conserve. Remember, too, that ventilation has a higher priority than lighting, and so the first use of electric power must be to operate ventilation systems.

Communications

The importance of communications cannot be overemphasized. Both external and internal communication are vital. External communication is a link to the outside world, a source of guidance, and an essential factor in many day-to-day shelter functions. Internal communication keeps shelter occupants advised about everything from the latest outside information to basic instructions about the tasks, the responsibilities, and the regulations that govern shelter life.

Security

The maintenance of orderly behavior is essential. Routine security and maintenance of order functions are handled by shelter staff; the most urgent matters are performed by local law enforcement personnel.

Fire Prevention

Overcrowded conditions and possible water shortages make fire a major safety threat. Although shelters have available the capabilities of local fire services, 24-hour fire watches should be established within the shelter.

Decontamination

In the event of a nuclear or other industrial accident necessitating evacuation, decontamination units may be established adjacent to or as a part of the shelter facility. Government authorities are responsible for designating shelter and decontamination sites and are responsible for the training and the assignment of monitoring personnel. The predisaster planning process is normally a coordinated effort between the companies involved, the government, the medical authorities, and the Red Cross. The shelter staff does not normally undertake decontamination procedures. In Red Cross shelters, the role of health services personnel is to supplement the community's existing health care delivery system. To this end, a course has been developed entitled ''Providing Red Cross Disaster Health Services in Radiation Accidents.'' See Chapter 7 for decontamination information.

RESPONSIBILITIES OF A SHELTER MANAGER

The shelter manager is responsible for the overall organization and management of the shelter. It is the manager's responsibility to coordinate all of the functions into a smoothly working operation. The successful manager is simultaneously an administrator, a supervisor, and a leader. As an administrator, the manager must obtain any supplies or skills not available within the shelter. Obviously, everything cannot be done by one person. As a supervisor, the manager must quickly delegate authority to assistants for operational functions. Because shelter occupants look to the manager for guidance and reassurance, functional supervisors need assistance and coordination of their efforts—all of which test leadership qualities.

The major functions, such as family services, have a higher level supervisor located at headquarters outside the shelter. Functional supervisors report to their headquarters supervisor on all technical matters related to the correctness of carrying out their functional responsibility and on policy decisions about technical matters. As a functional supervisor, the shelter manager is an administrator overseeing appropriate and timely delivery of services to the shelter occupants rather than deciding the policies of those services. The functional supervisor, however, reports to the shelter manager on administrative matters. This reporting includes such matters as hours, statistics, progress on the job, and problems with other functions in the shelter that cannot be resolved directly with other functional supervisors.

If a shelter management team has been preselected and trained, an organizational plan will normally be ready to activate. If, on the other hand, you are organizing as the shelter opens, concentrate on what is immediately needed. Develop the organization after activation.

Allocation of Space

Normally, a shelter manager collaborates with available functional supervisors in the development of a floor plan. No single model exists for allocation of space. The floor plan can vary according to the size and the shape of the shelter, the number of occupants, and their estimated length of stay. An additional consideration is whether the shelter will house centralized facilities such as a fixed feeding center, a temporary infirmary, or a decontamination unit.

The shelter manager's office and the administrative office should be centrally located. They should be easily identified by and available to shelter occupants, visitors, and staff. Normally, the registration desk and a message board are located near the main entrance. Health services must be accessible to shelter occupants and yet give privacy and be of adequate size to contain the necessary supplies. Family services require the same arrangement. If separate rooms are not available for these two functions, screens should be used to block them off.

The food service area will be determined by the cafeteria facility and its location. When a gymnasium or other large area is used for sleeping accommodations, attempt to separate the sleeping area from the activity areas, either by a barrier or by physical distance. This arrangement is especially important if shift-sleeping is used.

Space for recreational or religious activities should be allocated on the basis of the activities planned for available facilities such as an auditorium or classrooms and for outdoor sports and play areas. Storage areas are determined by the availability of rooms or closets that can be secured by lock and key.

If the shelter is to be used for a centralized activity such as a fixed feeding station, a temporary infirmary, or a decontamination site, special consideration must be given by the appropriate authorities to the traffic flow through the shelter. In addition to maintaining ''controlled access,'' separate such activities from other functions and clearly identify them.

Scheduling of Staff

The shelter manager is responsible for seeing that the needed number of shelter staff are available to operate the shelter and to provide services as required. This responsibility may be only an indirect one for certain functions—health services, for example—inasmuch as scheduling is done within these functions in consultation with the shelter manager.

Approximately 47 staff members are needed to operate a shelter on a 24-hour basis for 200 occupants (Table 9–1). Shelter occupants, who are usually capable of filling 85 percent of the jobs, are the primary source of staff. A volunteer coordinator should handle recruitment to fill designated positions. Should it

Table 9–1 Sample Staffing Pattern for a Mass-Care Shelter

Function/Title	Number
Administration	
Manager	1
Assistant manager	2
Clerical*	1
Security/safety*	3
Messengers and communications	3
Volunteer coordinator*	1
Transportation coordinator*	1
Reception/registrar*	3
Health services	
Physician (on call)	1
Nurse	3
Ancillary (first aid)*	3
Clerical*	1
Family services	
Supervisor	1
Interviewers	3
Food services	
Cook	1
Cook assistant*	3
Kitchen helper*	4
Food server*	3
Sleeping accommodations	
Supervisor*	1
Recreation	
Activity leader*	3
Building maintenance	
Supervisor	1
Janitor*	2
Supply	
Storekeeper*	1
Total	47

Notes: The sample is designed for a shelter containing 200 occupants and operating on a 24-hour basis. These figures vary and do not include such activities as fire or night watch. Many of the functions or activities form "teams" that work on a part-time basis.
  *Filled by shelter occupants.

Source: Adapted by permission of the American National Red Cross.

Registration records (Exhibit 9–1) must contain up-to-date and accurate information. These forms should include family name and given names, age, sex, marital status, predisaster address and telephone number, family members not located in the shelter, and medical information. Upon departure, a postdisaster become necessary to hire staff, the hiring should be coordinated with the head-quarters to which the shelter manager is responsible.

A 24-hour coverage is required in both the manager's office and the health services' nurse station. Specific hours are arranged for other functions, which are limited to daytime and early evening hours.

An excellent source of personnel and equipment support in many communities is the National Voluntary Organizations Active in Disaster (NVOAD).[6] NVOAD is composed of more than twenty organizations—most of them with religious affiliation—whose purpose is to foster more effective service to people affected by disaster. The local Red Cross chapter often coordinates these efforts. The Church of the Brethren, for example, has a disaster child-care program that can be used for shelters. Another example is the American Radio Relay League—radio amateurs who volunteer their services and the use of their privately owned communication equipment for use at shelters.

Consider establishing a shelter advisory council if it is anticipated that the shelter will be opened for a prolonged period. The council is a small, informally structured group composed of shelter occupants who serve as a barometer for the shelter manager.

Obtaining Supplies and Equipment

The shelter manager is responsible for establishing a system to control purchasing and distribution of supplies and equipment. The system can be either a centralized or a decentralized approach and is based on the size of the shelter and the estimated length of operation. Financial responsibility is of the utmost importance. On small operations, credit accounts may be established with local merchants. The Red Cross uses a "disbursing order" to purchase all supplies and equipment. The disbursing order is also used by family services and health services for any individual assistance to shelter occupants. On large operations, central purchasing is established, and the shelter manager requests delivery of needed items from that source.

Preparing Records and Reports

Systematic administrative procedures are necessary and important; they help control and account for both shelter occupants and supporting services. The shelter manager has direct responsibility for records and reports. Because accurate records assist in the preparation of required reports, all services and activities should establish shelter logs. The Red Cross uses standard forms for registration and all reports. However, if the forms are not readily available, information should be recorded on a note pad or in some other manner.

address and telephone number should be obtained. This form can be used for noting an occupant's location within the shelter and whether that person has volunteered to become a member of the staff.

Each day, the shelter manager must send a statistical report (Exhibit 9–2) to the headquarters to which the manager reports. This report contains the number of persons sheltered, the number of meals served, the number of persons provided medical treatment and any major problems encountered. It also includes the number of staff members operating the shelter. This report is usually transmitted first by telephone and subsequently by either mail or courier.

Other records may include time sheets for staff, lists of borrowed or rented equipment, and financial commitments. It is possible that headquarters may want to receive reports of financial commitments on a scheduled basis.

A Manager's Checklist

Upon officially being notified to open a shelter, the manager proceeds immediatley to the facility concerned. The first member of the shelter management team arriving at the shelter takes charge until succeeded by a more qualified member. The following is a Red Cross checklist of the functions the manager must fulfill:

- Establish and maintain communication with higher headquarters.
- Arrange for identification of the shelter and staff.
- Appoint assistants for functional responsibilities.
- Control entry and begin registration.
- Allocate space and begin organization.
- Establish emergency medical care and screening of incoming occupants.
- Establish procedures for security, safety, and fire regulations.
- Inventory available supplies and order needed supplies and equipment from higher headquarters.
- Arrange for the care of pets if required.
- Arrange for law enforcement and fire services protection.
- Establish daily schedules.
- Activate all functional teams and coordinate their activities.
- Recruit additional personnel as required.
- Establish appropriate relationships within the immediate community.
- Establish log and procedures for record keeping.

PROBLEMS AND CONFLICTS IN SHELTER LIVING

Universal Problems

Living in a mass shelter has been described as unsatisfactory at best. Strangers from widely different backgrounds and living standards are forced to live side-by-

Exhibit 9–1 Disaster Shelter Registration

American Red Cross

DISASTER SHELTER REGISTRATION

Family Last Name

Names	Age	Medical Problem • Killed • Injured • Hospitalized	Referred to Nurse
Man			
Woman (Include Maiden Name)			
Children in Home			
Family Member not in Shelter (Location if Known)			

SHELTER MASTER FILE

Shelter Location

Shelter Telephone No.   Date of Arrival

Predisaster Address and Telephone No.

I ☐ do, ☐ do not, authorize release of the above information concerning my whereabouts or general condition.

Signature

Date Left Shelter

Time Left Shelter

Postdisaster Address and Telephone Number

AMERICAN RED CROSS   FORM 5972 (5-79)

Source: Reprinted by permission of the American National Red Cross.

Exhibit 9–2 Disaster Mass-Care Activity Report

American Red Cross	DISASTER MASS CARE ACTIVITY REPORT

Prepare two copies. Retain one copy; forward original to Mass-Care officer.

D.R. Number _____ Report Number _____ Date of Report (COB) _____
Location _____ Telephone Number _____

Facility Type: ☐ Shelter ☐ Fixed Feeding ☐ Mobile Unit ☐ Other

Number Sheltered (If applicable)
Start of Day _____ End of Day _____ Net Loss _____ or Net Gain _____

Feeding: ☐ Fixed ☐ Mobile
Number of Meals: Breakfast _____ Lunch _____ Dinner _____ Snacks _____

Medical:
Number Sent Hospital _____ Number Provided Medical Treatment _____

Supply:
Attached copies of *Requisition for Supplies* (Form 253-B), *Supply Memorandum* (Form 2000-B), *Inventory of Nonexpendable Property* (Form 2349), and receiving documents.

Staffing:
Number of Paid Staff _____ Number of Volunteers _____

Major Problems, Remarks, or Comments (If additional space is needed, use reverse side of form)

Name and Title of Person in Charge		Signature of Person in Charge	

AMERICAN RED CROSS FORM 5975 (5-79)

Source: Reprinted by permission of the American National Red Cross.

side. Social behavior varies with each family. Many may be upset by the effects of the disaster, the disruption of living patterns, and the uncertainty of the future. Some may be worried about the safety of family members who are not with them and with whom they cannot make contact. A few may have been emotionally or psychologically disturbed before the disaster, and their problems may now be aggravated. All of this is compounded by the unfamiliar and restrictive nature of shelter living, the lack of privacy, the lack of sleep, and changes in eating habits.

The majority of shelter occupants successfully adjust to shelter living. Some, however, may be troublesome and demanding. It is, therefore, essential to establish basic rules and regulations for a shelter and to see that they are enforced. The manager must quickly gain control of the shelter to avoid all kinds of problems. In conjunction with local law enforcement, the manager must control personal behavior that is disruptive—use of alcohol and other drugs, sexual behavior, fighting, gambling, smoking, and the inappropriate use of supplies and equipment.

For those persons who suffer more prolonged and serious reactions to stress, psychological first aid should be the order of the day. The shelter is not expected to provide a total mental health program; however, effective management (information and direction); sympathetic, friendly interaction with others; and something useful to do can go a long way toward stabilizing the situation.

Perhaps the most common problem encountered is pets that accompany owners to the shelter. For health and safety considerations, pets must not be allowed in the same space with people (except for the dogs of the seeing and hearing impaired). Care of pets can usually be arranged with the humane society, animal rescue, and veterinarians. Because people consider pets part of the family, many refuse to become separated. Accordingly, if space permits, areas may be set aside or even constructed for pets. Many occupants may keep pets in the vehicles they used for evacuation. It is common practice for a family member to remain with the vehicle for security purposes because it contains the family's personal possessions.

Policy Problems

The shelter manager is not a policy maker; however, it would be a rare operation in which no policy problems arose. Consequently, the importance of formal training cannot be overemphasized. Even so, when in doubt, the shelter manager should always query the headquarters that provides supervision—a government agency, the Red Cross, or another voluntary organization. Policies vary. For example, in a government operated shelter, the manager is considered "an extension of local government."[2(p81)] The Red Cross, as another example, "accepts no financial donations in a shelter."[3(p10)] Persons who want to contribute are urged to send their contribution by check to the local Red Cross chapter. Always remember that advice, direction, and control are yours for the asking.

Potential Conflicts

Consciously or unconsciously, every thought, every opinion, and every decision made is based on beliefs, attitudes, and values. The United States has long been considered the melting pot of the world. Why should a shelter be any different? Religious beliefs and cultural beliefs and practices vary. To an already confusing world shelter life adds strange, overcrowded surroundings with an uncertain future. The entire management team must strive for a nonjudgmental attitude. A basic understanding of values clarification and some active listening can alleviate many potential conflicts.

THE ROLE OF THE NURSE IN A SHELTER

Because maintaining the good health of shelter occupants is vital to the successful operation of the shelter, the nurse becomes an integral member of the shelter management team. The nurse should participate in the decision-making process from the inception of the operation. All health services activities must be coordinated with those of the local health authorities and the medical community. These activities can be divided into the phases of assessment, planning, implementation, and evaluation.

Assessment

The nature and the extent of the disaster determine the activities of health services. These vary according to the potential or real health hazards, the number of injured and ill, the severity of the injuries and illnesses, the number of homeless, the age of the shelter inhabitants, and the health services that are available. A disaster, for example, that has destroyed or neutralized medical and health resources within the community can create far different needs than one that leaves those same resources unaffected.

With this in mind, space allocation is determined within the shelter. Adequate supplies must be on hand or must be obtained as quickly as possible. Quantities must be sufficient to sustain the early operation of the shelter until additional supplies can be obtained. Appendix 9-A lists the components of a sample shelter kit. Keep in mind the health services goals for the shelter:

- to provide emotional support
- to protect health
- to prevent disease
- to provide a temporary means of caring for people until families can resume normal living patterns

Planning

During the planning process, anticipate some of the most common problems encountered in shelters:

- chronically ill people dependent on continued specialized medication who either enter shelters without it or in very short supply
- normal or existing incidents of illness, including such chronic illnesses as diabetes and heart ailments
- the spread of communicable disease brought into the shelter or developed after the facility was opened
- emotional and physical reaction to stress

Medical supervision and plans for 24-hour continuous nursing coverage are essential. At least one registered nurse must be present during each duty period and is designated as the nurse in charge. The number and type of additional health services personnel depends upon the size of the shelter, the number and severity of illness and injuries, and special health conditions among shelter occupants. In situations involving a small number of shelter occupants with no health problems, telephone coverage is frequently arranged.

The procedures for handling the seriously ill or injured must be determined. What hospital or infirmary is to be used? Who will do the transporting? What are the lines of communication?

Arrangements must be made for requisitioning or purchasing supplies and must include plans for secure storage. Some equipment may have to be improvised, borrowed, or rented. The quantities of equipment and supplies needed are determined by the assessment of the situation.

Certain reports are required on a daily basis (e.g., the total number of ill and injured). Individual records are kept on all occupants receiving care (Exhibit 9–3). Patients who are referred or transferred to other health facilities should have accompanying documentation.

Implementation

As soon as the shelter opens, the screening of incoming occupants begins. Alert health services personnel for health problems requiring immediate attention, isolation, or transportation to other health care facilities.

Make regular sick call a part of the daily schedule, and establish a system for monitoring shelter health care problems. The nurse must work closely with the manager and other supervisors to maintain regular health services and the highest possible sanitary standards. The responsibilities of the nurse in charge appear almost endless. Appendix 9-B provides a sample Red Cross checklist.

Evaluation

The evaluation process is ongoing and takes place throughout the entire operation. Check progress through day-to-day interactions, one-to-one conferences,

Exhibit 9-3 Disaster Patient Record

FAMILY NAME	MAN'S FIRST NAME	WOMAN'S FIRST NAME	PREDISASTER ADDRESS AND PHONE	DR. NO.

| PATIENT'S NAME | RELATIONSHIP | AGE | SEX | | |

NAME AND ADDRESS OF FACILITY ☐ HOSP. ☐ SHELTER ☐ EM. AID STATION ☐ OTHER

DIAGNOSIS AND CONDITION (Include date and time information obtained)

HOSPITALIZED? ☐ YES ☐ NO	DATE ADMITTED	DATE DISCHARGED	PHYSICIAN'S NAME, ADDRESS, TELEPHONE NUMBER

HOSPITAL EMERGENCY ROOM | DATE TREATED & RELEASED | INSURANCE? ☐ YES ☐ NO |

REFER TO: ☐ 1475 ☐ 2063 ☐ PUBLIC HEALTH ☐ OTHER (Specify)

OTHER PERTINENT INFORMATION RELATED TO TREATMENT: PHYSICIAN'S ORDERS, CONTACTS, REFERRALS, ETC. (When recording treatment, include nature of complaint, action taken, date and signature. Continue on back of form).

AMERICAN RED CROSS FORM 2077 (Rev. 3-78)

PATIENT RECORD

Source: Reprinted by permission of the American National Red Cross.

and routine staff meetings. Compile a final evaluation from narrative reports, which are normally required of all supervisors, and from exit interviews as appropriate. The "lessons learned" form a basis for increasing effectiveness on future operations.

REFERENCES

1. *Disaster Services Regulations and Procedures Series,* ARC 3000-3099. Washington DC, American Red Cross, Revised May 1980.

2. *How to Manage Congregate Lodging Facilities and Fallout Shelters.* Federal Emergency Management Agency, 1981–728–877, p 81.

3. *Disaster Services Regulations and Procedures: Administrative Regulations,* ARC 3003. Washington, DC, American Red Cross. Revised January 1984, pp 4, 10.

4. *Disaster Services Regulations and Procedures: Shelter Management: A Guide for Trainers,* ARC 3074. Washington, DC, American Red Cross, August 1976, p 3.

5. *Statement of Understanding Between the Federal Emergency Management Agency and the American National Red Cross,* ARC 2267. Washington, DC, American Red Cross. Revised August 1983, paragraph L.

6. *National Voluntary Organizations Active in Disaster.* Washington DC, American Red Cross. Revised April 1982.

SUGGESTED READINGS

A Handbook for Local Governments, CPGI-6. Federal Emergency Management Agency, 1981.

California Earthquake Response Plan (Draft). Sacramento, Calif, State of California Office of Emergency Services, July 1983.

Church Response to U.S. Disaster. New Windsor, Md, Church World Services Domestic Disaster Office, July 1978.

County of San Diego Emergency Plan. San Diego, Unified San Diego County Emergency Service Organization, August 1983.

Guide for the Development of a Mass Care/Shelter Annex/Support Plan. Sacramento, Calif, State of California Office of Emergency Services, March 1979.

Nuclear Power Plant Emergency Response Plan. San Diego, Unified San Diego County Emergency Service Organization, December 1980.

Appendix 9-A

Disaster Shelter First Aid Kit

The following items comprise one Shelter First Aid Kit. Material should be assembled and prepacked in readily available cartons or container, clearly marked *FOR DISASTER EMERGENCY USE ONLY*. An annual verification inventory should be made and items subject to deterioration replaced.

Qty	*Equipment and Supply Items*
2 ea	apron/coverall (paper)
5 ea	bag, grocery or equal
5 ea	bag, large (plastic) waste
4 pkg	baggies, plastic with twist top
2 ea	emesis basin
1 ea	basin, hand-wash, plastic
2 ea	batteries, flashlight
1 ea	flashlight
6 ea	bed pads, disposable
1 ea	bed pan, plastic
2 ea	blankets, infant
1 set	bottles, infant (disposable)
12 ea	bottles, infant (w/nipples & covers)
1 ea	brush, bottle
2 ea	candles
1 ea	can-opener (beer)
25 ea	cups, drinking (hot/cold)
3 pkg	diapers, disposable (1) small, (1) large, (1) medium
1 ea	tongs, kitchen

---

[1]*Source:* San Diego/Imperial Counties Chapter, American National Red Cross.

1 ea	hot water bottle
2 pkg	Kleenex
2 pkg	matches, container or book
25 ea	newspapers, folded (optional)
4 ea	thermometers (universal w/notebook)
1 ea	water pitcher
1 ea	pail (optional)
12 ea	pins, safety, large
1 can	powder, scouring (Ajax or equal)
12 ea	sanitary napkins (individual pkg.)
1 pair	scissors (snub-nosed)
1 roll	tape, masking (1″)
4 ea	thermometers (universal w/disposable covers)
2 rolls	toilet tissue
1 roll	towels, paper
1 ea	tweezers
1 ea	stethoscope
1 ea	Sphygmomanometer

First Aid Supplies

2 ea	bandage, elastic 3″
2 ea	bandage, 2″ Kling
1 ea	bandage, 3″ Kling
2 ea	bandage, stocking
2 ea	bandage, triangular
100 ea	bandaids, or equal
10 ea	bandaids, butterfly, large & small
20 ea	blades, tongue (individual wrapped)
	cotton balls
3 ea	dressing, barrier (large)
100 ea	dressing, sterile (4 × 4)
100 ea	preps., alcohol
1 box	Q-Tips or equal
1 roll	tape, 2″, nonallergenic
1 roll	tape, 1″, nonallergenic
50 ea	towelettes (Wash-&-Dri or equal)
50 ea	towelettes (Green soap)
4 ea	disposable ice bag—cold pack
20 ea	eye pads
1 ea	liquid soap
4 ea	hot pack

Medication Items

1 btl	antacid (Mylanta)
1 btl	eye wash or saline, normal
1 pkg	antacid (Mylanta tablets)
1 pkg	sodium bicarbonate
1 tube	antibacterial (Neosporin)
1 btl	alcohol 70%, 8 oz.
1 btl	aspirin, gr V (100)
1 box	cornstarch
2 btl	kaolin w/pectin (Kaopectate)
8 cubes	sugar (or 8 pkg.)
1 btl	mouthwash
1 btl	oil of cloves
1 tube	petrolatum
1 btl	pediculocide
4 cans	Seven-up
1 btl	acetaminophen (Tylenol), 325 mg
500 mL	normal saline or salt (1 tsp. dissolved in 500 mL water)
1 btl	liquid Tylenol (infant)
1 btl	infant aspirin
1 box	salt
1 btl	vinegar
2 ea	fine-tooth comb
25 ea	individual medication cups

Administrative Supplies

25 ea	Disaster Log (NP-1836)
25 ea	Patient Nursing Log (NPW 821)
25 ea	Nursing Memorandum (Form 1475)
50 ea	Patient Record (Form 2077)
25 ea	Release of Confidential Information (Form 5854)
2 ea	Medical and Nursing Protocols-San Diego/Imperial Counties Chapter
1 ea	Health Services Regulations and Procedures (ARC 3050)
1 ea	Annex 5 (Medical-Health) San Diego County Emergency Plan
1 ea	ARC Visual ID Kit (S3-23)
1 pkg	pressure sensitive ID patches (320600)
1 ea	clipboards w/ruled pad
1 box	paper clips
1 box	rubber bands
1 ea	stapler w/staples
1 roll	transparent tape

12 ea	file folders
6 ea	pens (ball-point) and pencils
1 ea	shelter kit contents list
1 ea	25¢ taped to inside cover of kit (telephone)

Appendix 9-B

Checklist for the Nurse in Charge of Health Services at a Shelter

_____ See that all persons seeking care are received with warmth, understanding, and honest reassurance; are given prompt treatments; and fully comprehend instructions for continuing treatment.

_____ Arrange with the physician for initial and daily health checks.

_____ Establish nursing care priorities and plan for health supervision.

_____ Plan with shelter manager for adequate emergency communication and transportation.

_____ Plan for appropriate transfer of patients to regular care facilities as necessary.

_____ Plan for separation of persons from families with suspected communicable disease.

_____ Plan for and procure needed supplies in collaboration with shelter manager.

_____ Plan for area and staffing of first aid needs.

_____ Constantly evaluate potential health care needs, and organize schedules for continuing care.

_____ Review Red Cross medical and nursing protocols, special treatments, and general health needs with the physician in charge, visiting physicians, and nursing staff.

_____ Determine needs and arrange for secure storage and accountability for medications, medical equipment (syringes, needles), and records.

_____ Assign nurses and other health services personnel to appropriate duties, and provide on-the-job training and supervision.

Source: Adapted with permission from _Disaster Services Regulations and Procedures: Disaster Health Services,_ ARC 3050. Washington, DC, American National Red Cross, revised February 1976, p 33.

_____ Supervise the preparation and distribution of infant formulas; consult with the food service supervisor about modified diets for health or religious reasons.

_____ Advise the shelter manager about appropriate arrangements to care for pregnant women, infants and young children, the aged, the chronically ill, and persons with suspected communicable disease.

_____ Discuss social, medical, and nursing aspects of family problems with family services as appropriate.

_____ Plan with shelter manager for initial and periodic health inspection of the shelter, including sanitary inspection in accordance with local public health regulations.

_____ Provide nursing personnel and facilities when immunization of shelter occupants is initiated by the public health department.

_____ Keep shelter manager and nursing supervisor or director informed of medical, nursing, and health situations, activities, needs, and plans.

_____ Plan with shelter manager regarding coordination of participation by agencies in caring for victims in shelter (i.e., public health, mental health, human resources, and ministerial associations).

_____ Recommend and help plan for appropriate resources to meet the needs inherent in good mental health practice.

_____ Plan for appropriate Red Cross identification for health services personnel and the facility.

_____ Report at end of duty period to the relief nurse and arrange for regular reporting to the disaster health services officer or designee at headquarters.

_____ Establish and keep a log of disaster health services activities.

Chapter 10

Functioning in a Community Health Setting

Kathleen H. Switzer, R.N., M.S.

During a disaster response, many nurses must function outside the acute care arena. Nurses in a community health setting may make home visits to houses, tents, huts, and shelters, where they conduct health screening, prevention activities, and education programs among the disaster population. They may staff clinics and participate in such disaster operations as refugee camps and emergency child care centers.

The purpose of this chapter is to discuss the problems that nurses may encounter in the case of a serious disaster. Concepts and ideas applicable to diverse populations and disaster situations will be presented.

The most important community resource in a disaster is individual preparedness. Nurses should be ready to assume new and expanded responsibilities and to delegate tasks they would normally perform. So that nurses may teach and counsel others, they must be prepared personally as well as professionally.

Nurses in a community disaster will be expected to synthesize public health and community health nursing principles under the stress of crisis. They must apply their knowledge and expertise to unique and rapidly changing disaster situations. They also need planning, management, and leadership skills, clinical competence, and cooperative effort with other community workers.

In the United States, as in other highly developed countries, a sophisticated level of health care is enjoyed by the majority of the population. Basic public health concerns, such as food, water, sanitation, and associated diseases are not

NOTE: The author wishes to acknowledge the help of the following persons: Harry L. Gibbons, MD, Director, Salt Lake City-County Health Department, Salt Lake City, Utah; Adele P. Nelson, RN, MPH, Director, Office of Community Health Nurses and Division of Community Health Services, Utah State Department of Health, Salt Lake City, Utah; Theresa Overfield, RN, MPH, PhD, Associate Professor, College of Nursing, Brigham Young University, Provo, Utah; Mary E. Spitzer, RD, MS, Major, Chief Food Service, US Army Reserves, 328th General Hospital, Ft Douglas, Utah; and Howard G. Wilcox, MD, Chief of Staff, VA Medical Center, Spokane, Washington.

often addressed on a large scale. During a major disaster, nurses can expect the standard of living to be disrupted and issues of basic health concerns to increase in importance to the community. Useful knowledge for the community health nurse is available from developing countries, from countries relying heavily on international aid in a disaster, and from American disaster events. Current information with case examples from these experiences will be presented. Nurses can apply this information to their own situations.

This chapter is aimed primarily toward nurses actively practicing in a community health role. These nurses possess a variety of backgrounds and preparation; some may have advanced education and specialized training. Nurses sent into the disaster area may function as members of preventive medicine teams or relief programs. There they may be joined by those already working in community health positions.

To augment community nursing programs, volunteers may be recruited from the local population of inactive nurses. These nurses have different amounts of current expertise but often have valuable knowledge of the community and its members. The potential pool of nurses available for community disaster relief efforts include the following:

- industrial/occupational nurses
- school nurses
- public health nurses
- home health nurses
- clinic or ambulatory care nurses
- discharge planning nurses
- other community agency nurses
- local volunteer nurses
- nurses from state, federal, and international organizations

The diversity among nurses in the community setting makes it impossible to define a single clear-cut role or set of responsibilities. However, this diversity is an advantage when the multifaceted demands of a disaster must be met. Nurses should act within the scope of their own training and their individual positions and adopt a flexible approach to implementing nursing actions. They should adjust their interventions to suit the situation and the organizational climate within which they are working.

NURSING ACTIONS

The achievement of the best possible level of health care for persons in a community affected by a disaster requires a variety of nursing actions:

- casefinding and referring
- providing direct care
- assessing and evaluating
- problem solving
- organizing and coordinating
- teaching and consulting

Because a nurse sometimes works alone in a community setting, no other health provider may be present during a crisis. Thus, nursing actions may be initiated and carried out independently; however, these interventions should always be part of a team approach.

Nurses should collaborate among themselves and form a mutual support network with those having the needed skills and specialties. Nurses volunteering their work should attach themselves to organizations having assigned responsibilities. These groups are discussed in more detail in Chapter 13.

Plans and interventions should be consistent with the overall disaster plan and the actions of other health care team members. Nurses may need to actively seek out the expertise and the participation of other providers in order to promote a multidisciplinary team approach.

Nursing actions in a community setting should reflect changing disaster needs and should be aimed at prevention, either primary, secondary, or tertiary (Figure 10–1). *Primary* prevention is the reduction in the probability of disease, death, and disability resulting from a disaster. *Secondary* prevention is the prompt identification of disaster problems and the implementation of measures to treat and to prevent their recurrence or complications. *Tertiary* prevention is rehabilitation, in order to restore the community and its population to predisaster status and to mitigate long term disability.

Natural disasters create a predictable sequence of problems throughout the various disaster stages, although these problems are modified by the type and severity of the event. Figures 10–2 and 10–3 illustrate the changing sequence of disaster needs that follow earthquakes and floods or sea surges. Each problem area must be addressed through specific team actions and prevention measures. For example, management of mass casualties is an immediate need during the first 2 or 3 days following an earthquake. By contrast, in a flooding disaster, evacuation of the population into temporary shelters assumes priority.

Primary Prevention

Primary prevention begins before a disaster occurs. It encompasses all aspects of planning for health care delivery and preparation for basic living activities under disaster conditions. Primary prevention considers potential safety hazards and

Figure 10–1 Cycle of Preventive Action in a Disaster

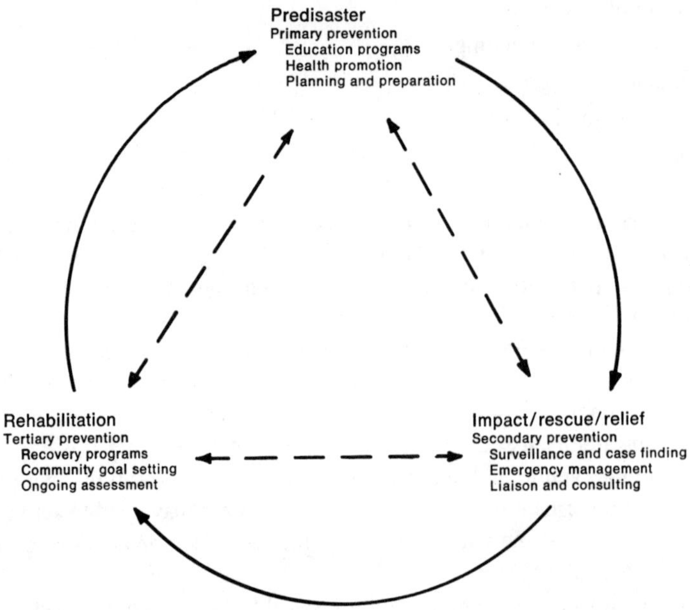

aims to reduce unsafe environmental conditions. For example, alternative food and water sources should be designated for use if usual supplies become contaminated or inaccessible.

Health promotion programs can be designed to encourage self-help measures, such as home storage of food and water and first aid training. Specific interventions, such as prevention of childhood diseases and provision of nutrition supplements to the disadvantaged, should help to keep community health levels high and to prevent some potential health hazards of a disaster.

Community social programs are important, because people enjoying a high level of emotional health have more resiliency in dealing with the crises generated by disasters. Communities are better able to adjust to new demands and difficulties if they have achieved stability and have provided their members with adequate physical and social supports.[1]

Primary prevention also reduces peoples' vulnerability by increasing their ability to respond to a disaster. Communities whose population has a heightened awareness of disaster possibilities are able to respond quickly and productively.

Secondary Prevention

Secondary prevention measures become important during the impact, rescue, and relief stages of a disaster. Because the acute care facilities may be overloaded

Figure 10–2 Earthquakes: Changing Disaster Needs

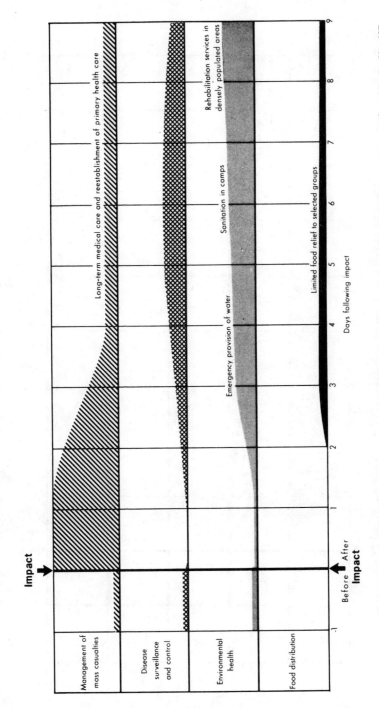

Source: Reprinted with permission from *Emergency Health Management After Natural Disaster*, Pan American Health Organization scientific publication No. 407. Washington, DC, World Health Organization, 1981, p 15.

Figure 10–3 Floods and Sea Surges: Changing Disaster Needs

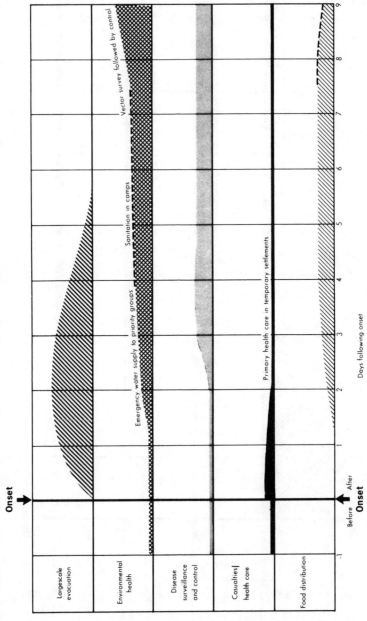

Source: Reprinted with permission from *Emergency Health Management After Natural Disaster*, Pan American Health Organization scientific publication no. 407, Washington, DC, World Health Organization, 1981, p 16.

with casualties, nurses in the community may organize and oversee nursing care for sick and injured persons at home or in shelters. These nurses may assume teaching and consulting roles, while volunteers and family members perform home health nursing activities.

Nurses should establish a liaison with acute care institutions for mutual consultation and problem solving. These arrangements can facilitate admission for acute cases and help ensure that those with early hospital discharges have adequate nursing care continued in the community.

Local resources may be supplemented by assistance from outside organizations and agencies. Casefinding and large scale screening for specific diseases and conditions need to be carried out. Follow-up programs need to be established to prevent complications and the recurrence of identified problems, and additional primary prevention measures need to be implemented. In many instances, existing programs for disease surveillance and sanitation must be immediately expanded.

Tertiary Prevention

Tertiary prevention is important during the recovery phase of a disaster, but the groundwork has been laid much earlier. Disaster planning and rescue efforts should be carried out with the long-term goal of restoring predisaster functioning. For example, when selecting refugee camp sites, workers should remember that evacuees sheltered far from their destroyed homes are less likely to return when the disaster is over. Therefore, establishing a camp site as close to the original community as possible encourages rebuilding and helps preserve community ties.

Exhibit 10–1 Case Example

In 1975, Vietnamese war refugees were relocated into several camps for eventual resettlement into other countries. This relief effort combined resources of all branches of the US military services and used voluntary organizations such as the Red Cross as well.[2,3]

On Guam, more than 86,000 refugees were given temporary food, shelter, recreation, and medical care as part of "Operation New Life." They were housed in a camp consisting of a hastily repaired World War II hospital annex and 3,275 tents. Many health services were offered, especially convalescent and general medical care, physical examinations, and public health programs. Health screening procedures, immunization programs for young children, and baby supply centers were established.[2,3,4]

Army community health nurses worked with the Vietnamese population. As one of their responsibilities, these nurses screened infants for signs of dehydration that might have occurred secondary to the heat, change in dietary habits, and possible diarrhea. Infants needing fluid replacement were referred to the hospital for care. Meanwhile, the nurses encouraged mothers to provide adequate formula, juice, and water for their infants and conducted teaching on the importance of these and other health measures.

Programs that were temporarily reduced during the crisis period need to be rejuvenated and restructured during the recovery stage. Some services are instrumental in assisting communities and individuals during the restorative process:

- nutrition counseling
- well child health care
- prenatal and postnatal health care
- chronic disease care
- communicable disease prevention
- routine health screening
- mental health counseling

Nurses may note signs that rehabilitation is not taking place. This type of casefinding is significant, and an epidemiological study may be needed to identify the continuing needs of community members. The long-term health effects of a disaster may vary according to the situation. Nevertheless, nurses will undoubtedly be dealing with the effects of the disaster and the prevention of long-term sequelae for some time afterwards.

Nurses remaining in the community after a disaster have the satisfaction of having followed the population toward normalcy. Schools, industries, and clinics will begin to reopen. Nurses should be involved with tertiary prevention activities and the reestablishment of their roles in a gradually normalizing environment. Primary prevention activities should assume new importance as nurses assist in revising plans for the next possible disaster and conducting disaster teaching programs.

ASSESSING HEALTH NEEDS

Nurses may be instrumental in determining health needs during all stages of a disaster. In addition to assessing the health status of individuals, nurses should participate in general community assessment and specific surveys or surveillance. They need reliable information to identify needs, formulate plans, and to assign resources.

General Community Assessments

Community assessments are used to give an overview of a community and to place problems into a broad context. Information from community assessments is usually multidisciplinary and is used by a variety of organizations and professional workers. Many groups outside the disaster area, such as government agencies or large voluntary organizations, require formal reports before providing assistance. Decisions about nursing services and programs are often based upon community assessments. These assessments are used in several stages of a disaster and include the predisaster preparation, emergency response, and recovery process.

Predisaster Assessments

Predisaster assessment should include an inventory of existing medical and social resources, an estimate of the community's vulnerability to disaster, and an examination of options to meet the potential health needs. During the emergency stages of a disaster, this predisaster information often provides the basis for an immediate response. Moreover, this preparation can be especially important when the disaster area has poorly developed communication systems or when these systems have been severely disrupted. Assessing and using community resources in disaster planning is discussed in detail in Chapter 13.

Emergency Assessments

After a severe disaster, an initial rapid assessment is usually performed by aerial survey. The military is often responsible for conducting this initial assessment. Their reports can be used by other outside resources for mobilization of relief activities.[5]

The more detailed multidisciplinary assessment that usually follows uses mobile survey teams. The collection of this information is extremely important to an effective disaster response. Adequate personnel and transportation, such as helicopters, need to be designated as teams for this purpose. The most qualified health professionals available should be assigned to these teams, inasmuch as their findings can determine major relief plans. Nurses who function on survey teams may experience conflict between their survey responsibilities and their desire to provide clinical assistance to disaster victims. They should be instructed to remain with their primary assignments unless their help becomes absolutely necessary.[5]

Information from these assessments can be used to determine health needs and to establish requirements for medical supplies, equipment, and personnel. Health programs and plans for distribution of resources should be based upon the data that are collected and reported.

Nurses may not have time to perform complete assessments during the emergency stages of a disaster. However, preexisting data on a community that experiences a disaster can be helpful. Nurses from outside the community should review information on community characteristics and on initial disaster reports. Information they may want to obtain includes the following:

- geographical extent of disaster area
- number of people affected

- major preexisting problems
- status of housing and shelter
- location and condition of health facilities
- condition and extent of water supply
- extent and distribution of food resources
- community morale and level of activity
- relief projects in progress

Nurses working with refugees or displaced persons should find it helpful to obtain information on the parent country or culture, as well as on the current living situation. Maps, demographic statistics, and the names and telephone numbers of key persons who might serve as consultants or contact points would be useful.

Ongoing Assessments

Interim assessments can be gradually supplemented during relief efforts or during the recovery process. Data collected should reveal the effects of a disaster on health, socioeconomic status, and cultural conditions. The findings should encourage teamwork and suggest multidisciplinary strategies for change.

Nurses may use a number of methods for collecting data:

- interview
- observation
- physical examination
- health and illness screening
- surveys (sample and special health)
- records (census, school, vital statistics, and disease reporting)

Nurses involved with community planning during the recovery stage will find a full assessment necessary to redesign and to refocus nursing services around changing community needs. An example of a nursing community assessment is listed in Appendix 10–A at the end of this chapter.

Specific Surveillance and Surveys

Technical surveys of specific problems must be conducted after a disaster. These surveys are especially important during the emergency stages and may continue until recovery is well under way. The study of health problems is usually performed as epidemiologic surveillance and can be used to determine the following:[6]

- number and proportion of injuries
- number and proportion of deaths
- incidence of communicable diseases
- incidence of mental health disorders
- inventory of remaining health facilities
- inventory of medical supplies

Because public anxiety and rumors can be expected, some selectivity is necessary in conducting surveillance. Priority should be given to high density populations, relocated populations, and deteriorating quality of life. Information about urban populations in which services have been severely affected, urban populations relocated into a rural area with few existing services, and rural populations newly congregated in camps or shelters should be included. Sparsely populated rural areas in which quality of life has deteriorated the least should have lesser priority.

A decision to initiate a specific surveillance investigation may be based upon casefinding, compilation of reports, and selective follow-up of rumors. An effort should be made to collect data systematically, even under disaster conditions. Reports should be submitted daily during the emergency stages of a disaster and weekly after the community has stabilized, until the potential risk of disease outbreak has passed.

Exhibit 10–2 Case Example

During earthquake disaster relief in Guatemala in 1976, epidemiologists from official agencies initiated a surveillance system for collecting, analyzing, and disseminating medical information. Six Peace Corps volunteer RNs made daily visits to selected hospitals, clinics, and public health centers located in the zone of greatest population and destruction. They collected specific information from the registration forms routinely used at these facilities, including age, sex, address, and diagnosis. Information on available acute care beds and new admissions was also compiled daily.[7]

Distribution of diseases was compared to information available from previous years and to reported diseases from unaffected areas. Over 30 reported epidemics were investigated. No increase in any disease was noted, despite persistent and rampant rumors. An increase in dog bites was documented the second week following the earthquake, and a program was successfully implemented to vaccinate dogs and to eliminate strays.[7]

More than 23,000 deaths and 77,000 injuries were caused by the earthquake and its aftermath. Over 20 percent of the population was left homeless. Information from epidemiological surveillance documented the course of medical needs. This information was used to guide key public health decisions about the use of resources, including deployment and planning for mobile health facilities and the distribution of vaccines and medical supplies.[7]

Nurses may participate in collecting data or preparing reports; they may assist in organizing the data collection process in situations that are otherwise chaotic and stressful. The observations of nurses may be important in interpreting data. Nurses should watch for situations that might affect the accuracy of the data or explain the findings, and they should document this information when preparing their reports.

The casefinding that nurses routinely perform in a community setting may be important in identifying the existence of specific cases that then become the basis for surveillance. Awareness of chance findings may uncover important health needs. The discovery of one case of a specific illness may indicate the existence of a widespread problem; further inquiry should then be made to see if other cases are occurring. The latest edition of *Control of Communicable Diseases in Man*, listed as a suggested reading at the end of this chapter, can be invaluable to nurses in performing this activity.

MAJOR HEALTH CONCERNS

Disasters create health concerns by disrupting the environmental standards of living. In addition to deaths and injuries, disasters may create conditions that increase the risk of illness and disease:

- overcrowding of the population
- decreased personal hygiene and sanitation
- increased personal injuries and malnutrition
- contamination of food and water
- disruption of public health services

Preexisting health levels often determine the occurrence of specific problems. However, the type, the severity, and the duration of a disaster also serve to modify the exacerbation of health problems. For example, earthquakes are likely to cause many deaths and overwhelming numbers of severe injuries requiring care, but they rarely create major population movements or disruption of food supplies. Conversely, food scarcity and evacuation of the population are common in floods, but there are usually few deaths and injuries.[5]

The longer any disaster disrupts a community and prevents recovery from taking place, the more cumulative disaster effects and health problems are likely to occur. Possible health effects of natural disasters are outlined in Table 10–1.

The specific health concerns that should receive attention during disaster relief operations are those that most disrupt community services and standards of public health. These services include water, food, sanitation, and care of the sick and injured.

Table 10–1 Health Effects Following Natural Disaster

Service	Most Common Effects on Environmental Health	Earth-quake	Hurricane/ Tornado	Flood	Tsuna-mis
Water supply and waste water disposal	Damage to civil engineering structures	●	●	●	○
	Broken mains	●	◐	◐	○
	Power outages	●	●	◐	◐
	Contamination (biological or chemical)	◐	●	●	●
	Transportation failure	●	●	●	◐
	Personnel shortages	●	◐	◐	○
	System overloading (due to shifts in population)	◐	●	●	○
	Equipment, parts, & supply shortages	●	●	●	◐
Solid waste handling	Damage to civil engineering structures	●	◐	◐	○
	Transportation failures	●	●	●	◐
	Equipment shortages	●	●	●	◐
	Personnel shortages	●	●	●	○
	Water, soil, and air pollution	●	●	●	○
Food handling	Damage to food preparation facilities	●	●	◐	○
	Transportation failure	●	●	●	◐
	Power outages	●	●	◐	◐
	Flooding of facilities	○	●	●	●
	Contamination/degradation of relief supplies	◐	●	●	◐
Vector control	Proliferation of vector breeding sites	●	●	●	●
	Increase in human–vector contacts	●	●	●	◐
	Disruption of vector-borne disease control programs	●	●	●	●
Home sanitation	Destruction or damage to structures	●	●	●	●
	Contamination of water and food	◐	◐	●	◐
	Disruption of power, heat fuel, water supply waste disposal services	●	●	●	◐
	Overcrowding	○	○	○	○

● Severe possible effect
◐ Less severe possible effect
○ Least or no possible effect

Source: Reprinted with permission from *Environmental Health Management After Natural Disasters*, scientific publication no. 430. Washington, DC, Pan American Health Organization, 1982, p 5.

Nurses can help community members prepare for home management of a disaster situation. Storage of food, water, and supplies all are parts of home preparation.

Water Conditions

For home preparation, water can be stored in either glass or plastic containers. Glass containers are resistant to permeable vapors and the leaching of chemicals into the water, but they are heavy and breakable. Plastic containers are easier to handle, but care should be used in selecting them. Any plastic containers that have been made for other purposes—ammonia bottles and plastic trash containers— should not be used to store water. Plastic containers that have been specially made to store water can be purchased. These should have been approved for food contact by the federal Food and Drug Administration.[8]

Stored water should be taken from the normal drinking supply. If it is to be stored for long periods of time, it should also be chemically disinfected first. Containers of water should be stored under the following conditions:[8]

- with a tight-fitting lid
- labeled with date and method of disinfection
- away from sunlight
- away from toxic substances (gasoline, kerosene, and pesticides)

During a disaster, uses for water will be expanded to mitigate disaster effects. Some of these increased demands are for activities such as the following:

- Industrial operations (heavy equipment use and emergency construction)
- Safety procedures (fire fighting)
- Decontamination operations (chemical and radiological procedures)

The community population will need a water supply in order to carry on the activities of daily living. This use includes water to drink and for domestic activities—cooking, preparing formula, bathing, laundering, and cleaning.

Because drinking is the most important use for water, the quality of drinking water is measured in terms of potability and palatability. *Palatable* water is water that is pleasing to the taste, but it may be contaminated by disease-causing organisms, toxic chemicals, radioactive material, or high amounts of organic matter. *Potable* water is water that is safe to drink and free from contamination. Some water cannot be used for drinking or food preparation because of poor palatability or low potability, but it can still be used for bathing or laundering or for other procedures requiring water.

Water Sources

The disruption of a normal water supply system necessitates the use of all available water sources. In addition to stored water, some emergency sources of home drinking water are usually considered safe:

- prefilled bathtubs and containers
- melted ice cubes
- liquid packed canned goods
- soft drinks and beer
- water heaters
- toilet tanks (not bowls)

The safety of water from prefilled tubs and containers, water heaters, and toilet tanks depends on that supply having been obtained before contamination. Running faucets or flushing toilets can introduce contamination from the main water supply. Water lines that are equipped with turnoff valves at their entrance to the house should be promptly turned off at the onset of a disaster to prevent contamination of water already in the house water system.

Waterbeds are not an acceptable water source because the plastic and the water usually contain pesticides to prevent the growth of algae, fungi, and bacteria.[8]

Some major water sources can often be made potable after testing and disinfection. They include the following:

- collected rain water
- melted snow and ice
- wells and springs
- lakes, rivers, and streams

Water from swimming pools also may be used if it has not been heavily treated to prevent the growth of algae. Industries such as ice plants, dairies, breweries, and food processing plants often have their own water sources and wells. Water from these sources may remain potable after the main water supply in a community has been damaged, and they represent an often overlooked supply of emergency water.

Water needs

When water is in short supply, all nonessential use—even bathing and laundering—should be curtailed in an effort to maintain an adequate supply of drinking water. The importance of keeping persons well hydrated under physical and environmental stress cannot be emphasized enough.

Adults can survive about 60 days without food, but few can live as long as 10 days without water. The adult body contains about 40 liters (42 qt) of water, and the absolute daily requirement for survival is about 1 liter (1 qt) per person.[9] Dehydration has serious effects on the body. For example, loss of about 2 liters (2 qt) leads to discomfort and inefficiency; loss of about 4 liters (4 qt) results in physical and mental disability; and loss of about 8 liters (8.5 qt) is fatal.[9]

The amount of water needed by an individual varies with the situation and is affected by a number of factors:

- body temperature
- amount of perspiration
- body size
- degree of activity
- fluid loss from illness

Extreme climates—hot or cold—create additional requirements for water. In very hot climates, body fluid losses from perspiration require large quantities of water for replacement. In severe cold climates, the person may not be aware of fluid loss because perspiration is quickly evaporated into the cold air or is absorbed into heavy clothing. In addition, personal hygiene in extreme climates requires more water.[10]

A special effort should be made to keep infants and the ill well hydrated. Because the body weight of infants contains a high percentage of water, much of it stored in tissue spaces outside the cells, infants are usually prone to dehydration. Treatment of conditions such as diarrhea and burns demands replacement of body fluids, proteins, and calories.

For a healthy population living under stringent conditions, 4 liters (1gal) of drinking water per person per day and an equal amount for personal use should be allowed for minimum planning purposes. Table 10–2 gives a more detailed estimate of water requirements under various environmental situations.

Water Disinfection and Sterilization

Because diseases such as typhoid, cholera, and dysentery can potentially be passed to humans by drinking water, nurses should understand the basic principles of ensuring a safe water supply and should be alert to possible disease cases. Remarkably few outbreaks of waterborne disease have been reported,[11] although some exceptions have been noted, such as the increase in giardiasis after the Utah flooding in 1983.

Table 10–2 Estimated Individual Daily Requirements for Water

Conditions of Use	Temperature/Cold Climate		Desert/Jungle Climate		Remarks
Activity Level:					
Minimum to normal	0.5–2 gal	2–7.5 L	2–3 gal	7.5–11 L	For eating and drinking periods not to exceed 3 days
	2 gal	7.5 L	3–4 gal	11–15 L	When dry rations are used
Normal to strenuous	3 gal	11 L	6 gal	23 L	Drinking plus small amount for cooking and personal hygiene
Living Arrangement:					
Temporary camp	5 gal	19 L	5+ gal	19+ L	Desirable for all purposes except bathing
Temporary camp with bathing facilities	15 gal	57 L	15+ gal	57 L	Includes allowance for waterborne sewage system

Source: Military Water Supply, Correspondence Course 160. Fort Sam Houston, Tex, Academy of Health Sciences, US Army, April 1981, pp 1–3; *Field Sanitation Team Training,* TC 8–3. US Dept of the Army, September 1978, pp 2–3.

In a major disaster, all free-flowing water sources should be considered contaminated until water testing has determined potability. There is no known safe method for decontaminating water containing toxic chemicals or radioactive materials but heat sterilization or chemical disinfection can make drinking water safe from most disease-producing organisms.

Heat sterilization. Water sterilization by boiling is the preferred method of treating drinking water whenever possible because most disease-producing organisms are killed at boiling temperatures. This method is especially desirable when the water is cloudy.

To heat-sterilize water, disaster victims should receive the following instructions:[8]

- Heat water to boiling and hold in a vigorous, rolling boil for 5 minutes.
- Use water for drinking after cooling. (Do not use ice to cool.)
- To improve taste, pour the boiled, cooled water back and forth several times to aerate.

Chemical disinfection. Disinfection of water supplies is an acceptable alternative if boiling is not possible and the water is clear, although this procedure may not kill all types of organisms. Particulate matter in cloudy water may shield organisms from the action of chemicals; therefore, sediment and cloudiness should be removed before chemical disinfection. Coffee filters, several layers of clean cloth, or a capillary siphon can be used to remove particulate matter or cloudiness.[8] Constructing and using a capillary filter is described in Figure 10–4.

Clear water can be chemically disinfected for drinking by using liquid bleach, iodine tablets, or halazone. All products should be fresh, because they tend to lose their strength over time. If bleach is more than 1 year old, it should be added in double the recommended amounts; if it is more than 2 years old, it should not be used for disinfection purposes.[8] Iodine tablets have a shelf life of 3 to 5 years and are gray when fresh. Halazone tablets have a shelf life of about 2 years, have an expiration label, and turn yellow if they have decomposed.

Iodine and halazone are commonly used for disinfection and can be easily purchased at sporting goods stores or drug stores. They come packaged with instruction for use. Liquid bleach, such as Clorox or Purex, can be used for home treatment of water. People should be instructed to use 16 drops of liquid bleach to 4 liters (1 gal) of water, or 1 teaspoon to each 19 liters (5 gal) of water. The treated water should be mixed thoroughly and allowed to stand for at least 30 minutes before using.[8]

Figure 10–4 Steps in Constructing and Using a Capillary Siphon

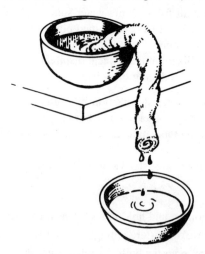

Notes: Make a long roll from a small, clean, terry-cloth towel. Place one end of the roll into a container of cloudy water, and drape the rest of the roll over the side of the container of cloudy water, hanging free. (The free end should hang lower than the water level in the container.) Place a clean container below the free-hanging end of the towel, and permit the water to drip from the end of the towel into the lower container. Particles causing cloudiness are left behind in the upper container and towel. Proceed with chemical disinfection.

Source: Emergency Water: Home Storage and Emergency Disinfection. Salt Lake City, Utah State Department of Health, Division of Environmental Health, May 1982.

Devices sold as water purifiers cannot be trusted to decontaminate water. They are intended for use with water that is already potable and should not be relied upon to provide safe drinking water during a disaster emergency.

Team Members

Environmental engineers and sanitarians are concerned with technical aspects of water sampling and treating. Microbiologists deal with laboratory identification of waterborne organisms. Nurses in the community have a role in instructing groups of people in water use and disinfection methods during a disaster and in determining individual needs to avoid dehydration. Besides, nurses may be in a position to perform casefinding and to report suspected diseases from contaminated water to medical authorities.

Cultural Considerations

In some developing countries, usual water sources may have levels of contamination from organisms that would be considered unacceptable in the western world. The surviving population in these countries have usually adjusted to the decreased potability of their water supply and appear to have some resistance to the expected waterborne diseases. In such situations, the level of water quality does not need to be increased over usual levels. In fact, the addition of disinfecting materials such as chlorine may create gastrointestinal upsets in groups not accustomed to treated water.

If water disinfection or sterilization methods become necessary, the local population may resist using them. In these situations, it is wise to work with local leaders and delegate the actual teaching to them. If a water source must be condemned, consider the use of food coloring to mark it. Otherwise, the population may continue using it, especially where a low educational level or a language barrier exists. However, community workers from outside the local area must have a high quality water source, inasmuch as they are likely to be susceptible to diseases not previously encountered.

Food Concerns

Problems associated with food may be encountered in a disaster. Scarcity and distribution; nutritional adequacy; sanitary handling, storage and processing; and cultural acceptability are some of the problems.

Home storage of food can be very important for disaster preparation. Certain foods are especially suitable for home emergency stores:

- ready-to-eat foodstuffs
- canned meats
- canned and dried fruits
- canned and dried vegetables
- peanut butter
- powdered and canned milk
- canned juices
- soups and crackers

Especially needed food items such as infant foods or special diet supplies should also be stored. Disposable plates and silverware, as well as utility knives and can openers, should be included. Foods should be in unbreakable containers.

Additional references and resources for nurses to use in assisting community members in preparing food for emergency storage can be found at the end of this chapter.

Scarcity

Scarcity of food supplies may result from flooding and tidal waves when farms and food stores are under water. Temporary shortages because of distribution problems may be experienced in any type of disaster. Groups that may be primarily affected by artificial shortages include the following:

- victims isolated in the disaster
- rescue workers without support
- institutions suddenly overloaded

Populations that have preexisting levels of hunger and nutritional disease may be especially affected by the destruction of fields and food stores and the disruption of transportation. If relief efforts cannot reverse the disaster damage, famine may be the long-term result.

The nutritional effects of a disaster can be mitigated by the maintenance of an adequate system of food distribution. Food distribution agencies are listed in Appendixes 13-A, B, and C. To provide adequate daily food supplies and to forecast future needs, however, these organizations need the following information:

- a census
- the percent of ill, elderly, women, and children
- the possible duration of the disaster

In refugee camps or evacuation centers, meal preparation areas or field kitchens can be established to prepare meals from all types of foods that may be available, to prepare meals for those who cannot cook for themselves, and to provide purposeful work for victims. In many situations, displaced families can cook their own food from local food sources or distributed goods. In such instances, special centers can be set up to provide formula and food supplements to pregnant mothers, infants, and those with special nutritional needs.

Nutritional Needs

Nurses should not be overly concerned with nutritional balance during the early stages of a disaster. In a 1983 flood in Utah, large quantities of donated foods arrived at designated shelters for those evacuated from their homes. These foods were largely high calorie items such as doughnuts, soft drinks, and fast foods. Although these foods do not fit the nutritional ideal, they were easy to transport, were readily accepted, and provided needed energy requirements.

During the first few weeks of a disaster, the main nutritional need is for calories, because calories are of primary importance in providing energy and in restoring body tissue composition.[12] Nurses should be able to teach others to recognize the available sources of calories in fats, carbohydrates, and proteins and to encourage their intake. Nurses may need to estimate the individual caloric needs required to sustain body weight in adults and to promote growth in infants and children.

Several rule-of-thumb formulas are available for use in quickly estimating average daily caloric needs. Infants between birth and 6 months of age require an average of 115 calories per kilogram (52 calories/lb); between 6 months and 1 year, 105 calories per kilogram (48 calories/lb). Breast milk or properly mixed formula usually supplies the necessary calories and nutrients for infants. Children up to age 19 require approximately 1000 calories, plus 100 calories for each year of life, on a daily basis.[13] As shown in Exhibit 10–3, caloric needs for adult men and women can be estimated by calculating the ideal weight from actual height.

Adjustments need to be made for activity levels. A sedentary adult male may require about 2000 to 2500 calories per day, while one doing light work may use an additional 500 calories. Men performing heavy work in a disaster, such as clearing rubble by hand, may need 4000 calories or more per day.[9]

Because emergency stored rations used in some disasters may be monotonous and unpalatable, strong encouragement may be needed to persuade people to consume enough to meet their caloric requirements.[14] Family members or others can be solicited to monitor the dietary intake of some persons to ensure that they consume enough calories.

When caloric intake falls below starvation rations, stored protein is used as an energy source. As body tissues are depleted, fat reserves disappear and muscles become visibly wasted.[9] Tissue maintenance demands calories; therefore, foods rich in protein should provide about 16 percent of the caloric intake.[15]

The typical North American or Western European diet provides more than an adequate number of calories from protein sources. For example, one slice of bread and one teaspoon of margarine equals about 2 grams of protein and approximately 115 calories. This one food item provides about half the protein requirement in a 1500-calorie food allowance.

Certain groups of people have an increased need for protein and calorie requirements. Community nurses should consider the following target populations:

- nonhospitalized sick and injured
- infants and growing children
- pregnant women and nursing mothers

Gastrointestinal upsets are commonly reported after a disaster. Nurses should consider maintenance of adequate protein and calorie intake as one primary prevention measure for diarrhea because there is evidence that diarrhea can be caused by inadequate intake of calories and protein.[15] Moreover, both nutritional requirements and nutritional losses can be increased by the stress of injury, infection, and illness.[15] The resulting diarrhea can cause further nutritional loss

---

Exhibit 10–3 Estimating Adult Daily Caloric Requirements

First, determine ideal weight from actual height:

Medium Frame: Allow *kg (lb)/first 152 cm (60 in)* plus *kg (lb)/additional cm (in)*

Female	45.5 kg (100 lbs)	2 kg (5 lbs)
Male	48 kg (106 lbs)	3 kg (6 lbs)

Small Frame: subtract 10%

Large Frame: add 10%

Then, estimate caloric needs:

calories/unit of weight
25–30 calories/kg (11–14 calories/lb)

For example:

Medium frame female 60 in tall = 120 lb ideal weight
120 × 11 = 1,320 calories estimated minimum daily requirement

Source: Zeman FJ: *Clinical Nutrition and Dietetics.* Lexington, Mass; DC Heath and Co, Collamore Press, 1983, p 1; Halpern SL (ed): *Quick Reference to Clinical Nutrition.* Philadelphia, JB Lippincott Co, 1979, p 296.

and dehydration. The effects of malnutrition and a suggested measure for diarrhea are outlined later in this chapter.

Infant feeding presents a special problem in a disaster. Existing stores of emergency rations may not be suitable for infants. The physical growth and development of the very young is susceptible to nutritional influences. Breast feeding of infants should be encouraged if at all possible. Breast milk, in addition to its nutritional advantages, also provides some protection against infectious diseases and does not require sanitizing. Pregnant women and nursing mothers need to receive additional rations and protein-calorie rich foods.

Vitamins and minerals are not primary nutritional concerns during the emergency stages of a disaster. Multiple vitamins can be used if they are available. However, persons who are well nourished before a disaster can usually maintain their nutritional status for several months with relatively few effects, even with a diet that is poor in vitamins and minerals.[12] Populations that have preexisting vitamin deficiencies need therapeutic doses of specific nutrients. These special needs can be predicted and calculated if the population's diet has been analyzed during predisaster planning.

Nutrition Assessment

A poorly nourished population is more susceptible then a well-nourished one to disease and the long-term effects of a severe disaster. The longer a disaster disrupts a normal food supply the more acute the problems become. Nutrition assessment becomes important in a disaster relief effort when the population shows signs of nutritional disease, especially when the food relief effort is inadequate to sustain basic body nutrition.

Some refugee populations may have problems with mass starvation or protein-calorie deprivation. These problems become serious in those who have diarrhea, intestinal parasites, or other demands on body stores. Severe protein-calorie malnutrition may result in deficiency diseases such as kwashiorkor and marasmus. These diseases are a major cause of morbidity and mortality among infants and children in many developing countries.[9,16,17]

Food Sanitation

Although gastrointestinal upsets are common in a disaster, few cases of food-borne illness have been documented.[11] However, nurses should be aware of this possibility and should be prepared to conduct teaching on the safe preparation of food. People should be instructed to cook all fresh meat and to boil raw milk. As a routine prevention measure in areas where sanitation is poor, fresh fruits and vegetables should be soaked in a weak solution of household bleach before they are eaten.

Sanitarians or veterinarians can evaluate the safety of food supplies that have been affected by a disaster. However, when these personnel are not immediately available, nurses can instruct the population in general food sanitation measures. For example, nurses should recommend that certain food products be thrown away or destroyed if they have come in contact with contamination or flood water:[18]

- fresh fruits and vegetables
- foods stored in cardboard or porous containers
- foods in corked or screwtop bottles
- leaking cans

Intact canned goods can be disinfected or sterilized by washing well with soap and water and then boiling the can for 30 seconds, or by wiping the top with full-strength household bleach.[18]

Failure of home refrigeration may lead to food spoilage. Foods such as cream-filled pastries, ham, luncheon meats, and leftovers should not be eaten after accidental thawing, and thawed food should not be refrozen. If freezer temperatures have remained higher than 10 °C (50 °F), other types of thawed food can be eaten if they are cooked thoroughly within a few hours.[18]

Foodborne disease occurs when food that contains microorganisms or toxic substance is eaten, or when poisonous animals or plants are mistaken for food.[19] The most common type of foodborne disease is bacterial. Organisms in the presence of food and moisture multiply to hazardous levels and cause contamination (Exhibit 10–4). The majority of bacterial contamination occurs in meats and fish, seafood, poultry, eggs, or milk products. These can support the rapid growth of microorganisms such as staphylococci, streptococci, and *Clostridia*.

Team Members

Because nurses in the community may come into contact with persons who have nutritional deficiencies and foodborne diseases, they have an important role in coordinating services with physicians and the medical treatment system and in conducting prevention programs. They should also collaborate with a dietitian or a nutritionist while performing nutrition assessments and planning teaching programs. Such specialists can provide special information on nutritional requirements. They can compute individual calorie needs from the basal metabolic rate, and they can provide information on specific diets, such as those for vegetarians.

Veterinarians or sanitarians can help by examining animals and perishable food supplies that are in the food distribution system. Food sources and supplies sent into the disaster area from outside countries must be certified for safe consumption.[20]

Exhibit 10–4 Factors Contributing to Foodborne Disease

Time and Temperature

1. Holding or transportating food without temperature control

    - Hot foods should be kept above 60 °C (140 °F).
    - Cold foods should be kept below 4 °C (40 °F).
    - Thawed foods should not be refrozen.

2. Excessive time between preparation and consumption

    - All foods should be eaten within 24 h.
    - Hazardous foods should be eaten within 3 h.

Hygiene and Sanitation

1. Infected food handlers or contaminated hands

    - Food handlers should be free of disease.
    - Food handlers should observe good personal hygiene such as hand washing and no smoking.

2. Unsanitary work surfaces, utensils, or equipment

    - Proper washing technique should be used.
    - Wash and rinse water should be hot.
    - Utensils should be air dried and properly stored.

3. Contamination from insects and rodents

    - Insects or animals should be kept out of food area.
    - Food should be covered, wrapped, or placed in enclosed containers for storage.

Source: Food Service Sanitation, study guide 163. Fort Sam Houston, Tex, Academy of Health Sciences, US Army, April 1978, p 87.

Cultural Considerations

Donated food supplies are often received in dehydrated form and must be reconstituted with water. It is important that the correct volume of water be added to powdered drinks, such as infant formula or those that furnish electrolytes. A mixture that is too dilute does not deliver sufficient nutrients, and a solution that is too concentrated may upset the body's electrolyte balance.

Disaster victims may not add sufficient liquid to powdered drinks if drinking water is in short supply. Mothers may use excessive drink or formula powder if they are worried about their infants' nutrition or if they are preparing drinks according "to taste."

Nurses may need to demonstrate the correct measuring and mixing technique, using improvised containers of the approximate needed size. Visual observation of this activity can be an effective teaching tool for populations that have low educational levels or for those who have difficulty reading in the language of the packaged instructions.

Whenever possible, diets should be composed of foods that the population usually consumes. Some of these foods contribute to good nutrition, even though they may be strange to the palates of outside relief workers. For example, cassava and taro are roots that are high in calories from carbohydrates, and insects are often rich in protein.[21]

During the Vietnamese relief effort on Guam in 1975, the US military dining facility served rice, a staple of that population. However, it was not well received initially, because the Vietnamese normally use a different type of preparation. Consultation with Vietnamese representatives was necessary in order to modify the cooking technique in a way that was acceptable to the population.

Nurses should remember that unfamiliar food often goes uneaten, even in the face of hunger. It may be wasted or used as barter for items the population values.

Items that are foreign to the prevailing culture may contribute to gastrointestinal upsets or nutritional deficiencies. For example, children who usually drink only whole cow's milk may get diarrhea if they are introduced to formula obtained through disaster relief supplies. In India and Bangladesh, children living in refugee camps and receiving donated skim milk were noted to have a high incidence of blindness from xerophthalmia. Very low levels of retinol were observed in the population's diet, and the skim milk had removed a scarce source of fat soluble vitamin A from the children's food supply.[22]

Introduction of quantities of donated food may also have a disruptive effect on the local economy—especially if it is agriculturally based. Use of local food sources from farms or from the existing food distribution system can help feeding efforts. This procedure can have a positive effect on both feeding programs and the local economy.

Sanitation Issues

Sanitation is often overlooked as an emergency need during a disaster. During floods and earthquakes, sewer systems are often disrupted, and the contamination of ground and water supplies by sewage creates a health hazard (Exhibit 10–5). Sanitation is a concern in refugee camps; overcrowding is common and personal hygiene may be marginal. In addition, garbage, refuse, and dead animals and bodies create a perfect climate for the proliferation of insects and rodents.

Exhibit 10–5 Case Example

Typhoons that struck Manila in the 1970s flooded sewers, septic tanks, and cess pools. The overflowing water contaminated wells and distributed refuse through the streets. Lack of useable water made personal hygiene difficult. Heavy damage to houses created leaking roofs, and some homes were totally without overhead cover. Those persons who were physically able worked to repair houses and to procure food and water. The waterwork authorities superchlorinated the water supply while flood waters receded and the system was reestablished.[23]

Latrines

When sewer lines are broken or blocked as they were in the 1971 earthquake in San Fernando, California, residents may be instructed to stop using their toilets and sinks. Garbage pickup can sometimes be combined with excreta disposal if urban sanitation service can be maintained and expanded. Residents can use plastic bags, tying them firmly when they are full. Sanitation crews should give priority to picking up these sacks.[24]

An emergency home toilet can be improvised from a plastic bucket with a tight fitting lid. A diaper pail lined with plastic bags may be suitable. A supply of plastic bags, ties, toilet paper, moist towelettes, and disinfectant such as household bleach should also be stored with home emergency supplies.

Other alternatives are usually public or communal and include the following:[24]

- packaged sanitation units
- trench, pit, or bore-hole latrines
- mobile latrines
- chemical latrines
- bucket latrines

Latrines should be properly located to prevent contamination of food and water. They should be at least 90 meters (100 yards) from any food service area or water source. Besides, they should not be dug into the water table or be placed where they can drain into the water supply.[25]

Approximately five to six seats or squat plates should be provided for each 100 persons. Emergency public latrines should also have the following features:[24]

- separate facilities for men and women
- usability for children
- adequate privacy

- good lighting at night
- sanitary maintenance
- water and soap for personal hygiene

In some disasters, such as earthquakes, urban dwellers may be evacuated to rural areas in which no sanitation facilities exist. In these instances, the main consideration is to select a private area away from cooking, living spaces, and sources of water. Human wastes should be buried or isolated so that insects, birds, and rodents can be prevented from spreading the excreta.[24]

Pests

An additional aspect of sanitation in a disaster is the control of pests. Insects and rodents can serve as vectors to humans. Pests to be controlled include scabies, mites, lice, fleas, bugs, ticks, flies, mosquitoes, sandflies, rats, and mice. Snakes may also be included; for although they do not carry disease, they may be poisonous and certainly are unwelcome visitors.

Community nurses can predict increased contact between the disaster population and pests during relief efforts. Pests may be forced by the disaster to migrate into living areas, or the population may be relocated into previously uninhabited rural locations containing animals and arthropods of all types.

Moreover, the environmental destruction secondary to a disaster may cause an ecological imbalance that favors proliferation of insects and rodents. Breeding sites for insects may be created by flooding or storms, by the disruption of piped water or drainage systems, and by the collection of standing water in rubble. Improvised water containers can also become breeding sites if they are not covered and if the water is not changed regularly.[24]

Rodents are very numerous in the wild population and are very quick to adapt to new environmental circumstances. During a disaster, the rodent population may increase dramatically until natural forces or vector control programs halt their multiplication. Rodents pass diseases to humans by bites, by contaminating water or foodstuffs, or by carrying small infected insects in their hair.[24]

The environmental imbalance leading to the increase in pests may be lengthy. During this time, the population faces an increased risk of diseases carried by vectors. Such diseases are plague, typhus, and malaria. Control of disease-bearing pests may be difficult in a disaster for several reasons:

- Normal pest control programs may be interrupted.
- Flooding may wash away pesticides and insecticides previously applied.
- Sanitation services and personal hygiene may decline.

Nurses in the community should be aware of the potential health hazard that pests present and should have some knowledge about their management. Pest control measures can be categorized as individual or group. Individual control includes good personal hygiene, the use of insect repellents, and dusting with insecticide powders. Group control includes the provision of specific areas for latrines or defecation; the prompt disposal of dead animals and bodies; proper disposal of rubbish, garbage, and human waste; surveillance of pest infestation; implementing insecticide and poison control programs; and the use of snake repellents around tent areas.

Buildings and Homes

After a disaster, fixed facilities may need to be razed because of structural damage or contamination. If a home must be destroyed, the former residents should be given a definite date for the razing so that they are given no false hope and have a definite time in which to remove possessions—if this is possible. Houses that have been submerged in flood waters must be completely washed down with a disinfectant if they are to be reinhabited.

Burial

The disposition of corpses after a disaster is closely related to issues of sanitation. Although bodies are not usually a direct source of illness, they encourage rapid proliferation of rodents, flies, and other pests that may carry disease to the population. Decomposing and unidentified bodies also create a serious mental health problem in the community.

Nurses are likely to encounter deaths during disaster relief efforts simply because every community normally experiences a certain number of deaths in any period. Although the mortality rate does not necessarily increase during a disaster, deaths from casualties may increase as the result of a serious disaster. Deaths during a disaster may become a problem because of special circumstances:

• concentration of deaths in a small geographic area
• high numbers of sudden fatalities
• disruption of usual funeral and burial services
• poor condition of bodies
• uncertain identification of bodies
• customs regarding death

If large numbers of casualties have occurred, special equipment may be required, such as hooks, slings, stretchers, trucks, and bulldozers. If refrigerated trucks are available, they may be used to hold bodies until they are identified.

Public health officials are often in charge of the morgue, and they supervise the bagging and disposition of bodies.

Funeral directors and clergy can be assisted by volunteers and organized teams of workers at the site. Workers usually wear perfumed surgical masks and gloves. They can expect to experience nausea, vomiting, loss of appetite, and sleeplessness.[26] Workers from outside the community can usually tolerate this type of assignment for about 1 week, but locals need to be rotated every day.

Bodies can be disposed of most easily during a large disaster by use of funeral pyres or mass graves. This practice may sometimes be necessary; however, many cultures find this objectionable. Traditions of death call for a personal identification and burial of each body with approprirate rituals. Thus survivors often make efforts to uncover bodies well buried under many feet of rubble, even at the risk of injury to workers, so that bodies can be identified and reburied with ceremony in shallower graves.[26]

The human need to personalize death with rites and rituals results in a burial process that moves slowly.[26] This characteristic must be balanced against the immediacy of disaster conditions and the necessity to expedite burials.

Procedures usually call for some separation between the living and the dead, such as controlled areas for temporary morgues. Bodies are individually laid out and personal effects are carefully handled.[26] It is important that personal belongings remain with the body to facilitate identification. In the United States, sophisticated methods of identification, such as dental records and medical histories, may also be used. Upon identification, statistical information on name, age, date, and cause of death are collected. Then the family or friends can begin making arrangements for burial.

Team Members

The establishment of sanitation programs in a disaster requires close cooperation with local leaders to provide the services of personnel and to obtain space and supplies. Disposition of dead bodies involves teamwork among the clergy, funeral directors, health officers, and community workers and may require allocated facilities and equipment.

Sanitation programs need specialists such as sanitarians, veterinarians, and environmental engineers. Public health nurses with official agencies may find it useful to acquire a sanitarian license through their state licensing boards. They can then assist the community in meeting increased sanitation needs by officially assessing the disaster effects on environmental health and by implementing emergency interventions.

Nurses often have an important role in conducting education activities on sanitation issues. They may also be instrumental in offering emotional support to people whose loved ones have been killed and to those persons whose homes have been damaged or destroyed.

Cultural Considerations

Sanitation problems in a disaster touch on several personal and sensitive issues:

- need for privacy
- practices of personal hygiene
- beliefs about cleanliness
- feelings towards objectionable pests
- emotions concerning loss of homes and belongings
- customs of death and burial

Sanitation problems often represent a difficult challenge, inasmuch as this area is one in which existing cultural habits may need to be modified or changed so that adequate standards of health can be achieved.

The nurse may need to conduct teaching programs on handwashing, disposal of dirty diapers, and the use of toilets and toilet paper. People of some cultures may save toilet paper unless they are provided with small cans for disposal and given instruction in its use. Others may prefer to squat and may resist use of the American-style toilets provided in evacuation centers and camps.

People of cultures accustomed to defecating or urinating in the open may be reluctant to give up their habits. As an acceptable compromise, they may be allowed to use a designated area well away from shelters if they agree to use established latrines when in camp. Arrangements for privacy may be critical and difficult to achieve in a disaster.

A nurse must avoid misunderstandings while conducting teaching on sanitation issues and while attempting to understand local customs and attitudes. Adequate translating can be very important, because words may have several entirely different meanings in dialects or languages that are related.

When death occurs, an effort should be made to personalize the situation as much as possible. It is important to morale and public relations that an attitude of respect be maintained. Brief eulogies should accompany all burials—even those in mass graves. The importance of sanitation issues must be balanced against the cultural acceptability of those measures and against the need to promote both physical and emotional well being.

Illness and Injury

Nurses in the community should be concerned with preventing illness and injury secondary to a disaster and with promoting health into the recovery stage. During the emergency stages of a disaster, acute care facilities may be overloaded, and so unusually sick persons may have to be cared for at home. If medical supplies are disrupted, those with chronic illnesses may be without medications and may become symptomatic. References on home nursing and the care of illness in the community are listed at the end of this chapter.

Although nurses cannot possibly address all health needs in a disaster, they may be useful in teaching others to care for the sick and injured at home, by participating in immunization programs, by screening persons for serious health conditions, and by promoting good habits of daily living. Table 10–3 lists potentially serious communicable diseases encountered in a disaster and public health methods of control. Information on interventions and control measures likely to be needed in a disaster can help nurses in meeting their responsibilities.

Immunizations

Immunizations are usually not needed for short-term disaster relief efforts, although tetanus toxoid serum may be required for those sustaining injuries. Whether immunization programs are to be undertaken during the recovery stage of a disaster depends largely upon the success of sanitation measures and the outcome of surveillance programs. Sometimes a disaster relief effort can be used for a one-time health promotion program, such as boosting childhood immunizations for polio, diphtheria, tetanus, whooping cough, measles, mumps, and rubella.

The population is usually very concerned about the possibility of an epidemic, and rumors are common. Public pressure may demand visible action and an immunization program, even when it is not indicated.

Surprisingly, few epidemics have been reported during disaster relief efforts (Exhibit 10–6). Mortality and morbidity levels have usually remained fairly constant.[12,23] However, because of the potential for widespread illness and the anxiety of a population, surveillance should assume importance—particularly when crisis services begin to phase out—because the risk of disease begins to rise at about that time. Outbreaks are possible for years after the impact has passed, especially if public health programs are slow in reorganizing and resuming service. Some population groups, such as refugee camps, require surveillance indefinitely.

Because decisions to conduct immunization programs are made on the basis of the interpretation of technical data, all mass immunizations should take place through government agencies that have official responsibility in this area. Nurses should reassure overly worried people and should dissuade volunteer groups from unilaterally undertaking immunization programs.

Nurses should be aware that immunizations tend to give an artificial sense of security to some people, who may thus ignore more effective preventive measures such as personal hygiene. Manpower and other resources may also be shifted away from more important programs such as surveillance and environmental sanitation. Other undesirable effects of poorly planned immunization programs also exist:

Table 10–3 Control of Potentially Serious Communicable Diseases in a Disaster

Disease	*Public Health Measures*
1. Water or Food-Borne Diseases	
Typhoid and paratyphoid fevers	Adequate disposal of feces and urine
Food poisoning	Safe water for drinking and washing
Sewage poisoning	Sanitary food preparation
Cholera	Fly and pest control
Leptospirosis	Disease surveillance
	Isolation and treatment of early cases (typhoid and paratyphoid fevers, cholera)
	Immunization (typhoid fever and cholera)
2. Person-to-Person Spread	
Contact diseases	Reduced crowding
Shigellosis	Adequate washing facilities
Nonspecific diarrheas	Public health education
Streptococcal skin infections	Disease surveillance in clinics
Scabies	Treatment of clinical cases
Infectious hepatitis	Immunization (infectious hepatitis)
Respiratory spread	Adequate levels of immunization before the disaster
Smallpox	
Measles	Reduced crowding
Whooping Cough	Disease surveillance in clinics and community
Diphtheria	
Influenza	Isolation of index cases (especially smallpox)
Tuberculosis	
	Immunization of entire population (smallpox) or children (measles)
	Continue primary immunization of infants (diphtheria, whooping cough, tetanus)
3. Vector-Borne Diseases	
Louse-borne typhus	Disinfection (except malaria and encephalitis)
Plague (rat flea)	
Relapsing fever	Vector control
Malaria (mosquito)	Disease surveillance
Viral encephalitis	Isolation and treatment (no isolation for malaria)
4. Wound Complications	
Tetanus	Tetanus toxoid immunization
	Postexposure tetanus antitoxin

Source: Reprinted with permission from Western KA: *Epidemiologic Surveillance After Natural Disaster,* Pan American Health Organization, Scientific Publication No. 420. Washington, DC, World Health Organization, 1982, p 10.

Exhibit 10–6 Case Example

When an earthquake struck southern Italy in November 1980, hospital admissions and the occurrence of infectious diseases were monitored. Typhoid and whooping cough were among the diseases usually reported in small numbers in this area. Although 32 suspected epidemics were reported, only two were confirmed after investigation and statistical comparison with previous disease levels. One of these was an outbreak of 39 cases of gastroenteritis in a group of firemen, and the other was the occurrence of 6 cases of viral hepatitis in a province adjacent to the earthquake zone. When admissions for pulmonary disease were examined and compared to those of previous years, a normal winter trend was found.

This surveillance program succeeded in distributing resources carefully in some cases. However, in other instances mass immunizations were given despite indications to the contrary. Public pressure forced expenditure of resources to deal with problems that did not exist. Relations with the press became strained because their reports exaggerated the risk of epidemic and spread fear among the population.

This survey also accurately reflected the incidence of trauma injuries requiring hospitalization during the first few days following the disaster. Some admissions for frostbite and hypothermia were documented.

Reports were made daily for approximately 3 months and then were made weekly as the community began returning to normal.[27]

- Routine immunization programs with known benefits may be curtailed.
- Vaccines may be poorly distributed and diverted from areas that really need them.
- Vaccines may be stockpiled in huge quantities and become outdated.
- Vaccines may be stored improperly and lose potency.

When immunizations are given, they can cause local and systemic reactions that temporarily impede activities of daily living. Their effectiveness may be diminished because of the following:

- Populations at highest risk are often not accessible and are missed.
- Two injections of a vaccine may be needed for effectiveness, and it is difficult to find the same persons twice in a disaster.
- The immune response may not reach an acceptable level until the disaster is over.

Drug Therapy

Preventive treatment with drugs such as antibiotics is rarely practical in a disaster, for the following reasons:[11]

- Drugs are effective against only specific diseases.
- Drugs would have to be taken indefinitely to be effective.

- Administration of drugs would have only a temporary benefit in areas in which diseases are endemic.
- Risk of side effects is not warranted.

Generally, drugs are prescribed only for the treatment of individual disease cases and should be administered according to established medical protocol. Only a few exceptions may be indicated, such as the first aid use of antibiotic ointment for minor burns and skin wounds.

Common Problems

The illnesses most commonly reported after a disaster are respiratory infections and diarrhea. These illnesses are related to the concerns about water, food, and sanitation described earlier in this chapter.

Overcrowding is the major cause of respiratory disorders. If people can be relocated and regrouped in confined areas, their illness normally runs its course, treated with a conservative approach of fluids and aspirin or acetaminophen.

Some of the causes of diarrhea have been discussed. In addition, diarrhea may follow antibiotic therapy or gastroenteritis. To recultivate the intestinal flora after the use of antibiotics, nurses can recommend buttermilk or live culture "natural" yogurt. After a gastrointestinal infection, persons may experience a transient lactose intolerance—a disorder that causes cramping, bloating, and diarrhea when milk products are ingested. In these cases, capsules of the enzyme lactase can be added to dairy foods to aid digestion.[28]

The dehydration that may occur as a result of diarrhea is a serious problem. Nurses should teach other community workers the following signs of dehydration:[21]

- little or no urine
- dark yellow urine
- sudden weight loss
- sunken and tearless eyes
- sagging "soft spot" in infants
- loss of elasticity or stretchiness of the skin

Dehydration can be prevented by forcing large amounts of fluid. Oral therapy may be needed when early signs of dehydration appear or when hospitalization is not available because of the effects of a disaster. The World Health Organization (WHO) has developed premeasured packets—oral rehydration therapy (ORT)— which are useful in large scale disaster operations. These packets are premeasured, have a long shelf life, and are easily distributed. The rehydration drink (Figure

10–5) can also be prepared by disaster victims using common household ingre-
dients.

At least 1 glass of the rehydration drink should be taken for each water stool. A
large person should consume at least 2 liters (3 qt) per day; a small child needs at
least 1 liter (1 qt) per day. If vomiting occurs, nurses should encourage small sips
every 5 minutes around the clock, until the patient begins urinating normally.[21]

Potassium is furnished for further electrolyte balance if orange juice, coconut
water, or banana is added. Infants should continue breast feeding in addition to
receiving the rehydration drink.[21]

Foods should be added as soon as a person is willing to eat, even if it temporarily
causes a slight increase in the frequency of stools and nausea. Foods high in
protein and calories are especially important so that the vicious cycle between
diarrhea and protein-calorie deprivation can be avoided.[21] These foods are outlined in Table 10–4.

Community nurses staffing a clinic can use a quick and reliable technique for
determining the degree of malnutrition when laboratory tests are unavailable. The
patient's actual weight and ideal weight are compared as follows:[16,29]

Figure 10–5 Rehydration Drink to Prevent and Treat Dehydration

Rehydration drink — to prevent and treat dehydration

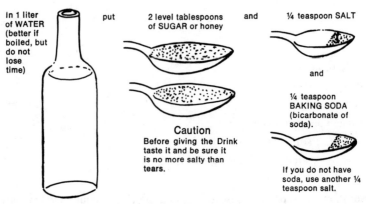

If available, add half a cup of orange juice or coconut water
or a little mashed ripe banana to the Drink.

Source: Reprinted with permission from Werner D: *Where There Is No Doctor.* Palo Alto, Calif, The
Hesperian Foundation, 1977, p 152.

Table 10–4 Foods for a Person With Diarrhea

When the person is vomiting or feels too sick to eat, he/she should drink—	As soon as the person is able to eat, in addition to ingesting the drinks listed at the left, he/she should eat a balanced selection of the following foods or similar ones:	
	Energy foods	*Body building foods*
• teas, rice water	• ripe bananas, papaya	• milk (if no lactose intolerance exists)
• chicken, meat, egg, or bean broth	• crackers, rice, potatoes	• chicken (boiled or roasted)
• Kool-Aid or similar sweetened drinks	• oatmeal or other grain (well cooked)	• eggs (boiled)
• rehydration drink	• fresh corn (well cooked and mashed)	• meat (well cooked, without fat or grease)
• breast milk	• applesauce (cooked)	• beans, lentils, or peas (well cooked and mashed)
		• fish (well cooked)

Do not eat or drink—

• fatty or greasy foods	• beans cooked in fat	• alcoholic drinks
• most raw fruits	• highly seasoned foods	• any kind of laxative or purge

Source: Adapted with permission from Werner D: *Where There Is No Doctor.* Palo Alto, Calif, The Hesperian Foundation, 1977, p. 155.

$$\frac{\text{Actual weight}}{\text{Ideal weight}} \times 100 = \text{percent of ideal weight}$$

Eighty to 60 percent of ideal weight indicates moderate malnutrition; below 60 percent of ideal weight signifies severe malnutrition. Irreversible and fatal tissue loss occurs when weight falls below approximately 50 percent of ideal body weight.[29,30]

The appearance of persons with protein-calorie malnutrition may vary according to the severity and the duration of an inadequate diet and in response to individual factors. Most appear semistarved, haggard, and pale. They are easily susceptible to dehydration and the effects of heat and humidity.[15,16] In areas where protein-calorie malnutrition is common, the people are smaller than usual. Although diminished body size results from an inadequate diet, this feature also protects individuals against a poor food supply by lowering the body's requirements.

The severe forms of malnutrition are most commonly seen in children, and are recognized as kwashiorkor (the edematous type) and marasmus (the non-edematous type). Other suggestive signs include the following:[16,31]

- Hair is dry and hypopigmented, thin and sparse, and easily plucked.
- Muscles are wasted and weak.
- Skin shows dirty brown patches or hypopigmentation, poor turgor, and little fat in subcutaneous tissue.
- Vital signs reveal a slow pulse, low blood pressure, and low temperature.

Adults with chronic protein-calorie malnutrition may not show specific clinical signs of kwashiorkor or marasmus. However, this condition leads to a reduced energy output, which results in suboptimal work performance and limited social activities. Men in developing agricultural countries may fall far short of receiving the calories necessary for physical labor. Women suffer from poor weight gain during pregnancy, small-for-date infants, and poor lactation. These problems perpetuate a lack of social progress and can impair restoration after a disaster.[29]

People affected by starvation usually respond spontaneously to the availability of food and have enormous appetites. Those who suffer from diarrhea, anorexia, or vomiting may respond to the rehydration drink and foods outlined in Figure 10–5 and Table 10–4. At least one study has shown that malnourished persons can be treated with intensive field feeding programs as effectively as with standard hospital treatment.[32]

First Aid

Injuries vary with the type, the location, and the severity of the disaster. Mortality rates can be extremely high in some types of severe disasters, but injuries are often not as high as expected. Because serious injuries often result in death, the healthy and the slightly injured survivors remain. By the time outside help has arrived, then, the majority of acute injuries remaining have undergone triage and are under care.

Nurses in the community encounter primarily injuries and accidents that arise from temporary and disorganized living situations. They should be prepared to teach basic first aid so that community members can be better prepared to care for themselves and each other. The American National Red Cross publishes several excellent references, which are listed at the end of this chapter. Needed skills include the following:

- cardiopulmonary resuscitation
- Heimlich manuever

- dressings and splints
- control of bleeding: pressure points and tourniquets
- treatment of snake and animal bites
- treatment of heat and cold injuries

In preparation for a disaster, some first aid and home supplies adequate for at least a 72-hour period should be made. They should include such items as the following:

- sleeping bags and blankets
- flashlight, batteries, and candles
- fire extinguisher
- battery-powered radio
- shovel and ax
- wood, coal, or other sources of heat
- garbage bags

Exhibit 10–7 lists the items that might be included in a home first aid kit.

Team Members

Nurses in the community must be concerned with preventing illness and injury secondary to a disaster and with promoting health into the recovery stage. This

---

Exhibit 10–7 Suggested Home First Aid Supplies.

Aspirin or acetaminophen
Antibiotic ointment
Petroleum jelly
Baking soda and salt
Assorted bandaids
Elastic bandages
Sanitary pads (double as dressings)
Assorted gauze pads and rollers
Handkerchiefs and small towels (double as triangular bandages)
Disposable diapers (double as dressings or padding)
Tape and safety pins
Thermometers
Scissors and tweezers
Soap
Personal medication and supplies

preparation requires cooperation with other community professionals and with health care providers in the acute care setting. In unfamiliar communities, it is important to establish an immediate liaison with local public health workers, because they may know what problems are usually found in their area and whether there is an increased incidence of the problems.

At times, nursing services may be dependent on decisions by local authorities; so programs undertaken may appear to be political rather than therapeutic. Nurses should remain flexible and realistic in their assessments and interventions and should strive to cope with the political and the psychological variables in the situation.

Nurses may perform an important function in mobilizing community members to join the team. The personal contact that nurses make with various groups and their leaders can greatly facilitate community action. Nurses themselves may function as leaders or as expert consultants. Assessing and using community organizations is discussed further in Chapter 13.

Cultural Considerations

In some cultures, family members care for each other during illness and injury. This form of self-help should be encouraged in all instances, unless an unusual illness requires isolation from others.

Many persons rely on favorite remedies or folk medicine for relief. This practice should be permitted and encouraged for the psychological comfort it provides— even in the absence of any known benefits. Only practices known to be harmful should be discouraged.

Nurses in the community may be very useful in facilitating the flow of information between various agencies, acute care facilities, and the population served. Casefinding and first-hand knowledge add to the surveillance of the health status of a population. An understanding of the living conditions, cultural variables, and specific concerns of the group should assist in the implementation of disaster relief efforts.

MAKING EVALUATIONS AND SETTING PRIORITIES

When presented with the chaos of a disaster and its aftermath, nurses may feel overwhelmed by the number of health needs to be addressed. The generalist role used routinely by many community health nurses may give them flexibility in meeting diverse situations. Nurses cannot respond in a rigid predetermined way; they must be ready to adjust to changing situations as they occur and to important problems as they are identified. However, nurses in the community may feel fragmented in the face of multiple demands.

During the pressure of crisis, nurses should find that a logical approach to problem solving is invaluable—like that offered by the four steps of the nursing process:

1. assessment
2. diagnosis
3. intervention
4. evaluation

Even when time for formal problem solving is not available, an awareness of the nursing process should assist in maintaining a sense of perspective and enhancing the positive effects of nursing actions.

The steps of the nursing process can be performed concurrently on a variety of simultaneous problems and can help to identify changing disaster needs. The nursing process can also help nurses to determine the information and expertise that may be needed from other health care professionals and to integrate that knowledge into their nursing actions.

Setting priorities should also help to focus nursing services and help to ensure that efforts achieve the desired result. Reviewing underlying assumptions and characteristics of community health nursing and applying them to the disaster situation should be helpful. Programs and services should meet the following criteria:[33]

- Refrain from doing what people can do for themselves.
- Be directed toward eventual independence.
- Complement or supplement, but do not duplicate other resources.
- Produce a documented effect on the prevention, control, cure, or rehabilitation of problems.
- Be directed toward target populations or individuals—those having the greatest positive impact on the community and those at greatest risk for developing health problems.

Priority should be given to problems created or intensified by the disaster and to restoring persons and communities to a predisaster level. Nurses should distinguish carefully between chronic or indigenous problems in the community and those associated with a disaster. It is tempting, especially when one is working in a deprived socio-economic setting, to intervene in preexisting problems. To intervene is usually to allocate disaster resources poorly, because disaster programs are very costly and are designed to be temporary.

Selective interventions may be carried out to alleviate preexisting problems, especially when acute disaster needs are intensified by these underlying problems.

However, nurses should be aware that inappropriate intervention into preexisting conditions often exacerbates the resentment disaster victims commonly feel toward workers in the later phases of a recovery effort. Nurses need to consider carefully the cultural context of their actions to help preserve the integrity and social fabric of the affected community and to ease their own transition into their disaster roles.

SUMMARY

Nurses working in a community setting during a disaster relief effort may come from a variety of clinical backgrounds. They may be part of the affected community or country, or they may have been sent into the area to assist. They will be called upon to work as part of several multidisciplinary teams, applying principles of community health nursing and public health to new and changing situations.

Nurses can contribute to disaster preparation by updating their knowledge about basic community concerns in a disaster response. Primary, secondary, and tertiary prevention measures all need to be considered in a context of varying locations, diverse populations, and different types of disasters.

Actions must be part of a process that includes specific assessments and application of knowledge, adjusted as ongoing evaluation indicates the need for new intervention strategies.

REFERENCES

1. Hoff LE: *People in Crises: Understanding and Helping*. Menlo Park, Calif, Addison-Wesley Publishing Co Inc. 1978.

2. Armstrong A (ed): *The Island Ark: Operation New Life on Guam, USA*. Pamphlet published by Marianas Naval Officers Wives Club, 1975.

3. *Operation New Life: Task Force Bobcat*. Pamphlet prepared by 1st Batallion, 5th Infantry, US Army.

4. Shaw R: Health services in a disaster: Lessons learned from the 1975 Vietnamese evacuation. *Milit Med* 1979;144:307–311.

5. *Emergency Health Management After Natural Disasters*, Pan American Health Organization scientific publication no. 407. Washington, DC, World Health Organization, 1981.

6. Assessment of health needs following natural disasters. Paper from Fourth Annual Meeting for Designated Epidemiologists, Pan American Health Organization, Washington, DC, May 1978.

7. Spencer HC, Romero A, Feldman RA, et al: Disease surveillance and decision-making after the 1976 Guatemala earthquake. *Lancet* 1977;2:181–184.

8. *Emergency Water: Home Storage and Disinfection*. Salt Lake City, Utah State Department of Health, Division of Environmental Health, May 1982.

9. Davidson S, Passmore R, Brock JF, et al: *Human Nutrition and Dietetics*, ed 7. New York, Churchill Livingstone, 1979.

10. *Military Water Supply*. San Antonio, Tex, Academy of Health Sciences, 1981.

11. Western KA: *Epidemiologic Surveillance After Natural Disaster*, Pan American Health Organization scientific publication No. 420. Washington, DC, World Health Organization, 1982.

12. Beckjord PR: Public health aspects of preventive medicine and disaster. *JAMA* 1959;171:212–217.

13. Zeman FJ: *Clinical Nutrition and Dietetics*. Lexington, Mass, The Collamore Press, DC Heath & Co, 1983.

14. Eicherly EE: Nursing in a thermonuclear disaster. *Nurs Clin North Am* 1967;2:325–335.

15. Coale MS, Robson JR: Dietary management of intractable diarrhea in malnourished patients: *J Am Diet Assoc* 1980;76:444–450.

16. Van Itallie TB: Starvation and protein-calorie malnutrition, in Thorn GW, Adams RD, Braunwald E, et al (eds): *Harrison's Principles of Internal Medicine*, ed 8. New York, McGraw Hill Book Co, pp 449–452.

17. Dahlberg K: Medical care of Cambodian refugees. *JAMA* 1980;243:1062–1065.

18. Speers JF: Prevent disease resulting from floods. *J Iowa Med Soc* 1969;59:355.

19. Gilchrist A: *Foodborne Disease and Food Safety*. Monroe, Wis, American Medical Assoc, 1981.

20. Fernandez M: Veterinary public health and disasters. *Disaster Preparedness in the Americas*, Issue No. 8. Washington, DC, Pan American Health Organization, July 1981.

21. Werner D: *Where There Is No Doctor*. Palo Alto, Calif, The Hesperian Foundation, 1977.

22. Lechat MF: The epidemiology of disasters. *Proc Royal Soc Med* 1976;69:421–426.

23. Velimirovic B, Subramanian M: The pattern of morbidity after typhoons in a tropical country. *Int J Biometeorol* 1972;16:343–360.

24. *Disaster Prevention and Mitigation*. New York, Disaster Relief Coordinator, Office of the United Nations, 1982. vol 8.

25. *Field Sanitation Team Training*, training circular No. 8-3, US Dept of the Army, September 1978.

26. Blansan S, Quarantelli EL: *From Dead Body to Person: The Handling of Fatal Mass Casualties in Disasters*. Columbus, Ohio. Disaster Research Center, The Ohio State University.

27. Greco D, Faustini A, Forastiene F, et al: Epidemiological surveillance of diseases following the earthquake of 23rd November 1980 in southern Italy. *Disasters* 1981;5:398–406.

28. Kastrup EK, Boyd JR, Olin BR, et al (eds): *Facts and Comparisons*. St Louis, JP Lippincott Co., 1984.

29. Blackburn GL, Bistrian BR, Maini BS, et al: Nutritional and metabolic assessment of the hospitalized patient. *JPEN* 1977;1:11–22.

30. Halpern SL (ed): *Quick Reference to Clinical Nutrition: A Guide for Physicians*. Philadelphia, JB Lippincott Co, 1979.

31. Goodhart RS, Shils ME (eds): *Modern Nutrition in Health and Disease*, ed 6. Philadelphia, Lea & Febiger, 1980.

32. Mason JB, Hay RW, Leresche J: Treatment of severe malnutrition in relief. *Lancet* 1974;1:332–335.

33. *Community Health Nurse in the Army*, FM 8-24. Headquarters, US Dept of the Army, 1980.

SUGGESTED READINGS
American Red Cross: *Advanced First Aid and Emergency Care*, ed 2. Garden City, NY, Doubleday & Co Inc, 1979.

Beneson AS (ed): *Control of Communicable Diseases in Man*, ed 13. Washington, DC, American Public Health Association, 1980.

Computer computation of family food and water needs. General Board of Relief Society, 76 North Main, Salt Lake City, Utah, 84111.

Essentials of Home Production and Storage. Salt Lake City, The Church of Jesus Christ of Latter-day Saints, 1978.

American Red Cross: *Family Health and Home Nursing*. Garden City, NY, Doubleday & Co Inc, 1979.

Recommended Dietary Allowances, ed 9. Washington, DC, Food and Nutrition Board, National Academy of Sciences, 1980.

American Red Cross: *Standard First Aid and Personal Safety*. Garden City, NY, Doubleday & Co Inc, 1979.

Appendix 10–A

Community Assessment

Population characteristics

- size and density
- age and sex
- distribution
- transiency or stability
- educational level

Cultural characteristics

- religion
- language or dialect
- customs

Housing

- quantity and quality
- location
- composition of typical household

Economy

- industries
- occupational groups
- income level

Health statistics

- births and deaths
- incidence and prevalence of diseases
- distribution of diseases
- immunization levels

Public services

- utilities
- schools
- transportation
- communication systems
- health care facilities
- organizations

Geography

- location
- prominent topographical features
- climate conditions

Government

- leaders
- type of system
- distribution of power
- political considerations

Disaster characteristics

- type and magnitude
- existing plans

Chapter 11

Development and Design of Disaster Educational Programs

Loretta Malm Garcia, R.N., M.S.N. *and*
Roseann P. Lindsay, R.N., B.S.N.

Successful response to a disaster is dependent upon the preparedness of both individuals and relief agencies. Preparation through learning in a well-designed curriculum is essential for disaster planning.

Nurses can anticipate being called upon to present disaster educational programs frequently. These programs may be required in a variety of settings such as acute care facilities, nursing homes, industry, schools, and public health departments. The general principles outlined here are applicable in a wide variety of programs. Chapter objectives are to assist nurse educators in the following:

- defining critical areas of need in disaster education
- assessing staff learning needs by designing an appropriate assessment tool
- incorporating adult education concepts when developing and presenting a curriculum
- using the large variety of available teaching methods and resources for instructors
- evaluating results to determine the effectiveness of programs and the needs for further continuing education

CRITICAL AREAS OF NEED IN DISASTER EDUCATION

Nurses need a basic knowledge that they can apply to a disaster situation. The general areas of preparation and readiness have changed very little over the years. In 1963, the National League of Nursing published Mary V. Neal's three-year study, *Disaster Nursing Preparation*, aimed at improving preparation of nurses for the functions they were expected to assume during disaster.[1] The report indicated that nurses need to know how to do the following:

- organize under chaotic conditions
- manage large wards with little or no professional assistance
- use volunteer help, both trained and untrained
- adapt and develop nursing care procedures to meet the demands of a disaster situation
- adapt and develop public health functions to meet demands of the situation.

Nurses unfamiliar with disaster response often conceptualize the practice of disaster nursing as frantic triage and dramatic lifesaving in battlefield-like conditions. However, disaster nursing encompasses more than triage skills and emergency medicine. There are roles for nurses in all phases of disaster response—planning, warning, impact, and recovery. Disaster nursing is not an isolated specialty; it is an extension of everyday practice. Nursing skills and principles remain the same but are adapted to meet the special physical, social, emotional, and spiritual needs of disaster victims and the special areas of management that a disaster creates.

Exposure to disaster preparedness and management should be a part of all basic nursing curricula. However, research indicates that little positive action has been forthcoming to establish disaster preparedness solidly in basic nursing programs.[2] Curriculum development has been slow and uncertain for several reasons:

- The problems of disaster appear to be overwhelming.
- Trained faculty are scarce.
- The agency responsible for providing this content is not clearly identified.

State and local governments, universities, and national nursing organizations have been recommended as providers. Participation in local disaster response can provide students with an opportunity to study this expanded nursing role in a complex and challenging community setting.

Content For A Disaster Teaching Unit

Basic information presented in a teaching unit should assist course participants to form an overall view of the community's response to a disaster, to perceive their agency's role and contributions relating to overall disaster response and management, and to assess risk in the community and identify resources for assistance. The topical outline for this book can provide a useful guide for a curriculum. Ellison recommends including the following material in disaster curricula:[2]

- definition of disaster and the philosophy of disaster care (Under this heading, causes, effects, phases of disaster, survival, and self-help should be addressed.)

- care of mass casualties, communication, organization, and coordination problems; triage; psychological effects of disaster; human behavior; and shelter living
- the role of the nurse, specifically the leadership function, in assessment of health needs and use of personnel and supplies to provide health care
- evaluation of care and services provided

The in-service instructor can then build from this base and incorporate information and skills exclusive to the agency's needs.

Design of a Disaster Teaching Unit

The nursing process provides an ideal structure for designing a disaster teaching unit. Steps consisting of assessment, diagnosis, intervention, and evaluation are guides in program development (Exhibit 11–1).

ASSESSING STAFF LEARNING NEEDS

Preassessment

It is imperative for the instructor to complete preassessment of learners before beginning instruction. Preassessment determines what Knowles terms "educational need." Knowles describes educational need as a gap between (the learner's) present level of competencies and a higher level required for effective performance as defined by himself, his organization, or his society.[3]

Preassessment also allows adult learners to participate in determining their learning needs. This opportunity significantly increases motivation for learning. More specifically, assessment determines whether learners have the necessary prerequisite skills, already know some of the material, and need some individualized instructional activities. Consequently, the results of preassessment should provide information as to whether students should be required to master prerequisite skills before beginning instruction, as to whether any students may omit any of the instructional objectives, and for prescribing specific instructional activities for specific students.

Choosing An Assessment Tool

Assessment tools have various purposes. Some tests determine present levels of competency versus asking desired levels. In considering the design of a preassessment tool, many options are available to the inservice instructor. Two models are

Exhibit 11–1 The Nursing Process Applied To Disaster Teaching

Assessment

- uses assessment tools
- determines learning needs
- involves participants

Diagnosis

- uses behavioral objectives
- based on assessment needs
- provides specific learning outcomes

Intervention

- based on behavioral objectives
- uses lesson plans
- develops strategies for achieving objectives
- provides methods and activities
- implements adult learning concepts

Evaluation

- completed by learners and instructors
- measures learning
- reassesses learning needs
- based on continued achievement

presented as alternatives: (1) Likert scale tool (Exhibit 11–2), (2) survey of knowledge (Exhibit 11–3).

The American Red Cross Self-Assessment Tool (Exhibit 11–2) exemplifies the Likert scale technique as it is applied to a specific learning needs assessment. Likert scales are the most common form of attitude measure. This type of tool gives the instructor specific information about each participant's entry level skills.

Disaster nursing quizzes follow traditional testing format. The example provided in Exhibit 11–3 uses true/false and multiple choice questions. Answers are easily scored and can identify learning needs. Quizzes can easily be adapted to a pretest or a posttest format.

Disaster Nursing Preparation, the NLN study completed by M.V. Neal, provides some examples of disaster curricula that could be modified to meet your needs.

Exhibit 11–2 Self-Assessment Tool (Likert Scale)

Please assess your degree of knowledge for each of the following items by checking the appropriate box. (1 is low; 5 is high)

Degree of Knowledge
I Feel I Have

1 2 3 4 5

1. Phases of disaster
2. Effects of disaster on the community
3. Effects of a disaster on the health care system
4. Psychological effects of disasters on victims and workers
5. Physical effects of disaster on victims and workers
6. Nursing process
7. Crisis intervention techniques
8. First aid practices
9. Community health resources
10. Role of government agencies in disaster relief
11. Concepts of Red Cross disaster relief
12. Chapter disaster health service plans
13. Red Cross administrative health services regulations
14. Supplementary role of Red Cross Disaster Health Services
15. Role of health service personnel in various disaster assignment settings
16. Disaster health services records and reports
17. Emergency assistance
18. Your experiences in chapter disaster health services preparedness

Source: Reprinted with permission from American National Red Cross, Form 1082, Application to Teach Nursing and Health Services—12/81.

INCORPORATING ADULT EDUCATION CONCEPTS

Planning an educational program for adult learners without incorporating adult education concepts dooms the program to failure. No matter how interesting or well planned the curriculum is, adults have different needs and expectations for their learning experiences. As you plan your program, keep in mind that adults need or have the following:[3]

- a learning climate that is physically and psychologically comfortable
- respect and acceptance by other students and instructors

Exhibit 11–3 Disaster Nursing Quiz

---

1. In a mass emergency situation, which blood type will be used for transfusions until facilities for typing and cross matching are established?

   a. A+   c. AB+
   b. O+   d. O−

2. Personnel from the Federal Emergency Management Agency (FEMA) can provide individual assistance to disaster victims by asking the Internal Revenue Service to postpone tax payments and amend income tax returns. (True or False)

Instructions: You are assisting with triage of casualties in a receiving area of a hospital near a building explosion. The standard Civil Defense categories for priority of treatment are being used. Please record the letter of the appropriate category with the number on the answer sheet. (Multiple Choice)

Question	Categories
3. Closed fracture of the femur	a. Minimal
4. Partial amputations	b. Immediate
5. Contused kidney	c. Delayed
6. Sucking chest wound	d. Expectant
7. Closed fracture of radius and ulna	
8. Third degree burns of both legs, hands, and forearms	
9. Penetrating wound of the abdomen	

Source: Adapted with permission from Neal MV: *Disaster Nursing Preparation: Report of a Pilot Project.* New York, National League for Nursing, 1963.

- a perception of the instructor as a guide or facilitator; someone approachable
- a vast resource of experience as individuals
- a desire to participate in planning and implementing the learning process
- habits and patterns of living, working, learning and at times resistance to change

Build on the Principles of Learning

When designing an educational program for adults, the planner must bear in mind the principles of learning. Knowles has identified superior conditions of learning:[3]

- Learners feel a need to learn (motivation).
- Learners perceive the goals of a learning experience to be their goals.

- Learners accept a share of the responsibility for planning and operating a learning experience and, therefore, have a feeling of commitment toward it.
- Learners participate actively in the learning process.
- The learning process is related to and makes use of the experience of the learners. (The more useful the information, the more it is retained. Past experiences are rich resources.)
- Learners have a sense of progress toward their goals.
- Learners have a sense that the more they see, hear, and do, the more they learn.
- The learning environment is characterized by physical comfort, mutual trust and respect, mutual helpfulness, freedom of expression, and acceptance of differences.

Learning Theories

Two learning theories—overlearning and simulation—apply to the situation in which increased retention of material is the objective. Both theories are teaching strategies especially suited to disaster training. In a disaster response, nurses must act quickly without extensive reflection. They must continue performing at an adequate level despite fatigue and stress; behaviors must be very familiar and almost instinctive.

Overlearning is a teaching technique whereby trainees are provided with continued practice far beyond the point at which the task has been performed correctly several times. Continual pairing of a response with a stimulus strengthens the stimulus-response bond, thereby making the response more reflexive. Overlearning is also valuable because it causes a response to become automatic. As a result, nurses are more likely to maintain the quality of their performance in times of emergency and added stress. It helps transfer material learned to job settings. Real world events are reduced to dynamic, safe, and efficient settings such as triage practice or mass casualty drills.[4] Overlearning theory is relevant to activities that must be practiced under simulated conditions because the real situation is too expensive or too dangerous. Practice and repetition are even more crucial in those tasks for which individuals cannot rely on lifelong patterns—for example, emergency procedures such as triage and crowd psychology in disaster settings. Frequently such situations are foreign to practicing nurses. Overlearning applied to a simulated environment is helpful in mastering these skills.

The triage practice cards can be especially useful to practice in overlearning. Small groups are formed of three to five persons. Each member, given several cards, decides on a triage category for each. Then the small group reassembles and arrives at a consensus. After ''paper drills'' are completed successfully and consistently, participants practice triage decision making on moulaged patients in a disaster drill. Role playing situations can be completed in a similar manner.

Simulation is an especially effective method with adult learners. Simulation creates a real-life situation with which the learner actively works and attempts to solve. From the instructor's point of view, simulation gives insight into how participants are grasping and developing new knowledge and skills. For the participant, simulation creates a comfortable, safe atmosphere in which experimentation in problem solving can take place. Role playing, games, and participative case studies are ways to incorporate simulation into the curriculum. In the near future, the increased availability of computers in the classroom will provide new and exciting avenues for learning through simulation.[5]

Program Design

After the learners' needs have been determined, a curriculum is tailored to meet those needs. Planning consists of translating diagnosed needs into specific educational objectives (or directions of growth), designing and conducting learning experiences to achieve those objectives, and evaluating the extent to which those objectives have been accomplished.[3]

Today, education has become behaviorally-based or performance-oriented. The advent of continuing education for nursing relicensure has made this particularly true. Learning needs to be measured at this time.

Behavioral objectives are tools that provide the instructor and the learner with specific, measurable, time-referenced learning outcomes. According to Monroe and Quinn, behavioral objectives are useful to educators because they do the following:[6]

- indicate the learning needs of students
- serve as targets of instruction
- guide the evaluation process
- reflect student gains
- reduce student competition

In the overall design of a program, objectives are essential because they become the criteria by which materials are selected, content is outlined, instructional procedures are developed, and tests and examinations are prepared.[6]

Richard Burns' *New Approaches to Behavioral Objectives* or Robert Mager's *Preparing Instructional Objectives* are excellent resources for learning to develop and use behavioral objectives.

Behavioral objectives form the basis for planning each lesson. Formalized lesson planning provides an excellent strategy for conceptualizing overall achievement of those objectives. Content, method, resources, activities, and evaluation combine in timely progressions for a visible working plan.

Teaching Strategies

Preparing an educational program that is informative and interesting depends upon integrating a variety of teaching methods. To increase retention of material, Edgar Dale stresses the importance of switching stimuli sources and the value of participation in the learning process. Reading and lecturing provide retention levels of 10 to 20 percent, while hearing, saying, seeing, and doing types of experience increase retention to 70 to 90 percent.[7]

Beyond routine lecture, many teaching methods are available to the in-service instructor:

- group discussion
- demonstrations and practice periods
- case studies
- triage practice
- audiovisual programs
- guest speakers
- out-of-class assignments
- written assignments
- computer simulation exercises
- panel discussions
- participation in mass casualty drills
- field trips
- role playing

A well-designed curriculum provides learners with varied learning stimuli. Adults benefit from 'doing' types of experiences. It is also essential to remember that every individual has a personal method of studying and learning new information. While some may enjoy and do well with reading and lecture, others may need audiovisuals and demonstrations. This insight can be especially helpful when slower learners are in the class. The instructor can explore individual needs with each student and determine which learning experiences are most valuable.

RESOURCES FOR INSTRUCTION

Classroom Studies

Instructors. Virtually every community has persons and agencies with expertise in disaster management. Tapping these resources can add diversity and enrichment to a program.

Guest speakers are excellent resources for disaster classes. It is always wise to engage a speaker well in advance. When engaging a speaker, request a specific topic and delineate the time period for the guest. Provide speakers with overall course objectives and written objectives for their presentation. This material helps keep them on track. Appendix 11–A provides suggested resources for guest speakers.

Audiovisual Resources. Audiovisuals are an invaluable resource for assisting participants in visualizing and feeling the impact of disaster and its consequences. They can be used to set the tone for a presentation, provide the basis for discussion, and allow participants to observe disaster situations and the strategies for intervention and relief. Also, audiovisual aids are an optimal learning tool for independent course work. Many of the resources listed in Appendix 11–A can also provide audiovisuals.

Development of one's own audiovisuals, particularly transparencies, slides, and flip charts, is encouraged. Materials such as these are easily tailored to the specific course features and points of emphasis. Some useful audiovisuals may already exist in your organization.

Handout Materials. Brochures, posters, and booklets are concise sources of information. It is helpful to obtain a sampling of these materials in the planning stages of the programs. They are also excellent handouts for course packets. Again Appendix 11–A can assist you in obtaining these materials. Also, Appendix D of Chapter 13 provides addresses of additional disaster resource centers.

Related Course Activities

Adult nurse learners really enjoy practical hands-on experiences. As a finale of the course, assign a task force to organize a triage exercise or a mass casualty drill (see Chapter 12). The objective would be to have participants demonstrate learning outcomes. It is important to provide content and skills practice sessions to emphasize roles and expectations before holding a drill. Additionally, "starting small" and working from simple to more elaborate drills can be helpful. It is essential to walk through roles and activities in a small drill, then to evaluate it, and finally to repeat the drill, using a more challenging situation. Encourage nurses to participate in various roles (e.g., planner, health care provider, victim, and evaluator).

Additional activities can be field trips to the county EOC and a visit to a working military field hospital. Casualty collection points and supply stations can provide excellent observational experiences. Nurses can volunteer to run Red Cross shelters (after completing prerequisite training) or can accompany Red Cross staff on field visits. Obtaining EMT certification can really enlarge one's emergency care skills and confidence levels. EMT courses provide excellent disaster drills.

THE EVALUATION PROCESS

In the designing of an educational program, an evaluation of learning is just as important as performing the needs assessment. Evaluation should be a part of the program design. It is developed at the same time as objectives, content, methods, and resources. It determines areas of weakness and strengths for learners and the program itself, and it measures the need for further continuing education. For adult learners, self-evaluation is more meaningful than arbitrary grade assignment or instructor critique. Adults enjoy being involved in evaluating their own achievements. This sense of partnership with the instructor de-emphasizes the traditional instructor-student relationship. It gives the participant a sense of equality and respect that is part of adult learning relationships. Participants are thus enabled to see their own progress toward objectives.

Knowles reports,

> I find myself now thinking less and less in terms of the evaluation of learning and more and more in terms of the *rediagnosis* of learning needs, and I find that, when my adult students perceive what they do at the end of a learning experience as rediagnosis rather than evaluating, they enter into the activity with more enthusiasm and see it as being more constructive. Indeed, many of them report that it launches them into a new cycle of learning, reinforcing the notion that learning is a continuing process.[8]

Appropriate participant evaluation methods should encompass checklists, questionnaires, planned observations, interviews, pre- and posttests, rating scales, inventories, and on-the-job consultations. These methods can be used to determine progress of the participant in learning concepts, memorized facts, knowledge application, problem solving, improved job performance, development of new interests, and changes in attitudes.[9] One can also evaluate performance in simulated conditions such as mass casualty drills, role playing exercises, and so on.

The evaluation tool should be developed at the same time as the needs assessment. An evaluation tool can follow a format similar to that of the preassessment tool (open-ended questionnaire, posttest survey, verbal critique, and so on). The following are effective evaluation methods:

- evaluation by participants (self and peer evaluation)
- pretests and posttests
- evaluation by an outside agency
- use of videotrainers

- evaluation of behavioral objectives
- on-the-job consultation

The use of several evaluation styles gives the instructor a better overall view of the learning that has (or has not) occurred in the program. Comparison of these results reveals areas of strength and weakness in the instructor and in the program itself. The need for further continuing education can be determined.

SUMMARY

The process of designing and presenting an education program based on staff learning needs can be challenging, fun, and rewarding. A program individually tailored to the needs of the organization should incorporate the general principles of disaster management and knowledge of overall community response. The in-service educator is encouraged to use adult education theories when developing the curriculum. The nurse should tap community resources and incorporate a variety of teaching methods to stimulate interest in and excitement about the program. Past experiences of participants can be invaluable. If at all possible, trainees should be afforded opportunities to participate in many practice settings. Disaster management skills can be enhanced by hearing, saying, seeing, and doing types of activities. In turn, retention can be increased to approximately 90 percent. Confidence level, knowledge base, primary care, and problem-solving skills can all increase.

Disaster exacerbates many common problems: communication breakdown, disorganization, and lack of or misuse of trained professionals. The problems and challenges of disaster management should be identified through historical research and incorporated into comprehensive educational programs. Clearly, tomorrow's disaster response will be the outcome of today's educational preparation.

REFERENCES

1. Neal MV: *Disaster Nursing Preparation: Report of a Pilot Project*. New York, National League for Nursing, 1963.

2. Ellison D: Education for nursing care in disaster. *Nurs Clin North Am* 1967;2:299–307.

3. Knowles, MS: *The Modern Practice of Adult Education: From Pedagogy to Andragogy*. Chicago, Association Press/Follett Publishing Co, 1980, pp 46–121.

4. Wexley KN, Lathan GP: *Developing and Training Human Resources in Organizations*. Glenview, Ill, Scott Foresman & Co, 1981, p 58.

5. Duke RD: *Gaming: The Future's Language*. New York, Sage Publications Inc, 1974, pp 55–65.

6. Monroe B, Quinn JB: Planning for instruction with meaningful objectives, in Klevins C (ed): *Methods and Materials in Adult Education*. New York, Klevens Publications Inc, 1972, pp 38–51.

7. Dale E: Cone of experience, in Wiman RV, Mierhenry WC (eds): *Educational Media: Theory Into Practice*. Columbus, Ohio, Charles E. Merrill Publishing Co, 1969, pp 160–161.

8. Knowles, MS: *The Modern Practice of Adult Education: Andragogy to Pedagogy*, ed 2. Chicago, Association Press/Follett Publishing Co, 1970, p 43.

9. Popiel ES: Assessing and determining training needs, in *Nursing and the Process of Continuing Education*. ed 2. St Louis, The CV Mosby Co, 1977, p 187.

SUGGESTED READINGS

Burns RW: *New Approaches to Behavioral Objectives*. Dubuque, Iowa, William C Brown Co Publishers, 1977.

Butman AM: *Responding to the Mass Casualty Incident: A Guide for EMS Personnel*. Westport, Conn, Educational Direction Inc, 1982.

Mager RF: *Preparing Instructional Objectives*. Belmont, Calif, Fearon Pitman Publishers Inc, 1975.

Mahoney R: *Emergency and Disaster Nursing*, New York, MacMillan Inc, 1969.

Resources For Guest Speakers and Informational Materials

Agency	Areas of Expertise
American Red Cross: staff and volunteers	Nursing roles in disaster Shelter management Assistance to individuals and families Family and corporate disaster preparedness Mass feeding and damage assessment
Comprehensive Emergency Management Personnel (CEM)—State	Role of the state in disaster mitigation & relief Relationship to local and federal agencies Financial and medical assistance plans
County Office of Emergency Services (OES)—in some areas, called the Office of Disaster Preparedness	Role of local government Relationship to state and federal agencies Emergency welfare services Coroner's services Public safety inspections Debris removal
Emergency Medical Services (EMS)	Coordination of medical response to mass casualty incidents Role of various agencies involved Disaster planning and disaster drills
Federal Emergency Management Agency (FEMA)	Role of federal government Temporary housing options Low interest loans Job placement Unemployment compensation Food stamps and other services available

Fire Department	Role of local fire department Services provided: rescue, first aid, extrication Coordination with other communities
Law Enforcement Department	Role of police Warning, evacuation, safety Crowd and traffic control Transportation and communications
Local Emergency Communications Network (e.g., Civil Air Patrol)	Role of agency(ies) Communication maintenance
Mental Health Workers	Crisis intervention Effect of disaster on adults, children, and elderly personnel Disaster related stress syndrome for victims and care providers
Military: Active duty, Guard and Reserve Personnel	Role of each facet in peace and wartime Assistance to the public sector Supply, personnel, and transport resources Use of temporary, mobile or inflatable hospitals Nuclear, biological and chemical decontamination
Paramedics/Emergency Medical Technicians (EMT)	Their backgrounds in emergency care & triage Communications Stabilization for transport Rapid assessment skills Planning mass casualty drills
Public Health Department	Medical and nursing roles Disease prevention Immunizations Public safety inspections Food and water sanitation

Agency	*Possible Subjects*
Environmental Protection Agency (EPA)	Environmental disasters Transportation of hazardous materials Decontamination procedures

Office of US Foreign
   Disaster Assistance (AID)
	U.S. relief assistance abroad
	Coordination of voluntary/governmental
	   assistance in foreign disasters

Safety Committee Industry	Coordination of medical response to mass casualty incidents Role of various agencies involved Disaster planning Disaster drills

World Health Organization/
   Pan American Health
   Organization
	Public health management of disasters
	International relief coordination
	International health
	(Much training material is also available
	   upon request)

National Institute of Occupational Safety and Health (NIOSH), Cincinnati, OH

Occupational Safety and Health Agency (OSHA) State and Regional Offices

Occupational and Environmental Health Education Resource Centers (Divisions of NIOSH—usually affiliated with a university setting)

Occupational Health Centers of various universities

Emergency Management Information Center (EMIC) Librarian*
Learning Resource Center, NETC
16825 South Seton Avenue
Emmitsburg, MD 21727
(800) 638–1821, X6032.
*Try to obtain material through state CEM office first.

Natural Hazards Research and Applications Information Center
Institute of Behavioral Science #6
Campus Box 482
University of Colorado
Boulder, CO 80309
(309) 492–6818
   To obtain information on the use of computers in hazards research and management; support for emergency decision making; and computer simulation of fire, hurricane, and cyclone disasters, contact:
The Society for Computer Simulation
P.O. Box 2228
La Jolla, CA 92038
(619) 459–3888

Appendix 11–B

Suggested Readings

(Available from the Pan American Health Organization)
525 Twenty-third Street, N.W.
Washington, D.C. 20037 U.S.A.

Disaster Preparedness Update: A Computerized Index of an Emergency Preparedness and Disaster Relief Bibliography, PHSP/83–121.

Disaster Preparedness Update: A Computerized Index of an Emergency Preparedness and Disaster Relief Bibliography of Interest for Latin America and the Caribbean. PHSP/83–25.

Selected Scientific Articles on Disasters (Abstracts, analyses and critiques), Part I and Part II, PAHO/ WHO, Emergency Preparedness and Disaster Relief Coordination Program, 1984.

Medical Supply Management After Natural Disaster, Scientific Publication No. 438, 1983.

Health Services Organization in the Event of Disaster, Scientific Publication No. 443, 1983.

Emergency Vector Control after Natural Disaster, Scientific Publication No. 419, 1982.

Environmental Health Management after Natural Disasters, Scientific Publication No. 430, 1982.

Epidemiologic Surveillance after Natural Disaster, Scientific Publication No. 420, 1982.

Emergency Health Management after Natural Disaster, Scientific Publication No. 407, 1981.

Assar, M: *Guide to Sanitation in Natural Disasters*. Geneva, World Health Organization, 1971.

DeVille de Goyet C, Seaman J, Geijer U: *The Management of Nutritional Emergencies in Large Populations*. Geneva. World Health Organization, 1978.

Various Disaster Reports are available, e.g., *The Effects of Hurricane David, 1979, on the Population of Dominica*. A study conducted by the Pan American Health Organization. 1979.

Chapter 12

Planning Mass Casualty Drills

David B. Lehnhof

What is the purpose of staging mass casualty or disaster drills for the professionals who deal with crises daily? Traditionally, the purpose has been to discover problems, weak points, and faults in the system.[1] However, the initial purpose may become the eventuality—on the principle that a fault looked for will be found. Accentuating the negative produces negative results. On the contrary, an exercise designed and carried through on a positive note will produce positive results. To further ensure a successful exercise, specific goals and objectives must be set on a positive note. Stated, then, in positive terms, the primary goal of staging mass casualty or disaster drills is education, and the objectives are these:

- the promotion of confidence
- the development of skills
- the coordination of activities
- the coordination of participants

The selection of the coordinator or committee head for the disaster drill is another most important step toward a successful exercise. Never make this decision, however, on the basis of a person's title. Nursing supervisors, physicians, or assistant administrators, although well qualified for the positions they hold, do not necessarily make the best coordinators for disaster drills; rather, persons trained or experienced in handling mock exercises should be placed in the control position. If such a person is not available, select a small group—two to four people—to plan the exercise. Choose persons ambitious enough to be daring but also diligent enough to do the work necessary to ensure success.

After the coordinators have been selected, do not allow the "big brother" attitude to develop. Pressure and interference can only serve to smother creativity and accomplishment. The group should be allowed to arrive at its conclusion. This

293

approach does not mean that help or guidance should not be given, only that it should be asked for. Scheduling regular follow-up or progress meetings is a good method to ensure the proper rate of progress without interfering.

DISASTER DRILL PHASES

Like all planned processes, a disaster drill or mass casualty exercise has distinct phases. They are planning the event, coordination before the event, implementation of the drill, and evaluation of the goals and objectives.

Planning

Disaster drills, like all organizational programs, should be designed to complement the goals, the purpose, the mission, the objectives, and the strategies of the organization.[2] When planning a mock exercise, always follow the four basic steps of planning:

1. Establish the goal of the exercise.
2. Determine the present situational need.
3. Determine the aids and barriers to the goal.
4. Develop a plan to reach the goal.

The goal (that which the exercise is intended to achieve) must first be clearly defined; then objectives or steps toward reaching that goal can be determined. Aids or barriers to meeting the objectives should be discussed and the best alternatives selected. At this point, a plan of action can be chosen (Figure 12–1).

This format can produce a plan of action that is functional and educational and that leads to a successful exercise. Determination of the goal of the exercise is vital to the success of the exercise.

The establishment of goals requires, moreover, an assessment of the organization's needs. For example, if the organization is to be responsible for the field triage of patients, then the need could be to familiarize personnel with triage tags and methodology or to determine the patient load capacity of the staff or the facility. However the assessment should not be based solely on skill demonstration. Assume, for example, that training has been produced for triage in the disaster setting. The exercise goal is to examine the effectiveness of the training and to reinforce the lessons learned, rather than how well the personnel can perform triage. This goal can be accomplished by designing a situation in which many patients rapidly undergo triage. Individuals or small groups of the staff are processed through the situation. The evaluation is based then on how well the staff

Figure 12–1 Format for an Action Plan

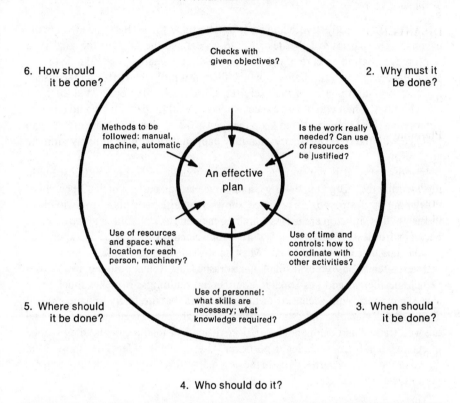

1. What must be done?

Checks with
given objectives?

6. How should
   it be done?

2. Why must it
   be done?

Methods to be
followed: manual,
machine, automatic

Is the work really
needed? Can use
of resources
be justified?

An effective
plan

Use of resources
and space: what
location for each
person, machinery?

Use of time and
controls: how to
coordinate with
other activities?

5. Where should
   it be done?

Use of personnel:
what skills are
necessary; what
knowledge required?

3. When should
   it be done?

4. Who should do it?

learned the triage program, not on how well individual staff members performed triage.

Participant Pretraining

Production of a successful exercise is dependent on the training and the ability of the participants. Without effective pretraining, the drill is doomed to failure before it begins.

Disaster drills should be a functional part of any training program for emergency medical organizations. Weeks before an anticipated drill, initiate training toward the organization's goals. Use the drill to enforce or to evaluate the effectiveness of the training program. If the organizational goal is that all staff members become well versed in triaging methods or in the priority of patient treatment, the training should reflect that goal. An exercise to evaluate the effectiveness of that training is thus a natural segment of the training program.

Scenario Design

Another step in effective planning is to determine the scenario needed for the exercise. The purpose of the design is to accentuate the goal. If the goal is to reinforce the definitive care of disaster victims, the scenario should not be that of an airplane crash in a rural area in which there is a prolonged effort in the rescue and transportation phases of the exercise. A food poisoning episode at the local church social, when you would expect a mass of walk-in patients, would be more appropriate. The key point is to keep the scenario realistic. It is more effective to practice with the type of scenario that may happen than with an unlikely ultimate cataclysm.

In most areas, it is not unusual for system-wide drills to present the scenario representing the "Big One"[1]—e.g., a massive earthquake in which 80 percent of everything is destroyed. Experience shows that effective plans for what will happen in this situation are useless: nothing happens as it should, and the exercise becomes fruitless. Moreover, this unrealistic scenario is a frustrating experience for the health care professional. Most professionals are regularly faced with disasters such as bus wrecks, small plane crashes, apartment building fires, multi-vehicle accidents, and gas leaks in commercial buildings. It makes much more sense to practice with scenarios of these disasters that are likely to happen.

The same principle applies to all disasters, regardless of their size. If personnel are well trained and can handle the 20- to 50-patient load incidents, they will be effective when larger scale incidents occur. Use smaller incidents like those listed above or the types reported daily in the newspaper for designing scenarios to meet your objectives and goals.

Sources of "Victims"

Many sources are available for the "victims" of a mass-casualty incident; you need to know only where to look. Boy Scout groups are often willing to participate as a public service project, and first aid and EMT classes frequently help as a means of gathering patient care experience. The local National Guard or other reserve units are another source of participants. Consider also involvement of some of the local nursing or physician staff. Their participation will provide not only a dual training experience for all participants but also an eye-opening experience for the professionals.

One final, but qualified, suggestion is the use of retired persons, the elderly, or nursing home patients. These people are often willing to participate, and the experience can provide them a break from their routine, can provide a form of exercise, and can elicit a feeling of worth. In return, these older persons can provide many things. First, they are often good actors. Many have had illnesses or accidents, and so they have the experience to portray problems realistically. Moreover, they enjoy helping and feeling involved with such community projects.

The primary area of concern during the planning is to protect the health and the well-being of the "victims." Some may have health problems, and most are somewhat fragile. However, by explaining your expectations and then listening to their response, you can quickly learn the limits of what is acceptable and possible. Most people readily tell what they can do and cannot do.

Environmental Considerations

Another step in the planning process is referred to as environmental considerations. Little credence is gained for a wildfire scenario if the exercise is carried out during a torrential downpour or a snowstorm. There just cannot be ice on the freeway when the temperature outside is 100 °F. The weather is a factor to be considered when planning the scenario. Consideration must also be given to the preparation necessary to contend with the weather. Prepare the participants to work or to be a victim in the prevailing conditions. Nor should all exercises be planned for warm sunny days. There is a greater probability for disasters to occur at night or in poor weather than on the nice days. For cold or wet weather exercises, provide protection for the victims.

Advise volunteers to dress warmly, when necessary, or to wear old, loose fitting, dispensable clothing. Alter the play of the exercise to fit the conditions (e.g., do not remove coats until the patient is in a protected area if it begins to rain). If the weather is unstable, plan a scenario that could happen in good or bad weather conditions, such as a bus wreck.

Coordination

The coordination of the disaster drill is an essential key for the success of that drill. After careful planning and before the actual implementation of the event, much coordinating must be done. The making of arrangements and the over-all responsibility should be the purview of the planning group. Divide responsibilities evenly among the chairman and persons coordinating the event. Some of those responsibilities involve arrangements for the site, liability, moulage, transportation, and special effects.

A suitable place must be found in which to carry out the exercise—particularly when dealing with an on-site scenario. Choose a site that corresponds with the scenario, and secure permission for its use.

Liability must also be considered at this time. Who is liable for property damages? Specify who is liable in a signed agreement between the owner or manager of the site and your legal advisors. Liability for injury to the participants or the victims must also be considered. Arrangements for this type of insurance coverage are often made through the hospital administrator or the local municipality. Waivers should always be signed, but these afford practically no legal protection if taken to court.

Arrangements must also be made for the moulage supplies. Gather and prepare them at least one week before the event. Persons who have agreed to act as victims should come prepared for moulage. They should wear appropriate clothing—something that can be thrown away after the exercise—and should be aware that moulage is to be used. Boy scouts tend to be nervous unless they have been forewarned about what is to be expected of them and why it is necessary.

Transportation to and from the site of the incident must also be arranged. The movement of the people involved in the exercise is an important consideration. Much cohesiveness is lost if 35 scouts must bicycle to and from the event and then go home in tattered clothing and Halloween-like makeup.

Smoke, fire, and explosions can make a disaster drill exciting and realistic. However, these special effects must be controlled by qualified and experienced people; otherwise the harmless, well-intentioned effects can turn the drill into a nightmare. Smoke can be effective, but great care must be taken that not too much is used and that it is nontoxic. Fire and explosions can also be simulated for effect; they too can be dangerous. Contact the local stuntmen's association for help in special effects. If there is no local association, contact the fire or police departments. The safety of all people involved and the community at large is the top priority.

A checklist can help the persons responsible for the drill to coordinate the event most effectively. The disaster coordination worksheet displayed in Exhibit 12–1 provides a sample list that can be adapted to local needs.

Implementation

Plans must also be made for the implementation of the event. It is imperative for success. Again, development of a checklist (cf. Exhibit 12–1) can assist in the effective implementation of the event. The following examples show its value in implementing five aspects of the event:

1. *Site*

   - Has the site been selected?
   - Have all equipment needs been met?
   - Have all safety considerations been addressed?
   - Have all legal liability factors been considered?
   - Has the site been prepared for the drill?

2. *Patients*

- Have the patients been arranged for?
- Have the patients been prepared?
- Have the patients been coached in their roles?
- Has the site been mapped out for patient positioning?

3. *Scenario*

- Has the scenario been prepared?
- Do all the patients understand their obligations?
- Do the rescuers understand their roles?

4. *Script* (operational plan)

- Do you have a plan for what you want to happen? (This need not be a detailed word-for-word document, as in a stage play, but it should indicate who is supposed to do what and at what time. This step should also coincide with the pretraining program.)
- Do all patients have appropriate injuries?
- Where are they in the site?
- Do the moulaged injuries fit the scenario?

5. *Special Effects*

- Are special effects necessary for the scenario?
- Have arrangements for the safe application of the effects been made?

Control

Disaster drills, like all activities, must have a beginning. One popular method is to run a mock call through the standard notification system; however, this notification should be prearranged to prevent misunderstanding by the dispatcher. Adequate communications are imperative for controlling the event. If the exercise is in-house, the on-site notification system can be used. However the event begins, it must be initiated according to the overall plan. The specifics depend on the scenario and the system, but they must be well planned to ensure a successful event. An illustration of the effect an exercise's beginning has on its control is depicted in the following hypothetical example. A drill has been planned to exercise the triaging capability in the emergency department. The scenario calls

Exhibit 12-1 Checklist for Disaster Drill Coordination

		Coordinator	Date	Site	Organization
		Dave	May 22	U of U	HE 595
			Goals & Objectives		Scenario
			Triage and Moving of Pts. by Priority		Explosion in Chemistry Lab.

	Scenario	Site	Liability	Patients	Supplies	Transport	Sp. Effects	Script	Initiation	Termination	Cancellation	Equipment	Moulage	Umpires	Communication
Planning	Tom	Tom		Bob	Jill	Bob	Tom	Tom	Bob	Bob		Jill	Jill	Tom	Jill
Date completed	Mar 1	Mar 1		Mar 5	Apr 5	Apr 5	May 1	Mar 1	Mar 5	Mar 5		Mar 5	Apr 5	Apr 5	Mar 5
Coordination		Tom	Jill	Bob	Jill	Bob	Tom	Tom	Bob	Bob		Jill	Jill	Tom	Jill
Date arranged		15	15	15	11	15									

	Implementation	Date set	Evaluation	Date completed
	Tom	May 22		
	Tom	May 20		
	Jill	May 15		
	Bob	May 15		
	Jill	May 20		
	Bob	May 18		
	Tom	May 15		May
	Tom	May 11	Dave	May 20
	Bob	May 22	Dave	May 22
	Bob	May 22	Dave	22
	Dave	May 22		
	Jill	May 20		
	Jill	May 20		
	Tom	May 18		
	Jill	May 18		

Comments:

for multiple patients with various injuries from a gang fight. The exercise could begin with the patients, the police officers, and the rescue workers crashing through the front doors unannounced. This approach may provide excitement; however, it may not produce the effect desired to augment the training program.

A more practical approach would be to gather the patients, the police, and the rescuers about a block from the site. The ambulance crews begin the exercise when they call in by radio, describing the number and the type of injured they are bringing into the hospital. Thus, the staff is alerted that a disaster-proportioned incident has occurred and that they must deal with it. The staff can then proceed to implement the disaster plan for the situation. This beginning can lead to a more fruitful exercise than the former.

Termination

It is also important to plan the termination of the exercise. The scenario should not be allowed to just wind down until the problem no longer exists. Set a general time limit that corresponds to the purpose of the drill. A more detailed script and problem requires more time in which to complete the exercise.

Another common mistake is to allow persons who have played out their parts in the exercise to wander around aimlessly. They interrupt the progress of the event and discourage the other participants who have not played out their roles. An area must be set aside to which these people can go when their part in the exercise is finished.

A test of the entire system (from the initial call for help to the posting of surgery patients into the ward) generally results in the failure of the drill. More can be learned about the capability of the system by exercising the various parts or groups, not the whole system. In the more complex systems, this system-wide approach produces not only a disaster of its own but also negative feelings and attitudes toward the disaster drill concept. Therefore, set a limit to the test, and provide a discernible point at which the exercise ends—whether the time limit has been reached or not.

For example, if the purpose of the drill is an exercise in triage for the emergency department, look for the point at which the patients have undergone triage and the treatment phase has begun. At this point, the exercise should end. The goal is to evaluate the triage training, not the treatment; it will accomplish nothing to continue. Evaluate only what has been set as goals or objectives.

Cancellation

It is never too late to cancel the exercise. To apologize for the circumstances that caused the cancellation is always preferable to carrying out a program that will fail to produce the designated experience. Cancel the exercise as soon as possible to avoid inconveniencing as many people as possible. If the participants feel their time was wasted by having to finish a nonproductive exercise, they will lose the positive cooperative spirit needed for future drills. Everyone may feel bad about time commitments made for a canceled drill; however, honesty in the explanation of why the goals can not be met will gain their respect when the project is completed successfully later.

Moulaging

The type and amount of moulaging needed for the exercise depends on the type, size, and needs of the scenario. If the objective is to test the rapid assessment of patients' injuries, only very simple moulaging is necessary. Pain can be simulated by the patient and the wounds can be drawn on with water color markers. This technique is simple and effective for training in rapid assessment.

As the scenario changes, so does the need for more complex moulaging. If the emergent treatment of injuries is the goal, realistic wound moulage becomes necessary. Moulaging is a true art form that can become mastered through training and patience.

Classes in theater costuming and makeup are generally available through local colleges and universities and are a good means of acquiring training in this field. The same basic principles apply for making someone look better as apply for making someone look worse or injured. Books on makeup and design may be available at the local library. Some libraries also have reference material on disaster makeup and moulage.

Most of the commercial moulage kits (e.g., those produced by Simulaids, Inc.) include directions on the use and development of moulaged wounds and are nice to use, although expensive. These kits are frequently advertised in the nationally published magazines for EMS personnel. After a certain amount of skill has been developed by the use of these kits, turn to supplies available from any theatrical supply house. Exhibit 12–2 contains a list of the supplies necessary to build an adequate moulage kit that costs approximately $150.00.

Umpires

Umpires or judges are used to help evaluate the effectiveness of the exercise and the performance of personnel participating in the drill—their actions, their reactions, and the treatment they give. Occasionally, have an umpire who is not obviously grading the event. This person can act as one of the patients, as a rescuer, or simply as an innocent bystander. The purpose of the umpire is not to spy on the participants but rather to provide another point of view and to evaluate the effectiveness of the event in meeting the objectives of the pretraining. To keep this critique from degenerating into reproach, then, develop a means of grading the performance standard. A performance standard must list the desired goals and

Exhibit 12–2 Moulage List

2 tubes or cans of white base makeup
2 tubes or cans of blue base makeup
1 tube or can of brown base makeup
1 tube or can of black base makeup
1 tube or can of dark green base makeup
2 tubes or cans of red base makeup
4 cans of morticians wax (or substitute)
1 bottle of honey mask—6 oz (for burns)
1 small ½ oz pot of dark red lip gloss
1 small ½ oz pot of bright red lip gloss
2 dozen wooden tongue depressors
1 dozen cotton swabs
1 bottle of glycerin—4 oz (for the wet look)
1 bottle of alcohol—2 oz (for thinning)
2 paint brushes with stiff bristles—¼ in wide
10 blood bags with tubing and hand pumps
5 femur wounds
5 tibia or humerus wounds
4 bottles of dark red food coloring—3 oz (for making blood)
2 qt of Karo or syrup base (for thickening blood)
4 empty 1-gal plastic jugs (for mixing blood)

objectives for the exercise in accordance with the general scenario. This standard should also list the skills or qualities the participants are expected to display.

The qualifications of those acting as umpires is another factor that requires careful consideration. Those chosen must be knowledgeable in the field or training area to be examined. To have umpires without experience grade the performance in a field exercise is not beneficial. The evaluation sought will not be provided. Moreover, appropriate selection of umpires or judges is a crucial factor in extending the learning experience of the exercise. Again, titles are no criteria for choosing the best umpires. Physicians and supervisors, although well qualified to evaluate medical expertise, generally make poor evaluators of a field exercise. Local persons with specific knowledge in the area of training should be secured for this evaluation. Umpires with this knowledge and an appropriate performance standard provide a proper evaluation of the event and the participants.

Evaluation

To adequately analyze the effectiveness of the disaster drill, begin by reviewing the planned goals and objectives.[2] This is the criterion against which the effectiveness of the drill should be evaluated. The only truly important factor is whether or not the objectives were met and the goals were achieved. Do not expect to be completely satisfied with every aspect of the exercise. Remember, disaster drills are designed to be a part of the total training program and, therefore, a learning process for everyone involved.

When developing the critique format, keep in mind again that the drill is only a part of the training program. The critique, then, should be treated as a part of the training program. Begin by trying to isolate the factors that led to the objectives not being met; then eliminate the personality from the review. Take out the "you did this, and you did that" from the situation. Design the critique format to display the problems and negative factors as problems in the exercise, rather than as individual faults. These problems are simply areas in which the training program needs support or further work. With equal enthusiasm, list and demonstrate the favorable factors that led to the objectives being met.

Be honest in the format. Prepare to discuss all factors that led to the objectives not being met. Faults in planning or execution must be as available for critique as are those factors related to the performance of the participants in the exercise. One method of designing the critique is to follow the outline used in the development of the event itself. This approach provides a step-by-step formula for the review process and allows for an orderly method of obtaining feedback from the participants.

Finally, during the critique, brainstorming should develop probable solutions to those problems discovered in the exercise.[3] As problems are identified, workable solutions to those problems are developed. This procedure prevents the critique from becoming a fault-finding session so that it remains a learning experience.

All the work in planning pays off at the time of postdrill communications. Gather together all participants, the umpires, and the observers, and thank them for their participation. The exercise could not have been completed without them. Open a controlled discussion of the goals and objectives and freely discuss obstacles in reaching those objectives. Input received from the participants and any preconceived solutions should then be combined to determine new objectives and goals for the training program. This action must be a joint decision. The participants will not only feel better about solutions in which they have had input; they will be more likely to implement the desired changes when they are part of the process. After the problems are dealt with, it is time to accentuate the objectives that were met. Play up these factors as a means of building the participants' morale and feelings about their involvement in this and future disaster drills.

The critique should then be wrapped up with a review of the new objectives and goals for this scenario and future drills. One method for doing this is to divide the participants into small groups with their respective umpires and observers. Encourage a short review of the drill with the objective of establishing what happened, how this drill could be improved, and how to implement the new objectives in future drills. The participants will feel more comfortable and open with their communications in a small well-controlled group and will offer even more input than in the large group. After a predetermined time, bring together the whole group to share any new ideas or suggestions developed in the smaller discussions.

RETRAINING

After a few days of rest and recuperation, gather the original planning group for an in-depth evaluation of the disaster drill. The key emphasis of this evaluation is to design a plan for retraining, and to begin planning for future drills. This evaluation should include a review of the training program, the drill, the problems discovered in the exercise, and the solutions derived in the critique. Detailed descriptions of those solutions should then be explored and combined into a plan for new training.[1]

When proven methodology is followed, disaster drills can be productive, educational, and effective. By implementing the methodology of planning, organizing, directing, controlling, and evaluation, exercises can be tailored to the needs of all types of training programs. Different situations, scenarios, and better or more realistic moulaging will not only lend themselves to many types of training, but they will improve with experience. When mass casualty exercises are properly prepared, they develop, improve, and consistently produce a desirable adjunct to a training program. A series of small drills, designed to evaluate specific areas, can prepare the way for a large system-wide drill that actually works and that produces the same type of benefits as the small-scale exercises.

In conclusion, remember that the purpose of a disaster drill or any casualty incident exercise is to augment the training program or to be a part of the training of emergency medical systems. The purpose is not to tear down parts or individuals or to meet requirements for certifications; it is to build and to develop the system.

REFERENCES

1. Butman AM: *Responding to the Mass Casualty Incident: A Guide for EMS Personnel.* Westport, Conn, Educational Direction Inc, 1982.

2. Smith WE: *Impact: Planning is Problem Solving,* syllabus. Ogden, Utah, Health Sciences Administration and Education, School of Allied Health Sciences, Weber State College, 1983.

3. Schottke DE: Organizing disaster drills. Presented at Disasters: Problems and Solutions in their Management, a course sponsored by the Florida chapter of the American College of Emergency Physicians, Kissimmee, Fla, January 25–27, 1982.

Chapter 13

Disaster Planning: Assessing and Using Community Resources

Kathleen H. Switzer, R.N., M.S.

Nurses can play a significant role in enhancing a community's disaster response by planning, assessing, and using community resources. Nursing participation requires an understanding of various groups, organizations, and agencies, as well as knowledge of disaster planning, principles, and research. The purpose of this chapter is to present information on these topics and to discuss specific disaster services and issues.

To provide the stimulus or initiative within a community for disaster planning, nurses can be instrumental in a number of ways:

- developing and teaching education programs
- writing and practicing disaster plans
- establishing relationships with agencies and organizations
- functioning as part of a community disaster response

Individual preparedness is the foundation of disaster planning. Nurses, as disaster workers, need to practice and to teach prevention and preparedness on a personal and a professional level. The more knowledge nurses acquire about community disaster planning and organizational characteristics, the better they can facilitate the disaster operation as a whole and the more effectively they can function within the established system.

Note: The author wishes to acknowledge the help of the following persons: Harry L. Gibbons, MD, Director, Salt Lake City-County Health Department, Salt Lake City, Utah; Theresa Overfield, RN, MPH, PhD, Associate Professor, College of Nursing, Brigham Young University, Provo, Utah; Mary E. Spitzer, RD, MS, Major, Chief Food Service, U.S. Army Reserves, 328th General Hospital, Ft Douglas, Utah; and Howard G. Wilcox, MD, Chief of Staff, VA Medical Center, Spokane, Washington.

NURSING PARTICIPATION

In an actual disaster response, nurses participate in both clinical activities and management responsibilities. They may need to expand and adapt their usual duties to include the following:

- assigning and supervising various levels of workers to patient care duties
- participating in the triage and transportation of patients
- overseeing distribution of medical supplies
- organizing disaster relief efforts
- coordinating actions with others

Nurses often assume additional responsibility and provide leadership in carrying out these activities and responsibilities. They also become an integral part of disaster teams that involve many disciplines and types of community health workers. In some instances, nurses may need to adapt to local leadership or to unaccustomed supervision by nonhealth personnel (e.g., police, military officers, or civil defense officials).

Clinical Activities

The clinical activities of nurses in a disaster are discussed at length in other chapters. Direct services to disaster victims need to be dovetailed in a multi-faceted, integrated approach (Exhibit 13–1). Nurses should be aware of the patterns of community disaster responses and the strengths and weaknesses of existing community resources while carrying out their clinical responsibilities.

Management Responsibilities

Nurses have increasing opportunities to participate in planning, implementing, and evaluating disaster services (Exhibit 13–2). Nurses are included on multi-disciplinary planning boards, working groups, or task forces—usually as representatives of a professional organization or agency.

The expertise of nurses can be used in local communities to provide leadership and management skills (Exhibit 13–3). During a disaster relief effort, nurse administrators are involved in implementing their agency's part of the disaster plan. In the absence or incapacitation of other local leaders, nurses may have inordinate degrees of responsibility and authority thrust upon them.

Exhibit 13–1 Case Example 1

A visiting nurse from New York was active in the organization of an 18-member team of physicians, nurses, and medical students who served under the International Rescue Committee. This team staffed the admissions ward, or emergency room, of a 1000-bed field hospital at a Thai holding camp for displaced Cambodians. The medical services offered by that team were part of a medical care system that included about 200 nurses and 80 physicians; personnel represented a number of relief organizations from more than a dozen countries.

The team found a population of more than 120,000 Cambodians crowded into huts. Many familes had been fragmented by separation or death; more than 1200 children were living in camp orphanages. Despite primitive and makeshift living conditions, the team saw a remarkable community organization in place, with the functioning of local leaders, the delivery of basic services, and the continuity of local customs. This organization was attributed to the spirit of the Cambodian people and the combined efforts of disaster agencies, including the Thai government, the United Nations, the International Committee of the Red Cross, and a number of voluntary agencies.

The camp was organized to provide facilities for water and food distribution, outpatient health clinics, schools, police stations, and orphanages. Cambodian workers constructed huts, hospital wards, and latrines. Other camp members participated in immunization programs, performed laboratory procedures, and acted as translaters.

The medical team treated a variety of conditions, especially respiratory and gastrointestinal infections. Family members stayed with hospitalized children to assist with their care and to keep families intact. Nurses and physicians dealt with many psychosocial problems and integrated their health care services with traditional Cambodian practices that used monks and shamans.

Preventive medicine included disease surveillance, investigation of health problems, and control measures such as immunizations and spraying for insects. Sanitation and safe food and water were a primary concern. Malnourished children and pregnant or lactating mothers were given supplemental nutrients. Even a family planning program was well received, although a few Cambodians regarded it as an attempt to reduce their population.

Education on topics of sanitation and personal hygiene was carried out. Many team members participated in training provided for Cambodian health workers; this training included a three-month program in nursing and a course in communicable disease control.

The high quality of services, much improved over those normally found in that area of the world, created some friction with the Cambodian's Thai hosts. As a result, some clinics and public health programs were expanded into adjacent Thai communities.

These combined relief efforts appeared to be highly successful in meeting both the immediate needs of the Cambodians and in building upon their existing culture and knowledge to achieve health benefits.[1]

Exhibit 13–2 Case Example 2

Anne G. Hargreaves, R.N., M.S., assistant deputy commissioner and executive director, nursing services and education, for the Boston Department of Health and Hospitals, was a member of a fact-finding team sent to El Salvador in 1983. Other members of the delegation included five physicians and a health educator. This group met with health professionals, political officials, and representatives of various local and international relief agencies. Visiting hospitals, prisons, rural clinics, and a refugee camp, they evaluated living conditions and health standards and identified serious problems. Anne Hargreaves later presented the findings in testimony before the House Committee on Foreign Affairs.[2]

Exhibit 13–3 Case Example 3

In March 1979, the nuclear reactor at Three Mile Island, Pennsylvania, malfunctioned and threatened an area within a 20-mile radius. Nursing supervisors and directors had major responsibilities for the safety, care, and evacuation of patients within that area.

A nursing home director had the dual challenge of finalizing plans to discharge or to evacuate current patients while stretching resources to care for additional elderly members of the community. She made difficult decisions about details of transportation, issues of nursing care, and priorities for skeletal staffing.

An emergency room supervisor implemented the hospital disaster plan by recalling her staff and making arrangements to handle radiologically contaminated patients. Simultaneously she prepared for the evacuation of her own family.

The nurse who was public health director for the area worked with state and federal advisors to implement the community response plan. Priorities for evacuation, establishing temporary shelters, and relocating hospitals and health care facilities were major concerns. Because emphasis was given to transportation and communication, a multifaceted approach with many types and levels of organizations was necessary.

This crisis tested the nurses' administrative skills as well as their professional and personal values.[3]

PRINCIPLES OF DISASTER PLANNING

Each disaster is a unique situation determined by the following factors:

- type and cause of the disaster
- magnitude and extent of the damage
- duration and geographic location of the event

Nevertheless, some generalizations about disasters can be made, and these can be applied to planning in a systematic way.

Basic principles of disaster planning are outlined in a publication from the Defense Civil Preparedness Agency, Department of Defense. Planning includes the following:[4]

- a continuous process
- a knowledge base
- a focus on principles
- anticipatory guidance
- reducing unknown situations
- evoking appropriate actions
- overcoming resistance

It is natural for persons to resist believing they will be subject to a disaster. Nurses have an important part to play through educational activities and disaster exercises in changing attitudes as well as in developing competence in functioning.

Disaster plans, which are discussed in more detail in Chapter 14, should never be considered complete. Plans need to be practiced and updated on a regular basis. A plan that is not revised at periodic intervals may create a false sense of security and may actually be counterproductive in a real emergency.

Planning can be done on the basis of known problems and issues that are likely to occur. Although plans can help trigger a desired response to disaster conditions, they cannot actually prevent most disaster problems. The situations most likely to arise are discussed throughout this book and this knowledge base should be used to formulate a disaster plan.

Many community needs are the result of the cumulative effects of a disaster and its sequelae. These events, which tend to occur in a domino fashion throughout the course of a disaster, potentially involve every agency and organization within a community and sometimes lead to requests for help outside the affected area. Countries with marginal resources and low socioeconomic levels may be especially susceptible to cumulative disaster effects. This situation is illustrated by the two-year progress of events and the community needs that stemmed from a cyclone striking East Pakistan (now Bangladesh) in 1970.

Most disasters do not reach that degree of severity. Nevertheless, disaster planning should include anticipation of the cumulative effects of disasters and the potential need for both local and outside resources, which last well into the rehabilitation stage of the disaster.

ORGANIZATIONAL CHARACTERISTICS

The characteristics of organizations functioning in a community have been studied.[5] They have been categorized according to their structure and the kinds of activities they perform in a disaster (Table 13–1).

Nurses belong primarily to established and voluntary organizations, but they may also be part of more informal organizations categorized as established affiliations and emergent citizen groups.[5] Other cultures and social settings may not reflect this system of categorization, but nurses should find this model helpful for understanding the organizational process during disasters in this country.

Established Organizations

Established organizations are formally structured and have definite characteristics:[5]

Table 13–1 Community Disaster Organizations in the United States

Organizational Type	Disaster Tasks

Established Organizations
  police force, hospitals
  fire departments
  public utilities
  health departments
	Assigned

Voluntary Organizations
  Red Cross chapters
  sheriff's posse
  church auxiliaries
  civil defense agencies
	Assigned

Established Affiliations
  Boy Scout messengers
  church-operated shelter workers
  veterans post traffic managers
	Assumed

Emergent Citizen Groups
  special interest groups
  search and rescue teams
  emergency coordinating councils
  ad hoc committees
	Assumed

Source: Quarantelli EL, Dynes RR: *Different types of organizations in disaster responses and their operational problems.* Columbus, Ohio, Disaster Research Center, The Ohio State University, 1977, pp 2–12.

- clear-cut lines of authority
- specific tasks and duties
- definite channels of communication
- explicit decision-making roles

Many community services are provided by established organizations. Those that would provide health care during a disaster include hospitals, nursing homes, and government agencies, such as health departments.

These organizations usually change relatively little during a disaster. Although decision making tends to occur at a lower level of the hierarchy during the disaster and some internal operating adjustments may be made, these organizations tend to be remarkably stable and function with relatively few problems. Established organizations seem actually to resist change. Although the work load increases, they assume few new disaster tasks and return to traditional duties as soon as possible. They use primarily their own personnel, perhaps because of the technical training needed. If volunteers arrive to assist, they may be turned away or released to other types of organizations.[5]

The operating stability of these agencies may create a public image problem. When the demands of the disaster cannot be met by public service organizations, they may be seen as being unresponsive to the community needs. However, this characteristic helps prevent disaster demands from overwhelming their capability to provide services.

Voluntary Organizations

Voluntary organizations are those that have a staff and perform routine tasks during normal times. They also possess a latent emergency capability and, during a disaster, perform new disaster related tasks with an augmented, largely volunteer work force. For example, Red Cross volunteers may have many important roles such as assisting families, maintaining lists of injured and deceased victims, and performing assigned duties at morgues and shelters.

Voluntary organizations undergo great changes in structure, personnel, and functions during relief operations. Their volunteers may have varying levels of training and usually have no experience working together as a group. These organizations typically encounter high stress and increased problems during a disaster effort.[5]

In contrast to established organizations, voluntary organizations have poorly defined boundaries of operation. Their emergency capabilities are usually stated in general terms during planning, which allows them considerable latitude in meeting community needs. However, workers often extend the limits of their work indefinitely, increasing their vulnerability to the stress of fatigue and overwork.

Indefinite operating limits also create situations in which volunteer workers announce credit for the work of another group, and in which persons operating in the name of the organization are unknown to the main staff. In some disaster situations, several voluntary organizations have undertaken the same disaster functions independently and simultaneously. The normal operating staff often spend considerable energy attempting to overcome the problems arising from these situations.

Established Affiliations

Established affiliations are the most numerous types of organization in a disaster situation. The members have existing affiliations with community organizations, but they form a new group in order to assume disaster related tasks. For example, church members may become shelter workers under Red Cross supervision. Clubs or fraternal orders with strong goals of community service may form new subgroups to assist other organizations.

Established affiliations may be difficult to recognize despite their common occurrence, because they are intermingled with established and voluntary organizations. However, they have unique organizational characteristics. They may provide enormous quantities of needed help and have a strong humanitarian purpose. In some instances, they can create operating problems because their primary loyalty belongs to their original affiliation and they do not easily come under the control or supervision of agencies having assigned disaster responsibilities.[5]

Although this divided loyalty may create conflict and can make management of activities difficult, these groups represent a valuable disaster resource. Nurses should be alert to the possibilities for using this type of organization effectively and creatively.

Emergent Citizen Groups

Emergent citizen groups are loose collections of individuals who form together for a specific purpose or to meet a special need. This type of organization tends to occur in a disaster when the following conditions are present:[5]

- major organizations lack coordination
- various disaster activities lack central control
- community members lack information

Emergent citizen groups frequently function in a disaster as a committee, task force, or special team. Many times, representatives from outside the disaster area simply attach themselves to an established organization and become part of their operations. At other times, an organization is formed when various representatives join together to deal with diverse and multiple disaster needs.

For example, a public health nurse often encounters special problems when dealing with the health needs and social adjustments of refugees; consequently, the nurse establishes a working relationship with hospital discharge coordinators and agency social workers. Informal meetings may be held to exchange information and coordinate plans for this special population. In some instances, concerned persons may form an emergent citizen group to address community issues they perceive as unresolved. These groups are usually coalesced around a specific community problem such as health symptoms arising from suspected contamination of air, water, or food.

Membership in emergent citizen groups often shifts, and their purposes or functions may also change as situations progress. They usually dissolve when the disaster or emergency situation abates; however, some groups become formalized into established or voluntary organizations. The Red Cross is an example of an emergent citizen group formed by a nurse, Clara Barton, to address the unmet needs of sick and injured soldiers during the Crimean War. It has become a well-established organization on a local, national, and international level.

The need for emergent groups should be anticipated and included in disaster plans. For example, communities can approve an emergency center as a contingency for major disasters. Designated key personnel operate this center to coordinate and to control all disaster functions, including public information. In this instance, the emergent group has assigned tasks and assumes characteristics of an established agency.

Nurses should consider forming and participating in emergent citizen groups when working in disaster situations needing control and coordination of activities and information. Networking through organizational groups is important in meeting disaster demands.

Emergency Response

The four types of organizations seem to respond to a disaster situation according to a hierarchy of unmet need.[5] If an emergency can be managed by established organizations, others are not mobilized and the community operations continue intact. A true disaster can outstrip the normal capabilities of the public service agencies, so voluntary organizations are called next to expand into their latent emergency functions. When these two types of organizations are insufficient to meet the community threat, groups of individuals affiliated with other community organizations usually respond to help meet the problems. A major disaster is characterized by the formation of emergent groups to perform special functions during the disaster relief effort.

Nurses will find that their particular organization has predictable characteristics during a disaster. The behavior of other groups can be anticipated and understood also. This information, coupled with knowledge about the responsibilities of various organizations, can aid the nurse in assessing and using community resources.

MAJOR DISASTER ORGANIZATIONS

Major disaster organizations can be found on a local, state, national, and international level. They include hundreds of established and voluntary organizations who perform a broad range of activities needed for all stages of disaster relief:

- predisaster planning and research
- rescue and emergency services
- rehabilitation and recovery programs

In a disaster, these organizations differ considerably in the contributions they make and in their approach, commitment, and purposes. They have different amounts of financial backing, resources, and expertise.

The larger, more experienced organizations usually have a better understanding of disaster problems and needs. They may have working agreements already in operation with key agencies, or they may have local development projects ongoing before the disaster.[6]

Improvised and spontaneous relief efforts are less likely to be successful, especially if they originate outside the disaster area. They can create confusion and duplication of effort. Services are more likely to be based on misconceptions rather than on documented need. Poorly conceived relief efforts, however well intentioned, place additional pressure on local organizations and divert attention and resources away from the disaster itself. Disaster relief efforts should be channeled through organizations with assigned responsibilities, unless additional assistance is specifically requested.

International Disaster Assistance

All nations should plan to meet their disaster needs independently; however, there are instances in which international assistance is necessary to relieve suffering. This need occurs most often in areas in which severe natural disasters are likely to occur, such as the Americas, or in areas in which resources are barely adequate to sustain normal living and cannot be extended to cover disaster relief, such as some third world countries.

Organizations that are experienced in international disaster services include those under the United Nations, large voluntary organizations, and various national governments. Some international organizations have national and local chapters in many areas of the world. Examples of organizations offering international disaster relief are given in Appendixes 13–A, 13–B, and 13–C. Additional information on disaster relief can be obtained from organizations listed in Appendix 13–D.

Requests for international disaster assistance are usually sent through specific channels, either from government to government or through health ministries, disaster relief offices, or coordinating agencies. Some delay in obtaining relief is inevitable because large organizations need time to review requests and to respond. Success in obtaining aid may depend upon using established lines of communications and on appropriately directing the request to the organization that furnishes the needed service.

Government organizations often have legal limits on their activities, and may require a formal declaration of emergency or a site visit by official representatives before they can act. They usually must account to a political body for funds and find it easier to respond to disasters with strong public appeal—especially those humanitarian projects with high visibility.[6]

Military Disaster Services

The military represents a source of disaster relief services on an international, national, and state level. Activities may include the following:

- fire protection
- law enforcement
- communications
- transportation
- debris clearance
- health and medical services

For example, the US Air Force and the US Army assisted the Nicaraguan government in a joint disaster relief operation after the earthquake in that country in 1972. A survey team and two field hospitals provided medical care and performed medical regulating and coordinating responsibilities.[7]

In the United States, the National Guard, reserves, and active duty military are often assigned to disasters. For example, the US Army Corps of Engineers and the Utah National Guard built dams and bridges during the Utah flooding disaster of 1983. In another situation, U.S. Army community health nurses and other medical personnel were sent to provide health services in the camps established for Cuban refugees entering the United States in 1975.

National Relief Activities

National disaster assistance in the United States is designed to supplement the services and activities of state and local governments and other community resources. To become available, some services require a presidential declaration of a major disaster or emergency situation. Federal agencies assist and cooperate with local authorities in the affected area, but they do not carry primary control of relief activities.

Decentralized operations like those in the United States occur in well-developed nations in which abundant local resources are available for relief efforts. In contrast, countries with low standards of living have disaster operations that are highly centralized, and the national agencies have strong control functions.

National organizations in the United States have many coordinating functions and are supportive to local and state programs. They include both national voluntary groups and established organizations.

For example, state and local health departments may request assistance from the Centers for Disease Control (CDC). This organization, which is part of the US Public Health Service, provides on-site programs and specialized services such as the following to prevent or to control the spread of communicable diseases in disasters:[8]

- epidemiologic surveillance
- laboratory assistance
- personnel for immunization programs
- vaccines and chemicals
- technical information
- advisory services and training

The Federal Emergency Management Agency (FEMA) is a national point of contact for the management of many disaster activities. This organization assists state and local governments in disaster planning and response, and develops national policies. FEMA has also been active in the development of nationwide contingency systems for disaster relief.

In the past, plans for disaster medical services in the United States have existed primarily on a state or local level and were outlined individually for each possible disaster. However, programs are now being developed to coordinate disaster planning on a national level and to provide contingency systems for large scale responses to major disasters.[9,10] These can be activated when a local health care system is overwhelmed by a disaster, or when the federal health care system is overtaxed with military casualties.

The establishment of plans to coordinate disaster medical resources on a national level can be traced to the Civilian-Military Contingency Hospital System (CMCHS), which was formed in the early 1980s. This system consists of the voluntary enrollment of civilian hospitals to augment military and Veterans Administration hospitals caring for military casualties.

In a natural disaster, CMCHS is limited because only acute care beds can be provided. However, CMCHS has stimulated interest in emergency preparedness and the care of mass casualties and has provided a model for an even more relevant development—the National Disaster Medical System (NDMS).

The NDMS was created in response to a presidential mandate in 1981 to improve emergency preparedness in the United States. This system is designed to respond to a full range of natural and man-made disaster contingencies, according to the nature of the disaster, the number and the type of victims, and the capabilities of state and local resources. If necessary, CMCHS can be activated as part of this larger plan.

The NDMS consists of three major elements:[9,10]

1. medical response: providing medical assistance at the disaster site
2. evacuation: moving injured victims from the disaster site to medical care
3. medical care: providing definitive acute care for hospitalized victims

In the event of a major disaster, the medical response would be carried out by multidisciplinary Disaster Medical Assistance Teams (DMATs), formed by volunteers in interested health agencies and institutions. Personnel include volunteer physicians, nurses, technicians, and other professionals, as well as staff for activities such as litter bearing and food preparation. Two types of teams receive training to respond:[9]

1. casualty clearing-staging units

   - minimum of 103 personnel
   - triaging and stabilization of injuries
   - preparation of victims for transport

2. mobile surgical units

   - 215 personnel
   - surgery for emergent injuries

After evacuation, usually by military air transport, victims are to be distributed to participating hospitals through a coordinating center. It is estimated that 71 coordinating centers will eventually be established throughout metropolitan areas of the United States. The hospital system is projected to accommodate 100,000 designated beds nationwide.[9]

The formation of NDMS has required consideration of many issues. Some of those addressed in the implementation of this plan are the following:[10]

- area selection and expansion
- strategies for coordinating hospitals
- responsibilities of medical teams and mobile units
- medical evacuation procedures
- reimbursement and legal liability
- education and public information
- supply and logistics

As the NDMS continues to develop, nurses will find many opportunities to participate in planning, training exercises, and actual disaster responses. Large numbers of nurses are employed by the federal organizations affiliated with the NDMS. These agencies include the Department of Health and Human Services (HHS), the Public Health Service (PHS), the Department of Defense (DoD), and the Veterans Administration (VA). Community nurses in NDMS areas may also volunteer for teams. Although the NDMS is broad in its multidisciplinary approach, and represents a composite of various agencies and organizations, nurses should find that NDMS complements existing community plans and resources.

Several professional nursing organizations are also taking part in the development of disaster contingency systems:[10]

- American Association of Colleges of Nursing
- American Association of Nurse Anesthetists
- American Nurses' Association
- Emergency Department Nurses
- National League for Nursing
- Society of Nursing Service Administrators

Community Disaster Resources

Local and state organizations have traditionally played a direct role in providing disaster services in the United States. Disaster management is under the control of local authorities until the governor declares a state of emergency. At that point, state agencies assume primary responsibility and authority.

Some community organizations, both established and voluntary, have national or international ties; so they often request assistance and support from these larger disaster organizations. If disaster demands outstrip the resources of local and state organizations, officials may request a formal declaration of a national disaster emergency. Many other community groups represent unique local resources; they often are found as established affiliations or emergent citizen groups. The types of organizations found in a disaster have been described in more detail earlier in this chapter.

Community workers often have experience in multidisciplinary team work. For example, police and fire departments, emergency medical personnel, and hospital emergency rooms work together on a daily basis to handle isolated emergency events. Nurses should foster and develop these relationships; they can become the pattern for a larger disaster response.

Most communities have plans for an Emergency Operation Center (EOC).[11] Key community leaders report to a designated location to activate the center in an emergency. The EOC is usually located in a government facility or public building and is equipped with communication capabilities and emergency plans.

As shown in Figure 13–1, the EOC oversees all major community services during a disaster. It assists in coordination of relief activities and serves as a source of public information. The EOC also assesses the scope and the magnitude of the disaster and provides central direction for community disaster operations.

Health-related services that nurses may find in the emergency stages of a disaster include the following, which are grouped under three main categories:[12]

1. Medical care

   - system of priority treatment
   - identification and registration of injured
   - transportation of sick and injured
   - body identification and mortuary services

2. Health and sanitation

   - water supply and purification
   - vector control and waste disposal
   - safe and uncontaminated food
   - medications for chronic conditions
   - apprehension and disposition of animals
   - communicable disease control

Figure 13–1 Organizational Chart of Emergency Operation Center

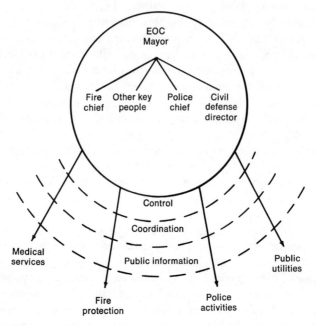

Source: *Disaster operations: A handbook for local governments.* Washington, DC, Federal Emergency Management Agency, 1981.

3. Mass care and feeding

- school shelters and kitchens
- food stamp distribution
- food supplies

COMMUNITY GROUPS AND BEHAVIORS

The nurse may encounter and may be part of one or several groups that exist in a community disaster relief effort. An accurate understanding of group behavior can be helpful in dispelling popular myths and in making disaster plans.

Victims

Group behavior of victims is often subject to misunderstanding. It is assumed that the social and psychological structure of a community disintegrates with the destruction of the physical environment.[13] It is falsely believed that the norms are personal panic, irrational and antisocial behavior, and complete dependency on outside resources and organizations.

Although the occurrence of multiple problems increases with the duration of the disaster and its aftermath, sociological research has shown that most behavior of disaster victims is purposeful and rational.[13] Panic and disorientation has been reported only in isolated instances and is usually short-lived. Antisocial behavior, such as looting and conflict, can be best predicted on the basis of what existed in the community before the disaster.[13] Although long-term sequelae may be identified during community rehabilitation, problems may actually be reduced during the rescue stages of a disaster.

In general, victims respond initially with a high degree of mutual aid and self help. They may enter the affected area in an effort to offer aid to others and may resist organized efforts to dissuade them. Although victims may show long-term psychological effects from the disaster and its aftermath, they typically respond actively to the emergency stages of a disaster with unselfishness and optimism.

This heightened morale may lead to a later stage of victim group behavior in which outside workers are excluded and become the objects of frustration and anger. Victims share an intense common experience or bond; their community identity is strengthened by the adversity.[14] They may resent efforts by those who have not felt the effects of the disaster in the same way, despite an obvious need for the skill and the expertise of the outside workers.

The typical stages of psychological reaction are described in Chapter 8. Nurses need to be prepared to adjust to the group behavior of victims and to foster self help efforts. In this way, victims can be used as a community resource to maximize nursing efforts toward recovery.

Workers

Workers in a disaster include community leaders, individual volunteers, and employees from organizations and agencies. Some of these workers may also be victims, and they may come from inside or outside the disaster area. Any of these groups of workers may include nurses.

Community Leaders

Some nurses may function as community leaders during a disaster. In other instances, leaders must be identified by the nurses. Officials may be absent or lost in the disaster; so new leaders eventually emerge. Community leaders may be subject to overwork and eventual exhaustion.[13] Even when they are physically present, these persons may become ineffective and make poor decisions because of fatigue.

Other problems encountered by community leaders may include conflict over organizational authority for new disaster related tasks, and competition between organizational groups over boundaries and powers.[15] Nurses need to be aware of the political climate in which they are operating and the characteristics of disaster leadership. Disaster plans and their implementation should be coordinated with community leaders because the exercise of authority is necessary and existing patterns of responsibilities form the basis of a community response.

Onlookers and Individual Volunteers

Onlookers may include the following:

- community members returning for belongings
- anxious relatives looking for family members
- curious citizens
- members of the media

During a major disaster, literally thousands of onlookers may arrive in an hour's time. Community workers may experience severe frustration as crowds of people watch them at work.

Coping with onlookers requires patience. Observation sites can be established at a distance so the curious can satisfy themselves and leave. An information desk can serve to field questions, to be used as a contact point for workers, and to screen incoming people.

Volunteers solicited from the onlooker group can be assigned needed tasks. Some of these workers may be professionals and most will be members of the local community. These workers show characteristic victim behavior and tend to be extremely active initially. Unless they are forced to rest, individual volunteers eventually become unable to work efficiently and begin to make serious mistakes. Local volunteers can also be excellent sources of information about a community or its culture; they can interpret the customs of the area and, when necessary, provide translation into regional dialects.

Agency and Organization Workers

Workers from agencies and organizations may be part of the affected community or may be called in from the outside to assist in disaster relief efforts. Nurses are often members of this type of group, which includes professionals, ancillary personnel, and trained volunteers. These persons are better trained and better able to pace their activity level. They are less subject to the exhaustion experienced by other groups.

However, workers from outside the community may show flashes of resentment toward the local population and may display sudden periods of low morale. It may be difficult for these workers to see the purpose or the end results of their labors. Information and feedback on the results of rescue efforts may be beneficial; work assignments need to be meaningful and challenging.

Role Conflict

It has been suggested that local disaster workers may experience conflicts between their families, personal responsibilities, and their work and that some individuals may leave their jobs during a disaster. Research into disasters in the United States has shown that this pattern of behavior is not common in this country.[15] Expected crisis behavior in families and organizations seems to minimize role conflict; so the worker may drop less important roles to focus exclusively on the demands of a disaster.[15]

In general, nurses can expect personnel to perform their duties in spite of personal concerns, as long as they are physically able to be present. However, certain individuals or groups of workers may be susceptible to stress from multiple and conflicting demands. Nurses should be alert to signs of psychological strain and conflict in their coworkers and their personnel.

PLANNING AND COOPERATION

Local planning is important because a community needs to rely entirely on its own resources during the early stages of a disaster. Outside resources, which take time to arrive, are mobilized primarily after local resources have been fully committed.

The likelihood of a potential disaster can be estimated by a community. For example, earthquakes, disasters, or floods are more likely to occur in particular geographic areas. Therefore, possible effects can be anticipated, and critical resources can be identified. Table 10–1 in Chapter 10 outlines the most common environmental effects of several natural disasters. These effects are modified by such factors as population density, type of building construction, and community preparedness. The potential disaster need can then be matched against existing resources.

Guidelines for setting priorities and allocating resources can be written, and steps to request outside assistance can be taken. Responsibility for specific tasks is defined and assigned by the following:

- legislation, regulations, and ordinances
- agreements or resolutions

- statements of understanding
- customary practice

Coordination Agreements

Agreements are outlined for the exchange and the assignment of services, personnel, equipment and supplies. These often take the form of a mutual aid response whereby local governments assist each other according to a prearranged plan and within legally defined limits.[16]

Voluntary organizations frequently draw up mutual agreements of cooperation, or statements of understanding. Although these are very general in nature, they establish a liaison with other voluntary organizations. Voluntary organizations may also have agreements to integrate their services with government agencies.

This cooperative effort begins in the predisaster stage and continues through the recovery or rehabilitation process. Under the pressure of a disaster emergency, coordination is more complex and, at the same time, more critical.

Distribution Problems

Distribution problems are common in a disaster. With the disruption of a community, the relocation of facilities such as shelters, camps, medical services, and emergency morgues assumes major proportions. Planning and coordination is important in minimizing distribution problems with supplies, food, water, victims, and personnel. Food scarcity and distribution is discussed in Chapter 10.

Distribution of Injured Victims

During nondisaster emergencies, distribution of the injured is normally done by taking the injured to the closest emergency department or by taking the person with a special injury to the facility offering that type of care. For example, a patient with massive multiple injuries may be transported to a hospital with a trauma unit, even when it is not the closest treatment facility.

In a disaster situation with many injuries, these approaches are insufficient and may increase the morbidity and mortality rates. The closest hospitals soon overflow; then patients must be transported farther and farther away before receiving definitive care. Consequently, patients with complicated or multiple injuries may be transported long distances before receiving adequate stabilization.

The distribution of injured victims has been addressed on a large scale in several overseas disaster efforts, including one in Nicaragua in 1972,[7] and another in Guatemala in 1976.[17] Information on the number of available hospital beds was done as part of a larger surveillance program. A system of moving patients among the different hospitals and coordinating the various medical services was devised.

A triage concept to distribute victims has been suggested by Butman[18] and is diagrammed in Figure 13–2. It is based on an urban situation often found in the United States in which one or two hospitals are usually within 5 to 25 minutes by ambulance. These are called "near hospitals." A larger group of hospitals, "far hospitals," are available within 45 to 60 minutes. In this system, the near hospitals receive all injuries for evaluation and stabilization. Ambulances at the disaster site transport only to the near hospitals, equalizing the number of patients to each facility as much as possible.

The near hospitals would not routinely admit all patients to their own wards as they would usually do. Instead, patients would be stabilized, reevaluated, and selectively transported to far hospitals for further treatment. The near hospitals would keep far hospitals advised of the patient load and flow; ambulances that normally service the far hospitals would transport patients from the near hospitals.

Figure 13–2 Triage System for Victim Distribution

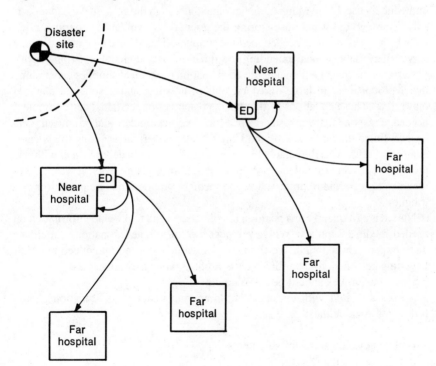

Source: Adapted with permission from Butman AM: *Responding to the mass casualty incident: A guide for EMS personnel.* Westport, Conn, Educational Direction Inc, 1982, p 141.

To assist with the management of supplies, ambulances transporting patients can also be used to bring medical supplies on the return trip.

This system resembles the military procedures for handling large numbers of casualties and coordinating levels of medical care. It forces reevaluation and stabilization in a favorable environment away from the disaster site. It spreads the work load and reduces each group's responsibilities to a realistic level, thereby improving care.

Management of Supplies

At the disaster site, the need for medical supplies parallels the distribution of patients, because the type and the number of casualties determine the amounts of drugs, dressings, and equipment used. Replacements for lost prescriptions, over-the-counter drugs for self-treatment, household first aid items, and vaccines for possible immunizations are also required.

A quick survey within the disaster area may show that many needed supplies are salvageable. For example, one million dollars worth of supplies was found to be immediately useable in Managua, Nicaragua, although the earthquake had reportedly destroyed the warehouse storing the goods.[19] Surveillance programs often include an assessment of needed medical supplies. This should be matched with a survey of available goods, extending coordination to the regional or national level.

At times the management and the coordination of medical supplies can assume major proportions. In large disasters, tons of unsorted and unsolicited material may arrive. These donations further tax the resources of personnel and equipment needed to respond to the disaster itself. Much may accumulate and be unused. One support function undertaken by the United States government during the Nicaraguan relief effort was the establishment of a medical supply depot to deal with this problem. This central collection point consisted of 23 large tents. It was used to identify, to sort, and to prepare donated medical supplies and equipment for distribution.[7]

Nurses are frequently in a position to collect data and to provide information on needed medical supplies. Whenever possible, unsolicited donations should be discouraged. Those that arrive should be forwarded to a central collection point. Diverting personnel for handling excess supplies when they are needed for patient care responsibilities should be discouraged.

Nurses affiliated with organizations preparing material for donation should follow these guidelines:[20]

- Give advance notice of shipments.
- Send only what is requested.
- Label all containers plainly with indelible printing in English and in a second language if required, with a clear destination, and without abbreviations.

- Color code all containers: *red* for foodstuffs; *blue* for clothing and household goods, and *green* for medical supplies and equipment.
- Do not send perishables or items which become outdated.

REPORTING AND COMMUNICATION

Each stage of a disaster, from predisaster preparation through warning, impact, emergency, and recovery, has communication requirements. Consequently, communicating information efficiently and effectively is a major concern in disaster planning and response. Aspects of that communication include the following:

- news media presentations
- public education programs
- official announcements
- warning and advisory services
- specialized communication capabilities
- reports and records
- informal information networks

Adequate communication is essential for control and coordination activities. In a disaster, government agencies may officially have all three functions. The EOC, which was discussed earlier in this chapter, is one example of a disaster organization specifically designated for control responsibilities, as well as for coordination and communication functions. Moreover, advisory services of the government provide monitoring, detection, and prediction of natural disasters. They also warn the general public. Voluntary agencies, broadcasting organizations, and the news media assume some public information responsibilities. The Federal Emergency Management Agency oversees the Emergency Broadcast System in the United States. In addition, international organizations disseminate and exchange information on major disasters around the world.

Predisaster Preparation

Predisaster preparation relies heavily on public education methods:

- posters and pamphlets
- public service announcements
- newspaper and magazine articles
- school educational programs
- volunteer training
- disaster drills

These methods are supplemented by stories from persons who have experienced a disaster. These stories are passed along by word of mouth and may sometimes be classified as folklore with varying amounts of factual base. Community members enter a disaster with different amounts and types of information gathered from these sources of communication.

Nurses need to be aware of communication patterns and systems that may be operating during a disaster. Whenever possible, emergency communication procedures, such as radio systems, special telephone lines, and call-up plans, should be used on a frequent or routine basis. These systems will then be well practiced and their use in a disaster will seem natural.

Warning Systems

Several types of warning or alerting systems are necessary at different times in a disaster. They can be either public alert systems or organizational call-ups. For a disaster that is imminent, most communities have adopted a standard warning signal to be used for alerting the public (Figure 13–3). This signal is usually given by siren, whistle, or horn. Persons are asked to take appropriate shelter upon hearing it and to turn on the radio to receive emergency messages with information and instructions.

The content of any disaster message is important. At times, information has been withheld or minimized in the mistaken belief that the truth would cause people to panic. However, research has shown that, during a disaster, persons are generally goal oriented, capable of self help, and oriented toward action.[13] Communication should be aimed, then, toward giving community members information they can use to understand the danger clearly and to prevent or minimize damage.

Figure 13–3 Standard Warning Signal for Imminent Disaster

Attention or alert signal	3 - 5 minute steady blast	Natural disaster or peacetime emergency

Attack warning signal	3 - 5 minute wavering sound	Only in case of enemy attack

Source: *In time of emergency* by Office of Civil Defense, Department of Defense, March 1968, pp 18–19.

Messages should meet certain standards:[21]

- be specific
- be urgent
- state consequences
- state immediacy
- be issued continuously

Persons are more likely to ignore messages that are vague and allow for rationalizing or postponement. They are also less likely to respond to messages that are inconsistent with each other or with environmental cues. For example, flood warnings may be ignored on a sunny, calm day unless the message specifically describes the flood source, such as melting snow, or dam leakage.

An adequate alerting or organizational call-up plan for personnel is an essential part of any disaster response. Frequently plans are not specific and notification is done on an ad-lib basis[18] that results in patchwork notification and breakdown in communication. The call-up plan may be implemented during the warning, the impact, or the emergency stages of a disaster (see Chapter 10).

Impact and Emergency Networks

During a disaster, communication flows heavily among all types and levels of organizations and from organizations to the general public. This flow is supplemented by an informal grapevine as persons attempt to clarify, to verify, or to interpret official messages.[21]

Convergence

The stricken area receives a convergence of supplies, personnel, and information. Radio stations may be deluged with questions about warning messages or offers of aid.[21] Hospitals, police, and other organizations usually receive volumes of incoming calls.

Telephone lines and switchboards may be so overloaded that call-up plans cannot be implemented. Some hospitals have installed separate lines to be used during an emergency. Emergency vehicle radios and portable radios can be used during the rescue efforts, although they operate on different frequencies. This difference is seldom a drawback as long as they are tied into a central dispatcher. In fact, some segregation of communication may help to prevent confusion.[18]

In a major disaster, all communication systems may be destroyed or damaged, interrupting the flow of information both inside and outside the disaster area. For example, when Cyclone Tracy devastated Darwin, Australia, on Christmas Day

1974, the city and its inhabitants were isolated from communication for many hours during the early part of the storm.[21] If the community is temporarily cut off, the convergence process takes longer to begin.

Reports and Records

In most disasters, adequate equipment is present and functioning, but problems occur when individuals fail to communicate properly. Messages may be unverified, fragmented, or generalized. A hospital may simply say, "Don't send more patients;"[18] however a status report would be more helpful. It should contain the following information:

- number of patients
- number of available beds
- needed personnel
- needed supplies
- operating capability

Another area of concern is that of keeping records on disaster victims. The injured may be moved several times as they progress through the established triage system. An "in-and-out" log can help family members locate their relatives and provide data for a status report. Record keeping is important in conducting morgue services—especially if emergency burials are necessary. The nurses in the community also provide the data on and assessments of the health needs of the disaster population (see Chapter 10).

Press and Other News Media

News media reports can have a major impact on disaster behavior. Rumors or misinformation, when given the weight of public broadcasting, can cause confusion and can seriously hinder the rescue effort. Attention to the following guidelines for the dissemination of public information[21] can help to eliminate the spreading of misinformation:

- Public information must be an organized part of any disaster operation.
- Staff must be assigned to monitor and to verify news media reports.
- Authentication and clearance for stories should be given quickly.
- Officials must be aware of the public need for information and must contribute it through releases, briefings, and interviews.
- News media personnel should be kept informed of the overall disaster situation and of the possible consequences of their reports.

Informal Networks

The community itself is a rich source and channel of communication. Information is generated by community members and passed through informal networks that are, nevertheless, structured along predictable lines. Persons tend to turn to close friends or relatives first, asking questions and sharing known information. The circle of communication then widens to include neighbors and other friends. Eventually, disaster victims begin a free interchange with complete strangers who are sharing disaster experience through activities such as sandbagging or shelter living.

This informal information network operates more quickly than formal channels. When individuals are receiving official instructions at about the same time they are being similarly informed by word of mouth, it is a sign that the formal communication system is working well. A personal list of community contacts can be very helpful for nurses to use in gaining access to the informal system.

Knowledge about the informal system that may be operating is essential for controlling rumors and implementing desired actions during a disaster. That incorrect or incomplete information from news media sources may feed the spread of rumors points to the need for good public information and communication plans. Understanding rumors can sometimes help in tracing their source and correcting the information.

Rumor or misinformation spread through the informal network, changing in detail as it is passed along. Rumors usually do not cross outside a given socioeconomic group. They are often passed within a family unit or to community members of the same sex. The rumor may have a specific source, but the teller is usually not concerned with the importance of the information.[21]

Nurses, especially those in community settings, may be in a position to use the informal system with persons not normally receptive to disaster planning and instruction. Minority groups may speak or read in a different language, or they may not relate to the cultural context in which information is presented. Other persons may be outside the mainstream of society or may be mentally handicapped.

Special materials and courses of instruction adapted to the target population can sometimes be used. At other times, the nurses can work through local leaders to gain acceptance for a course of action. In dealing with this aspect of disaster communication, the nurse is operating in the difficult area of influence and persuasion and is concerned with changing attitudes and opinions.

Recovery Process

During the rehabilitation efforts that take place after the acute stages of a disaster, communication may be aimed at the following:

- circulating information about disaster services
- reporting on community progress
- identifying needs for community restoration

Collection of information on the extent of disaster damage also needs to be done. This information can be used to plan recovery efforts and to determine the need for various types of aid. Nurses are among those who collect that data on community needs and make recommendations for allocation of resources.

Some leaders tend to minimize the effects of a community disaster in order to offer reassurance and to encourage pride in the community's ability to help itself. This minimizing of the disaster may create a false sense of security and may delay a needed response. Other persons may exaggerate the extent of the disaster out of emotion or in order to secure all possible funding and outside assistance for disaster relief. Accurate recording and reporting is important, however, in documenting the amount and the type of outside assistance necessary for community restoration.

INDIVIDUAL PREPAREDNESS

Demi and Miles have examined the role of nurses in disaster response.[22] In 1981, the skywalks at a hotel collapsed, killing 114 persons and injuring 188 victims. In studying this disaster, the authors found that the nurses who were most effective in leadership roles were generally those who had formal responsibilities in the disaster plan, and who had previous disaster training and experiences.

Individual preparedness is the most important disaster resource in a community. By assessing their own readiness and planning for their disaster role, nurses can assure that their expertise is used effectively.

Nurses can prepare themselves professionally for disaster readiness by participating in disaster planning at their workplace, by making contributions through their organizations, and by keeping their personal affairs in order. At the personal level, for example, nurses reporting to a disaster site need to assemble some items to take with them:

- a copy of their professional license
- personal equipment, such as a stethoscope
- a flashlight and extra batteries
- cash money
- warm clothing and a heavy jacket
- record-keeping materials
- string bags and plastic bags
- other personal items

They may also want to take pocket-size reference books. (Some suggested references are listed at the end of Chapter 12.) A local language dictionary can be particularly helpful, especially if it contains medical and health-related terms.

Before participating in a disaster response, nurses should expand their own knowledge base on disaster topics. Those who are interested in gaining more information about disasters can contact organizations about specific subjects, or they can request that their name be added to the mailing lists. (Some organizations that perform disaster research and distribute disaster information are listed in Appendix 13–D.) With this information, nurses can conduct disaster educational programs and can contribute to the development or the refinement of disaster readiness plans.

SUMMARY

Nurses participate in disaster planning through clinical activities and management responsibilities. They can be valuable in enhancing a disaster response by creatively assessing and using community resources.

Crisis strengthens a sense of community affiliation and belonging. Nurses will find that an understanding of existing community patterns and an awareness of typical group behavior facilitates their functioning in a disaster setting. Similarly, knowledge of organizational characteristics and responsibilities, general principles of disaster planning, and common response issues form a reliable basis for carrying out nursing functions.

As members of the health care team, nurses can be instrumental through formulation of plans, implementation of services, and evaluation of responses. Many nurses have the opportunity to participate in assessing and using community disaster resources either through their work setting or through their professional organization. Preparation on the part of individual nurses is vital in providing the experience and the training necessary for nursing leadership in a disaster.

REFERENCES

1. Levy BS: Working in a camp for Cambodian refugees. *N Engl J Med* 1981;304:1440–1444.

2. Hargreaves AG: Special report on health care in El Salvador. *Nurs Outlook* 1983;31:198.

3. Davis RW: Three Mile Island, a nursing dilemma. *Supervisor Nurs*, December 1979, pp 12–15.

4. Dynes RR, Quarantelli EL, Kreps GA: *A Perspective on Disaster Planning*, Defense Civil Preparedness Agency. US Dept of Defense, 1972.

5. Quarantelli EL, Dynes RR: *Different Types of Organizations in Disaster Responses and Their Operational Problems*. Columbus, Ohio, Disaster Research Center, The Ohio State University, 1977.

6. *Emergency Health Management After Natural Disaster*, Pan American Health Organization scientific publication no. 407. Washington, DC, World Health Organization, 1981.

7. Coultrip RL: Medical aspects of US disaster relief operation in Nicaragua. *Milit Med* 1974;139:879–883.

8. *Digest of Federal Disaster Assistance Programs*. Federal Emergency Management Agency, 1979.

9. *Facts on the National Disaster Medical System*. Rockville, Md, National Disaster Medical System, 1984.

10. Swetonic MA: The nurses' role in national medical preparedness: Civilian-Military Contingency Hospital System and National Disaster Medical System. Read before the 90th Annual Meeting of the Association of Military Surgeons of the United States, San Antonio, Tex, November 1983.

11. *Disaster Operations: A Handbook for Local Governments*. Federal Emergency Management Agency, 1981.

12. *Emergency Operation Plan*. Salt Lake City, Utah Offices of Emergency Services, State of Utah, 1977, vol 2.

13. Quarantelli EL: *Human Resources and Organizational Behaviors in Community Disasters and Their Relationship to Planning*. Columbus, Ohio, Disaster Research Center, The Ohio State University, 1982.

14. Hannigan J: *Conflict and Cooperation Content After Disaster: An Exploratory Analysis*. Columbus, Ohio, Disaster Research Center, The Ohio State University, 1976.

15. Quarantelli EL: *Structural Factors in the Minimization of Role Conflict: A Re-evaluation of the Significance of Multiple Group Membership in Disasters*. Columbus, Ohio, Disaster Research Center, The Ohio State University.

16. *Environmental Health Mangement After Natural Disasters*, Pan American Health Organization scientific publication No. 430. Washington, DC, World Health Organization, 1982.

17. Spencer HC, Romero A, Feldman RA, et al: Disease surveillance and decision-making after the 1976 Guatemala earthquake. *Lancet* 1977;2:181–184.

18. Butman AM: *Responding to the Mass Casualty Incident: A Guide for EMS Personnel*. Westport, Conn, Educational Direction Inc, 1982.

19. Assessment of health needs following natural disasters. Paper from Fourth Annual Meeting for Designated Epidemiologists, Pan American Health Organization, Washington, DC, May 23, 1978.

20. *Medical Supply Management After Natural Disaster*, Pan American Health Organization scientific publication No. 438. Washington, DC, World Health Organization, 1983.

21. *Disaster Prevention and Mitigation: A Compendium of Current Knowledge*. New York, Disaster Relief Coordinator, Office of the United Nations, 1979, vol 10.

22. Demi AS, Miles MS: An examination of nursing leadership following a disaster. *Top Clin Nurs* 1984;6:63–78.

Appendix 13–A

International Disaster Relief: United Nations Agencies

United Nations Disaster Relief Office (UNDRO)

- Furnishes information on relief requirements
- Mobilizes and coordinates relief services
- Maintains clearing house to match disaster services with needs and to exchange information
- Makes advance arrangements for future assistance from potential donors

Pan American Health Organization (PAHO)

- Acts as regional office for the Americas under the World Health Organization (WHO)
- Coordinates international health action in the Americas
- Provides technical cooperation to health authorities

  - assesses environmental and health needs
  - carries out epidemiologic surveillance and disease control
  - inventories and procures health relief supplies
  - formulates cost estimates and relief projects

United Nations Children's Fund (UNICEF)

- Promotes health, education, and welfare of children and mothers
- Provides emergency funds and supplies

Source: Emergency Health Management After Natural Disaster, Pan American Health Organization scientific publication No. 407. Washington, DC, World Health Organization, 1981, pp 63–64.

World Food Program (WFP): purchases, ships, and distributes food

Food and Agriculture Organization (FAO)

- Provides technical cooperation in long-term food development
- Assesses agriculture and food needs
- Provides emergency food supplies
- Participates in prevention of animal diseases

To order a case study, to contribute materials on significant disasters, or to obtain more information contact:

Emergency Management Information Center (EMIC) Librarian
Learning Resource Center, NETC
16825 South Seton Avenue
Emmitsburg, MD 21727
1- (800) 638–1821 ext. 6032

To obtain information on the use of computers in hazards research and management; support for emergency decision making; computer simulation of fires, hurricane and cyclone disasters contact:

The Society for Computer Simulation
PO Box 2228
La Jolla, CA 92038
(619) 459–3888

Appendix 13–B

International Disaster Relief: Voluntary Organizations

League of Red Cross Societies—a world federation of 126 National Red Cross, Red Crescent, and Red Lion and Sun societies

- Coordinates international disaster relief
- Obtains cash donations and emergency items
- Provides assistance through national societies

  - food and shelter
  - medical supplies
  - volunteer workers
  - field hospitals and medical teams

International Committee of the Red Cross (ICRC)—a private neutral Swiss organization whose basic concern is victims of war and civil conflicts

- Nutrition services
- Medical assistance

CARE (Cooperative for American Relief Everywhere)—a New York based organization that includes MEDICO, an affiliate, and whose policy is to cooperate with government authorities

- Provides emergency food, hand tools, and supplies
- Conducts rehabilitation and rebuilding

Source: Emergency Health Management After Natural Disaster, Pan American Health Organization scientific publication No. 407. Washington, DC, World Health Organization, 1981, pp 65–66.

- water supply systems and sanitary facilities
- houses and health facilities
- health care and training teams

CARITAS International (International Confederation of Catholic Charities)—a federation of 91 national organizations—stimulates, coordinates, and supports member relief efforts

Catholic Relief Services (CRS)—an American organization affiliated with ACRITAS

- Provides food, clothing, medical supplies, and shelter
- Employs public health advisors and nutritionists

Lutheran World Relief (LWR)—an American organization of various Lutheran denominations

- Provides assistance in kind
- Gives loans for long-term reconstruction

Mennonite Central Committee—an organization representing American Mennonite churches—Provides assistance for specific community projects; technical and financial support

OXFAM—an organization with autonomous affiliated agencies in five countries

- Provides expertise in housing and emergency sanitation
- Manages refugee camps
- Offers immediate disaster aid
- Provides nutritional assistance

International Salvation Army: Provides health care assistance and various supplies

Save the Children Fund/Federation: Assists in community nutrition and water treatment

Seventh-Day Adventist World Services (SAWS)

- Offers health programs
  - hospitals and dispensaries
  - child feeding
- Employs professionals overseas: physicians, dentists, and nurses

World Council of Churches—a fellowship of more than 270 Protestant and Ortho-
dox churches with headquarters in Geneva, Switzerland—has several components
including:

- Church World Services (30 United States churches) offers broad support for
  health projects
- Christian Action for the Caribbean (CADEC) coordinates disaster relief in
  that area

Appendix 13–C

International Disaster Relief: Governmental Organizations

Organization of American States (OAS)—an organization that uses the Pan American Health Organization (PAHO) as its health agency and distributes relief to its member nations

- Operates a fund from voluntary contributions
- Procures food, medical supplies, and other relief

European Economic Community (EEC)

- Provides relief goods from member countries

  - Medical supplies and water treatment equipment
  - Tents, blankets, and food

- Restores social and economic activities

  - Insecticides and fertilizers
  - Fuel, vehicles, and spare parts
  - Provides emergency food aid

Source: Emergency Health Management After Natural Disaster, Pan American Health Organization scientific publication No. 407. Washington, DC, World Health Organization, 1981, pp 64–65.

Appendix 13–D

Disaster Organizations: Information on Services

- The American Council of Voluntary Agencies for Foreign Service
  Technical Assistance Information Clearing House (TAICH)
  200 Park Avenue South
  New York, New York 10003

- Distribution and Sales
  Pan American Health Organization (PAHO)
  525 Twenty-third Street North West
  Washington, DC 20037

- National Office
  Federal Emergency Management Agency (FEMA)
  Washington, DC 20472

Chapter 14

Disaster Planning and Other Administrative Aspects of Mass Casualty Situations

Lloyd A. Schlaeppi, M.H.A. *and*
Michael J. Rogers, M.A.

The nurse must play a significant role in the medical aspects of disasters and the use of proper patient sorting, treatment, and processing techniques in mass casualty (MASSCAL) or disaster situations. However, nurses also need to consider the importance of the administrative aspects in preparing for and handling these same situations. Good administrative management, like good nursing care, does not just happen; it must be thought about, planned for, and rehearsed. For example, regardless of how skilled the nurse and other care providers of the institution are in performing triage and treating MASSCAL victims, it would be of little comfort to MASSCAL patients if none of the care providers were aware of the event because the notification procedures to alert the staff broke down.

The administrative requirements for handling MASSCAL situations can be incorporated into the "five Ps" of disaster management (Exhibit 14–1):

1. Plan the disaster plan (P^1)
2. Publish the plan (P^2)
3. Pre-position supplies and materials (P^3)
4. Practice the plan (P^4)
5. Perform evaluation (P^5)

Many of the aspects of processing MASSCALs stem from the care and treatment of numerous casualties generated simultaneously (or within a short period of time) on the battlefield. Indeed, many of the patient processing techniques and administrative suggestions put forth in this chapter stem from the military services. In fact, the need for planning (P^1), the need to keep everyone informed (P^2), the need to have proper equipment and to know how to get to it and use it in an emergency (P^3), the need to rehearse (P^4) and the need for after action evaluation (P^5) are military principles that evolved early in the history of warfare. The five Ps of disaster management are a natural derivative of these principles, which are still considered sound.

Exhibit 14–1 The Five Ps of Disaster Management

Planning the Disaster Plan (P^1)

- Understand the requirements of MASSCAL situations.
- Consider assumptions.
- Determine the concept of operations.
- Approach planning as a command-directed, multidisciplinary effort.
- Organize an emergency operations center.
- Consider regional, community, and environmental factors (see also Chapters 1 and 13).

Publishing the Disaster Plan (P^2)

- Keep the plan simple.
- Develop the hospitalwide plan.
- Develop procedures and instructions for alerting and notifying personnel.
- Develop individual functional annexes to the plan.
- Staff the plan internally and externally.

Pre-positioning of Supplies and Materials for MASSCAL (P^3)

- Identify supplies and equipment requirements.
- Determine storage locations and security.
- Prepare self-contained, easily transportable MASSCAL kits.
- Position MASSCAL kits and develop inspection requirements.

Practicing the Plan (P^4)

- Educate the staff to disaster management strategies.
- Test the plan independently at all levels.
- Practice the plan as a unit in a two-phase process.
- Schedule a drill concurrent with community or regional facilities.
- Test the alert and notification system.

Performance Evaluation of Casualty Exercises and Actual MASSCAL (P^5) (see also Chapter 12)

- Identify and prepare internal and external "evaluations" before an exercise drill.
- Require an on-the-spot debriefing and evaluation by key personnel at the conclusion of the exercise or actual MASSCAL.
- Require a written report by major activity chiefs.
- Prepare an institutionwide report on the drill or exercise and on lessons learned from it.
- Initiate corrective action.
- Monitor, reevaluate, update, and change the disaster plan as required.

In addition, the military services, the military reserves, and the National Guard have often been called upon to assist the United States and other nations who were faced with national disasters and MASSCAL situations, such as earthquakes, floods, fires, failures of man-made devices, and so forth. Regardless of the source of casualties, answering the following questions has always been a primary concern for personnel engaged in the medical support of MASSCAL:

- How do we get to the patients rapidly with competent help, equipment, and supplies?
- What is the best method of sorting (triage) the patients at the site so that a sensible "order of treatment" is established?
- How do we stabilize the patients and remove them from danger?
- How can we best transport these patients?
- How should we deal with bystanders, the news media, next of kin?
- What assistance can be obtained from local law enforcement personnel, the news media, and so forth?
- What is the best use to make of any lessons learned by the experience to capitalize on strengths and to minimize shortcomings?

This chapter provides guidance to nurses, physicians, and administrative personnel about internal disaster planning and other administrative aspects of MASSCAL or disaster situations. The primary objective is to prepare nurses and the rest of the medical team to care for and to administer to casualties, their loved ones and next of kin, and the public at large at the disaster site and at the treatment facility. Chapter 13 focuses on macrolevel planning and administrative requirements. It also concentrates on the regional aspects, the community resources available, and the requirements for coordinated and integrated disaster planning for the entire community in which the hospital is located. This chapter concentrates, however, on the microlevel issues (such as the institution's basic disaster plan, requirements for the MASSCAL kit, and short cuts for prompt patient processing) involved in preparing an institution to meet any MASSCAL situation. Regardless of the level, one overriding consideration precedes all disaster and MASSCAL planning—the requirement to be prepared. Disasters and situations leading to MASSCALs happen rapidly and often with no warning. Communities must be prepared for their occurence at all hours of the day.

PLANNING THE DISASTER PLAN (P¹)

In Lewis Carroll's *Alice's Adventures in Wonderland*, there is a delightful encounter between Alice and the Cheshire Cat that vividly points out the need to understand the requirements and the need for planning. Alice had become confused and lost during her journey through Wonderland when she came upon the Cheshire Cat. She asked him, "Which way do I go from here?" The cat replied, "That depends a good deal on where you want to go." When Alice confessed that she did not know where she wanted to go, the Cheshire Cat replied, "Then it doesn't matter which way you go!"

Understanding the Requirements

Without an understanding of the requirements and the proper planning for disasters or MASSCAL, nurses and their organizations would be as lost and confused as Alice. Personnel would be constantly reacting to situations (as Alice did) and would never find themselves in the proactive posture in which they should be. A number of factors focused in three questions should be considered by all institutions attempting to understand the requirements a MASSCAL would place on them:

1. What types of disasters are we most likely to encounter as an institution?
2. What are the JCAH's requirements for disaster planning, and what are those of state or other accreditation bodies that we subscribe to?
3. What are the capabilities and responsibilities of our institution?

Any determination of requirements that is based on the types of disasters most likely to be encountered by an institution must first of all take into account any unique weather patterns (floods, tornados, hurricanes) that may affect the geographical area. For example, during hurricane Frederick, Gulf Coast hospitals from Mississippi to Florida called in their staffs early, discharged and evacuated some patients, placed the rest in hallways and sheltered rooms, and increased supplies where possible. In spite of Frederick's 130 mile per hour winds, these actions spared patients and staff members from injury.[1] Consider also any potentially dangerous industries (chemical plants, munitions factories) located in the institution's patient area. The near disaster at the Three Mile Island nuclear plant in Pennsylvania (like hurricane Frederick) pointed up the need for hospital evacuation and disaster plans. A third factor that must not be overlooked is the presence nearby of large transportation terminals (airports, harbors) where accidents could generate large numbers of casualties. Finally, determine where within the institution's patient area large groups of people assemble. For example, in the United States several football domes have collapsed as a result of heavy snow falls. Fortunately, they were all unoccupied at the time and did not cause a MASSCAL situation; however, the potential exists. The JCAH requirements for disaster planning are comprehensive. The JCAH requires the member hospital to have a written plan for the timely care of casualties arising from both external and internal disasters, and the hospital must document the rehearsal of these plans.[2] Specifically, the JCAH requirements for external disaster plan are as follows:[2]

- The plan must be rehearsed at least twice per year.
- There must be evidence of a concerted effort to coordinate with the activities of local emergency services (see Chapter 12).

The requirements for the internal disaster plan are that it should fulfill the following:

- The plan must be written to cover internal disasters, including fire, explosions, bomb threats, and civil disturbances.
- The plan must be made available to all hospital personnel and must be displayed on appropriate bulletin boards at nurses' stations and other areas.
- The plan must be rehearsed at least quarterly for each shift (i.e., no fewer than 12 drills per year).

JCAH further requires that the external and internal drills must be realistic; must involve the physician, nursing, and administrative staffs; must use an efficient system to notify and to assign personnel; and must be concluded with a written report documenting the evaluation of each drill and the corrective action recommended.

Ultimately, however, any institution seeking to understand requirements placed on it by a disaster must consider its capabilities and responsibilities. A plan must be based upon the institution's capabilities, which may range from basic first aid to the most sophisticated shock trauma treatment available. Without unlimited funds, however, a hospital cannot realistically prepare itself for every kind of disaster. The planning process, therefore, involves some trade-offs. An institution also has a responsibility to inform the community (local police, rescue squads, etc.) of its capabilities and limitations in handling a disaster.

Considering Assumptions

When a person has acquired a sound understanding of the requirements for disaster planning, it is wise to formulate assumptions that affect the MASSCAL or disaster situation. Exhibit 14–2 lists some basic assumptions that usually apply to all MASSCAL or disaster situations. These assumptions must be kept in mind (as well as any assumptions that are unique to your hospital) during the planning process.[3]

Exhibit 14–2 Common Assumptions About MASSCAL or Disaster Situations

1. Disasters that cause MASSCALs occur with little or no warning.
2. As the population becomes more congested, the danger of a disaster with MASSCALs increases.
3. Disruption may occur in communications, utilities, and transportation. Therefore, a pre-planned alternative means of initial notification and management of operations is required.
4. Normal hospital operations may be disrupted in either an internal or external disaster situation.
5. Internal and external traffic control, internal security, and a public information center may be required.
6. The first casualties to arrive at the hospital from an external disaster do so within one hour of the actual disaster.
7. Planning and rehearsing for MASSCAL situations prepare a facility to respond better to the real thing.

Determining the Concept of Operations

Consider now some of the major aspects of how the institution will operate in disaster situations. Major items to be considered are the following:

- What will the chain of command be in a disaster mode? Who can order implementation of the plan?
- What will be the degree of expansion of the hospital during the disaster situation? Are there additional areas or beds that can be quickly activated to accommodate additional casualties?
- What notification and recall procedures will be implemented to ensure that the medical team is expeditiously informed when a disaster occurs?
- How can conservation of personnel resources be accomplished? Many facilities automatically revert to twelve-hour staffing (or hold over the off-going shift if the disaster occurs close to the change of shift) to ensure continuous personnel coverage for the duration of the emergency.
- What security measures will be used (and by whom) to minimize the presence of unauthorized persons and vehicles at the disaster and treatment sites?
- What security measures will be taken to reduce the threat of internal disasters (e.g., use of security guards, identification badges for all hospital employees, visitor's passes, package control)?
- How will the facility be evacuated if an internal disaster (or external disaster such as a chemical spill, tornado, flood) occurs? The concept of operation for evacuation of the facility must include patient safety, transportation, memo-

randums of understanding (MOUs) with the gaining facility and the community for extra personnel, vehicles, food, and shelter resources.

- Where will the centralized public information center be located, and who will be the designated spokesperson for the hospital?
- How will personnel be trained to perform their assigned tasks?
- How will personnel be informed about the location of pre-positioned supplies and materials for MASSCAL?

Approaching Planning as a Command-Directed, Multidisciplinary Effort

It is doubtful that an institution can or will have an effective disaster plan without the support of top management. Throughout this book, the concept of a medical team approach to disaster planning is stressed. The more each discipline is involved with planning within the organization, the better the plan will probably be. This approach to planning calls for a central plan that emphasizes the major concept of operations and chain of command—a plan that sets the institutional tone for responding to MASSCAL situations. The plan should be a succinct, readable document that could be used to orient all new employees. Department, service or activity levels should also develop subplans to cover the ''how-to'' aspects of their respective disaster activities. Although these subplans should be more detailed than the central plan, simplicity is still the key. The best subplans seem to be those written in a cookbook style. They use a checklist approach that addresses item-by-item (function) what is required at the department, service, or activity level to ensure that the unit functions smoothly in a disaster.

Organizing an Emergency Operations Center

A hospital emergency operations center (EOC) should be established and activated concurrently with the implementation of the disaster plan. Its function is to act as the command and control element.[4] The staff of the EOC is appointed at the discretion of the facility, but it may include the director of nursing service, the director of emergency medical services, the (assistant) hospital administrator, and the director of public information.

The EOC should provide a unified medical command in which information is constantly available and updated through electronic communication and personnel pool runners. Typical EOC activities include the following:

- maintenance of information about critical supply inventories
- maintenance of bed census or patient accountability and the number of beds available

- maintenance of surgical backlog (in hours and by type, etc.)
- maintenance of medical capability information (loss or gains of specialty capability due to personnel or equipment)
- preparation of public information and news releases
- handling the press

PUBLISHING THE DISASTER PLAN (P²)

Keeping the Plan Simple

According to a military anecdote, Napoleon kept a simpleton (often referred to as Napoleon's idiot) with him at all times. His only purpose was to be the first recipient of all military orders before they were dispatched down the chain of command. If the simpleton failed to understand an order, it was not released; it was modified or reworded until even the simpleton could understand it.

There is much to be said about the value of keeping the disaster plan simple. A 1,000-page plan that covers every conceivable circumstance will not be read, and so it is a disservice to the institution. One of the requirements of good planning is to ensure that the plan is understood, that it is disseminated, and that it works. Accreditors and surveyors who examine an institution are quick to spot whether a plan is viable, or whether it is merely decorative—a plan that can be brought out to make the right impression at the right time.

Developing the Hospital Plan

You have now reached the point in the planning process at which you understand your requirements, have a good grasp of the assumptions, understand what your concept of operations is going to be, and know the value of simplicity. Is there anything else to be considered before you start writing the hospital plan? One thing worth considering is to approach other hospitals similar to yours and to request copies of their disaster plans. Most institutions are more than eager to share their plans and, in fact, are proud of their planning efforts. Certainly, plans from hospitals of similar size and location should stimulate thinking, should trigger ideas, and should offer additional insight into the planning process. (See also Chapter 4.)

Developing Notification Procedures

One of the subplans to the central disaster plan should be the facility's procedures for alerting and notifying personnel. A good reason for placing this subplan immediately after the central disaster plan is the requirement that alert and notification rosters be reviewed and updated frequently. Personnel, telephone numbers, and addresses change in even the most stable work environments. Alert and notification rosters should be verified at the department, service, or activity level at least every quarter to ensure that they are accurate.

The procedures for alerting and notifying personnel during and after work hours should outline the institution's plan and responsibilities. The plan should, as a minimum, address the following concerns:

- authentication instructions for the hospital staff member receiving initial hospital notification of a disaster
- the importance of recording the name and telephone number of the source of information
- the importance of questioning the source of information about where, how, and when the disaster occurred
- the importance of requesting as much information as possible about the number and nature of casualties
- the importance of verifying initial telephone information by a call back to the source (Mass casualty hoaxes are frequently initiated on unsuspecting institutions, the most common being false bomb threats.)
- the importance of rapidly transmitting the information to the person authorized to initiate alert procedures and to activate the disaster plan
- the importance of prompt notification of key personnel through the use of call rosters

The use of telephone call rosters to alert key personnel—especially after duty hours—are highly recommended. Most facilities do use call rosters, and the most popular format seems to be the telephone cascade roster (Figure 14–1). The advantage of the cascade format is that, when properly used, it permits rapid dissemination of information to a large number of persons. In the sample call roster, Jones starts the alert process by calling Slever and McKnight who in turn each alert two additional employees. This process is called the cascade effect because each new person starts additional information chains.

Three basic rules must be followed to ensure that the roster functions properly:

1. **The chain must not be broken**. If the person to be alerted cannot be reached, the caller contacts the next person in line. The caller also passes on to the next person in line the name of the person who could not be reached so that this information can be passed throughout the chain and ultimately relayed to the originator. For example, Slever, unable to reach Rover, would

Figure 14–1 Sample Alert Call Roster (Cascade Format)

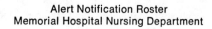
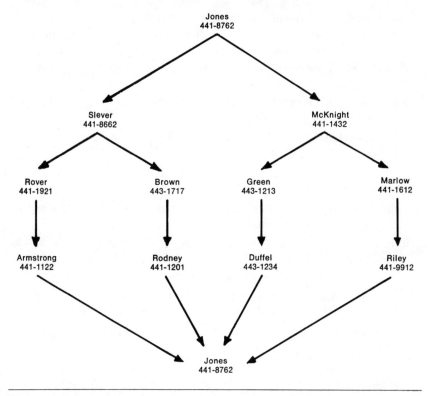

Alert Notification Roster
Memorial Hospital Nursing Department

Jones
441-8762

Slever
441-8662

McKnight
441-1432

Rover
441-1921

Brown
443-1717

Green
443-1213

Marlow
441-1612

Armstrong
441-1122

Rodney
441-1201

Duffel
443-1234

Riley
441-9912

Jones
441-8762

call Armstrong and relay the alert message; he would also notify Armstrong
to pass the information on that Rover could not be reached (see Figure 14–1).

2. **The originator completes the alert process**. When the process is completed, the person originating the alert process should be the last person with
whom contact is made. For example, Jones starts the alert process by
contacting Slever and McKnight. At the conclusion of the alert process,
Jones should receive a call from Armstrong, Rodney, Duffel, and Riley,
which would indicate that the alert process had been successful. Jones
should also receive information from the last person in each chain of any
members who could not be reached (see Figure 14–1).

3. **Frequent practice makes perfect**. Alert call rosters must be kept current,
and each member on the roster should keep a copy of the roster available at
home to ensure a quick response.

Developing Individual Functional Subplans

One of the advantages of a central disaster plan with individual functional subplans at the department, service, or activity level is the involvement of the whole organization in the planning process. Just as top management must be intimately involved in the central plan, so department, service, and activity chiefs must be involved in their respective annexes to the central plan. These subplans must cover the "how-to" aspects of operation in an external or internal disaster situation.

The number of subplans varies from institution to institution and depends in part on how the facility is organized. However, usually as a minimum, the functional areas of hospital command, administration, professional services, nursing, radiology, pathology, pharmacy, supply and services, patient administration, and food service are addressed in separate annexes. Likewise, the subplans are structured in a variety of formats; there is no single way to develop them. Nevertheless, a good test of whether the nursing subplan is adequate is to ask the question: Does the annex answer the who, what, when, where, why, and how aspects for the nursing activities?

Staffing the Plan and Subplans

Staffing for all individual subplans must come from the departments, services, or activity levels concerned. Obviously, there is already much interdependency between these elements in a routine situation, but this interdependence is greatly heightened in a disaster situation. In short, the subplans should enhance and promote the theme of the central plan.

Also coordinate the disaster plan with external community agencies, such as other hospitals within the community, law enforcement authorities, fire protection agencies, civil defense authorities. Request these agencies to provide comments and recommendations. This coordination effort usually brings excellent results because external coordination of the plan increases the dialogue between the medical facility and other community facilities and agencies with which it must work in a disaster. Furthermore, reviewing each other's plans increases the chances that shortfalls will be spotted and corrected. The end result should lead to improved plans and subplans.

PRE-POSITIONING SUPPLIES AND MATERIALS (P³)

The very nature of a disaster or MASSCAL situation causes disruption to routine administrative and logistical procedures. Because the number of patients and the intensity of their treatment requirements expand logistical support requirements, other administrative procedures (e.g., medical record processing and personnel or property accountability) must be abbreviated or streamlined. It becomes apparent then, that careful consideration must be given to identifying the types and volumes of supplies, forms, and equipment required and to determining whether and where they can be pre-positioned. The facility must ensure the prompt availability of adequate basic utilities and supplies and essential medical and supportive materials.

Storage Locations, Security, and Rotation of Supplies

Lists should be developed that identify the supplies and equipment needed, the quantities required, and the locations at which they are to be stored and maintained. Supplies and equipment that can be packaged or incorporated into kits or sets should be pre-positioned and maintained to the extent possible at the anticipated work site. These items and their locations should be identified in the plan (or its subplans), together with maintenance and inventory requirements. Packing lists should be developed and maintained with the kits or sets at the storage area, and procedures should be established to ensure that appropriate periodic checks or inventories are made and recorded. The kit should be conspicuously labeled: *Emergency Procedures/MASSCAL Only*. Pre-positioned supplies and equipment should be used only in support of true emergency procedures, not as a temporarily convenient method to effect routine resupply. However, the subplan must define which supplies are to be rotated to ensure that shelf-life integrity is maintained.

Documents and Records

In addition to the pre-positioning of medical supplies and equipment, much time can be saved and efficiency can be enhanced by using preassembled and pre-positioned medical records, related forms, and documents for patient and personal effects accountability. To streamline and to hasten medical records and documentation procedures, consider the creation of an abbreviated, preassembled disaster medical record. Consider also the use of preassembled, pre-positioned MASS-CAL packets that contain medical records and other administrative items and are stored in a chest or a footlocker.

Figure 14–2 shows recommended materials required at the major triage and treatment sites. A copy of the disaster plan and appropriate subplan should be placed in a document protector or annotated envelope and affixed to the inside cover of the chest. Assemble MASSCAL packets for each patient—enough to accommodate the maximum anticipated number of casualties to be received or treated. Prenumber each packet with a serial number that becomes the patient's registration and accountability number; record this number on the exterior of the packet and on each item it contains. A block of registration numbers should be

Figure 14–2 Contents of a MASSCAL Kit

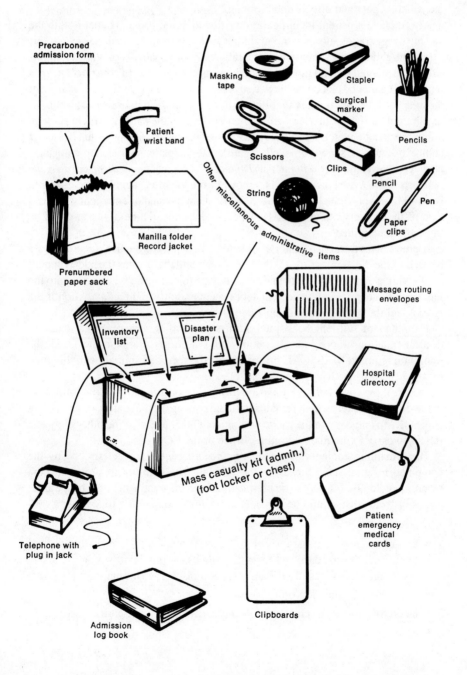

reserved and designated for MASSCAL situations. A large paper sack can serve as the envelope for each prenumbered packet, and also as a convenient repository for the patient's personal effects and clothing.

Also include a patient identification wristband in the packet. Label it with the patient's registration number and highlight with a vibrant colored magic marker. The highlighting makes it easy to differentiate between patients previously admitted and accounted for and those admitted during the disaster. In some instances, a wristband cannot be placed on the patient because of time constraints, the nature of the injury, or the loss or unavailability of the wristbands. In these cases, write the registration number with a surgical marker directly on the patient's forehead or an uninjured area on which it can be readily seen. (A surgical marker is the device of choice because it shows up well regardless of a patient's race or coloring.) However, *never affix a patient's wristband or emergency medical card to the patient's litter*. When the patient is removed from the litter, the identification link is lost. Moreover, if the litter is reused while the wristband or emergency medical card of the former patient is still attached to the litter, the next victim could be improperly identified.

A prenumbered standard manila folder or other suitable medical record should be used as the disaster record jacket. The plain manila folder has the added benefit of allowing a carbon copy of the admission form to be imprinted directly onto the face of the folder. This practice enhances accountability and reconciliation if the patient and the record become separated.

The standard full-length hospital admission form is sometimes used during disaster situations to preclude later duplication of efforts. If this form is used, the minimum required MASSCAL information to be recorded should be highlighted for the benefit of the triage admissions clerks.

Prepare three copies of the admission forms. The original copy of the form stays in the disaster packet, which remains with the patient. Remove the two remaining copies. Keep one copy in the triage or treatment area, and give the other copy to a runner to carry to the main admitting office or the EOC.

The remaining contents of the disaster record packet are determined by the combined hospital staff; however, they should take care not to proliferate the records needlessly. Forms can be pre-positioned in the treatment or the triage area. Types of forms that should be considered for inclusion are the following:

- an abbreviated summary sheet for documentation of care (Most federal facilities use a standardized form that allows for physician's orders, nurses' notes, progress notes, TPR data grid, and discharge summary.)
- physician's medication order forms
- laboratory forms for chemistry, hemotology, urinalysis, and so forth
- transfusion forms

- consent forms
- x-ray request forms
- inventory forms to document patient funds, valuables, and clothing

A plastic patient recording card embossed with the MASSCAL patient registration number should also be included in the packet for use at treatment sites. To expedite processing, include "death packets" in the kit. They could also be preassembled and maintained in the morgue or another designated area. Other supplies recommended are various required administrative items such as extra blank forms, pens, pencils, and surgical markers. These, too, should be pre-positioned with or in the MASSCAL kits.

Having well-constructed and pre-positioned MASSCAL kits available during an emergency minimizes the time required to process patients and enhance patient care accountability.

PRACTICING THE PLAN (P⁴)

Disaster preparedness is not a necessary outgrowth of a well-designed and well-constructed disaster plan. The plan cannot provide the orderly and effective response needed to deal with all aspects of the disaster. The plan must be known, must be understood, and must be managed by a competent, confident hospital staff. After a disaster has occurred, there simply is no time to learn new procedures and to implement untested sequences of events.

The key to effective disaster planning is in viewing the process as a dynamic, continuous cycle of events[3]—analysis followed by discussion, followed by trial testing, followed by problem analysis, followed by discussion of the methods for improvement, followed by revision of the documented plan, followed by practice or testing of the revised plan, and so on (Figure 14–3). The cycle of events must continue to turn in order to keep pace with changes in personnel, procedural requirements, automation, and other technological advances.

The Grand Plan vs Small Scale Drills

The overall hospital disaster plan is a complex multidisciplinary mesh of separate, concurrent, yet interfacing and overlapping actions and spheres of influence. The central plan must be tested on occasion by a real or simulated disaster of such magnitude as to render normal routine procedures ineffective. Such rehearsal or testing is both necessary (JCAH requirement) and useful, but it can be disruptive to required health care delivery.[5] Premature hospitalwide disaster drills can also undermine morale and confidence and can even cause unnecessary conflicts. The overall plan cannot succeed and should not be tested until each

Figure 14–3 Disaster Planning Viewed as a Dynamic Cycle

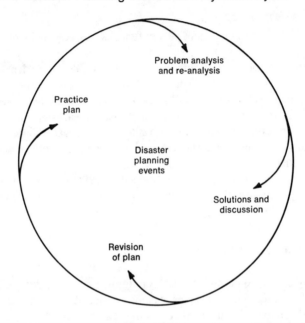

of the interdependent parts (subplans) have been tried and tested. Personnel must be familiar with their individual roles and with those that are dependent on or interrelated to their actions. Informal, then formal, small scale, internally developed departmental drills best satisfy this requirement. Such drills should be scheduled for all shifts.

Just as the actions of individual staff members interface, so do the activities of various sections and departments of the hospital interrelate. Interdepartmental drills are the next step then toward a hospitalwide disaster rehearsal. These drills identify redundancies and gaps in responsible areas, broaden the perspectives of the staff, and build trust and confidence within the facility.

Although the entire impetus of disaster planning is intended to enable the hospital to deal with a large scale disaster that produces casualties with little or no warning, many facilities tend to place too much importance on unannounced, large scale drills. It is certainly important to test the ability of the entire hospital to be alerted and to respond rapidly to a disaster; however, for the most part, this requirement can be largely satisfied by smaller scale recalls and telephone alerts that determine shortfalls in notification chains, schemes, and communications equipment.

Scheduled or preannounced drills invariably foster greater vertical and horizontal staff involvement and concern, and so they have heightened training value.

Inform personnel, however, that they are expected to review the plan and that they are responsible for its implementation. Community participation is also desirable and should be included in larger scale exercises.

Evaluation and Critique

The dynamic, continuous cycle of events (see Figure 14–3) demands identification of problem areas and the subsequent analysis of proposed solutions and revisions to a disaster plan. Therefore, regardless of the relative scale or magnitude of the drill, it should always provide a means of evaluation and critique. Development of checklists, questionnaires, and other critique forms is an absolute necessity for objective assessment and evaluation. Where possible, comparison against established standards and the use of external evaluation should be included. Some excellent sources of external evaluators are firefighters, police, and nursing and administrative personnel from other hospitals in the area.

Every drill should be followed by a formal critiquing session that focuses on the adequacy of the plan, its strengths and weaknesses, and the lessons learned. It should never be allowed to become adversarial or a finger-pointing session; rather, it should concentrate on events, actions, and methods of improvement. It is important to assess what has taken place and the reasons and causative factors involved while the drill is fresh in the minds of the participants and can be accurately recalled.

Resource-Saving Practices

Practicing the plan (P^4) need not always involve the use of precious time and personnel resources (Exhibit 14–3). One successful way to practice is to use locally developed videotapes. These should be kept short (15 minutes) and can be sequentially or departmentally based. A tape can be run continuously in the cafeteria throughout the day or during prime dining times. These tapes are useful for in-service education, or they can be broadcast in waiting areas and at selected worksites.

PERFORMANCE EVALUATION (P^5)

Detailed guidance for performance evaluations of casualty exercises is given in Chapter 12. In general, evaluations should be accomplished before any exercise is concluded. A required on-the-spot debriefing should be conducted by key personnel at the conclusion of the exercise or the actual MASSCAL. In addition, designated activity chiefs should submit formal, written after-action reports after

Exhibit 14–3 Resource-Saving Disaster Plan Practices

Videotape recordings

- cafeteria broadcasts
- broadcasts at scheduled worksite and in waiting area
- inservice educational broadcasts
- learning resource library video tape for in-house viewing or home viewing

Mandatory refresher training
Take-home practical exercises and self-pace programmed tests
Disaster preparedness questionnaires
Quarterly disaster preparedness newsletter
Preemployment training

the exercise or disaster. These should serve as the basis for the institutionwide report. The major reasons for detailed after-action reports are as follows:

- They serve as the basis for formally documenting casualty exercises and actual MASSCAL events.
- They allow for monitoring, reevaluating and updating and changing the disaster plan and subplans as they are required.
- They serve as the best means to identify corrective action where it is required.
- They allow for the entire operation or event to be placed in proper scope.

SUMMARY

Planning is generally considered to be one of the most important functions of management. Disaster planning, then, by its very definition takes on an added importance and urgency. It is an imperative that the contemporary health care facility simply cannot ignore.

A multidisciplinary approach with broad participation under strong leadership can go a long way toward ensuring effective disaster planning and the subsequent implementation of plans. The plans must be simple and flexible and must be based on normal procedures as much as possible. Disaster planning must be dynamic, and the written plan should never be thought of as being truly finished. Consideration of a simple disaster planning framework such as the *five Ps* aids in focusing on the continuous cycle of events necessary to ensure the effectiveness of disaster preparedness efforts. A well-planned, well-rehearsed, and orderly response to any disaster situation is a goal within the grasp of any facility and involves minimum disruption of facility routine. Undue expenditure of valuable resources is not required. Attaining that goal can be professionally enriching and can greatly enhance the facility's service to the community.

REFERENCES

1. Richards G: Focus on hospital preparedness: When bad winds blow. *Trustee,* November 1979.

2. *Accreditation Manual for Hospitals/85.* Chicago, Joint Commission on Accreditation of Hospitals, 1984.

3. Lansky GY: Disaster! Planning for the worst. *Health Serv Manager,* May 1982, pp 1–3.

4. Katz IB, Pascarelli EF: Planning and developing a community hospital disaster program. *Emerg Med Serv,* September/October 1978, p 70.

5. Williams DJ: Major disasters: Disaster planning in hospitals. *Br J Hosp Med,* October 1979, pp 308–317.

SUGGESTED READINGS

Cowley RA (ed): Mass casualties: A Lessons Learned Approach: Accidents, Civil Unrest, Natural Disaster, Terrorism. Proceedings of the First International Assembly on Emergency Medical Services, Washington, DC, US Dept of Transportation, 1982.

Keller EL: A realistic approach to disaster planning. *Hosp Med Staff,* May 1977, pp 18–23.

Schultz R, Johnson AC: *Management of Hospitals.* New York, McGraw-Hill Book Co, 1976.

Seaver DJ: Coping with internal disaster is a hospital priority. *Hospitals,* July 16, 1977, pp 167–172.

Chapter 15

Legal Implications of Nursing Practice in a Major Disaster

Marilyn M. Pesto, R.N., M.S.N., J.D.

To assure that all resources are concentrated on the medical problems presented during a disaster, the actions of health care providers must not be unduly influenced by legal considerations. However, matters of law that may apply to disaster situations should be determined and disseminated as part of disaster planning and preparedness. The law does make allowances for the special circumstances presented by emergencies and disasters: however, it is very difficult to make generalizations. Furthermore, laws are constantly being modified by new statutes and case rulings. The material presented here should be used primarily as a starting point for determination of the current, detailed legal limitations that apply to a particular location and circumstance. Local counsel should always be consulted for specific advice on liability.

DEFINITION OF DISASTER

The first problem in discussing the legal implications of disaster nursing is precise definitions. Much of the terminology that has an apparently well understood medical or lay definition may have quite a different legal definition or have no legal definition whatsoever. Of particular importance is the difference between an *emergency* and a *disaster*. Webster's Dictionary defines an emergency as "a sudden, generally unexpected occurrence or set of circumstances demanding immediation action," while a disaster is "any happening that causes great harm or damage; serious or sudden misfortune."[1] Although ever disaster is an emergency, every emergency is not necessarily a disaster. Various medical and relief organizations have defined disaster by its causation and magnitude. The International Red Cross defines a disaster as "a castastrophic situation in which the day-to-day patterns of life are suddenly disrupted and people are plunged into helplessness and suffering, and as a result, need protection, food, clothing, shelter, medical care, and other necessities of life."[2] A more medically oriented definition has been offered by Rutherford,[3] who suggests that "a minor disaster is one involving at least 25 people or at least 10 patients requiring in-patient treatment in a hospital; a moderate disaster is one involving at least 100 people or at least 50 patients requiring in-patient treatment; a major disaster is one involving at least 1000 casualties." The general sense of these definitions is that a disaster is an emergency situation of a magnitude that overwhelms the resources available to handle "normal" emergencies.

In a legal situation *emergency* and *disaster* may have very specific meanings valid only within the context of an individual statute or jurisdiction. The Federal Disaster Relief Act and the California Emergency Service Act provide illustrations of this point. The Federal Disaster Relief Act defines a *major disaster* as

> any hurricane, tornado, storm, flood, high water, wind-driven water, tidal wave, tsunami, earthquake, volcanic eruption, landslide, mudslide, snowstorm, drought, fire, explosion or other catastrophe in any part of the United States which, in the determination of the President, causes damage of sufficient severity and magnitude to warrant major disaster assistance . . ., to supplement the efforts and available resources of state, local governments, and disaster relief organizations in alleviating the damage, loss, hardship or suffering caused thereby.[4]

The California Emergency Services Act defines three levels of emergencies. A *local emergency* is a

> duly proclaimed existence of conditions of disaster or of extreme peril to the safety of persons and property within the territorial limits of a county . . . or city caused by such conditions as air pollution, fire, flood, storm, epidemic, riot, drought, sudden and severe energy shortage, plant or animal infestation or disease or earthquake or other conditions . . ., which conditions are or are likely to be beyond the control of the services, personnel, equipment, and facilities of that political subdivision and require the combined forces of other political subdivisions to combat.[5] The same statute also defines *state of emergency* and *state of war emergency*.

As in the case of the Federal Disaster Relief Act, it is important to note that a disaster may not be a disaster in the eyes of the law until it is officially proclaimed as such by the appropriate governing agency or persons. Such a proclamation can have a significant legal bearing. In California, a physician, hospital, or nurse cannot be held liable (within certain limits) for acts performed at the request of any responsible state or local official during a duly proclaimed emergency.[6] Note that there is little uniformity from state to state as to what constitutes a disaster or how one is legally recognized. This information must be obtained by the parties responsible for disaster planning, examined for relevance to the local plan, and periodically checked and updated.

DEFINITION OF NURSING PRACTICE AND STANDARDS

No law specifically defines the scope of nursing practice as it pertains to disaster situations. However, other sources can be used to determine guidelines for nurses who may be on a disaster response team or who may find themselves called unexpectedly to attend to victims of a disaster. Guidelines can be drawn from the following sources:

- nurse practice acts
- opinions of states' attorneys general
- joint association agreements
- professional organization standards
- current custom and practice
- common law

States' Nurse Practice Acts

The most obvious place for such guidelines should be the state nurse practice act. However, the language of most nurse practice acts is usually general, often vague, and sometimes ambiguous. For example, the *Missouri Nurse Practice Act*[7] states that

> professional nursing is the performance for compensation of any act which requires substantial specialized education, judgment, and skill based on knowledge and application of principles derived from the biological, physical, social and nursing sciences, including, but not limited to:
> (a) Responsibility for the teaching of health care and the prevention of illness to the patient and his family; or
> (b) Assessment, nursing diagnosis, nursing care, and counsel of persons who are ill, injured or experiencing alterations in normal health processes; or
> (c) The administration of medications and treatments as prescribed by a person licensed in this state to prescribe such medications and treatments; or

(d) The coordination and assistance in the delivery of a plan of health care with all members of the health team; or

(e) The teaching and supervision of other persons in the performance of any of the foregoing.

This definition permits nurses to perform nonspecific tasks (such as assessing, coordinating, and teaching), but it does not allow them to medically diagnose or treat. It offers little assistance in defining what a nurse may do in a disaster. For example, is starting an IV on a severely burned patient considered diagnosis and treatment? The practice act does not answer such questions. Furthermore, a quick survey of other nurse practice acts shows that most of the acts define nursing functions in broad general terms as consisting of patient observation, data recording, and implementation of treatment orders of physicians.[8] Some states, such as Connecticut, have revised their nurse practice acts, giving nurses more definite guidelines. The Connecticut Nurse Practice Act gives the nurse the right to diagnose, teach, refer, and collaborate with other professionals in rendering health care services.

Opinions of States' Attorneys General

A second source of guidelines is the opinions of states' attorneys general. Often legal questions concerning practice arise that the state board of nursing cannot answer in its capacity; at such a time, an official opinion is requested of the state's attorney general. One criticism that has been made of such opinions is that, because of the changing nature of nursing, the legal interpretation of nurse practice laws are well behind the realities of nursing.[8]

Joint Association Agreements

A third source of guidelines is joint association agreements. Unlike the attorney general's opinions, joint association agreements are not legal opinions. However, these agreements may serve as evidence for persons trying to prove that their actions were within the scope of their practice. In other words, a nurse might point to the practice agreements between professional associations to prove that the nurse was operating within accepted standards.

Joint association statements may provide clarification to questionable areas of practice. For example, the state board of nursing and the board of healing arts may agree that nurses may administer IV medications and that both professional bodies consider this a nursing function within the scope of the nurse practice act.

Professional Organizations' Standards

A fourth source of guidelines is the standards promulgated by the professional organization. Although the American Nurses' Association has not published guidelines for disaster nursing per se, the Division on Medical Surgical Nursing Practice and the Emergency Department Nurses' Association have developed standards of emergency nursing practice that define the practice area and outline the scope of nursing activities.[9] Because disasters often generate emergencies and emergency nurses are called to respond, it is useful to be familiar with the standards for emergency nursing.

The standards indicate that "the scope of practice of the emergency nurse encompasses activities that are directed toward health problems of various levels of complexity. Rapidly changing physiological or psychological status may be life threatening, and it requires assessment, intervention, ongoing reassessment, and supportive care to significant others. Life support, health education, and referral are among the several roles and responsibilities."[9]

Standard III of American Nurses' Association for emergency nursing[9(p7)] delineates several goals:

> The goals for emergency nursing care are prompt assessment of the problem presented by the individual and appropriate definitive intervention *within established legal parameters,* directed toward physiological and/or emotional stabilization. If the goals are realized the nurse will observe the following outcomes:
>
> (1) the individual's physiological and/or emotional status is stabilized.
> (2) the individual is referred for appropriate follow-up care.
> (3) the individual or responsible party demonstrates a knowledge of the nature of the importance of follow-up care.
> (4) the individual is free from preventable adverse effects that may be directly related to nursing intervention.

The seven standards outlined by the American Nurses' Association for emergency nursing provide guidelines and boundaries for nursing practice in emergency situations. Although these are professional standards (not legal standards), one would be hard pressed to prove that a nurse operating within the bounds of professional standards was not practicing within legal boundaries.

Current Custom and Practice

A fifth source of guidelines is derived from the current custom and practice of similarly situated nurses. Professional nursing is constantly changing and increasing in accountability and responsibility. Current professional literature keeps the profession's members abreast of such changes, roles, and responsibilities. For example, suggested requirements and qualifications of a triage nurse have been published (Exhibit 15–1 and 15–2). Nurses who hold themselves as being able to perform triage during a disaster might find themselves being held to criteria published in the literature.

Common Law

A sixth source of guidelines is the common law as it relates to disasters or emergencies in general. In a compilation of case law, Prosser (a noted authority in tort law) states the following: "The courts have been compelled to recognize that an actor who is confronted with an emergency is not held to the standard of conduct normally applied to one who is in no such situation."[10(p169)] He indicates that it is eminently clear that this special rule for emergencies is based on the fact that the

---

Exhibit 15–1 Requirements of a Triage Nurse

The triage nurse must—

- be able to function well under stressful situations;
- be able to make accurate assessments about patient care;
- have a working knowledge of the internal operations of the emergency department;
- know intradepartmental policies;
- be able to make rapid and sound decisions;
- have firm convictions;
- possess good communication skills;
- be able to offer emotional support to others;
- be able to think ahead;
- be able to supervise others;
- be an on-the-spot teacher;
- be able to control traffic flow;
- possess good crisis intervention skills;
- have a working knowledge of the prehospital care system;
- be able to avoid conflict and loss of temper;
- represent the hospital and the emergency department to the public;
- assist in discharge planning;
- be able to handle telephone triage;
- be able to deal with patient communication problems, such as those arising in patients who have expressive aphasia, the intoxicated patient, the belligerent patient, and those who are deaf or do not speak English.

Source: Reprinted with permission from Budassi S, Barber JM (eds): *Emergency Nursing: Principles and Practices.* St Louis, The CV Mosby Co, 1981, p 91.

Exhibit 15–2 Qualifications of a Triage Nurse

In order to function in the role of triage nurse, one must—

- possess a valid state registered nurse license;
- be certified as a mobile intensive care nurse (if that certification is available);
- be certified in basic cardiac life support and, preferably, advanced cardiac life support;
- have a minimum of 2 years of critical care nursing experience, with at least 6 months of this being in the emergency department;
- have at least four training shifts in the triage position with a senior triage nurse;
- have at least three evaluation shifts in the role of triage.

Source: Reprinted with permission from Budassi S, Barber JM (eds): *Emergency Nursing: Principles and Practices.* St Louis, The CV Mosby Co, 1981, p 91.

actor is left no time for thought or that he is reasonably so disturbed or excited that he cannot weigh alternative courses of action and must make a quick decision based on impulse. Prosser relates that, under these conditions, the actor cannot reasonably be held to the same standard of conduct as one who has had full opportunity to reflect.

It should be noted that this does not mean that any different standard of conduct is to be applied in an emergency. Prosser succinctly states this in the following paragraph:[10(p169)]

> The conduct required is still that of a reasonable man under the circumstances, as they would appear to one who was using proper care, and the emergency is only one of the circumstances. An objective standard must still be applied, and the actor's own judgment or impulse is still not the sole criterion. He may still be found to be negligent if, notwithstanding the emergency, his acts are found to be unreasonable. The "emergency doctrine" is applied only where the situation which arises is sudden and unexpected, and such as to deprive the actor of reasonable opportunity for deliberation and considered decision. A further qualification which must be made is that some emergencies must be anticipated, and the actor must be prepared to meet them when he engages in an activity in which they are likely to arise.

In other words, a nurse who is confronted with an emergency is not held to the same standard of conduct as that normally applied to a nurse who is not faced with an emergency. The general reason given for this policy is that the nurse has no time for thought, cannot weigh alternative courses of action, and must make a speedy decision. In essence, the ''emergency rule'' holds that the nurse in an emergency setting cannot be held to the same standard of conduct as one who had had full opportunity to reflect.

This general rule does have limitations. First, the emergency doctrine applies only to cases in which the situation is sudden and unexpected. For example, a nurse working in an emergency department would not be surprised to find an emergency; thus, this emergency rule would not apply. Secondly, the conduct required is still what would be expected of a reasonable person under the circumstances. If the nurse does not act reasonably, then the nurse may be found negligent.

These very general rules of law provide the disaster nurse with a cursory overview of the applicable law pertaining to this field of nursing. This law in turn provides the outer limits of the scope of practice. An in-depth analysis of general liability principles can further assist the practitioner in determining a safe as well as legal scope of practice.

GENERAL LIABILITY AND COMMON LAW

Before an examination of the effects and ramifications of statutory enactments (laws made by legislators), such as the Good Samaritan Acts, it may be useful to determine nonstatutory liability, which is ascertained through case law (laws enacted by courts). The traditional elements (Figure 15–1) providing a cause of action for negligence to be brought against a nurse can be stated briefly:[10(p143)]

- a duty or obligation, recognized by law, requiring the actor to conform to a standard of ordinary care for the protection of others against unreasonable risks

---

Figure 15–1 Traditional Elements Providing Basis for Nursing Malpractice Action

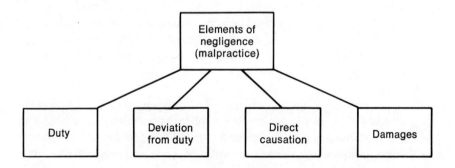

- a failure on the actor's part to conform to the standard required
- a reasonably close causal connection between the conduct and the resulting injury
- an actual loss or damage resulting to another

In other words, a person bringing successful malpractice action against a nurse must prove that there was a departure from the accepted standard of care and that this deviation caused the complainant's injury. Examining each of these four elements in detail provides a better understanding of their applicability to disaster nursing.

Duty

Deeply rooted in the common law is the doctrine that a person owes no duty to aid another in distress and, more specifically, that, in the absence of some special relationship, he owes no duty to render assistance to one for whose initial injury he is not liable.[11] As one court expressed it, "the law of the land does not require a man to rescue a drowning child, no matter how little personal risk it might involve."[12] In other words, "with purely moral obligations the law does not deal."[13]

If there is no relationship between the parties, then there is no duty. If, however, one party decides to offer assistance to the victim, the law holds that the act of rendering aid creates a duty on the part of the rescuer to use reasonable care.[14] If the rescuer happens to be a nurse, a nurse-patient relationship is formed, and the nurse is required to exercise the degree of care that other nurses would have exercised under the same or similar circumstances.[14] A rescuer also has a duty to avoid any affirmative act that makes the situation worse.[15] For example, nurses who have not been trained in triage procedures should not attempt to triage disasters; they should limit themselves to procedures within their current competency.

A duty may also be established through a contractual arrangement. For example, a nurse may agree to be on a response team for the disaster preparedness organization. If this nurse breaches the agreement by not responding as expected, the nurse may be liable for damages. However, it should be noted that suits for breach of contract in the health care field are minimal. The predominant cause of action is the tort action for negligence. If the victim can show that the nurse had an agreement to respond to disasters, the victim is likely to be successful in proving that there was a duty and thereby meet the first element of the tort case of action.

As previously noted, the existence of duty implies a degree of skill:[16(p324)]

> This duty is the possession and exercise of that reasonable degree of skill ordinarily possessed by others of his profession practicing in similar

circumstances. Although a direct test in court as to requisite skill in an emergency has not been set forth, the cases justify certain generalizations:

(1) A specialist in fact, who also holds him/herself out as a specialist, would be held to the skill of the up-to-date specialist in his particular field.
(2) A general practitioner would be held to the standard of a general practitioner. Perhaps a specialist in fact who did not hold him/herself out as anything but "a nurse" when responding to an emergency call would need only meet this general standard.
(3) Nursing students would be held to the standard commensurate with their particular level of training and experience.
(4) Persons who have particular training in first aid would presumably have this considered when a judge or jury weighed their conduct.

Deviation from Duty

Once a duty has been established, a deviation from the standard must be shown. The deviation may be one of malfeasance or nonfeasance. *Malfeasance* is an affirmative act that does not meet the acceptable standard of care.[17(p863)] An example of malfeasance might be a situation in which a nurse moves a patient with spinal column damage without properly immobilizing the patient first. A *nonfeasance* is a failure to act when acceptable standards of practice dictate certain appropriate action to be taken.[17(p950)] An example of a nonfeasance might be the failure to apply a tourniquet to a patient who is hemorrhaging or the failure of a professional disaster response team member to respond to the call of the disaster.

The victim's lawyer generally shows deviations from practice by indicating to the trier of fact—whether it be judge or jury—what a reasonably prudent nurse would have done in the same or similar circumstance. This course of action is then contrasted to the conduct of the nurse who allegedly deviated from the standard. If there is a major difference in the conduct of the reasonably prudent nurse and the conduct of the nurse who has been accused of wrongdoing, then the judge or jury may find that the nurse has committed malpractice and is liable.

Direct Causation

The third element that the victim must show is a causal connection between the breach of duty and the injuries. The defendant nurse's conduct is a cause of the event if it was a material element and a substantial factor in bringing it about. It should be noted that where the conclusion of causation is not one within the common knowledge of layperson, expert testimony may provide a sufficient basis for reaching a determination.[10] This procedure is often the case in medical malpractice. An expert witness, generally a physician or a nurse, must testify to the trier of fact (the judge or jury) that the deviation caused the damage alleged by the victim. For example, an expert witness may testify that had the nurse sufficiently immobilized the fractured femur, the artery would not have been lacerated and the patient would not have died. In contrast, a nurse expert would not be necessary to testify to a jury that a nurse deviated from the standard of care in allowing a patient to roll off a stretcher and injure himself. A jury could draw such a conclusion independently without the assistance or interpretation of an expert witness.

Damages

The fourth element that the plaintiff-victim must show is damages. Actual loss or damage resulting to the interests of the victims must occur.[10] Negligent conduct in itself is not such an interference with the interests of the world at large that one has any right to complain of it or to be free from it, except in the case of some person whose interests have suffered.[10] In other words, a plaintiff would not have a cause of action to sue the nurse if the negligent act did not produce some actual injury to the person involved.

LIABILITY AND GOOD SAMARITAN STATUTES

Under the common law, as was previously noted, when a person attempts to render assistance to another and that assistance is later deemed to have been performed in a negligent manner, liability can be imposed. The Good Samaritan statutes may alter this harsh result of the common law. The doctrine that a person owes no duty to aid another in distress is deeply rooted in centuries of law and nurtured by the extreme individualism typical of Anglo Saxon legal thought.[11] As far back as 1898 our courts in *Buch v Amory*[13] gave expression to this doctrine when they said:

> Actionable negligence is the neglect of a legal duty. The defendants are not liable unless they owed to the plaintiff a legal duty which they neglected to perform. With purely moral obligations the law does not deal. For example the priest and the Levite who passed by on the other side were not, it is supposed, liable at law for the continued suffering of the man who fell among thieves which they might, and morally ought to have, prevented or relieved.

To emphasize its point, the court stretched the argument to its unappealing extreme with almost ruthless consistency. Suppose *A*, standing by a railroad, sees a two-year-old babe on the track and a car approaching. He can easily rescue the child with complete safety to himself. And the instincts of humanity require him to do so. If he does not, he may perhaps justly be styled a ruthless savage and a moral monster, but he is not liable in damages for the child's injury or indictable under the statute for its death.[13]

Many explanations have been offered for the inception and continuation of the common law approach. One author attributes it in part to the fact that "the courts were far too much occupied with the more flagrant forms of misbehavior to be greatly concerned with one who merely did nothing, even though another might suffer harm because of his omission to act."[10]

Another rationalization for the long life of the common law approach is the difficulty in formulating and administering a new rule. The law has been reluctant to recognize nonfeasance as a basis of liability in the absence of some definite relationship between the parties sufficient to create a duty. The absence of this special relationship has relegated the omission of such cases to the status of moral obligation, which the law disclaims any power to enforce, no matter how bizarre or offensive the result.[18]

Despite the deeply rooted common law doctrine, there were, as early as 1908, legal scholars proposing the existence of a duty in rescue situations. Professor Ames proposed that "one who fails to interfere to save another from impending death or great bodily harm, where he might do so with little or no inconvenience to himself, and the death or great bodily harm follows as a consequence of his inaction, shall be punished criminally and shall make compensation to the party injured, or to his widow and children in case of death."[19]

More recently, contemporary legal authorities have echoed the feelings of Professor Ames. Purver[11(p304)] illustrates this attitude in the following statement:

> In flagrant cases of omissions to rescue it is not a misuse of language to say that the injury occurred because of the bystander's inaction. The distinction between misfeasance and nonfeasance in rescue situations has been perpetuated by reasoning which is lame, limp, and lackluster and that the ebbing of the strongly individualistic philosophy of the early common law and the increasing dependence of one societal unit upon another make a strong case for the legal recognition of a duty to rescue.

Thus we begin to see an argument being made for a change in the early common law which held that there is no duty to rescue. Because society's value of the individual began to shift to group or community needs, the law accordingly needed to change. Failure to stop and help became less acceptable. Slowly, rescue has become recognized as being socially desirable—an activity to be promoted and encouraged. The first Good Samaritan act was passed by the state of California in 1959. Since that time, every state and the District of Columbia have followed suit and have adopted similar Good Samaritan statutes.

The legislative purposes of the Good Samaritan acts are generally twofold: first, they are meant to encourage people, including nurses and physicians, to respond to medical emergencies when they are under no obligation to do so and thus to provide medical care to emergency victims who would not otherwise receive it; second, they are meant to protect the Samaritan from suit or liability through grants of immunity.[20]

The court in *Colby v. Schwartz*[21] described Good Samaritan acts as follows:

> The enactment of Good Samaritan legislation represents the resolution of competing interests. On the one hand, there is an interest in the vindication of the rights of the malpractice victim. On the other hand, there is a need to encourage physicians to render emergency medical care when they otherwise might not. Where applicable, the legislation favors the latter over the former.

Although Good Samaritan statutes share many similarities, they vary so much from state to state that, literally, no two states are alike.[22] Nonetheless, five common elements have been identified:

1. identification of the protected class
2. requirement that the Good Samaritan act is in good faith
3. requirement that care be rendered gratuitously
4. identification of the zone of protection
5. identification of the standard of care

Problems of Interpretation

It is fair to say that if nurses meet the requirements of the state statute under which they are practicing, they are thereby provided immunity. However, disputed factual situations and interpretations of the statutory language may prompt litigation in determining whether immunity is in fact provided. Frequent sources of dispute are the two prerequisites in all Good Samaritan legislation: (1) the need for the aid to occur at the "scene" of an emergency, and (2) that a relationship (i.e., duty) not preexist the emergency.[14]

It would be easy to envision general scenarios in which disaster nurses would be provided immunity as well as scenarios in which they would not be provided immunity. For example, a nurse who happens upon a disaster unexpectedly, where there has been no previous planning, and sets about to render aid or nursing care will probably be immune from liability. On the other hand, a nurse who has been designated as part of a response team and is called accordingly in response to a disaster, whether it be to render aid in a shelter or in a hospital, is probably not protected under the Good Samaritan statute (Figure 15–2).

These two examples give the two ends of the continuum in which it is easiest to deal in absolutes. However, there are many factual situations between these two extremes. Nurses need to know whether the Good Samaritan statute protects them in these situations.

Some states provide answers by delineating specific situations that are covered by the statute. For example, three states have defined *scene of an emergency*. The Washington and Minnesota definitions exclude hospitals and doctors' offices, but the California physicians' statute provides that the scene of an emergency includes hospital emergency rooms, but only when a "medical disaster" duly proclaimed by local or state authorities is in effect. Eleven states—Florida, Kentucky, Maine, Nevada, Kansas, New York, Ohio, Rhode Island, Washington, Louisiana, and the District of Columbia—have specifically excluded hospitals, clinics, and doctors' offices from the scope of immunity, while two others—Alaska and Texas—specifically include hospitals but exclude clinics or doctors' offices. Seven states place no restrictions at all on where immunity applies.[22]

Because statutory language seemingly places greater weight on exclusion than on inclusion, it can be inferred that in other jurisdictions, such as Alabama and Illinois, a hospital is also excluded. A good many states simply define the location

---

Figure 15–2 Immunity Provided by Good Samaritan Statutes

Continuum of Immunity

Immunity	Possible Immunity	No Immunity
Example: RN encounters an accident on the highway and stops and renders aid. RN is traveling in winter when a snowstorm traps many people. She offers assistance.	Example: An OB nurse on a surgical unit is visiting a friend during her lunch hour when the patient in the next bed has a cardiac arrest. She initiates CPR.	Example: RN is employed by a professional disaster response team.

as the *scene of an emergency* or combine this phrase with other more specific language. For example, the California statute defines an emergency occurring within a hospital as "a situation whether or not it occurs in the emergency room, requiring immediate services for alleviation of severe pain, or immediate diagnosis and treatment of unfavorable medical conditions, which, if not immediately diagnosed and treated, would lead to serious disability or death.[23] It also defines the *scene of the emergency* as "including, but not limited to, the emergency room of a hospital in case of a medical disaster."[14,23]

It has been said that the most comprehensive and noteworthy Good Samaritan act was enacted by the Michigan legislature. There, civil immunity is provided by two different yet interlocking statutes. One provides immunity to nurses and physicians voluntarily responding to emergencies in general, while the other is specifically addressed to hospital emergencies. It should be noted that both statutes place primary emphasis upon the question of the preexisting duty.[14] The Michigan statute is as follows[24]:

> (1) In instances where the actual hospital duty of that person did not require a response to that emergency situation, a physician, dentist, podiatrist, intern, resident, registered nurse, licensed practical nurse, registered physical therapist, clinical laboratory technologist, inhalation therapist, certified registered nurse anesthetist, x-ray technician, or paramedical person, who in good faith responds to a life threatening emergency or responds to a request for emergency assistance in a life threatening emergency within a hospital or other licensed medical care facility, shall not be liable for any civil damages as a result of an act or omission in the rendering of emergency care, except an act or omission amounting to gross negligence or willful and wanton misconduct.
>
> (2) The exemption from liability under subsection (1) shall not apply to a physician where a physician-patient relationship existed prior to the advent of the emergency nor to a licensed nurse where a nurse-patient relationship existed prior to the advent of the emergency.

Interpretation by Case Law

Because all Good Samaritan statutes are not as clear and concise as Michigan's, one must frequently look to case law for interpretation of the statute in ascertaining applicability. Such interpretation was provided California's Good Samaritan act by the California courts in two separate cases: *Colby v Schwartz*[21] and *McKenna v Cedars of Lebanon Hospital*.[25] *Colby* discusses whether California's Good Samaritan statute can be applied to a hospital emergency room, while *McKenna* considers whether hospitals can be included within the meaning of the "scene of an emergency" for purposes of civil immunity.[14]

In *Colby,* two emergency room physicians operated on a patient who had been involved in an automobile accident as a part of their normal course of practice. When they were later sued for malpractice, the physicians argued the defense of immunity under the Good Samaritan statute. The court rejected their argument and held that, as members of the emergency call panel, the physicians owed a duty of care to all potential patients requiring such emergency care. Consequently, section 2144 would be inapplicable. The court stated that section 2144 was "directed towards physicians who, by chance and on an irregular basis, come upon or are called to render emergency care."[21]

The court also expressed its concern that in situations in which the duty preexists the emergency circumstances, providing immunity would deprive malpractice victims of legal remedies and would potentially cause a lower quality of medical care.[14]

The court in *Colby* appears to create a dichotomy of duties: those that are undertaken "by chance and on an irregular basis" and those that are part of the practitioner's "normal course of practice." The Good Samaritan act applies to the former and not to the latter.[14]

Although the Colby case applies to an emergency department situation, the dichotomy of duties that the court enunciates could easily be extrapolated to a disaster setting, leading one to conclude that the nurse who renders aid in the normal course of practice is not provided immunity under the Good Samaritan act.

In *McKenna,* a physician on a hospital floor where he usually did not work responded to an emergency call summoning him to the room of a patient having seizures. He responded and treated the seizures; however, the patient went into cardiac arrest and died 11 days later. A malpractice suit was filed against the responding physician. At trial, the jury was instructed that "no licensed physician, who in good faith renders emergency care at the scene of the emergency, shall be liable for any civil damages as a result of any of his acts or omissions in rendering the emergency care."[25] Like the *Colby* court, the *McKenna* court focused on the preexisting relationship. The court stated that inasmuch as no prior duty was shown to exist, the responding physician "was truly a volunteer"[25] and that application of the Good Samaritan act would be consistent with the legislative purpose.

In ascertaining a preexisting duty to render aid to the emergency patient, the court in *McKenna* set forth various situations or relationships that could occur within a medical center by which such a duty would be created. That court stated that a person would have a prior duty to render aid in emergencies if the person were a member of the hospital team whose job it is to respond to emergencies.[25]

The *McKenna* court went one step further and stated that when no doctor-patient relationship preexists the emergency, the immunity offered by the Good

Samaritan act should apply regardless of where the emergency occurs.[25] The locus of emergency is significant because, as mentioned previously, it is one of the controlling prerequisites in all Good Samaritan statutes. What constitutes the scene of an emergency for the purpose of qualifying for Good Samaritan civil immunity must be ascertained.

In accordance with the scene-of-emergency prerequisite, disaster nurses need to ascertain whether a disaster would meet the criteria for their qualifying for immunity. Again, one could easily envision situations that would meet the scene-of-emergency criteria. For example, a volcanic eruption occurs; a nurse goes immediately to the scene and begins to administer aid. The nurse would be immune to suit. However, another situation with slightly different facts would probably not qualify as the scene of an emergency. Consider the same volcanic eruption, but now the victims are brought to a shelter, at which the disaster nurse renders aid as part of a response team. The nurse would probably not be immune due to the preexisting duty.

Good Samaritan acts do not prevent disaster nurses from being sued; however, they might provide civil immunity from such an action, should the nurse meet the prerequisites of the statute. Because each state has its own form of the Good Samaritan act and because some states have case law interpreting the statutory language, local law should be reviewed for applicability.

CONCLUSION

Two sets of conclusions, one applicable to institutions planning for an organized response to a disaster and one applicable to individuals involved in disaster response by circumstance, may be drawn. Institutional disaster planning, by the very nature of the activity, involves foresight and careful consideration of institutional and individual roles. Any credible plan assures training and duties appropriate to intended functions during an actual disaster. Except in those few states that specifically grant certain types of immunity during declared disasters, it is doubtful that Good Samaritan statutes would protect individual members of a disaster response team. This is because the existence of the plan may be used to infer the preexistence of a duty, as well as to infer that the disaster was not unexpected. Even if all conditions are met, all Good Samaritan statutes apply to individuals—not institutions. Note that institutional liability is a separate issue not addressed by this chapter. This is, of course, not to imply that individuals who respond in a preplanned and organized manner to a disaster are to be held to nondisaster legal standards. As was previously noted, common law requires only that the actions be similar to those of "responsible persons" under similar circumstances; i.e., in this case, disaster situations. More precise legal considerations can and probably should be incorporated in disaster plans by consultation with hospital risk managers, in-house attorneys, and attorneys for disaster relief umbrella organizations such as the Red Cross and Civil Defense. It is again emphasized that the law varies drastically from state to state and is undergoing constant modification.

In the case of an individual nurse involved by circumstance in a disaster, statutory protection by Good Samaritan acts is clearer. Such a nurse would, by definition, not be a preplanned, specially trained member of a disaster response team, but rather a true volunteer, thrown into an emergency or disaster situation by the necessity of the moment. Probably the most interesting aspect of this situation is whether or not the local Good Samaritan statute allows a hospital to be a recognized emergency site. Comparatively few states recognize a hospital as such. Again, the common law recognition of the special circumstances presented by a disaster will always apply.

REFERENCES

1. *Webster's New World Dictionary*, college ed 2. New York, World Publishing Co, 1976.

2. Trey R, Safar P (eds): *Disaster Medicine*. Berlin, Springer-Verlag, 1980, vol 1.

3. Rutherford WH: Planning for major disasters, in Birch CA (ed): *Emergencies in Medical Practice*, ed 11. New York, Churchill Livingstone, 1981, p 92.

4. 42 USC §5122 (1974).

5. Cal Gov't Code §8558 (1982).

6. Cal Gov't Code §8659 (1982).

7. Mo Rev Stat §335.016 (8) (1981).

8. George JE: *Law and Emergency Care*. St Louis, The CV Mosby Co, 1980.

9. American Nurses' Association, Division on Medical-Surgical Nursing Practice and Emergency Department Nurses' Association: *Standards of Emergency Nursing Practice*. Kansas City, American Nurses' Association, 1975, p 7.

10. Prosser WL: *Law of Torts*, ed 4. St Paul, West Publishing Co, 1971, pp 143, 144, 169, 170, 240, 334.

11. Purver JM: Duty of One Other Than Carrier or Employer To Render Assistance To One for Whose Initial Injury He Is Not Liable. *33 ALR 3a 301* (1978).

12. *Union Pac R Co v Cappier*, 66 Kan 649 (1903).

13. *Buch v. Amory Mfg Co*, 69 NH 257 (1898).

14. Steipel HR: Good Samaritans and hospital emergencies. *S Cal L Rev* 1981;54:419–445.

15. Poole DW: The Good Samaritan and the law. *Tenn L Rev* 1965;32:287–293.

16. Cady EE: Medicolegal considerations, in Stephenson HE, Kimptom RS (eds): *Immediate Care of the Acutely Ill and Injured*, ed 2. St Louis, The CV Mosby Co, 1978, p 324.

17. *Black's Law Dictionary*, ed 5. St Paul, West Publishing Co, 1979, pp 863, 950.

18. White MR: Duty to rescue. *Pittsburgh L Rev* 1966;28:61–75.

19. Ames J: Law and morals. *Harv L Rev* 1908;22:97–113.

20. Helminski FJ: Good Samaritan statutes: Time for uniformity. *Wayne State L Rev* 1980/81; 27:217–267.

21. *Colby v Schwartz*, 78 Cal App 3d 885 (1978).

22. Mapel FB, Weigel CJ: Good Samaritan laws—who needs them?: The current state of Good Samaritan protection in the United States. *S Tex L J* 1980;21:327–354.

23. Cal Bus & Prof Code §2144 (1980).

24. Mich Comp Laws Ann §691.1501 (1980).

25. *McKenna v Cedars of Lebanon Hospital,* 93 Cal App 3d 282 (1979).

SUGGESTED READINGS

Barry J (ed): *Emergency Nursing.* New York, McGraw Hill Book Co, 1978.

Berg DA, Hirsch HL: The physician's duty to treat: Taking the plunge without leaving the ground. *Leg Aspects Med Pract* 1983;11:4–5.

Bianco EA: The physician-patient relationship. *Leg Aspects Med Pract* 1983;11:1–3.

Creighton H: *Law Every Nurse Should Know,* ed 4. Philadelphia: WB Saunders Co, 1981.

Flowers T, Kennedy W: Good Samaritan legislation: An analysis and a proposal. *Temple L Q* 1965; 38:418–430.

Grant HD, Murry RRH: *Emergency Care,* ed 3. Bowie, Md, Brady Publishing Co, 1982.

Habeeb WR: Construction of Good Samaritan Statutes Excusing from Civil Liability One Rendering Care in Emergencies, 39 ALR 3d 222 (1971).

Hemelt MD, Mackert ME: *Dynamics of Law in Nursing and Health Care,* ed 2. Reston, Va, Reston Publishing Co Inc, 1982.

Holden AR: *Medical Malpractice,* ed 2. New York, John Wiley & Sons Inc, 1978.

Lanros NE: *Assessment and Intervention in Emergency Nursing.* Bowie, Md, Brady Publishing Co, 1983.

Murchison IA, Nichols TS: *Legal Foundations of Nursing Practice.* New York, MacMillan Inc, 1970.

Oberstein NS: Torts: California good samaritan legislation: Exemptions from civil liability while rendering emergency medical aid. *Cal L Rev* 1963;51:816–822.

Rains ML: Legal considerations in the emergency department, in Budassi SA, Barber JM (eds): *Emergency Nursing: Principles and Practices.* St Louis, The CV Mosby Co, 1981, pp 35–50.

Rund DA: *Essentials of Emergency Medicine.* Norwalk, Conn, Appleton-Century-Crofts, 1982.

Rund DA, Rausch TS: *Triage.* St Louis, The CV Mosby Co, 1981.

Appendix A

Managing Hazardous Materials in Disasters

Resources for determining the hazard characteristics of hazardous materials:

CHEMTREC—Telephone (800) 424–9300
Chemical Industry (shippers, manufacturer, etc.)
Rail transportation industry
Bureau of Explosives—Telephone (202) 243–4048
National Response Center—Telephone (800) 424–8802
Emergency action guides

Common Emergency Action Guides:

1. *Emergency Handling of Hazardous Materials in Surface Transportation Hazardous Materials—Emergency Response Guide*
   Available from—
   Bureau of Explosives
   Association of American Railroads
   1920 "L" Street, NW
   Washington, DC 20036
2. *Fire Protection Guide on Hazardous Materials*
   Contents—Flashpoint Index of Trade Name Liquids
   NFPA 325M—Fire Hazard Properties of Flammable Liquids, Gases and
             Solids
   NFPA 491M—Manual of Hazardous Chemical Reactions

Source: Information compiled by N. Jean Myers, RN, Assistant Director of Nursing, and John A. Papasodero, RN, BSN, Clinical Supervisor, both from the Emergency Department of the Medical Center of Beaver County, Beaver, Pennsylvania.

NFPA 704—Recommended System for the Identification of the Fire Hazard
of Materials
Available from—
National Fire Protection Association
470 Atlantic Avenue
Boston, MA 02210
3. *Hazardous Materials—Emergency Response Guidebook*
Available from—
Department of Transportation
Office of Hazardous Materials Operations
2100 Second Street, SW
Washington, DC 20590
4. *Hazardous Chemicals Data* (U.S. Coast Guard CHRIS System)
Available from—
Superintendent of Documents
US Government Printing Office
Washington, DC 20402
Order Number: 050–012–00147–2
5. Stutz DR, Ricks RC, Olsen MF: *Hazardous Materials Injuries, a Handbook for Prehospital Care*. Greenbelt, Md, Bradford Communications Corp, 1982.
6. *Environmental Protection Agency Regional Solid Waste Offices*
Available from EPA regional solid waste office

Region 1
Solid Waste Program
John F. Kennedy Building
Boston, MA 02203
617–223–5775

Region 4
Solid Waste Section
345 Courtland Street, NE
Atlanta, GA 30308
404–881–3016

Region 2
Solid Waste Section
26 Federal Plaza
New York, NY 10007
212–264–0503/4/5

Region 5
Solid Waste Program
230 South Dearborn Street
Chicago, IL 60604
312–353–2197

Region 3
Solid Waste Program
6th and Walnut Streets
Philadelphia, PA 19106
215–597–0980

Region 6
Solid Waste Section
1201 Elm Street
First International Building
Dallas, TX 75270
214–767–2645

Region 7
Waste Management Section
324 East 11th Street
Kansas City, MO 64108
816–374–3307

Region 8
Solid Waste Section
1860 Lincoln Street
Denver, CO 80203
303–837–2221

Region 9
Solid Waste Program
215 Fremont Street
San Francisco, CA 94105
415–556–4606

Region 10
Solid Waste Program
1200 6th Avenue
Seattle, WA 98101
206–442–1260

Index

H

Halazone, water disinfection, 246
Hazardous material, management of,
resource list, 385-387
Head-to-toe assessment, 25, 37-43
pregnant women, 135-136, 137
Head trauma, 120-122
assessment of injuries, 120
cerebral hypoxia, treatment of, 121
Glasgow Coma Scale, 120-121
Health conditions, 259-268
communicable disease, control of,
261
cultural factors, 268
dehydration, 263-264
diarrhea, 250-251, 263
drug therapy, 262-263
immunizations, 260, 262
injuries, 266-267
malnutrition, 264-266
post-disaster effects, 240-241, 250
respiratory infections, 263
specialists involved in, 267-268
Heat sterilization, water, 245
Helicopters, 129-131
landing zone, characteristics of, 130
safety rules, 130-131
Hematology, pregnant women, 136,
138, 140
Hemorrhage, pregnant women,
management of, 145-146
Hemothorax, 115
History, medical
obtaining, 112-113
pregnant women, 136, 138
Hospital nurses, 11, 12
Hospital, fire in, 79, 80
Hospitals, external disasters, 79-98
assessment procedure, 82
disaster notification form, 81
emergency department, 89-90
emergency, nurse managers' role, 90
equipment/supplies, stocking of,
83-84
nursing units, 95-98

notification of, 95-96
patient discharge system, 96-97
space allocation, 96-97
specific emergency treatment areas,
90-95
triage area, 85-89
disaster tag, 88, 89
evaluation of patients, 87
team in, 85-87
See also Specific emergency
treatment areas.
Hospitals, internal disasters, 74-79
assessment procedure, 75-76
evacuation, 76-79
Hypertension, pregnant women,
159-160
Hypoxia, cerebral, treatment of,
121

I

Immediate auscultation, 24
Immunizations, 260, 262
Impact phase, 9-10
psychologically geared interventions,
190
reactions during, 190-191
Infants, calorie requirements, 249
Injuries, first-aid for, 266-267
Insects, 256
Inspection, in assessment, 24
Internal bleeding, 109
assessment of, 21
Internal disasters
fire, 79, 80
See also Hospitals, internal disasters.
International disaster services,
316-317
governmental organizations, 342
United Nations Agencies, 337-338
voluntary organizations, 339-341
Iodine, water disinfection, 246
Irradiated patients, *See* Radiation
disaster.

About the Author

Loretta Malm Garcia grew up on a farm outside of Wahoo, NE. She graduated in 1975 as a Diploma RN from Lincoln General Hospital School of Nursing, Lincoln, NE.

In 1975, she joined the US Navy Nurse Corps and was stationed at Naval Regional Medical Center, Camp Pendleton, CA. She worked a variety of clinical settings ranging from Neonatal ICU to orthopedics and surgery.

After leaving the Navy, she moved to Utah where she completed her BSN in 1980 at the Extended Baccalaureate Nursing Program of the University of Utah in Ogden, UT. She completed her Masters in Nursing Administration in 1982 from the University of Utah. She currently holds ANA Certification in Nursing Administration, Advanced.

Studies in disaster began as her graduate school research project, titled *Disaster Management Skills: Results of an Alternate Teaching Method*. Based on this project, she went on to win the Army Nursing Research award in 1982—The Phyllis J. Verhonik Memorial. She has been co-conference leader of two major disaster conferences in SLC. These were co-sponsored by the 328th General Hospital, her Army Reserve unit, and the University of Utah College of Nursing.

Ms. Garcia just finished a 4½ year assignment as the Assistant Chief Nurse, Active Guard Reserve, of the 328th General Hospital. She currently teaches disaster management skills at the University of Utah College of Health Division of Continuing Education and does consulting in disaster management.

DATE DUE

4/17/c			
AG 26 '92			
NO 0 9 '94			
NO 2 8 '94			

DEMCO 38-297